All Things Made New

DIARMAID MacCULLOCH

All Things Made New

The Reformation and Its Legacy

OXFORD
UNIVERSITY PRESS

OXFORD
UNIVERSITY PRESS

Oxford University Press is a department of the University of Oxford. It furthers
the University's objective of excellence in research, scholarship, and education
by publishing worldwide. Oxford is a registered trade mark of Oxford University
Press in the UK and in certain other countries.

Published in the United States of America by Oxford University Press
198 Madison Avenue, New York, NY 10016, United States of America.

Library of Congress Cataloging-in-Publication Data

Names: MacCulloch, Diarmaid, author.
Title: All things made new : the Reformation and its legacy / Diarmaid
MacCulloch.
Description: New York : Oxford University Press, 2016. | Includes
bibliographical references and index. | Description based on print version
record and CIP data provided by publisher; resource not viewed.
Identifiers: LCCN 2016020307 (print) | LCCN 2016011764 (ebook) |
ISBN9780190616823 (updf) | ISBN 9780190616830 (epub) | ISBN 9780190616816
(hardback : alk. paper)
Subjects: LCSH: Reformation—England. | Reformation.
Classification: LCC BR375 (print) | LCC BR375 .M287 2016 (ebook) | DDC
270.6—dc23
LC record available at https://lccn.loc.gov/2016020307

1 3 5 7 9 8 6 4 2
Printed by Sheridan Books, Inc., United States of America

For Felicity Bryan and Stuart Proffitt

Contents

CONTENTS

PART III

Looking Back on the English Reformation

List of Illustrations

1. The west front of Bath Cathedral Priory, *c.* 1500. Photograph: istockphoto

2 and 3. Details of angels on the west front. Photographs: Alamy

4. Lucas de Heere, *The Family of Henry VIII: An Allegory of the Tudor Succession*, *c.* 1572. National Museum of Wales, Cardiff. Photograph: Bridgeman Images

5. Anon. (English school), *The Somerset House Conference*, 1604. National Portrait Gallery, London. Photograph: Stefano Baldini/ Bridgeman Images

6. The opening of Psalm I, from the Psalter of Henry VIII, 1530–47. British Library, London (Royal 2 A. XVI, f.3). Photograph: Bridgeman Images

7. Title-page of *The Byble in Englyshe*, sixth edition, November 1541. Cambridge University Library (Bible Society, Anderson Room, BSS.201.B41.8). Reproduced by kind permission of the Syndics of Cambridge University Library

8. Gerhard Flicke, portrait of Thomas Cranmer, 1545. National Portrait Gallery, London. Photograph: Alamy

9. Portrait of Thomas Cranmer from Gilbert Burnet, *The History of the Reformation of the Church of England*, 1679–82, Vol. 1, facing p. 179. Photograph: University of California Libraries

Preface

Reformation history has been a huge growth industry over the last
three decades: university libraries are bursting with a wealth of scholarship, but a lot of it is difficult to grasp and still very specialist.
What I have tried to do in the varied essays in this book is to reflect
on all that scholarship and then interpret it for a wider audience. I
have divided the book into three sections of essays spanning my
work over the last quarter-century: some are book reviews; some
freestanding studies of particular topics. All have appeared in print
before, though one of them so far only in Spanish; I am very grateful
to the editors and publishers who have agreed to their reproduction
here. I have chosen versions of the essays which reflect what I wanted
to publish, rather than the texts which those with purer taste first put
into print; I have also removed some over-detailed criticism of certain books, and smoothed out the immediacy of some contemporary
references. Overall, in my choices of what to include, I have avoided
over-technical studies or essays with a more local than national or
international focus, but I have included one long piece on Robert
Ware of Dublin because it is a bizarre tale and a detective story, which
reveals how even good historians can fall for a con man. Some who
know my work will look in vain for one of my better-known essays,
'The Myth of the English Reformation'. It has become a casualty of
its later influence on my arguments and the discussion around them,
as the ideas in it inform much later writing. Its text would seem repet-
itive alongside other pieces included here, besides the fact that it
would represent an early and only partly formed version of my
thoughts. Its conclusions on the myth-making of Anglican history
remain fundamental to my presentation of the Reformation.

These essays reflect my belief that the proper study of history has a purpose, indeed (to be portentous), a moral purpose: it forms a powerful barrier against societies and institutions collectively going insane as a result of telling themselves badly skewed stories about the past. I have concentrated my efforts over the years on the sanity of Anglicanism, which like all belief-systems making a claim to special authority, has frequently based its claims on skewed stories. But these essays are not just directed to Anglicans, and I would be offended to be described as an Anglican historian – rather than as a historian who is also an Anglican. I hope that readers will find glimpses of sense in what follows, as well as entertainment and perspectives on the past which seek to look past accumulated prejudices, including my own.

These essays are dedicated to two people who have benevolently shaped my career in writing and have become good friends in the process: my literary agent Felicity Bryan and my publisher at Penguin, Stuart Proffitt. They commissioned none of the essays gathered in this volume, so it is offered to show them what I was up to when I should have been getting on with writing for them.

Introduction: all things made new

The old things are passed away, behold all things are made new.

        2 Corinthians 5:12, Douay-Rheims New Testament

When at the beginning of the 2000s I took on the task of writing the history of all sixteenth-century Europe, I initially gave it the title *A House Divided*. My wise publisher, realizing that this might puzzle some potential purchasers and therefore adversely affect our sales, made me turn this into the subtitle for the book which appeared as *Reformation: Europe's House Divided, 1490–1700*. But the point remains. If you study the sixteenth century, you are inevitably present at something like the aftermath of a particularly disastrous car-crash. All around are half-demolished structures, debris, people figuring out how to make sense of lives that have suddenly been transformed. It has taken me several decades to lift my eyes off that great cataclysm – which was no less a cataclysm because many will be celebrating and cherishing its good results in its half-millennium in 2017 – to consider how things were before it.

The most noticeable characteristic of Western Europe in what we call the Middle Ages was its cultural and religious unity – unity through a common alignment with the pope in Rome, and a common language for worship and scholarship, Latin. Western Europeans who know anything about their history tend to take this united medieval phase of it for granted, in the way that when we are growing up, we take for granted the environment around us as the norm by which everything else is judged. But this obscures the fact that it is unique in human history for a region to be so dominated by a single form of monotheistic religion and its accompanying culture for so long. Only the Wahhabi variety of Islam in what is now Saudi Arabia comes close to such a claim to exclusive dominance, and for a far shorter period; I would challenge you to name another example of similar intensity. Islam has the concept of the *umma*, the shared community of Muslims, but this has not resulted in the sort of unity possessed by medieval Western Christendom. The dominance of the Church which looked to the Bishop of Rome was a freak in human experience, albeit a freak with profound consequences for the present day. Its break-up in the sixteenth century was a return to the normality of human history.

Many people who want to understand Christianity are often bewildered by the assumptions and preoccupations of Christians, and why Christians believe what they do. One of the arguments of *Reformation: Europe's House Divided,* and now of this book also, is that we will not understand the Christianity we find in modern Europe and America without travelling back in time to the Reformation. And once there, there is more to study than Protestantism. The Reformation was an explosion of different concerns: many discontents, many excitements came together, but then also developed in all sorts of directions, so there was a Roman Catholic Reformation just as much as a variety of Protestant Reformations. Indeed, the Roman Catholic Church was transformed while Protestantism was created, in what is often called the Counter-Reformation – more accurately if a little more vaguely, the Catholic Reformation. The old Church had an enormous shock when it was confronted by Luther and his fellow Reformers, and it had to make a great effort of renewal in order to survive.

There is an important qualification to make here. The old Western Church was not in the terrible state of decay which has formed the foundation of traditional Protestant narratives of the Reformation (and indeed of some self-congratulatory narratives of the Counter-Reformation as well). That was especially true in the kingdom of England, but it was also the case in less predictable parts of the Church, such as in England's uncomfortable neighbour Ireland. Even though the ecclesiastical organization of medieval Ireland was chaotic and dysfunctional, from about a century before the Reformation there were plentiful signs of an extraordinary religious revival, especially in the Gaelic west of the island. It was spearheaded by Franciscan friars, who have left the ruins of their friaries all over the western parts of

Ireland. This was not a dying religion, but one in a process of vigorous transformation without Luther's help.

It is therefore a Protestant myth that this old Church was in such a tottery state, that all that was needed was to put a little finger on it, and it would fall over and collapse. Not so: it satisfied most people. The Protestant Reformers destroyed a powerful, self-confident institution. That makes the Reformation and Reformation theology so much more interesting. Only ideas and their independent power could so dramatically have brought down such a strong structure.

So the Reformation was not caused by social and economic forces, or even by a secular idea like nationalism; it sprang from a big idea about death, salvation and the afterlife. God was all-powerful, and therefore He was the Lord of Death as well as of Life: nothing that human beings could do, nothing of the intricate structure of intercessory prayer for the dead maintained by the late medieval Western Church, could alter His decision, born of His own mercy and judgement. That is the thought that seized the German friar Martin Luther (1483–1546) and inspired so many people in Europe, and that is what brought this immense and powerful structure down. It was not the religiously indifferent who became Protestants, but rather those who like Luther who had believed passionately in the old Church's road to salvation, and who were then convinced that they had been cheated. White-hot Catholics became white-hot Protestants – that is why so many clergy of the old Church became leaders of the Reformation, for they suffered a double agony. Not only had they been cheated over salvation, but they had cheated others in their preaching and ministry, and now they must make atonement. Hence their deep bitterness against the old structure, and hence, also, the bitterness of those who fought back to defend the old structure. Since Luther's struggle involved an attack on the power which the Church claimed to help people in gaining their salvation, it became a power struggle in a much wider sense.

More remarkable still was that behind Luther's thoughts were those of two men who were centuries dead before his time: first the Apostle Paul, a contemporary of Jesus Christ, and then the African theologian of the fourth century, Augustine, Bishop of Hippo (354–430). It is impossible to over-estimate Augustine's importance to Western Christianity, both Catholic and Protestant. Augustine read what Paul had written centuries before his own time, especially in the Epistle to the Romans, and what he saw was a picture of an all-powerful God, and humanity which is utterly fallen, utterly corrupt. Augustine called a human being such as himself 'a lump of perdition' – a lump of lost-ness. There is nothing that a lump of perdition – people like you and me – can do for our own salvation. We need God to do it all.

That was the centre of Augustine's thought, and although the theme had repeatedly resounded in the thought of medieval Western Christianity, Luther returned to it anew as the motor of his theology, but he also saw the Church of his day telling people they could do things for their salvation, like paying for masses for the good of their souls and the deceased whom they had loved. That enraged him, filling him with compassion for their helplessness and scorn for their deceivers. He had believed in that same system of ideas, and now he thought it a confidence trick, a cheat. That is the basis of the Protestant Reformation. It was saying loud and clear what Augustine had said long before.

So the Reformation was based on a profound sense of pessimism about human beings. For that reason, it had a difficult relationship with the other great movement of thought in its time, what we now call the Renaissance. The Renaissance discovered new potential in human beings – its exponents and scholars were called humanists, because of their interest in *humanae litterae*, the civilized and civilizing literature of ancient Greece and Rome. The word 'humanist' did not then have its modern implication of atheism or agnosticism. The humanist writers, artists and scholars of the Renaissance were overwhelmingly Christians who wanted to emphasize that human beings have a value: God has given them skills and graces which they can take up and use for God's glory. Someone like the great humanist Erasmus of Rotterdam (1466/9–1536) would certainly not have taken the view that human beings were 'a lump of perdition'. He was saying something very different from Luther – and of course also different from Augustine, a man whom I think Erasmus secretly loathed.

That meant that there was a serious internal conflict for Protestant Reformers who were also humanists. Take the Swiss reformer of Zürich, Huldrych Zwingli (1484–1531). He was a humanist, but that did not stop him becoming a Protestant. Zwingli has been marginalized in popular memories of the Reformation in comparison with Luther. Yet he is fascinating because he believed that Christianity is about here and now, that it is concerned to improve contemporary society. He found the writings of Erasmus inspiring, but like Luther he was still also Augustine's man, and torn between humanism and the Reformation. Zwingli wanted to say that his own city, Zürich, could be the perfect Christian Commonwealth, but at the same time to affirm that human beings were also completely fallen. The Swiss Reformation was constantly working its way through that paradox, much more than Luther in his purer Augustinian pessimism needed to. It was a movement of social reform far more than Luther's Reformation, and generally it had a broader appeal beyond the governing classes who embraced and sustained Lutheranism in northern Europe. That social consciousness has remained one of the characteristics of 'Reformed' (that is, non-Lutheran) Protestantism, sometimes inaccurately known as Calvinism.

One of the reasons that it is important to re-present the Reformation for our own times is to remind modern Westerners of the sheer strangeness of the sixteenth century. There is no question that the English need to be reminded of that more than the Scots or the Welsh, certainly more than citizens of the United States of America, but even those who think that they know what the Reformation was about generally do not. In the sixteenth century Europeans burned one another for denying that bread could become God, or that Jesus was fully God, or fully God and fully human, while some hanged others for not believing in government by bishops. In the past, they did indeed do things very differently.

The past also catches up with us in unexpected ways and places. Another fascination of Reformation Europe is how far it resembles great swathes of culture across the world at the present day. Western Christianity has largely cut the links between church and state, so that we now think it odd or inappropriate that monarchs and politicians should interfere with church affairs. But that is certainly not the case in modern Islamic cultures, which retain a much more integrated view of society. Within the Islamic world, rulers or monarchs do make a difference in religion, and Islamic societies show many analogies with sixteenth-century Europe. This is particularly worth remembering in the United States, where there is such lively debate as to whether or how politics and the Christian Churches should mix.

It is always difficult to predict which beliefs from the Reformation past will suddenly re-emerge. One of the big themes in the Reformation of the sixteenth and seventeenth centuries was that the Last Days predicted in the Bible were about to happen very soon. That is one of the reasons that the Reformation was such an urgent, bloody affair, because it was vital to get things right with God before the Last Days. Now large parts of the Christian world once more emphasize the Last Days. We see this in Africa and Asia, but particularly in the United States; after the nineteenth-century addition of a particular sub-theme, the 'Rapture' of the saved, Last Days have come to play a major part in American conservative Evangelical Protestantism, affecting world politics once again. For a while at the beginning of the twenty-first century, this theme threatened to become a major motor in the foreign policy of the United States, for example, in the Christian right's attitude to the Israeli–Palestinian question. The powerful link-up between the American right and Israel is rooted in a Protestant preoccupation with biblical predictions of the Last Days, because an essential precondition for Christ's Second Coming is that the Jews must be converted. So an intimate relationship with the Jews is necessary (and whatever the government of Israel may think of the reasoning, it is not displeased with the resulting friendship).

Equally important is the effect of Last Days thinking on questions of world environmental damage. If the Last Days are coming, it is a profane distraction to bother with problems of pollution or exhaustion of natural resources, which in any case have been supplied in God's providence for humans to use. Hence the Christian Right's long-standing lack of interest in a matter which may bring the Last Days on human civilization, but not in the manner it anticipates. Europeans have mostly forgotten Reformation theological topics like the Last Days, so they find it difficult to understand what is going on in American politics. For me, a European, it is crucial to see just how different the United States is, and how close it is to the Reformation, compared with the sort of world in which I live in the United Kingdom, or in which the Scandinavians, the French or the Germans live.

This great cultural divide is all the more strange because modern Western Europe and the United States are both societies created by the Enlightenment, the aftermath of the Reformation. The background was the series of wars of religion in the seventeenth century, in particular the very bloody Thirty Years War, which exhausted European society and led it to the beginnings of a kind of tolerance. Europeans were sickened by the violence, and the experience of just how futile it is to kill people in the name of religion was one of the reasons why Europe turned towards the Enlightenment. Enlightenment rethinking of old certainties involved a reassessment of what a sacred book is, and it suddenly seemed despicable to persecute people because they read that book in a different way. Many people went to North America just to escape the misery of persecution, but now most of their descendants in the United States still go to church, while most of the later generations in Europe have ceased to do so. American church-going may now be showing signs of following a European pattern, yet the long-standing and continuing difference is one of the greatest puzzles in the modern history of religion, and it lies at the heart of why Europe and America still find it so difficult to understand each other.

Nevertheless, the United States did not invent toleration, and neither did Western Europe. In the sixteenth century there were wide areas of toleration in Europe which we have forgotten about, because they were in eastern Europe – in Poland, Transylvania, Hungary. During the sixteenth century there were so many different religions competing in these areas that their rulers decided they would be best advised to exercise a broad tolerance of variety. The statements about toleration which we take for granted, and tend to associate with the Enlightenment, had already been made in Reformation Poland and Hungary. It is sad that we remember the former eastern European principality of Transylvania for Count Dracula, who never existed, rather than as the first Christian polity officially to declare that everyone ought to be able to worship God in their own way without interference. The Transylvanian Diet (that is, its Parliament) spelled this out as early as 1568, in a Declaration made in the parish church of a town called Torda, a place which should be more of a centre of pilgrimage than it is:

ministers should everywhere preach and proclaim [the Gospel] according to their understanding of it, and if their community is willing to
accept this, good; if not, however, no one should be compelled by force
if their spirit is not at peace, but a minister retained whose teaching is
pleasing to the community ... no one is permitted to threaten to
imprison or banish anyone because of their teaching, because faith is a
gift from God.

So what did the Enlightenment do to move on, and make Europe so
different after the Reformation? The wars of the Reformation had
been about how to read a book, and the chief importance of the
Enlightenment for Christianity was a revolution in how to read that
same book. To use the jargon of my scholarly trade, it was a change
in historical technique: a subjection of all texts, whether or not they
claimed to have a sacred character, to new criteria of authenticity, in
which historical context mattered as never before. This was a peculiarly Western phenomenon, and its effect over two centuries has been
to polarize Western Christianity between those who embrace and
those who reject the Enlightenment. This polarization has now over-
shadowed the divisions of the Reformation. It places conservative
Roman Catholics and conservative Protestants on the same side in a
culture war. In recent decades, that war has been focused particularly on debates about sexuality – but there could be many other
issues, if we chose to change the battleground. The overarching issue
is one of authority. Do we arrive at truths as a matter of individual
judgement, or through deference to authoritative church leaders or
to an infallible sacred text?

I have been acutely aware of this new shift of alliances while I have
been writing what is gathered here, and I always knew that there was
a need to say a lot about Roman Catholicism in order to talk about
the Reformation. Half my *Reformation: Europe's House Divided* was
about the Counter-Reformation, which was just as much a Reformation as anything led by Martin Luther, Huldrych Zwingli or John
Calvin (1509–64). Moreover, Counter-Reformation Catholics turned
Christianity into a truly worldwide religion, taking it to America, Asia
and to subtropical Africa. They began their missions well before the
Protestants, who had enough on their hands working out who they
were and what they believed, and fighting the Catholics for survival.

So the Reformation/Counter-Reformation story ranges to the jungles of South America, the ports of Japan and the kingdoms of Africa. Already in the very first decade of the sixteenth century there was a son of a king of the Kongo in central Africa who became a bishop of the Catholic Church.

We have not only to remember this story, but also tell it in both its glory and its horror, because soon, in Africa and America, Western Christian expansion became tangled up with one of the greatest crimes in Western history, the organization of the slave trade across the Atlantic. Good Christians created that trade and sustained it for three centuries – Catholic and Protestant alike. And they were happy to do so because, whether Catholic or Protestant, they heard the Bible telling them that they could. Up to the late seventeenth century, no Christians challenged the existence of slavery as an institution. If you had taken a straw poll in any Christian gathering before that date, such as from the University Church of St Mary the Virgin in my own home city of Oxford, and asked whether slavery was evil, not a single Christian hand would have gone up to say yes, it was evil. That is because the predominant voices in the books of the Bible accept slavery as part of the God-given fabric of the world. Now it is entirely the other way round: not a single Christian alive, I think, would defend slavery, and so in this respect, all Christianity is now out of alignment with the Bible.

Counter-Reformation is also a vital theme for the present-day Church alongside Reformation, because for more than thirty years, the Church of Rome was headed by consciously Counter-Reformation popes, John Paul II (1978–2005) and Benedict XVI (2005–13). The weakness of this variety of Catholicism is that it has continued to regard the Enlightenment as its enemy, and has sought to exclude Catholics who take a different view. Now, under Pope Francis, the atmosphere has suddenly become very different, even if so far little has formally changed. The next few decades are going to be an interesting phase in the life of the Roman Catholic Church. It was already noticeable in the half-century after the Second Vatican Council (1962–5) how many Protestant themes were suddenly taken up by the Roman Church: the liturgy in the vernacular, Bible-reading, popular hymns in church, ordinary people encouraged to sing and Communion offered in both kinds. The last two popes were unmistakeably opposed to much of this, and were against new ways of seeing authority: it was in that sense that they led a Counter-Reformation papacy. Their tragedy was that they did not learn the lesson which King Canute tried to teach to his courtiers, that you cannot push back the tide of the oceans. In raising expectations, Reformers may well find themselves swept away by them; Pope Francis deserves good wishes for trying to ride the tiger. Whether or not he succeeds, another Reformation may be in prospect within the Catholic Church, yet it is unlikely to be another Counter-Reformation.

Eastern Christianities, the Churches of Orthodoxy and Oriental Orthodoxy, have something of a walk-on part in any Reformation story. There is a simple reason for this: so far none of them has experienced a Reformation. Back in the eighth and ninth centuries many of them were convulsed by an 'iconoclastic controversy', which hinged on one of the great issues to reappear in the sixteenth-century Reformation – whether images were a help in worshipping God or a hindrance. But in the case of the Orthodox, the status quo was restored and not partially overthrown as it was in the West in the sixteenth century – images came back. It was also very important that the Greeks had always heard the Gospels and the Epistles of Paul in their original Greek. The West had translated the New Testament into Latin, and it was a huge shock for scholars when they first experienced the text again in Greek at the end of the fifteenth century. It was one of the biggest challenges to the Western Latin Church's authority that it had been presenting the New Testament in a language other than the original: even without Martin Luther, that would have caused a significant upset. That single fact may explain why Orthodoxy has never had a Reformation.

That leads to a second observation about Orthodox Christianity: it has not experienced the Enlightenment either. Now in the twenty-first century, there are strange new experiences to face. As they do so, Orthodox Christians may benefit from contemplating the Reformation story, because they are now encountering the same Enlightenment culture as Protestantism and Roman Catholicism without ever having had the experience of Reformation. In an irony of history, Orthodoxy was protected from modernity by its enemies, first because the Ottoman

Turks marginalized it when they conquered the Byzantine Empire, then because it was cruelly persecuted by Russian Communism. In those circumstances, it needed all its courage and spiritual resources to survive, and it could not afford the luxury of thinking creatively about either Reformation or Enlightenment. But now Orthodoxy has no excuses in confronting the pluralism and primacy of choice which characterize the modern West, and the experience is likely to be traumatic. It is depressing watching current events in Russian Orthodoxy: the way that the Moscow Patriarchate dances to the tune played by President Putin and the Kremlin, delighted to have its place back in the limelight, with no sense of the dangers of power. Protestants, Muslims, Jehovah's Witnesses are all once more facing repression in Russia and other parts of the former Soviet Union. Perhaps now Orthodoxy will experience its own Reformation, but the omens so far are not good.

Are Western Christians all more or less now Protestants? The Reformation has become a central part of the Western legacy for both Europe and the United States. Perhaps the most precious thing the Reformation left as its legacy is something that Martin Luther probably never said: 'Here I stand, I can do no other.' It was actually some years after his death that those words were first written down, but Luther ought to have said them, because they sum up a little of what it is like being a Protestant. The idea became the central creed of the Enlightenment too. In the United States, even the Roman Catholic Church is a church of individualists who make their own decisions. They do not listen to their bishops, particularly when the bishops lecture them against the use of artificial contraception. If you follow Luther's supposed words, you stand alone, before your God, before your destiny (or however you want to put it), and ultimately you do not have the help of a tradition. You find your own matrix: that is the Western privilege and dilemma, the terrifying gift of being part of Western Enlightenment civilization. Luther already knew that feeling of terror.

The curious thing is that this emphasis on individual decision contradicts various other hopes and aims which were dear to the Reformers. The Reformation tried to be certain about religion. Just like the Roman Catholic Church, it wanted a single truth, and its quarrel with Rome was that Rome had distorted that truth. There is a tragedy in laying down clear, firm patterns, which give people a sense of rootedness and value, because religious belief is always open to change, to variety, to nuance, to subtlety. Great religious leaders are very often temperamentally inclined to discount subtlety. But God is often just out of reach – Luther, indeed, often talked about a hidden God. Most religion has a representational quality; it does not provide clear answers. It is instructive to see how a certain sort of conservative Protestantism and a certain sort of Counter-Reformation Catholicism both love the clear answers, how they very often say much the same things, particularly on sexuality. Listen to the late Dr Ian Paisley and the late Pope John Paul II on the subject of sex a few years back, and there were remarkable similarities, as there are in the case of their admirers. The two traditions, which in many ways hate each other, both chase similar certainties.

Those who call themselves religious traditionalists tend to be those who do not know enough about their religious tradition, or who have edited out those parts which they do not like. Moreover, their pro-claimed traditionalism too often turns out to be a tradition of saying no rather than yes. A proper traditionalism contemplates the whole range of its past. It is happy to say that past Christians, and past Christian dogmas, were as often wrong as they were right. Looking at the tangled story of the Christian past, I am not tied to an assumption that my little corner of belief has some innate advantage over any other. 'Blind unbelief is sure to err,' sang the Christian hymn-writer William Cowper (1731–1800). Historians are likely to retort that blind belief has a record even more abysmal, and that clear-sighted doubt might be the most healthy state of all. That is history's gift to the Church, and in a curious, topsy-turvy way, it is a gift that we owe to the Protestant Reformation. Let's be grateful for it.

PART I

Reformations across Europe

I

Christianity: the bigger picture

Christianity, as I have remarked elsewhere,[1] is in essence a personality cult. At the centre of its message is an individual person, Jesus – and his historical rooting as a person in a particular time and place is emphasized by the very ordinariness of that name for the Jewish society into which he was born. 'Jesus' is more properly 'Jeshua', the name of an ancient Jewish hero, who appears in anglophone Christian Bibles as Joshua (no doubt so that Christians may distinguish him from his later namesake). This Mr Average of Galilee has acquired what we might mistake for a surname, so he is called 'Jesus Christ'. But Christ is not a name but a title, significantly not in the Aramaic which Jesus spoke, but in Greek. It means 'the Anointed One' and is the translation of a Hebrew term meaning the same, a word familiar even to those beyond Judaism and Christianity as 'Messiah'.

Christians believe that the Christ who is an aspect of the God who was, is and ever shall be, is at the same time a human being set in historic time. History matters a great deal in Christianity, which is why it is so important to try and get the history right, and not be misled by shoddy versions of it. History was there from the start, given that Jesus would have grown up with a welter of stories about his Jewish past and its significance in God's purpose, many of them contained in the Hebrew Scripture which Christians call the Old Testament. The first surviving specifically Christian literature was a story or set of stories about how Jesus died: these are the 'Passion narratives' which are now embedded in the four Gospels, which are themselves a set of stories seeking to throw different spotlights on the God who was made man. Christians in our own age also believe that they can meet with this human being in as real a fashion as the disciples who walked with him in Galilee and saw him die on the Cross. They tell stories about themselves on the basis of these stories from the past – more Christian history.

Christian history is also the story of a book, the Christian Bible (which is actually a library of books – the Greek word *Biblia* is in the plural, meaning 'books'). When in the seventh and eighth centuries CE the Anglo-Saxons had to create a brand-new vocabulary in their own language for the theory and practice of Christianity, they considered what word they should use to describe this Bible, and they came up with 'biblioðece', which is the same word as the French still use for 'library'. Books are the storehouses for human ideas, and the Bible is no exception: whatever one thinks of its claims to authority, it is the record of one of humankind's attempts to access and understand the divine.

Ideas are independent variables of the human mind, which need to be taken seriously and understood in their own terms. Christianity has a huge capacity to mutate, like all successful major world faiths. Christians do not like being reminded of this, particularly those who are in charge of the various religious institutions which call themselves Churches, but that is the reality, and has been from the beginning. It will be better for the mental health of the followers of the great religions if they come to recognize this diversity as a virtue and not as a vice, an opportunity and not a threat.

Christianity was a marginal branch of Judaism whose founder Jesus left no known written works; Jesus seems to have maintained that the trumpet would sound for the end of time very soon, and in a major break with the culture around him, he told his followers to leave the dead to bury their dead. Yet, remarkably quickly, his followers seemed to question the idea that history was about to end: they collected and preserved stories about the founder. Within a few decades, they also survived a major crisis of confidence at the end of the first century, when the Last Days did not arrive. This was perhaps one of the greatest turning points in the Christian story, which shaped it into a very different institution from that of its founder or even of its great apostle, Paul, complete with an institutional hierarchy, a collection of credal statements and a closed canon of scripture; but we know little about it. Christianity, unlike Judaism, its parent faith, was not inclined to write about disappointment in its sacred literature.

A basic element in this chameleon-like character of Christianity is an instability which comes from its two-fold ancestry. Far from being simply the pristine, innovative teachings of Jesus Christ, it draws on two much more ancient cultural wellsprings: Greece and Israel. The story must begin among the ancient Greeks and the Jews, a thousand years before Jesus, hence the title of my general history of this religion, which I published as *Christianity: The First Three Thousand Years.* The first thousand of those three thousand years was in fact a pair of millennium-long histories marching side by side. Both Jews and Christians thought that they had a uniquely privileged place in the world's history. The extraordinary cultural achievements in art, philosophy and science of the ancient Greeks gave them some good reason to think this; more surprising was the fact that the constant experience of misfortune and destruction did not kill the Jews' faith in their own destiny. Instead it drove them to conceive of their God not simply as all-powerful, but passionately concerned with their response to Him, and passionate in anger as well as love towards them.

Such an intensely personal deity who was nevertheless the God for all humanity was very different from the supreme deity who emerged from Greek philosophy in the thought of Plato: all-perfect, and there-fore immune to change and so devoid also of the passion which denotes change. The first generations of Christians were Jews of the Eastern Mediterranean who lived in a Hellenistic world, shaped by Greek elite culture at least from the time of Alexander the Great's conquests, four centuries before. They had to try to fit together these two irreconcil-able Jewish and Greek visions of God – and the results have never been and can never be a stable answer to an unending question.

Most Christians alive in the world today are Catholics or Protes-tants, together more than 80 per cent of all Christians (if you lump in the Mormons). Another 10 per cent or more call themselves Ortho-dox, with some other local label attached – Greek Orthodox, Russian Orthodox, Romanian Orthodox and so on. That does not leave much over, as my schoolboy arithmetic tells me. But that sliver of alternative Christianity, the few per cents after you have added up all the Chris-tianities which I have just named, was once the future of the Church. It is the ancient Christianity of Africa and Asia, flourishing still in Ethiopia and India, finding an uneasy place in national life in Egypt, hanging on for dear life elsewhere in the Middle East, or unhappily, more often, finding exile in America or Australasia. That is a lost Christian history, which Western Christians need to know about if they are to have a proper perspective on their own history.

Because most Christians now are Catholics or Protestants, they give priority to their own history, which is the story of the Western, Latin-speaking Church, once so marginal, so provincial and unsophisticated in its thinking. But there was a time when the outcome looked very different. In the year 451, the Roman emperor, or rather his wife Pulcheria, a lady with whom it was unwise to trifle, summoned a Council of Bishops to a town called Chalcedon. It is no coincidence that Chalcedon was within easy reach of the imperial palace troops in Constantinople; you can still reach it on the Bosphorus ferry from Pulcheria's former capital Istanbul in forty minutes or so.

The issue at Chalcedon was a complicated argument about the natures of Jesus Christ: the balance between Jesus the man and Christ the divine Son of God. The imperial government was desperately concerned in this, because the arguments about it threatened to split the Empire in two. So the emperor offered the bishops a deal which was a deliberate compromise: steam-rolling a settlement through the middle of the opposing sides. At the centre of it was what has come to be known as the Chalcedonian Definition of the Natures of Christ: an intricate and extended juggling of technical theological language about 'nature' and 'persons' to capture the elusive combination of divinity and humanity in human language.[2] It is what Catholics, Protestants and Orthodox alike classically believe about this matter, which is, after all, at the heart of Christian belief.

In the traditional reading of the history of Christianity, the Council of Chalcedon of 451 has usually been seen as the culmination of the Early Church's story: a sort of Hercule Poirot denouement in the drawing room, where, after all the complications of the Early Church plot, the truth is revealed and then the credits roll. But this story of triumph is an illusion. Chalcedon was a catastrophe, a disaster. Fully two-thirds of the Church refused to sign up to it, in part at least, because they did not trust the emperor to do theology. Because it was a compromise, those who rejected it were on either wing, so they detested each other as much as they detested the emperor's Church, and actually, as I discovered when filming my history of Christianity in the Middle East, they still do.

So these refuseniks founded their own Churches, led by their own bishops; their snooty enemies in the emperor's Church gave them condescending names – Nestorians and Monophysites – and because those names are condescending, it is worth replacing them with admittedly clumsy labels which these Christians themselves might just find acceptable: Dyophysites and Miaphysites. They themselves, of course, would simply call themselves *Orthodox*. To the people we Westerners call Orthodox, and to Western Christians themselves, they were and are Unorthodox. Yet they are still with us. Far from the time that they and not the Church of the Roman and Byzantine Emperor seemed to represent the Christian future, the emperor's Church has descended into Roman Catholicism, Protestantism and Orthodoxy.

The outcome was long in the balance. It was much swayed by the astonishingly rapid early conquests of the Muslims in the seventh century; yet the first Muslim rulers did not regard their enterprise as promoting their faith in a missionary manner, and in fact Dyophysite Christianity flourished under their rule. When the Abbasid dynasty founded a great new Muslim capital and named it Baghdad, Dyophysites provided much of its intellectual life. The Dyophysite Church of the East was a think tank for the Muslim Abbasids in Baghdad. Because the Church of the East was so used to arguing about the natures of Christ with other Christians, and so adept at translating Greek philosophy and theology into its own Syriac language, it had all the intellectual equipment which the Arab Muslim rulers needed to access the wisdom of the past. Without the Church of the East, and its translation of Mediterranean Greek classics into Arabic, we would not have regained our access to much Greek philosophy, or even got to know about what we in the West call Arabic numerals (they actually came from India).

And the Church of the Middle East became the Church of the Far East. It reached to China, so outside the ancient imperial capital now called Xi'an, in the heart of the Chinese countryside, you can stand in the precinct of a Christian monastery from the seventh century, still called by the Chinese phrase for the Roman Empire, and so named Ta Qin. It is possible that there might be similar experiences on offer in monasteries in Korea, and even in Kyoto in Japan, which have been transformed into Buddhist shrines. But steadily, bit by bit, this future of Christianity was eroded. Plague, massacre, victimization by mad or bad monarchs: Islam faced all these disasters too, but in the worst times, Islam found more powerful friends in Asia than the Christians. It might have taken just one more Mongol warlord to listen to his Dyophysite Christian mother or sister, and central Asia would have become Christian rather than Muslim – but it was not to be. So bishops in Tibet found no successors, and monasteries in Mongolia crumbled into dust.

Into the vacuum stepped others, in particular the Bishop of Rome, the Pope. I called that section of my *Christianity: The First Three Thousand Years* which does catch up with the Western story, 'The Unpredictable Rise of Rome'. My point was that there was nothing inevitable about the modern papacy, and the claims that it makes for its special authority have only been remotely plausible for about half of Christianity's history. The early Church looked to five patriarchs, not one, and there is still another pope in Alexandria. It has not been good for the spiritual health of the Roman Church to look to a single leader, however much it helped to pack the pews throughout the world in the last century. Moreover, the more recent history of the Roman Catholic Church (that part of the Western Church which remained loyal to the pope in the sixteenth century) contains a paradox: from the early nineteenth century, popes became more autocratic, just at the time when, throughout most of Europe, autocracy was giving way to democracy. The Catholic Church turned its back on a medieval 'conciliarist' current of thought which stressed a much wider sharing of power and decision-making, through councils of Church leaders and maybe even laypeople. Additionally, the accident of the French Revolution severely crippled the power of rival focuses of authority within the Church: it had destroyed the Holy Roman Empire, removing its emperor and the prince-bishops who had had a tendency to treat papal claims to monarchy with a sceptical eye. The pope then stood alone like a post when the rest of the building has collapsed, and recent papal claims to authority are based on that historical circumstance. Now, in the wake of the second Vatican Council of the 1960s, we have witnessed half a century of struggle between

Catholics who wish to defend that papal monarchy and those who wish to restore the conciliarist programme.

Is it worth the effort to refocus the history of Christianity in such ways as these? Emphatically yes – because in the last forty years religion has thrust itself into the consciousness even of secular Europe. When I was an undergraduate at the end of the 1960s, the future of religion was commonly yoked to the word 'secularization': the assumption that religion's power to influence the mind of humanity was waning in the face of increasing secular-mindedness, and that it would retire gracefully out of the political or public world into the private sphere. But in 1977 the first born-again Christian President (Jimmy Carter) took office, in 1978 a Counter-Reformation pope, John Paul II, was elected, and in 1979 the Ayatollahs seized control of the Iranian Revolution. I could extend the chronology year by year into a relentless succession of events. Europe, far from setting the pattern for the world in secularization, has proved the exception to the worldwide reassertion of religion. One or another form of religion matters desperately to the overwhelming majority of human beings alive, and if historians ignore that plain fact, they are ignoring reality.

I also think of modern worldwide controversies which historians may help to unravel. Take the furious modern rows about sexuality. In the present day, many conservative Evangelical Protestants refuse to accept new configurations of human sexuality, in the name of faithfulness to the Bible. What they often fail to notice is that they have already assisted in one major rejection of biblical authority, one of the most significant so far in the history of Christianity. In the eighteenth and nineteenth centuries a crucial minority of Evangelicals successfully campaigned for the abolition of slavery, in defiance of that same Bible, in which there is a clear and consistent acceptance of the permanent existence of slavery. The same Evangelicals who proclaim biblical certainties are proud of an achievement which defied biblical certainties. This will not be the last occasion on which there will be such a dramatic change of direction. Christianity is a mere two thousand years old, a tiny fraction of human experience over millennia. It is a young religion, finding its way; that is what makes it exciting to contemplate.

It is always worth emphasizing the diversity and the unexpected, crabwise evolution of Christianity, or indeed of any religious system. One of the most unattractive features of a certain sort of religious outlook is its insistence that it represents the only true or authentic face of the religion of which it is a part. Of course, this is not the exclusive property of religion. Sébastien-Roch Nicolas de Chamfort, who managed to preserve his sense of humour through the French Revolutionary Terror, wearily paraphrased its slogan 'Fraternity or death' as the proposition 'Be my brother, or I'll kill you'. One could read the history of the world after the French Revolution in terms of the tidy-mindedness of certain pathological forms of the Enlightenment: a dogmatism which fuelled Fascism and Stalinism, and has brought measureless misery to the world.

This common human pathology of dogmatism, religious or non-religious, is based on pride. The most plausible doctrine of Western Christianity, depressingly, is original sin, and at the root of all sin is pride. If historians are prophets (and they should be, in the original meaning of the Hebrew equivalent of that word, 'spokespeople'), then their principal prophecy is against pride, a characteristic that is also the target of the court jester. The good historian and the successful court jester have much to say to each other.

2

Angels and the Reformation

Angels, so splendidly introduced to us by a team of essayists commanded by Professors Marshall and Walsham, are a fairly natural outcrop of the problem faced by all humans who wish to affirm an all-powerful God, wholly other than themselves and the divinely created cosmos around them. How could a creator beyond all worlds have any relationship to the created? The discovery of angels provided a satisfying answer. The word 'angel' echoes the Greek for 'messenger', which in the Hebrew scripture, the Tanakh (called the Old Testament by Christians), appears as *mal'ak*; so an angel is the accredited agent of communication used by the deity. Scattered through the Tanakh, angels perform various useful chores for God – one intervenes, for instance, countermanding God's first order to Abraham to sacrifice his son Isaac with a last-minute pardon for the boy (Genesis 22:9–12). Later, according to Genesis 28:10–12, the sleeping Jacob observes angels going about their everyday business, up and down a ladder to heaven. These angels are famously sculpted on the early sixteenth-century west front of the Priory Church at Bath, ascending and descending their turret-ladders like holy termites; those heading for humankind, still burdened with the contents of God's out-tray, are portrayed upside down (see Plates 1–3). The ensemble at Bath engagingly commemorates a dream about a dream, since the church's complete rebuilding was the result of Bishop Oliver King of Bath and Wells contemplating Jacob's ladder in his sleep.

The usefulness of angels increased as Judaism was confronted with Hellenism. Because of the prestige of Greek learning among the Jews, the grittily personal Yahweh of the Jews, by turns wrathful and loving, had now to be envisaged in terms of the distance, passionlessness and perfection which characterized the ultimate deity in Platonic philosophy. Early Christians, puzzling over their new claims that a man Jesus was somehow that ultimate deity, and having at their disposal the Tanakh plus the man-in-the-street's version of Platonism, gratefully turned to the angels in their new narratives of divinity. Most memorable was the appearance of an angel at that tricky moment of union between the divine and the human: the Annunciation of the coming Nativity to the Mother of Jesus (Luke 1:26–38), a scene of intimacy which became one of the staples of Christian sacred art, once Christians decided to indulge in sacred art. Some angels in both the Tanakh and New Testaments gained distinctive personalities through having names, Gabriel of the Annunciation for example; alongside him were Michael, a useful colleague in a scrap, and Raphael, who was good to have around if one was feeling under the weather. Much later, in late medieval Germany, the over-imaginative Benedictine Abbot Johannes Trithemius envisaged Raphael presiding over the invention of writing and the popularization of music, both of which can indeed be enjoyable concomitants of convalescence.

And there was another angel who gained not one but several names: for reasons best known to himself, he went freelance in the messenger business, and took various other angels with him. His first appearances in the Tanakh did not quite fit the angel mode, but then there was no single mode to begin with. He was called the Adversary, Hassatan, and although he was a fairly insignificant nuisance in the Hebrew Scriptures, he grew in status in later Jewish literature, particularly among writers who were influenced by other religious cultures which told of powerful demonic figures. Hassatan caught the imagination of the Christian sects in Judaism, and by the time that the Christian Book of Revelation was written towards the end of the first century CE, he had become a figure of cosmic significance and was now called Satan or Lucifer (see Isaiah 14:12). In Revelation 12:7–9, his fall from Heaven, as described by Isaiah and Ezekiel, was turned into a more circumstantial story of warfare in Heaven, and Christians saw him as the final adversary for God in the end-time. The fallen angel Satan/Lucifer, a shapeshifter who might become a dragon or a King of Tyre or even a beautiful good angel, is a frequent visitor to the pages of both the volumes under review, and rightly so. Angelology goes hand in hand with demonology, which has frequently excited Christians more, and hence the essayists are also led into discussion of witchcraft. What is pleasing about the present pair of books is that witches, almost over-researched in the last half-century, are kept in their place in the course of the two volumes' innovative investigation of a theme in early modern Christianity which might be seen as even more important.

How should an idea of personality be developed in relation to angels from the starting-point of their names? Names imply some resemblance, however distant, to human beings. As messengers were prone to be males in ancient society, angels were habitually regarded as male, though not very male. In the Tanakh they were prone to look like human beings, as when Abraham entertained three of them to dinner, with propitious consequences (Genesis 18:1–22 – though it was not clear whether, in actuality, the Deity himself was moonlighting on this occasion). Given angels' constant gadding to and fro from Heaven, it was not surprising that Christians, short of experience in portraying the sacred, took a hint from Greek and Roman figures of Victory and gave angels wings. Soon a problem was beginning to arise for the Early Church: from the time that Christians began considering that certain deceased human beings were also potential go-betweens with God, initially because of the impressively heroic nature of their deaths, there was a problem of demarcation.

How did the developing cult of the saints relate to the tasks performed by the likes of Gabriel, Raphael and Michael? It was so difficult to keep the work of angels and saints apart that the named angels came to be treated as saints, and in the Western Latin Church, one even gained a universally observed feast-day. I am writing this on Michaelmas Day, still fossilized in English law as one of the most important financial nodal points of the year (Gabriel did not do so well, but he also gained a festival for a while in the English diocese of Exeter, thanks to the enthusiasm of one fifteenth-century bishop). As the Western Roman Empire crumbled into something else during the fifth century, Michael, the soldier-angel, took his place along soldier-saints, almost equally insubstantial figures like George or Sergius and Bacchus, whose cults enjoyed enormous popularity in a world all too familiar with unsaintly soldiers. Michael made up for his lack of capacity to provide saintly relics for the faithful's devotion by acquiring an extraordinary array of holy high places across Europe, all dedicated to him, so that churches of St Michael-in-the-Mount can be found on the European map in a rich variety of languages. Still Michael and his angelic fellows kept their wings, which remained a useful instant visual distinction from those fleshly saintly beings who had entered heavenly bliss with no questions asked at the gate.

Just at the time that Michael was seizing the imagination of fifth- and sixth-century Christians, there came the intervention of a Syrian monk. He was so obscure that we have never discovered his real name, but he has proved one of the most important thinkers in the history of Christian Churches, in both east and west. Indeed, he claimed to be an associate of the man who might well be described as the most important Christian thinker after Jesus Christ, the apostle Paul. He took on the name and personality of Paul's chief convert in the largely unreceptive city of Athens, Dionysius the Areopagite, who had lived some four centuries before the Syrian monk's own time. There was good reason for this protective clothing, because one remarkable fact is apparent from Pseudo-Dionysius's writings: in terms of both Catholic and Orthodox Christianity, he was a heretic (a fact, as far as I could see, noted neither by Feisal G. Mohamed nor any of Marshall and Walsham's essayists). The pseudonymous writer's theological outlook was Miaphysite: in other words, he rejected the compromise formula which the imperial family steam-rollered through the Council of Chalcedon in 451, a rejection shared by the overwhelming majority of Christians to the east and south-east of the Roman Empire at the time. And yet he was enormously influential; he flits through the pages of these two books as frequently as does the Devil, though with a rather different effect. His respectability was aided in the Western Church when a ninth-century abbot of Saint-Denis near Paris creatively confused him with the identically named French bishop who was patron saint to Abbot Hilduin's own abbey. Nevertheless, this was as much effect as cause, part of an enthusiastic first reception of Pseudo-Dionysius in the West which, from then on, fed a mystical tradition previously little-resourced by Western theology. An essential element in Dionysius's impact was his dragooning of the angels into hierarchies (in fact he seems to have invented the word 'hierarchy', as Mohamed points out, although his suggested etymology of it at p. 9 is eccentric – it simply means 'rule by a priest'). This layered procession of beings from high to low kept the Deity safely corralled away from created substance: a Platonist strategy which would have gladdened the hearts of gnostic Christians back in the second century CE.

Blithely ignoring that dismaying thought, not to mention the Miaphysite milieu of Dionysius's writings, medieval Western Christians lapped up the pseudonymous Syrian's tidy-minded mapping of celestial society. After all, they lived in a hierarchical world, and it was natural to suppose that the world beyond was even better organized. In fact, many of them improved on Dionysius's scheme, revelling in further complexity. Mohamed helpfully provides a tabulated comparison of how the thirteenth-century Franciscan theologian Bonaventure elaborated Dionysius, and he also reproduces part of Dean John Colet's equally complex manuscript diagram from nearly two centuries later. Bonaventure is another writer weaving his way throughout these two books, and his speculations are a good illustration of the way in which discussion of angels became a nose of wax: a convenient dump for whatever theological point a theologian wanted to make.

Chief among these points was the tendency of clergy in every age to take themselves very seriously. One reason why those medieval Western clerics embraced Dionysius with such enthusiasm was that he had designed his hierarchy as a parallel to the sublunary world of ecclesiastical sacraments and offices in the Church, as indeed the etymology of 'hierarchy' implied. For Dionysius, bishops equated to 'Dominations' among the angels, ranking just below the dominical sacraments, and from there the clerical orders descended to lay catechumens, whose equivalents among the angels were not dignified with any other particular term of art. Obsession with angels thus frequently lined up with hyper-clericalism, as it certainly did in the case of John Colet. Yet if clergy were thus seen as close to angels, it gave them a frightening responsibility. Just as pseudo-Dionysius's contemporaries among

Syrian monks expressed their sense of closeness to God by the most savage mortification of their bodies, so Colet lashed out at the failings of his fellow clergy with a relish that Protestants later mistook for anti-clericalism; it was in fact precisely the reverse.

Even those Renaissance humanists who had no vested interest in boosting the role of clergy bought into pseudo-Dionysius – though their emphasis was slightly different. Intoxicated with their own excitement at their rediscoveries in ancient philosophy and magic, they saw Dionysius's vision as offering all humans the chance to resemble angels. Reading in the Marshall and Walsham volume Bruce Gordon's entertaining dissection of the discussion of angels in the Renaissance is a sobering reminder of what terrible old nonsense clever people will create if they put their minds to it: the writings of Pico della Mirandola and Johannes Trithemius are particularly instructive in this regard. Yet one has to remember that they were trying to use words to describe that which is beyond description: not merely the nature of an angel, but the being of God. Their torrent of words and celestial categories should perhaps be compared to musical composition – meaningless in one sense, yet in another the only way of capturing the meaning of the sublime.

It is not surprising that the Reformation brought challenging times for angels. The Dionysian tradition had entangled them in the pretensions of the old clerical hierarchy, and popular devotion had embedded them deep in the cult of the saints, so Protestants needed to do a great deal of furious rethinking about them, among much other fury. The saving grace for the angels, in contrast to the saints, was that they were indisputably prominent in the Bible, and their constant occupation fighting their former colleagues, the followers of Satan, was a thoroughly congenial theme to Protestants, whose mindset was one of struggle and whose thoughts so frequently turned to Antichrist. So angels survived, as demons survived: there were even guardian angels for elect Puritans. In fact, as is revealed successively by Peter Marshall ('Angels around the deathbed'), Raymond Gillespie ('Imagining angels in early modern Ireland') and Joad Raymond ('"With the tongues of angels": angelic conversations in *Paradise Lost* and seventeenth-century England'), English and Irish Protestant Dissenters were liable to be much more extravagantly enthusiastic for the powers and potential of angels than members of the Protestant episcopal Established Church.

Predictably, Luther and Calvin took up radically different stances, as Philip Soergel's essay on 'Luther and the angels' reveals. The divergence was very like their split on their respective views of Mary the Mother of the Lord – hardly surprisingly, in view of Mary's intimate links with angels, both with Gabriel and those who visited the shepherds after the Nativity. Luther never lost his warm devotion either to Mary or angels; with characteristic energy, he took delight in remoulding these feelings to bolster his deep Christocentricity. Calvin, preoccupied with the dangers of idolatry, was sour about both Mary and angels, grudgingly unable to deny their place in God's purpose, but unwilling to make undue fuss about it in case it gave people the wrong idea.[1] Calvin's reductionism was echoed by Archbishop Ussher of Armagh, balancing profound historical scholarship, rugged Reformed Protestantism and a conviction of the rightness of episcopacy when in the year of peril 1641 he argued that the angel of the Church in the Book of Revelation, Chapter 1, was no more nor less than a flesh-and-blood bishop, not unlike himself.

It is easy to understand the feelings of Reformed theologians – not just Calvin – when one contemplates the lush developments of angels in the Roman Catholic Counter-Reformation. One can hardly imagine its triumphal atmosphere without the host of bewinged and gilded beings, as resplendent and all-pervasive in Mannerist, Baroque and Rococo church interiors as butterflies in the rain-forest – right down to the fag-end of the Pseudo-Dionysian system represented by the two little bored cherubs who are a staple of modern greeting-card shops. There is a rich seam of information in Walsham/Marshall on the multiple ways in which angels assisted the resurgent Church of Rome. Fernando Cervantes excitingly opens up their usefulness in mopping up or countering identities from among the multiple deities encountered by the Spaniards in the New World; he is aided by a striking image (provided by the editors) of an angel from Lake Titicaca, fashionably dressed as a gentleman, complete with broad-brimmed hat, cheerfully brandishing a gun, his wings somewhat superfluous to the requirements of a jaunty young Spanish grandee.

The late Trevor Johnson shows how the Jesuits in this, as in so much else, quietly forgot their early risky speculations about angels in the course of their hugely successful makeover as the Papacy's most loyal assistants. It is reassuring to learn from the Society that Ignatius probably shared with Our Lady the privilege of having a guardian archangel rather than merely an angel: a necessary precaution, in view of the attacks which the Jesuits faced on all sides 'by heretics and even by Catholics'.[2]

María Tausiet concentrates on the combat with demons in Spain, who, particularly on the borders with French Protestants, could be appreciated as a gift of God, demonstrating the power of the true Church, when they were eventually vanquished. Robin Briggs also introduces us to preoccupations with demons, this time in the writings of Jean Bodin. From the age of thirty-seven, Bodin had constant guidance from a spirit who appeared to be a guardian angel. The sage's eagerness to make sure that witches were persecuted was a useful smokescreen for his own very peculiar and eminently punishable heresies. The afterlife of Reformation and Counter-Reformation is glimpsed in Elizabeth Reis's presentation of New England, where angels gained something of a boost from the eighteenth-century Great Awakenings. There is irony here, because (as Alexandra Walsham reminds us) the same George Whitefield who was so important in the Awakenings back home in England proved the nemesis of angels in the little Suffolk town of Bildeston (not Bidleston as in the text). The churchwardens, inspired by Whitefield's preaching, arranged for the hacking-down and burning of the angels carved in the splendid medieval nave roof of their church; the damage can still be seen.

Owen Davies notes the peculiarity that English folklore in the nineteenth and twentieth centuries seems almost entirely innocent of angels, despite the continuing prevalence of the guardian angel in the consciousness of many children, and he speculates that spiritualism has come to provide a more reliable and democratic path to the other world than arbitrarily arranged angelic visitations.

Feisal Mohamed's book reads like an extended version of an essay from Marshall's and Walsham's book (to which, indeed, it makes generous and appropriate reference), and is a useful study of the literary and theological presence of angels in English Protestant thought from Richard Hooker to John Milton. Mohamed rightly emphasizes the importance of Pseudo-Dionysius to this theme, although for the most part his story is of good Protestants following Calvin in their scepticism about the Areopagite's fantasies. Colet is a prolegomenon to these English Reformed writers, to stress just how different and how medieval he was (Colet's stock as morning-star of the Reformation has crashed in recent years, aided by Jonathan Arnold's demonstration of his mediocre performance as Dean of St Paul's).[3] Milton, as Mohamed points out (p. 106), accepted Pseudo-Dionysius as a Father of the Church only so that he could sneer at all the Church Fathers. Milton is the star of this study, occupying around half of its text, and Mohamed provides detailed examination of his treatment of Raphael and Michael. He leaves the reader with a convincing picture of the perplexities faced by a sensitive and cultured Reformed Christian in sorting out from two thousand years of religious experience what should be valued, and what should be junked, in order to create an epic for his own time.

3

The Virgin Mary and Protestant Reformers

Let us contemplate Thomas Cranmer, Primate of All England, sitting on an altar to preside over the trial of Anabaptist heretics. The time is May 1549; the altar, unceremoniously covered over to support the judge, is that of the Lady Chapel in St Paul's Cathedral in London: several of the heretics on trial have denied the Catholic doctrine of the Incarnation, and one will later be burned at the stake. In a compelling paradox, an archbishop tramples an altar of Our Lady in the course of defending the Incarnation. One witness in the crowd of onlookers was a pious and scholarly Welsh Catholic, Sir Thomas Stradling, who later wrote down his reactions to the occasion. He interpreted it as the uncannily accurate fulfilment of an eleventh-century prophecy to be found in a manuscript in his own library: Cranmer, he pointed out, went on to be punished for his blasphemy first by the 1549 rebellions and then by his fiery death at the stake.[1]

The scandal of Cranmer on the Lady altar tells us a good deal about the ambiguous feelings of the Reformers for Our Lady. On the one hand they saw it as a major work of piety to demolish and demystify the cultic and devotional world of which she was the centrepiece. On the other, they needed her as a bastion to defend the Catholic faith against the more militant forces which the Reformation had unleashed. They wished her to play her part in the biblical narrative which they were proclaiming to the world, and which they felt was threatened from the two opposed forces of papistry and radicalism. But in the ambiguity of their feelings towards Mary, they were being true to what they found in the biblical text: here was a story of Mary which not only was restricted in scope but also contained elements of both praise and reserve. The Reformers' task was one of restoration as much as destruction.

Since so much of the Reformers' relations with Mary were determined by the scriptural text, it is inevitable that the prehistory of their attitudes lies in the mind of Desiderius Erasmus. The young Erasmus, innocent of his later career as a biblical scholar, did what any young humanist cleric with conventional ambitions would have done – he wrote elegant Latin verse in praise of Mary. His *Supplication to the Virgin* has the extravagant note which one expects in late medieval literature: he calls her 'my salvation, my sole and certain refuge'; 'the beautiful moon, sister and mother of the eternal sun'. In his *Paean*, written at much the same time, he styled Mary 'a true Diana', as he also did in the *Supplication*; yet by 1528, in his *Ciceronian*, the mature biblical critic and doyen of humanists was ridiculing those who might seek to portray Jesus as Apollo and his mother as Diana, and his earlier poetry clearly embarrassed him.[2] That note was sounded in a letter to Thomas More even before he had got very far in his biblical study, and in the same year his Christocentric devotional work, *The Enchiridion*, pioneered an observation which became a cliché of Protestant moralizing: 'No devotion is more pleasing to Mary than the imitation of Mary's humility.'[3] In another classic statement, Erasmus pointed out the obvious, but also left a timebomb for the Western Church: 'Christ is the anchor of our salvation, Mary is not.'[4]

When Erasmus turned his scrutiny onto the text of the Bible, his work proved a devastating broadside against much of the critical structure created by the doyen of biblical commentary, Jerome, which had been formative in the development of Mariology. If readers of the Bible note allegory in its text, they should do so with due caution, and direct it aright. Erasmus came to deplore the use of wisdom material from the Song of Songs or the Book of Sirach in relation to Mary; if there was allegory in the figure of the beautiful bride or the pre-existent wisdom, this should refer to the Church and its relation with the saviour. Protestant commentaries would ram home this message.[5]

An issue over allegory which proved more troublesome to Protestants was the perpetual virginity of Mary: much of the traditional case for this belief was based on a directly allegorical use of Ezekiel 44:2, on the shutting of a gate through which only the Lord could enter, bolstered by a Latin reading of Isaiah's prophecy of a young woman conceiving the son Immanuel (Isaiah 7:14). Erasmus could not read these as Jerome had done. In response to shocked complaints about his comments, he set out a precise position: 'We believe in the perpetual virginity of Mary, although it is not expounded in the sacred books.'[6] Other insights of Erasmus proved crucial to the revolution in soteriology which was to come. In his 1519 revision of his New Testament edition, he rewrote the Latin version of the angelic salutation which was quoted devotionally in the 'Hail Mary'; now the Virgin became '*gratiosa*' rather than '*gratia plena*', and thus less available as a prop for the theology of merit.[7] He sneered at the misguided piety which led some to use Luke 2:51, the statement that Jesus was subject to his parents, to affirm that Jesus still owed obedience to his mother. This outbreak of common sense might sound trivial, but it was of huge importance, since it was a wedge to split apart the edifice of intercession by Mary to her son which had become so all-pervasive in Western popular devotion.[8]

After such rethinking of the fundamentals, it was inevitable that the cults of Mary and indeed of all the saints should come into Erasmus's sights. Famously in his *Colloquies*, he turned his pilgrimage to Walsingham and Canterbury into light comedy for the public.[9] This was part of a vigorous debunking of the physicality and tactility of late medieval popular piety which reflected Erasmus's distaste for lay devotion; for all his loudly proclaimed vision of the labourer reading the Bible at the ploughtail, and his strictures on the clericalism of his age, he was profoundly repelled when he observed the everyday reality of Western Christendom's layfolk grasping at the sacred. His nausea would become naturalized in Protestantism, particularly in its Reformed variety.[10] The intellectual genealogy is clear. Erasmus attacked the excesses of the cult of relics, devoting particular wit to the easy target of relics of milk from the Virgin: a particularly heavy-handed (not to say offensive) version of this sarcasm can be found in John Calvin's anti-relic tract of 1544.[11] Erasmus developed the topos of the saints having replaced pagan deities: St Anthony had taken over from Aesculapius and the Virgin Mary had staged a *coup d'état* against Proserpine. In the *Colloquies* and elsewhere he sneered at sailors in distress who used titles for Mary like 'Star of the Sea, Queen of

Heaven, Mistress of the World, Port of Salvation'.[12] All this can be found echoed in a classic and influential demolition of the cult of saints and relics by Heinrich Bullinger, *De origine erroris libri duo*, which, via its 1539 edition, came to be plagiarized around 1560 in the longest single reference to Mary in all the Homilies of the Church of England: a purple passage in the blockbuster-length *Homily against Peril of Idolatry*.[13]

One must point out that Erasmus's revisionism on Mary, together with his irritable sallies of defence against the sniping of conservatives, has to be balanced with expressions of apparently genuine devotion to the person and work of the Virgin, to be found liberally scattered through his writings throughout his career. Even one of his very last works, a collection of prayers of 1535, is careful to include a notably traditional prayer to the Virgin.[14] As the consequences of his attacks became plain in the first decade of the Reformation, Erasmus had drawn back in alarm and done his best to reaffirm some old certainties. One of the most unexpected of his writings after the Luther explosion is his *Votive Mass of Notre Dame of Loreto*, a venture into liturgy unique for him, published in 1523 at the request of a friend who was the parish priest of Porrentruy, not far from Basel. However, what is noticeable in this apparent attempt at reconciliation with the world of holy places is the emphasis on the Passion of Christ, together with a complete absence of any positive celebration of the Holy House, something which is quite an achievement in the circumstances. Erasmus included a homily in the mass which managed to dwell on the common late medieval theme of the sufferings of Mary, while at the same time criticizing some of the devotion and iconography which it had attracted: 'She suffered at her son's suffering, but by force of character she restrained the human feelings of her heart, she smothered her sighs, she held back her flowing tears, and while the rest of the disciples fled in fear, she alone stood with John beside her son's cross. Those pictures, which show her fallen down and stricken with fainting, dead with suffering, are damaging. She did not wail, tear her hair, beat her breast or cry out that she was unhappy. She drew more comfort from the redemption of mankind than suffering from the death of her son.'[15]

Here was a possible direction in which reformed Catholicism might

travel. Erasmus's biographer Léon-Ernest Halkin has indeed suggested that his revised Mariology made him the predecessor of
Muratori and the Catholic Enlightenment.[16] There might have been a
future for a Mariology drawing on the Christocentric theology of the
Passion in a Catholicism which had not been traumatized by the Reformation. If one considers the *Spirituali* in Italy in the 1530s and
1540s, for instance, there is the example of Vittoria Colonna, lay theologian and patron of Michelangelo. Inspired by Michelangelo's gift
to her of a drawing of a *Pietà*, one among his artistic meditations on
the Sorrows of the Virgin, Colonna wrote poetry which concentrated
on this theme of the bond between mother and son in the Passion,
which so illuminated for her the way in which Christ's death transformed death, and the son's body, caressed by the Virgin, showed
forth the divine gifts of the Spirit. Her Mariology could therefore
become an organic part of a theology which emphasized the *spirituale*
themes of the death, resurrection and the work of the Holy Spirit:
themes which strike a chord with the Reformed spirituality of the
north. However, it is striking that such Marian themes do not emerge
when Colonna corresponded with another outstanding humanist
writer, Marguerite of Angoulême. Both women might have been
expected to draw on the well of feminine models provided by Mary;
the five extant letters between this distinguished devotional pairing
bulge with scriptural allusions, yet those relating either directly or
allegorically to the Virgin are noticeable by their absence.[17]

Moreover, the fate of *spirituale* piety was to be driven to the margins of Catholic spirituality, to face systematic suppression or to seek
refuge in Protestantism. The *Spirituali* became a might-have-been of
Catholic history. A contrast and significant pointer to what would be
the actual future is provided by the career of one contemporary of
Erasmus who sought to follow in his revisionist or mediating path:
the Franciscan friar from Avignon, François Lambert. Around 1520,
Lambert published *La couronne de Notre Seigneur Jésus-Christ*, a
devotional work modelled on the rosary, but transferring its Marian
focus to the person of Christ: it contained thirty-three mysteries of the
life of Christ. Yet the work still referred to Our Lady, and sought her
intercession as well as those of the angels and saints: it affirmed the
Immaculate Conception, and prayed devoutly for the Pope.[18] Not

long afterwards, in summer 1522, Lambert took it upon himself to travel to Zürich in the middle of the ferment of its Reformation, and he preached in the Fraumünster, on the subject of intercession by Mary and the saints. This was the famous occasion on which Huldrych Zwingli heckled the preacher, bellowing out *'Bruder, da irrest du'* ('That's where you're wrong, Brother'). On the following day Lambert was involved in debate with Zwingli; it was the last time that the friar wore his Franciscan habit, and after that he was launched on his own brief but intensely active life as a champion of Reformation. No more talk of Our Lady's intercession from him.[19]

Lambert's apostasy brings us at last to the Reformation itself, and the double legacy of destruction and affirmation which Martin Luther bequeathed to its various outworkings. Erasmus had refocused scripture, subverted pilgrimage and saintly intercession and emphasized the Passion and saving work of Christ. All this was welded into a potent and destructive force by Luther's fiery and single-minded promotion of justification by faith only. It was unlikely that the mediation of the saints would have for long escaped a clash with his message, but the very liveliness of the pilgrimage industry brought immediacy to the contest. Already in one of his key declarations of war on the old world of devotion in 1520, the *Address to the Christian Nobility of the German Nation*, Luther drew attention to the most recently and dramatically created Marian shrine in Germany. This was the 'Beautiful Mary' of Regensburg, a Frankenstein's monster created (with nice historical irony) by the future radical Balthasar Hubmaier. Hubmaier, then a highly traditionalist preacher at the cathedral, had in winter 1519 incited an anti-Jewish pogrom in Regensburg, after which Our Lady was drafted in to cure a workman badly injured during the demolition of the synagogue. Fifty thousand pilgrims were reputed to have visited the makeshift shrine chapel within a month of its completion on the Feast of the Assumption, 1519. Hubmaier's unappealing combination of anti-Semitism and Marian fervour (both of which he later regretted) was to have a dire effect on the place of Mary in Protestant Europe: it was the equivalent of Johann Tetzel's indulgence campaign in catalysing a violent reaction in Luther. The year-old Beautiful Mary fired Luther's fury: it formed the climax of his list of offensive shrines that should be 'levelled' ('*vorstoret*') as he launched a bitter diatribe against pilgrim-age in the *Address*.[20]

Luther had thus given one particular cue for destructive action to the many people who were beginning to look to him for guidance. There was one further connection which needed to be made to complete the logic of destruction: shrines often centred on a statue, and Marian shrines invariably did. It was Luther's colleague in Witten-berg, Andreas Karlstadt, who made the link between shrines and the evil of images generally. In January and February 1522, with Luther away in the Wartburg, crowds destroyed images in some of the churches of Wittenberg, inspired by Karlstadt.[21] Luther promptly stopped this in March, but the following year Zwingli's parallel Ref-ormation in Zürich followed Karlstadt's lead, turning popular vandalism into an orderly and thorough-going cleansing of the churches. Naturally, images of Mary, so prominent in the iconography of medieval church interiors, were prime targets in this process: vic-tims of what, by analogy with *hyperdulia*, might be styled *hyperphobia*. Luther had little time for either Karlstadt or Zwingli's Zürich, but he could hardly unsay what he had said about pilgrimage in the *Address to the Christian Nobility of the German Nation*. In 1522 Wolfgang Russ preached at the Bavarian shrine of Our Lady of Altötting against Marian devotion and miracles: it was the beginning of nearly half a century of eclipse for the shrine until the Counter-Reformation put a special effort into reviving it.[22] Russ's echo of Luther's call for action was repeated throughout northern Europe: over the next couple of years, images of Mary which were special focuses of pilgrims' devotion became prime symbols of what needed to be destroyed. In March 1524, enthusiasts for the Reformation in Allstedt were inspired by their preacher Thomas Müntzer to turn on the nearby Marian shrine at Mallerbach; they terrorized its hermit custodian into flight and ended up burning the place down.[23] In the same year, far to the north in Riga, a similar group of the godly denounced as a witch the much-venerated statue of the Virgin in the cathedral, uprooted it and ducked it in the river: since the wooden object floated, they pronounced it guilty and burned it at Kubsberg, the customary place to punish witches.[24]

This carnivalesque mixture of the spontaneous, the calculated and the ritualistic, set the pattern for what happened in Reformed Protestant lands over the next century and into the general mayhem of the Thirty Years War: from England, one could multiply examples of exemplary destruction of Marian images from the time of Thomas Cromwell, Edward VI or Elizabeth I. These atrocities spawned a new genre of Roman Catholic Marian devotion, what might be styled cults of battered Marys: images which had been rescued after Protestant vandalism and were thus seen as especially worthy exemplars of the sufferings of Our Lady. One can cite particular examples from Paris in 1528 (rebattered in 1545 and 1551), pre-Calvinist Geneva in 1532, or Valladolid in 1600: this last battered Mary, victim of the ideologically fuelled English raid on Cadiz in 1596, was specifically renamed Santa Maria Vulnerata.[25] One has to emphasize, however, that this violent assault on the physical symbols of Mary was a phenomenon of Reformed Protestant Europe, of the heirs of Karlstadt and Zwingli; it died away wherever Protestantism was chivvied into that modified version of Luther's bundle of beliefs which has come to be styled Lutheranism. Luther's horror at the consequences of Karlstadt's actions in Wittenberg drove him furiously to think about the image problem, and led him to the conclusion that there was no problem. Once the more ridiculous or dangerous images had been put aside, the old statues, pictures and stained glass could be left to bring innocent delight and edification to the faithful.[26] The consequences can pleasurably be seen in Lutheran northern Europe to this day; two examples will suffice. In Lübeck Cathedral, the great Rood group has now survived both the Reformation and Allied air raids, so the attendant Mary and John still guard the crucifix on their fourteenth-century screen. Perhaps most memorable of all Mary's appearances in Lutheran church interiors is Veit Stoss's glorious suspended sculpture of the Annunciation which hangs above the high altar of the parish church of St Lorenz in Nuremberg (and restored in modern times to its original position after some years of discreet withdrawal).

Luther was not simply reacting to what he regarded as the crassness of Karlstadt. He quickly matched his assault on the Marian cult with a positive repositioning of Mary as part of his own announcement of the message of salvation. He first set this out in one of his most eloquent devotional writings, the *Commentary on the Magnificat*:

published in September 1521, it was begun even before he had left Wittenberg to defy the Holy Roman Emperor at the Diet of Worms.[27] It was no mechanical exercise for Luther to explore Mary's song. He showed how much of traditional devotion to Mary he was prepared to admit in his paraphrase of the angelic salutation: 'O thou blessed Virgin, Mother of God . . . Hail to thee! Holy art thou, henceforth and for ever . . .' 'Queen of Heaven' was a permissible title 'as much as it is certainly true', without making her a goddess.[28] All this could be preserved because it emphasized a paradox characteristic of Luther's theology: Mary's glory consisted, as she herself sang, in God having lifted her up from lowliness. Even before Karlstadt had forced him to face the practical question of images and iconoclasm, Luther was thinking out how devotional art might be redirected suitably to portray Mary, and as he meditated on this, he produced one of the most memorable passages of his work: a sustained contrast of 'the Divine glory joined with her nothingness; the Divine merit with her homage; the Divine greatness with her smallness; the Divine goodness with her lack of merit; the Divine grace with her unworthiness'.[29] Note that God had regarded Mary's lowliness and not her humility, which might be seen as a merit: Mary's momentous destiny was not given to her because of any merit of her own – a thought in which Luther's core theology coincided with the textual exegesis of Erasmus.[30] This radical repositioning effectively rescued Mary's humanity to emphasize both the reality and the enormous gift of the Incarnation: the huge error of medieval devotion, as was clear in the art which it had produced, was to contrast 'us with the Mother of God instead of her with God'.[31] Luther was then free as his commentary climaxed to 'pray God that He may offer us a right understanding of this Magnificat, an understanding which does not merely expound and shed light on it but burns and lives in body and soul. May Christ grant us this through the intercession and the intention of His dear Mother Mary. Amen.'[32]

Luther remained faithful throughout his career as a Reformer to the programme set out in his Magnificat commentary. In 1962 Walter Tappolet produced a remarkable anthology of passages on the subject of Mary from Luther, Zwingli, Bullinger and Calvin, *Das Marienlob der Reformatoren*. The very thoroughness of Tappolet's achievement reveals the imbalance between Luther and the three Reformed theologians:

Luther takes up nearly half the work, and in Tappolet's table of references, Luther scores eight pages, in contrast to the couple of pages encompassing Zwingli, Bullinger and Calvin.[33] Luther never wrote a specifically Marian hymn (indeed, he characteristically modified various medieval pilgrimage hymns in a Christological direction), but his hymnody is scattered with warm references to Mary in the context of the Incarnation. These allusions are unsurprisingly prominent in his Christmas hymns, but they also emerge delicately and beautifully in his sacred love-ballad from the early 1530s, '*Sie ist mir lieb, die werte Magd*' ('The worthy Maid is dear to me'). In this, Luther keeps three themes in exquisite tension: his controlling image is of the woman crowned with the twelve stars from Revelation 12, but the woman is traditionally both an image of the Church and an image of Mary; in all three guises she finds her child kept safe from the dragon of sin.[34]

Luther's warmth towards Mary continued to be expressed in his preaching, which remained tied to the liturgical year, because he kept so much more of the Kalendar than other churches in the Protestant world. Free to choose which he would retain of the festivals associated with Mary, he kept those which could be seen as centring on Christ rather than Mary: the Annunciation, the Visitation and the Purification. Tappolet points out that Luther preached on these feast-days until the end of his life, while by contrast his last sermon on the Conception of Our Lady was no later than 1520, on her Nativity 1522, and on her Assumption 1523.[35] The subject of the Magnificat remained a favourite with him, to be lovingly and regularly expounded on the feast associated with it in scripture – the Visitation – on 2 July. Luther's partiality for the Visitation contrasts with the one non-Lutheran Church of the Reformation to keep the shape of the liturgical year, the Church of England: curiously, when Archbishop Cranmer made his own selection of festivals, the Annunciation and Purification still got special liturgical mention, but the Visitation was dropped, even from the ceremonialist provisional rite of 1549. This was despite the pivotal dramatic role which the Magnificat continued to play in the English liturgy of Evensong; moreover, here was an instance in which Cranmer consciously ignored advice from Martin Bucer, who shared Luther's particular affection for the feast, and who advocated retaining it when he gave advice on revising the 1549 rite.[36]

If the Zürich Reformers were not so vocal as Luther in their praise of Mary, they still echoed the message of his Magnificat Commentary, a work which achieved wide popularity, no doubt in large measure thanks to the unusual lack of polemical edge in the work. Like him, they were conscious of accusations from their conservative enemies that they dishonoured the Virgin, and they were eager to make as positive noises as they could. In 1522, the same year that he shouted down Lambert in the Fraumünster, Zwingli preached and published a major sermon 'On the ever pure Virgin Maid Mary the mother of Jesus Christ our Saviour', a careful recounting of the scriptural material on Mary and a direct response to claims that he had denied Mary's virginity.[37] The Zürich authorities were gradualist in their approach to Marian devotion; the Marian liturgical feasts were not abolished until 1535; and, more surprisingly, one would have experienced a liturgical recitation of the scriptural portion of the Hail Mary in the Zürich preaching service right up to 1563, when Bullinger finally did away with it.[38] Bullinger could be surprisingly old-fashioned when he chose: unlike his mentor Zwingli, he seems to have been prepared to countenance the possibility of the Assumption of Mary, on the reasonable Protestant basis that Enoch and Elijah provided scriptural precedents for such an event. The discussion, admittedly casual enough, occurs in an unpredictable setting: the 1539 version of his well-known book (already cited above) attacking relics and pilgrimages. In the course of a rather tortured dialogue with the writings of Jerome, Bullinger affirms without apparent reservation, 'For this reason indeed we believe the sacred body of Mary, the most pure home and temple of the Holy Spirit, to have been carried by angels up to heaven.'[39]

It is significant that when an edition of Bullinger's *De origine erroris* was published in Geneva in 1549, this remarkable sentence was omitted from the text.[40] With Calvin, a more chilly overall attitude to Mary is perceptible than in either Wittenberg or Zürich. While Luther cheerfully remarked in 1523 that the Hail Mary was no danger to those of firm faith, and while its scriptural text continued to echo around the churches of Zürich, in 1542 Calvin bitterly denounced any use of it as 'execrable blasphemy', together with the titles of honour for Mary which Luther was happy to commend.[41] It is noticeable that the Angelic Salutation is never cited in Calvin's *Institutio Christianae Religionis* (his famous work of systematic theology, the *Institutes*): indeed, throughout the *Institutes* in its successive versions, the absence of any use of the standard Marian biblical passages, whether direct or allegorical, is very striking. There is only one passing reference even to the Magnificat.[42] Admittedly, when he was forced to face up to the Marian scriptural passages in his biblical commentaries, Calvin could be carried away by his interest in the text and used his imagination. For instance, in his commentary on Luke 2:48, he chose to defend Mary for telling off the boy Jesus for his truancy in the Temple: 'The weariness of three days was in that complaint,' he said sympathetically.[43] Yet such naturalism was not the attitude which the Queen of Heaven might have expected. Calvin's single-minded hatred of anything which could be regarded as an idolatrous obstacle to the worship of God skewed in a negative direction the delicate balance of attitudes to Mary which the Lutheran and Zürich Reformers had managed to sustain, and gradually Calvin's was the influence which coloured the spirituality of non-Lutheran Europe. It was noticeable in England, for example, that the first version of the English Bible to supplant the phrase 'full of grace' in the Angelic Salutation at Luke 1:28 was the Geneva translation of 1560: there it became 'thou that art freely beloved', and the Authorized Version did not return to the older phrase in 1611, opting for 'thou that art highly favoured'.[44]

This impact of Calvinism in later Tudor England fused with an older native English strain of negative comment on Mary: this was a mark of Lollard discourse, and it had in turn been distinctively reinforced by the charismatic preaching of Hugh Latimer, diffused into the Elizabethan age through publication. Latimer, as Bishop of Worcester in the 1530s, had taken a savage delight in the nationwide round-up and destruction of cultic images of Mary carried out in 1538, not least the venerated image in his own cathedral.[45] Freed from circumspection after the death of Henry VIII, he took up Erasmus's theme of the negative passages about Mary in scripture and infused it with a distinctly personal misogyny in his campaign to sweep out the remnants of the once-mighty English cults of Our Lady. The best thing about Mary for Latimer was that she was obedient: that was a positive womanly quality. However, she had not always shown the humility of the Magnificat: she had demanded to speak to her son, 'interrupting his sermon, which was not good manners'. Latimer took great delight in citing John Chrysostom and Augustine to prove his point that 'she was pricked a little with vain-glory; she would have been known to be his mother, else she would not have been so hasty to speak with him . . . The school doctors say she was arrogant.' She was even at fault for losing Jesus in the Temple, and she quarrelled with him afterwards 'like a mother' – this phrase might form a clue to Latimer's unconscious feelings. Christ's independent actions on this occasion illustrated for Latimer the limits of earthly obedience: *oportet magis obedire Deo quam hominibus*, 'It is better to serve God than human beings'. All this conveniently served to prove for Latimer, as Chrysostom's remark had already indicated to William Tyndale two decades before, that Mary could not have been conceived immaculately.[46]

'Magisterial' reformers – the Luthers, the Tyndales, the Zwinglis, the Calvins, who became the new ecclesiastical establishment in Protestantism – were nevertheless always uncomfortably conscious that they were skating on thin ice when they took to putting Mary in her place. They shared with their papist opponents a loyalty to the Church as it had emerged by the time of the Council of Chalcedon. But as the devastating response to Luther's call for the levelling of shrines had demonstrated, it was not always possible to predict or control which elements of the early Christian package would now be challenged by more radical spirits. Here the role of Mary was a major area of instability. Some of the reaction was a generalized hostility to what Mary had become in the devotion of the Western Church, and so it was allied to the destruction of shrines and images. All through the Reformation century, one can find offensive talk about Mary which was an extension (albeit injudicious) of some of the more extreme rhetoric of Calvin or Latimer – it was little more than posturing to show what a good Protestant the speaker was. It is unlikely, for instance, that when in 1605 a glover from Buckinghamshire ranted that 'the virgin Marie was the instrument of the divell', he was expressing any sort of coherent radical theology beyond too much beer and anti-Catholicism.[47]

But there was much more to Reformation radicalism than an effort to out-Calvin Calvin. The Reformation had turned back to scripture, and one obvious issue to rethink was the proposition about Mary most insecurely supported in scripture: her perpetual virginity. Any reader coming fresh to the appropriate references in the biblical text would draw the conclusion that Jesus had brothers and sisters, and that is the conclusion that many readers did come to in the 1520s. So in May 1525 an unidentified radical, probably Conrad Grebel, scandalized the town leadership of St Gallen because he 'slandered Our Lady with seven children'.[48] This biblicism might in itself seem of minor significance, but as we will see, the Reformers unanimously resisted it, partly because it was soon allied with a profound challenge to the Chalcedonian package of doctrine. The challenge was a denial of the Early Church's conclusions about the equality of persons in the Trinity, agreed at the Council of Nicaea (in 325), and of the Council of Chalcedon's carefully brokered compromise on the humanity and divinity of Christ, agreed in 451. Reassessing the significance of the Incarnation of Christ, as radicals did, was in itself likely to downgrade the role of Mary in salvation.

Several trains of thought converged on such an agenda, both recent and ancient. For many radicals, as for humanist theologians like Zwingli, the starting-point was not so much Mary but that other focus of late medieval Western devotion, the Mass. Erasmus had habitually stressed the spiritual against the physical; one of his favourite texts was John 6:63. Zwingli had followed him in warming to this affirmation that the spirit gives life and the flesh profits nothing, and he had built on it his Eucharistic doctrine of remembrance, denying the physical or corporeal presence of Christ in the Eucharist. It was not surprising that when such respected authorities distanced themselves from physicality, more adventurous spirits should combine that consideration with their loathing for the cultus surrounding both Mary and the Mass. If the body of Christ in the Eucharist was a spiritual and not an earthbound flesh, that had implications for his incarnation on earth: it was logical to suppose that his flesh in his earthly life was created not of the Virgin but in Heaven.

Besides this rooting in contemporary humanist scholarship, there were various older sources of this doctrinal departure. One strain within medieval mystical piety had affirmed and meditated on Christ's celestial flesh. A different medieval inheritance came from radicals like Lollards or Taborites who had been angered by the Marian cult and had sought to downgrade Mary; they often rationalized their anger by drawing on the ancient male fantasies about reproduction made respectable in Aristotelian biology, where a woman was considered merely as a vessel for the reception of male seed. If no male seed was involved in Christ's incarnation, it was logical that he did not partake of human flesh. The eighth-century iconoclast Byzantine Emperor Constantine V had expressed the 'vessel' theory of Mary in a vivid metaphor: 'When she bore Christ within her womb, she was like a purse filled with gold. But after giving birth, she was no more than an empty purse.'[49] The emperor's aphorism was destined to have a long history, although the many generations who repeated it over some eight centuries no doubt had little idea of its origin. In the Netherlands of Charles V, for instance, it could be heard on the lips of Pieter Florisz., a tailor in Gouda, who said that Our Lady was like 'a sack that had once held cinnamon, but now only retains the sweet savour'. In a rather less flavoursome version, Willem die Cuper said that she was like a flourbag from which the flour had been emptied.[50] The common variant motif among contemporary English radicals was the saffron bag, in which the smell of the precious contents would linger; Hugh Latimer was once accused of having used this metaphor and, true to form, he did not entirely repudiate it but did his best to turn it into an orthodox sermon illustration.[51]

The first known developed celestial flesh doctrine of the Reformation came from Alsace in 1524, much at the same time as the images of Mallerbach and Riga were being put to the torch: here the lay preacher Clement Ziegler developed in a series of tracts on the sacraments a theory of the celestial body of Christ pre-existent before his acquisition of visible human flesh at the Incarnation.[52] On this foundation were built a number of more thoroughgoing doctrines of celestial flesh, first in the contrasting proposals of Caspar Schwenckfeld and Melchior Hofmann in Strassburg. Hofmann produced an alternative metaphor for Mary to that of the bag, unconciously echoing the ancient Gnostic Valentinus in describing Christ as passing through Mary 'as water through a pipe'.[53] Hofmann's ideas were taken up by Menno Simons later in the decade, among the quietist radicals of the Netherlands, and the celestial flesh doctrine became characteristic of his followers, despite their own further disagreements as to its mechanics. It was Melchiorite or Mennonite Christology which led Joan Bocher to the stake in London in 1550, after the trial in which we have already met Archbishop Cranmer balancing on the Lady Chapel altar of St Paul's.[54]

Almost as soon as this series of celestial flesh solutions to the Incarnation problem developed, they were being confronted by the opposite form of radicalism in Unitarianism: Jesus was not God at all, but a human prophet. As much as any celestial flesh doctrine, this would downgrade the role of Mary in salvation. The belief was first picked up by scandalized mainstream Reformers at trials of radicals in Augsburg in 1527, and paradoxically it was given wider currency among radicals when official publication of statements from the trials deliberately or inadvertently ascribed the doctrine to the widely respected radical leader Balthasar Hubmaier – entirely without foundation.[55] While celestial flesh doctrine found its refuge in the Netherlands, Simons kept his followers distanced from Unitarianism or Arianism; these doctrines were instead to find a home among the persecuted evangelicals of mid-century Italy, before migrating for a long and tempestuous career in Central and eastern Europe.[56]

So both main forms of surviving radicalism were means of downgrading Mary far more drastically than did mainstream Protestantism. Perhaps that is why the radical social message of the Magnificat rarely seems to have been an inspiration to the radicals, when one would think that this scriptural text would have been an obvious stimulus to social idealism and a sacred reordering of society. It is significant that radical thinking rarely took the opposite course – to give Mary more honour than the old Western Church had done – even although there was no absolute reason why this should not have happened.[57] The exception to the rule was that wayward and original genius Paracelsus. Particularly in a couple of stormy years in Salzburg in 1524 and 1525, Paracelsus turned his thoughts to a fundamental rethink of the nature of the Trinity, and the relationship of Our Lady to it, in a flurry of theological speculation, none of which was published until much later.[58] Paracelsus was concerned to find the female principle in God: in his *Liber de sancta trinitate*, he called this the 'Gottin'. Although, in that work, he did not identify the 'Gottin' with Mary, he did take this further step in the various tracts on the subject of Mary which he wrote at much the same time. So in *De virgine sancta theo-toca*, probably of 1524, Paracelsus writes that Mary '*gehört in die Gottheit*' (forms part of the Godhead).[59] It was not surprising there-fore that he vigorously affirmed the immaculate conception and perpetual virginity of Mary. Equally remote from his Reformation contemporaries was Paracelsus's affirmation that Mary was of a dif-ferent order of creation to other women, or his readiness to follow the traditional exegesis which identified her with the figure of Wisdom in Sirach 24. He considered that her earthly life was a tiny span com-pared with her pre-existence and her life in Heaven; now she was the '*Fürstin der Himmelstadt*' (ruler of Heaven).[60]

In his later theological writings, Paracelsus became more cautious on the topic of Mary, and the theme of her mystical pre-existence receded. As much as his independent creativity could ever be catego-rized, after the 1520s he drew further away from the traditional Church and closer to the Reformers, which may have curbed his enthusiasm for the old devotional imagery and inclined him more to what magisterial Protestants were saying about Mary.[61] He might also have been somewhat chastened if he heard of the Marian antics of one of his south German contemporaries, the bigamous radical furrier Nicholas Frey, who may single-handedly have scandalized radicals out of interest in Mary. When Frey abandoned his first wife in Rot-tenburg and took up with an aristocratic widow, he saw his new relationship as a spiritual union with a new Mary and a new Eve, while he himself took the role of the Trinity. The territorial synod of Strassburg in 1533 begged to differ, and eventually decreed that the unrepentant Frey should be drowned: he did not have a following.[62] What is certainly significant is how little impact Paracelsus's early speculations about Mary were to have in the many and varied circles, largely Protestant, which became fascinated by assorted aspects of Paracelsianism. Take for instance the mystic Jacob Boehme. Like Paracelsus a half-century before, he felt the absence of a female prin-ciple in God, and he sought to define what that principle might be. However, in one of his most important mystical writings, *The Way to Christ*, it is striking how Boehme distances from the Virgin Mary his figure of the Virgin Sophia, through whom the soul might experience mystical union with God. Mary is given a conventional functional role as the vessel of the Incarnation, and in one long passage which is a detailed exposition of the Incarnation, Boehme emphasizes the human flesh of Mary, explaining that she was part of the corruption of human flesh which resulted from the Fall. In this, Boehme remains true to his Lutheran roots, and there is no hint of Paracelsianism.[63]

In the face of the varied forms of radicalism which threatened the Chalcedonian synthesis, the magisterial Reformers were anxious to show themselves true to beliefs which the early Church had affirmed about Mary. Many Reformers were happy to affirm the title Theotokos with the ancient Church, regarding it as much a defence against modern deviant Christology as it had been against Nestorianism.[64] They revealed different degrees of agnosticism towards the Assumption, with (as we have seen) Bullinger apparently more positive than most.[65] As to the doctrine of the Immaculate Conception, Protestants could simply stand back and enjoy the continuing row within the Roman Church on this topic.[66] The issue was simple for them: the Immaculate Conception was a late and illegitimate development of doctrine which clashed directly with Luther's assertion of justification by faith alone. Luther's paradoxical soteriology was at its most dramatic on the subject of Mary's sinful flesh: he revelled in the Saviour's genealogical connection to the incest of Judah and Tamar. 'God allows [Christ] to be conceived in most disgraceful incest, in order that he may assume the truest flesh.' Christ was born of a flesh truly 'polluted by Judah and Tamar', which was equally truly sanctified by the Holy Spirit.[67] Perhaps the most hard-hitting statement of this evangelical paradox came from Roger Hutchinson, an Edwardian chaplain to Archbishop Cranmer, who emphasized that no dishonour came to Christ's divinity because his humanity filled the Virgin's womb: 'For his divinity is not defiled thereby, no more than the sun shining upon carrion and filthy jakes is dishonoured or defiled through their stinking scents.' This was a remarkable meditation on the mystery of the Incarnation, and it is worth noting that it arose directly out of Hutchinson's disputes with the Melchiorite radicals of Edwardian London.[68]

It was, however, on the perpetual virginity of Mary that the magisterial Reformers showed themselves unanimously and adamantly conservative. This was despite the fact that their stance left them ideologically vulnerable both to Roman Catholics and to radicals.

Humanist Catholics like Thomas More could point to Erasmus's affirmation that the perpetual virginity was a matter of faith, yet still could not be found in scripture. If so, continued belief in it was a powerful argument for the validity of 'unwritten verities', the traditions of which the Church was a guardian, a doctrine which was roundly condemned by the Reformers.[69] By no means all Catholics agreed with Erasmus, and Thomas Swynnerton, an English polemicist of the 1530s, had some fun pointing up their divisions on the matter, but the challenge was a serious one.[70] More serious still was the radical challenge on perpetual virginity, because it was a dialogue between two parties who were likely to be committed to *sola scriptura*. The radicals could combine with Catholics to accuse the Reformers of stretching the biblical record in affirming the perpetual virginity; indeed, radicals would say that the biblical evidence pointed in precisely the opposite direction.

If biblicism was to determine the argument, then there was only one convincing line of defence for the magisterials: to follow the tendentious exegesis of the relevant biblical passages which Jerome had pioneered back in the fourth century, when he had faced similar objections from Helvidius, and had answered them in characteristically acid tones. This is what the Reformers did: they reiterated Jerome's contention that, contextually, the Synoptic Gospels' mention of Jesus's 'brothers' actually referred to his 'cousins', and that when Jesus was described in Matthew 1:24–5 as Mary's first-born son, it actually meant that he was her only son. Repeatedly and monotonously they sneered at the name of Helvidius, and took it as read that Jerome had demolished Helvidius's case.[71] Moreover, some Reformers could suddenly rediscover a taste for medieval allegorical interpretation and patristic exegesis which in other circumstances they would have regarded as distinctly suspect: they rejected the guidance of Erasmus and pointed confidently to the proof-texts Ezekiel 44:2 and Isaiah 7:14. Both Zwingli and Bullinger abandoned their humanism in this regard.[72] An alternative Protestant approach, useful against papists and radicals alike, was to express guarded agnosticism about the scriptural foundation of the doctrine, and then proceed to say that in any case it was a peripheral belief and not a matter of salvation.[73] But one never feels that the Reformers were very happy with this. Their doubts would only have been heightened if they were aware of a passage in the *Ecclesiastical Polity* by that Reformed Protestant gone to the bad, Richard Hooker: he cited the doctrine of the perpetual virginity of Mary as an example that 'even in matters divine, concerning some thinges we may lawfully doubt and suspend our judgement'.[74]

Why this neurotic attachment to the perpetual virginity among the magisterial Reformers? At one level, one can ascribe it to the general worries about sexuality which have been especially pervasive within Western Christianity: Jesus Christ, however much one safeguarded his humanity along with Nicaea I and Chalcedon, needed to be distanced from the more messy realities of human reproduction, along with his mother, if one was to show true love and reverence for him. At a more conscious theological level, the debate about interpreting scripture on the perpetual virginity might have relevance to arguments among the Reformers themselves: thus at the Colloquy of Marburg in 1529, when Zwingli was lamenting what he saw as Luther's literalist obstinacy about Christ's words of Eucharistic institution, he likened Luther's attitude to the wrong-headedness of Helvidius.[75] But the real impetus was the radical challenge – not merely because of radical views on the Incarnation which might bear on the perpetual virginity debate, but because of a different issue which was one of the other major concerns of radicals: the affirmation of adult against infant baptism. In both cases, the question of scriptural authority was the same. Beliefs which the magisterial Reformers felt passionately were valid and important – the perpetual virginity of Mary and the necessity of infant baptism – had distinctly shaky justification in scripture. Any admission of that meant toying unhappily with some notion of church authority in addition to the authority of scripture, and that meant vulnerability to radicals and conservatives alike. One Lutheran spokesman, Hermann Busche, innocently let the cat out of the bag when debating with Anabaptists at Münster, while debate was still possible there in 1533. After admitting that infant baptism was not explicitly found in the Bible, he said that there were many things 'not mentioned in the Bible which are still perfectly acceptable. For example the perpetual virginity of Mary or that the Bible nowhere mentions the baptism of the apostles.'[76] It was with such debates in mind that the perpetual divinity assumed the importance that it did. When Andreas Osiander wrote to Zwingli in 1527 that the sum total of religion consisted in the satisfactory proof of the Virginity of Mary, or when in the same year Johannes Oecolampadius told Zwingli in strikingly similar terms that the whole of Christendom stood or fell on the acknowledgement of Mary's perpetual virginity, it was because they wrote in the aftermath of the first radical assertions at Augsburg that Jesus Christ was no more than a prophet.[77]

We have followed a tangled story, and it is not surprising that the tangles gradually led to a general Protestant silence falling over Mary. The aggressive promotion of Our Lady by Rome as a symbol of its mid-century recovery did not help matters. In England, where the last official Hail Mary was heard in the wake of the death of Queen Mary I, people were discouraged from singing about the Virgin as their ancestors had done. The ballads which were put into print from the London presses, which admittedly may not be identical with those which were actually sung, are notable for what they do not contain: it was God's providence, not Our Lady's, which appeared in the lyrics.[78] Christmas carols, such as Luther loved and amplified, were controversial in England, associated with Catholic survival and infrequently published in Elizabeth's reign, although they began making a comeback in the early seventeenth century; English publishers produced no picture of the Holy Family before 1637. One might even see the popular carol 'Righteous Joseph' as an attempt to take the spotlight off Our Lady and redirect it onto her husband.[79]

Even within the Lutheran world, Luther's continuing devotion and his permission for religious art did not lead after his death to any flourishing modified Marian devotion. New pictures of Mary ceased to be placed in Lutheran churches after mid-century, while images of the Crucifixion continued to be a staple of Lutheran church art. Luther's own promotion of one central image of the Crucifixion was symbolic of this silence: one of the most well-known title-pages designed by Lucas Cranach the Elder for Luther's translation of the Bible centres on a very medieval depiction of Christ on the cross – but the flanking figures are no longer Mary and John, but Luther himself and the Saxon Elector Johann Friedrich. For the Reformed world, Mary took her place in the scheme of salvation because she was there in the scripture and in the creeds. But those who learnt their catechism in the Reformed world were not encouraged to think further or more than functionally on the subject, any more than they were prompted to dally long with the communion of saints departed.[80] On the eve of the Church of England's stealthy tiptoeing away from Calvin and the Reformed world in the seventeenth century, it is noticeable that the forerunner of that movement, Richard Hooker, said almost as little about Mary as did John Calvin.

This silence is particularly striking among activist Protestant women, who might have been expected to look to the Church's arche-typal woman for an example. Perhaps the problem was the limited range of models which Mary now offered. The few positively approv-ing mentions of her in the staple of English official preaching, the *Homilies* of 1547 and 1563, pointed to scriptural references concern-ing her humility and her obedience to lawfully constituted authority.[81] In this, England was only following other parts of the Protestant world (and indeed, much Counter-Reformation spirituality) in pick-ing up the theme of humility which Erasmus had highlighted; characteristically for the sixteenth century, official England also ignored the more radical messages contained in the Magnificat. A contemplative, passive model was not what the independent-minded Protestant woman was looking for; she needed stronger, more force-ful biblical exemplars, and very often she found them in the Old Testament rather than in the stories of Mary. For instance, in the writ-ings of the Strassburg hymn-writer and lay theologian, Katharina Schütz, wife of the Reformer Matthias Zell, the women who stand out are Judith and Esther, or from the New Testament Anna the prophetess, passionate Mary Magdalene, or busy Martha. The Virgin Mary is hardly visible.[82] When in London in 1582, Thomas Bentley edited a collection of descriptions and lives of biblical women as part of his proto-feminist anthology *The Monument of Matrones*, Mary came off badly. Old Testament women figure most, with Judith get-ting the longest entry at fifteen and a half pages, and even Sarah achieving five pages to the Blessed Virgin's four.[83] Nor was there any widespread impulse to draw on the traditional web of imagery around Mary for alternative Protestant purposes. There has been a good deal of exaggerated talk of Queen Elizabeth I of England taking on the attributes of the Virgin and becoming the centre of a substitute cult:

such discussion has been effectively brought down to size by the research of Helen Hackett, who has shown how peripheral, gradual and lacking in official encouragement was the development of any use of Marian imagery for the queen.[84]

It is around the time of the passing of Elizabeth of England, as the Nativity carols began finding their way back into print, and as cultured Protestant noblemen began risking pictures of scriptural scenes from the life of Our Lady in their private chapels, that one finds hints of a different voice within Protestantism.[85] With the passage of time, the heirs of the Reformation were better able to reflect on what might be missing in the Protestant devotional revolution. So, in the 1630s, the French Reformed pastor and popular devotional writer Charles Drelincourt was able to write a tract and a substantial follow-up book concerning the honour which was appropriate to the Blessed Virgin Mary, rather to the surprise of his Roman Catholic clerical contemporaries.[86] Above all, in England, the clerical party fostered by Lancelot Andrewes – the 'avant-garde conformists' who were being nicknamed 'Arminians' by the 1620s – gathered up Mary in their enterprise of rewriting the history and the theology of the English Church. But their devotional poetry, their liturgical adventures, or the statue of Our Lady on Oxford's University Church erected so controversially by the chaplain of Archbishop Laud, must remain another story. The last word is best given to John Jewel, a cosmopolitan champion of the whole European Reformation as well as defender of the English Church, in an aphorism generated by his long dialogue with his old school companion, the Catholic scholar Thomas Harding: 'Verily, M. Harding, to be the child of God it is a great deal greater grace than to be the mother of God.'[87]

4

John Calvin

Ambrose, Jerome, Augustine, Gregory: the Four Latin Doctors of the Church are a miscellaneous bunch. Three bishops, plus one scholar who failed in the eremetical life, which he nevertheless continued to extol; three successful politicians, one pioneer of missionary planning, one writer of hymns and one inspiration for the Western musical tradition. Plus, of course, in Augustine, one creative thinker of genius, who shaped Western Christianity for good, but who was virtually ignored elsewhere in the Christian world.

These are the men who stare in stern benevolence out of the panels of many a medieval pulpit. All their achievements are reflected in the achievements of John Calvin, with the exception of Jerome's failed effort at being a hermit. Truly, Calvin was heir to their inheritance, perhaps the most Augustinian theologian of the sixteenth century, creator of a Church which could in its peculiar fashion aspire to be the authentic voice of Catholicity in his time. Protestantism, I would hazard, was not a word which had great appeal to John Calvin; Catholicity would have aroused him a great deal more. Let us explore why Calvin might be placed alongside the Four Latin Doctors, if Rome were to erect some monumental equivalent of Geneva's great 'Reformation Wall' of theological heroes in a corner of Vatican City.

Calvin might be said to share one other characteristic with the Four Latin Doctors. They were innocent of the discipline invented by the medieval Western Church which he so despised: theology. No one had talked much of theology before Peter Abelard wrote the *Theologia christiana* in the 1120s, and by then the Latin Doctors were dead and gone, to be digested into the new theological discipline, to become its raw material. Calvin was at the other end of the medieval factory of theology, recycling ore from the scholastic waste-heaps. As a civil law-yer of modishly humanist learning, and with an acute humanist sense of history, he escaped the training in scholastic theology which nur-tured most of the early Protestant Reformers, from Luther to Zwingli to Bucer to Cranmer. Among the most well-known movers of the Ref-ormation, Calvin was only paralleled in this by Desiderius Erasmus and by Vadianus, the engaging lay reformer of Sankt Gallen.

That meant that Calvin found it easy to stand back from the scho-lastic achievement, and select from it what he wanted, which was not much. Bernard of Clairvaux was one of the few medievals who sur-vived his scrutiny, mainly by being effectively pre-scholastic in his approach to matters of divinity, and Professor Anthony Lane has helped us see just how selective Calvin could be in using Bernard. Once Calvin was exposed to Bernard's writings, he found material which could be judiciously adapted to back up his existing theological positions. Bernard the devout son of the Roman Church did not fea-ture, unsurprisingly, nor would one know from Calvin that Bernard was perhaps the most prominent monk of his age. In any case, Cal-vin's forty-one citations of Bernard hardly match up to no fewer than 1,708 quotations from Augustine of Hippo in Calvin's works.[1]

All in Calvin's teaching was, of course, directed in good humanist fashion *ad fontes*, to the wellsprings, and *ad fontes* meant scripture. In the course of delivering a brisk rhetorical kicking to that mysteri-ous early theologian known as Dionysius the Areopagite, Calvin provided a robust definition of what he felt theologians should and should not do:

> No one will deny that Dionysius, whoever he was, subtly and skilfully discussed many matters in his *Celestial Hierarchy*. But if anyone exam-ines it more closely, he will find it for the most part nothing but talk. The theologian's task is not to divert the ears with chatter, but to strengthen consciences by teaching things true, sure and profitable. . . . Therefore, bidding farewell to that foolish wisdom, let us examine in the simple teaching of Scripture what the Lord would have us know . . . [2]

Calvin was here actually borrowing his scepticism on Dionysius from Luther; but he was consistently much more relaxed than Luther about using the pre-Christian heritage on which scholastic theology had drawn when making his own reconstruction of the Catholic faith. Professor Irena Backus has pointed out the way in which Calvin's non-theological humanist intellectual background stayed with him in his exposition of theology. Long after his first publication, his textual commentary on Seneca's *De Clementia*, he retained his propensity to use philosophical terms drawn from the Stoics and from Aristotle, and his acquaintance with pre-Christian learning was not in the first place mediated by reading what the Fathers had said about them.[3] As Calvin taught himself theology, there remained some limitations: in all his intense concentration on biblical commentary, he very rarely used Hebrew sources at first hand, and the evidence for his having more than a passing acquaintance with Hebrew may charitably be described as scanty.[4]

Calvin's early saturation in civil law rather than theology has left its mark on the *Institutes*. From its earliest published version in 1536, this summary of the Catholic faith has a feature which makes it innovative among the early efforts of the Reformers to constitute doctrinal statements: where Luther's *Small Catechism* ends with a catalogue of Christian duties, the 1536 *Institutes* makes a systematic attempt to integrate a discussion of civil government with doctrine, and it does so in notably humanist and frequently non-scriptural terms. Calvin's famous if convoluted statement justifying resistance is not couched in scriptural terms at all, but refers to the institutions of ephors in Sparta, demarchs in Athens or the tribunes of the people in the Roman Republic.[5]

So the young evangelical academic took a fresh, non-scholastic approach to structuring his thinking on the great questions of Christianity, as he tried to create his own properly scriptural basis for the exposition of the Christian faith. The years 1536 to 1537 saw a pair of publications from Calvin, following the model made conventional by Luther's *Large* and *Small Catechisms*: they were principally structured by the Ten Commandments, Apostles' Creed, Lord's Prayer and sacraments. The shorter *Brève Instruction chrétienne* suffered rapid obscurity; in fact it was lost until 1877. The larger companion of which it was a digest was to enjoy rather more celebrity. Even its first version of 1536, the *Institutio* represented one of the most substantial efforts so far to provide a systematic basis for the emerging reform of the Western Church.

Of course, the *Institutes* changed much before their final majestic form, so comprehensively rearranged from that first catechetical work, but one constant feature in all editions was the Preface. It was dedicated to King François I of France, whose subject Calvin was in 1535, but who was long dead by the time that the last editions appeared in the early 1560s. This might seem strange, in view of the propensity of many humanists to change the dedications of their books to pursue congenial or generous patrons, and in view of the fact that as far as Calvin was concerned, King François was neither congenial nor generous. Why retain this passionate appeal to a monarch who was one of the greatest disappointments among many for the Reformers of the sixteenth century?

Timing was all in that Preface, which was so significantly dated August 1535, despite the *Institute*'s actual publication in Basel in 1536. By August 1535, all Europe would have known of the violent end to one of the most traumatic seventeen months in sixteenth-century European history, when in June of that year, the Anabaptist reign in Münster was brought to a violent end. A traitor led the combined forces of the bishop and the emperor through the city defences and captured its Anabaptist king, John of Leiden. The leaders suffered the exemplary sadism of punishment which affronted authority felt appropriate to the crime of rebellion at the time.

With those events in mind, it was essential for Calvin to show the French king how to distinguish his own loyal evangelical subjects – the true Catholics – from the Anabaptists of Münster. It would be easy for French traditionalists to link the destructive regime of John of Leiden to the radical vandals in France, who in 1528 had vandalized a much-loved image of the Virgin Mary in Paris, and in 1534 had shocked all right-thinking people by disfiguring prominent places with printed attacks on the Mass. Calvin was not that removed from these iconoclastic wretches, and his Preface to the king was a plea that he might recognize evangelicals as his friends rather than the self-styled Catholics who persecuted them. 'Elijah taught us what we ought to reply to such charges: it is not we who either spread errors abroad or incite tumults; but it is they who contend against God's power.'[6]

In 1536 Calvin was not to know that he would claw his way to a position in an alien European city in a fashion which had reminiscences of the rise of John of Leiden, similarly with a certain amount of bloodshed in the process, although more assured and long-term in its outcome. It is instructive to consider the similarities between Anabaptist Münster and the Geneva which Calvin helped to remould. In both cases, a prominent European city repudiated its traditional overlord, a territorial bishop, and in the confused aftermath of that rebellion, both cities invited in prominent foreigners to help create a religious Reformation, violently destroying much from the past in the process. In the wake of the charismatic foreign leaders, there streamed from regions far from the city a host of ideologically motivated immigrants. Apart from the crowds of ordinary laypeople who arrived in Geneva, all the ministers in the city were immigrants, mostly French; in fact, astonishingly, between the 1540s and 1594, the Genevan ministry did not include a single native Genevan. Both in Münster and Geneva, this exceptional situation triggered constitutional revolutions, both of whose outlines were to haunt European imaginations for centuries to come. Moreover, when Anabaptists talked of the Church, what they said was not that different from some of the things which John Calvin was inclined to say about it. His assertions that discipline and suffering were characteristic of the true Church were also Anabaptist themes.

Much of Calvin's subsequent development of his theology was designed to show how different he was from an Anabaptist; hence that Preface in the *Institutes*, and hence also that pioneering discussion of civil government, which in its first version trumpeted its support for monarchy a good deal more loudly than in later modifications.[7] Certainly, Calvin's place in Geneva contrasted sharply with that of John of Leiden in Münster. Rather than becoming a theocrat, his relation to the city authorities was distinctly reminiscent of that of Bishop Ambrose in Milan in relation to successive Roman emperors – wheedling, threatening, flattering, confronting, all against a background of constant detailed scrutiny of government as a busy pastor, preacher and teacher.

Calvin's Preface to the King of France was nevertheless a piece of self-deception. When preaching in Geneva on Acts 5:29, the crucial text about obeying God rather than man, he performed an unhappy balancing act. He told his listeners that this was a demand for resistance to the deceitful Church of Rome, but that Anabaptists 'and other fantasists' used it even though they 'only wished to govern themselves in accordance with their foolish brains, under the pretence of wishing to obey God'.[8] Many of Calvin's followers indeed proved over the next century that they could be as destructive and politically revolutionary as any Anabaptist, not least in the kingdom which François I bequeathed his successors.

When Calvin returned to scripture to repristinate the Catholic faith, he quickly discovered the pitfalls of returning *ad fontes*: he was not the first or last to find that 'the simple teachings of scripture' might need a little glossing. A crisis came for him only a year after the publication of the *Institutes*, and even though the facts about this affair have been easily available in modern scholarship for more than a century, they had been interestingly little noticed before an excellent piece of textual editing by Dr Marc Vial. The crisis was triggered by accusations made by Pierre Caroli. Caroli, like Calvin, was a refugee from France and had briefly been his colleague in Geneva before becoming chief minister in Lausanne. Caroli then accused his former French exile associates in Geneva, Calvin, Guillaume Farel and Pierre Viret, of being Arians. The accusation led to an examination of the case at a synod at Lausanne in May 1537, in which the three accused produced a confession of faith which explicitly condemned not only Arius but also his bitter posthumous opponent Macedonius and the contrary views of Sabellius, that father of modalist monarchianism, an even earlier deviant view of the Trinity.[9]

So far, so orthodox, but among other rash formulations, the Genevan trio's confession of faith adopted a strategy disastrous in terms of the Catholic and Orthodox traditions: it tried to use purely scriptural language, leaving aside the two terms 'Trinity' and 'person' as being unscriptural. This was precisely what many radical European Christians were beginning to do, on the perfectly reasonable scripturalist grounds that these crucial terms of developed Christian orthodoxy were not to be found in the Bible. Yet to abandon them was to abandon all Trinitarian language after the first essays in Western Latin Trinitarian theology by Tertullian, together with the whole inheritance of discussion worked out in the wake of the Council of Nicaea of 325. One historical development from such a strategy was the radical

Christianity which looked askance at any theology created in the post-Nicene age, regarding it as tainted by the fateful alliance between the Church of the Mediterranean and the Roman Empire. What followed from that attitude was the anti-Trinitarianism whose mid-sixteenth-century variants stretched from London to Lithuania. This movement fostered the developed Unitarian mode of thought which its opponents scornfully called Socinianism, and which in turn we now see as one of the founding elements of the Enlightenment.[10]

Such a future was the rather unexpected nemesis of a scrupulous scripturalism, and it has to be said that in the seventeenth century many Reformed Protestants helped the process on its way. At Lausanne in 1537, Calvin was forced into a corner, and not merely by his own devotional logic, but by his annoyance at being personally hounded by Caroli. This led him into the further rashness at the Synod of refusing to sign the Athanasian Creed, an act of extreme folly if he were to be taken seriously as a Catholic Christian. Oswald Myconius, minister of Basel, was among the influential voices expressing his displeasure, in particular in a letter to Heinrich Bullinger of Zürich.[11] The aftermath was a rapid retreat in the form of Calvin's two pamphlets published later that year. They reiterated his commitment to the use of the word 'Trinity' and emphasized that a further rash statement of the Genevan ministers' confession, identifying Christ with Jehovah, was only what the great, although equally contentious, Bishop Cyril of Alexandria had said amid the storms of the Miaphysite controversy back in the fifth century.[12] The resulting literary warfare rumbled on for a decade. As late as 1545, it was capable of making Calvin fall ill with worry, and of galvanizing him into writing a seventeen-thousand-word attack on Caroli in a few days.[13]

Thereafter, Calvin in his career as religious leader was haunted by two urgent polemical necessities, which were also profound questions about his theological identity. First was the need to place himself as far away as possible from the Anabaptists. That meant, secondly, claiming a position of Catholicity which could look respectably mainstream in terms enunciated by the Church of the first five centuries – therefore as far as possible from what the Early Church had defined as heresies. Let us see how he might have achieved this.

One way was through Calvin's rediscovery of the tradition of the

Church. Very quickly, the Protestant Reformers had rowed back from their initial confident rejection of Church tradition in favour of scripture alone, because Anabaptists had with perfect justice pointed out that scripture alone gave the most dubious foundation possible for something which magisterial Protestants much valued: the practice of infant baptism. That consideration had already affected the doctrinal formulations of Huldrych Zwingli in Zürich in the 1520s, and it can be seen to the full in Calvin's developing discussion of another vexing problem for the Protestant Reformation: where their Church had been before Luther. Calvin's initial reaction to that question was to say that for long, there had been no visible Church before Luther. From 1539, however, the *Institutes* asserted baldly that even in the worst times:

> the Lord used two means to keep his covenant inviolable. First, he maintained baptism there, a witness to this covenant; consecrated by his own mouth, it retains its force despite the impiety of men. Secondly, by his own providence, he caused other vestiges to remain, that the Church might not utterly die.[14]

Calvin did not argue the case as to why the sacrament of baptism had survived in such comparative lack of corruption, while the sacrament of Eucharist had been perverted into 'the greatest sacrilege'; he simply asserted as an axiom that this was how God had arranged affairs.[15] No matter that the Anabaptists asserted that the historical corruption of baptism was as great as that of the Mass: baptism as commonly practised on infants became the cornerstone of Calvin's case for the authenticity, the authentic Catholicity, of his reform. This was emphasized by the revisions on the subject of baptism and its efficacy as an instrumental sacrament which Calvin added to the 1543 version of the *Institutes*. They were part of a pattern. Calvin performed an even more radical about-face in 1543 on a ceremonial matter which was emphatically visible: the laying on of hands, especially in ordination. That custom, to which he had emphatically denied sacramental character in 1536, was now described as having a sacramental character. The 1543 version of the *Institutes* might be seen as the moment when the doctrine of the tradition of the Church came into its own in Calvin's writings.[16]

Randall Zachman frames his excellent discussion of such shifts in Calvin's theology in terms of 'dialogue with Roman Catholics', and he is sound in his instinct that they arose from conflict: Calvin's theology, like that of Augustine of Hippo, thrived on conflict. Nevertheless Zachman may be guiding our gaze in the wrong direction. In 1543 Calvin had to face a challenge from a different variety of radicalism from that of Münster Anabaptists: part of the spectrum of those within the very immigrant community of Geneva itself. Naturally they included independent-minded and articulate people with strong opinions, and one was the Savoyard Sébastien Châteillon (now more usually called Sebastian Castellio). In 1543 Castellio put himself forward for the ministry in Geneva, but he was known to have his own stance on a number of biblical and theological problems, the most irksome of which for Calvin was his refusal to accept that the Song of Songs should really be a 'canonical' part of the Bible. Calvin was determined to defend the canonicity of the Song of Songs; his theology was based on the principle that God's revelation of his Word was definitively contained within the Bible, and unlike Martin Luther he was not prepared to pick and choose where the Word was best expressed within the Bible's covers. The Bible was God's to define, however unpromising the sensuous lyrics of the Song of Songs might seem.

However, this raised the uncomfortable question of how the canonical boundaries of the Bible had been set in the early Church, as Calvin readily appreciated, given his humanist sense of historical perspective. At some point the Church had made decisions about what should be in the Bible and what should not. Calvin had Castellio's views condemned, but he was forced to talk afresh about the tradition of the Church: 'our first plea and entreaty was that he should not rashly reject the age-long interpretation of the whole of the Church' – this was only a couple of years before the Council of Trent was to make such age-long interpretation an equal source of divine revelation with the biblical text.[17] For all his talk of pleas and entreaties, once Calvin had won his point with the civil authorities, Castellio was sent packing from Geneva, to add his own acid voice to an increasing chorus assailing Calvin's reputation for posterity.

Once Calvin had seen the importance of tradition to his arguments, he was faced with the dilemma of all Protestants who made the same rediscovery: how to pick and choose among the rich storehouse of tradition which was thus afforded him. He had been badly bruised by the Caroli affair and its revisiting of the fourth-century conflicts on Incarnation and Trinity: how might he best enunciate his loyalty to Catholic tradition? He might have done what so many had done in the fourth and fifth centuries and emphasized the role of Mary, the Mother of Jesus. Mary was the symbol and the means of Christ's Incarnation, the miracle of Christ's coming in flesh and blood in his earthly life in Palestine. Both Zwingli and Luther had written movingly about Mary because they felt real love and reverence for her, and they saw her as a guarantee of the Incarnation.

Calvin showed nothing of the same spirit of reverence for Mary. His fixed hatred of anything he defined as idolatry made him determined to avoid distraction from the worship of God, so he was suspicious of any attempt to give honour to Mary the mother of God. In the whole of the text of the *Institutes,* so soaked in biblical citations, there is only one passing reference to the Magnificat, Mary's biblical song when she learned from the angel Gabriel that she would bear the Christ-child.[18] Calvin could not ignore Mary's part in the story of the Incarnation, for Christ was 'born of the Virgin Mary' and 'was incarnate by the Holy Spirit of the Virgin Mary', but he and his successors felt that when Christians had recited these statements in the Creeds, they should not dwell further on them in case idolatry loomed. It was not surprising, therefore, that Calvin should not warm to Luther's emphasis that Christ's coming in flesh by the Virgin could be experienced in every Eucharistic service.

So although Calvin naturally wanted to proclaim a Catholic doctrine of the Incarnation, he found Mary a problem rather than a reliable ally in this. Instead, he turned to the successive Councils of the early Church. The climax of these statements was the work of the Council of Chalcedon in 451, with its careful crafting of the 'Chalcedonian Definition' on the person and natures of Christ. Christ was one person in two natures inextricably linked: he was God the Son and so fully part of the Divine Trinity, while at the same time he was Jesus the human being, born in Palestine. Chalcedon had a particular significance for magisterial Protestants, who saw it as the last General Council of the Church to make reliable decisions about doctrine in accordance with the core doctrines proclaimed in scripture – magisterial Protestants were all the more inclined to respect the early Councils because the radicals of the Reformation rejected their legacy. In Calvin's case, Chalcedon might almost be seen as an organizing hermeneutic for his developed theology.

The balance of statements within the Chalcedonian Definition, with its emphasis on the indivisibility of the two natures of Christ, gave Calvin a model for that general principle which became very important to him: distinction, but not separation (*distinctio sed non separatio*). It was the perfect model to be used by this theologian so consciously striving for a Catholic balance: it can be seen, for instance, in Calvin's discussion of the Church, both visible and invisible, or of election, both general and particular – and above all, in what he says about the Eucharist. Already in 1536, Calvin faithfully reproduced the terms of the Chalcedonian Definition when he came to discuss the nature of the Incarnation and also of what it means to be human. But once more, it is the watershed 1543 edition of the *Institutes* in which explicit references to the Council of Chalcedon multiply.[19] And as Professor Backus has made clear, this emphasis on the ecumenical councils and the Fathers generally remained a distinctive feature of Reformed Protestant scholarship during the sixteenth century, far more than among the Lutherans. Perhaps the Reformed felt more need than Lutherans to justify their position against both Roman Catholicism and Reformation radicalism.[20]

Calvin, against his will, became the champion of a non-Lutheran Reformed axis on the Eucharist. He came to a Reformation already divided with distressing clarity since the Colloquy of Marburg in 1529. It was inevitable that Calvin, with his project to define the boundaries of a Reformed Catholicism, devoted much energy to finding a formulation about the Eucharist which would give it due reverence and also avoid saying either too little or too much about it. His first instinct had been to disapprove of Zwingli's ideas, and he continued to feel that Zwingli's presentation of the Eucharist lacked an appreciation of the mystery which it embodied, 'which plainly neither the mind is able to conceive nor the tongue to express'.[21] In his attempt to take a middle way in the controversy in a short treatise in that year of failed ecumenism, 1541, he said that Zwingli and Johannes

Oecolampadius 'laboured more to destroy the evil than to build up the good'.[22]

However, although Calvin found Zwingli's discussion of the Eucharist inadequate, he also strongly criticized Luther in his 1541 pamphlet. He deeply disapproved of Luther's insistence on finding the body and blood of Christ physically present in the Eucharistic elements. To understand why, we need to consider some of Calvin's other deeply held beliefs, for more than one consideration drove him to reject Luther's Eucharistic theology. First was Calvin's preoccupation with the dangers of idolatry. Paying undue attention to physical, visible objects obscured the worship of God 'in spirit and in truth' – this is a phrase from a passage in the fourth chapter of John's Gospel which scores frequent references in Calvin's *Institutes*.

With the 'distinction but not separation' principle in mind, Calvin made a firm distinction between 'reality' and 'sign', which nevertheless would not separate them. The old Church betrayed this principle by confusing reality and sign, attributing to the signs of bread and wine worship which was only due to the reality behind them. Luther, Calvin felt, had also wrongly attributed to the signs that which was only true of the reality: in particular, when Luther asserted that the physical body and blood of Christ were capable of being everywhere wherever the Eucharist was being celebrated in the world, Calvin devoted a substantial section in the final version of the *Institutes* to ridiculing the Lutheran doctrine of ubiquity.[23] He thought, on the other hand, that Zwingli had separated sign and reality too much. Calvin was firm against Zwingli by stating his conviction that 'in the sacraments the reality is given to us along with the sign'.[24]

Typically, Calvin returned to Augustine of Hippo, and like so many Reformers, he was grateful for the crisp Augustinian definitions of the sacraments as 'a visible sign of a sacred thing' or 'a visible form of an invisible grace'.[25] But lurking always behind his sacramental discussion is the fifth-century clash over the divine and human natures of Christ, so relevant to that famously distinctive feature of Calvin's thought, the *extra Calvinisticum* on the Trinity. Calvin, who always remained sensitive to Lutheran charges that he was repeating the errors of Nestorius, had already inserted into the 1539 *Institutes* an attack on both Nestorius and his extreme opponent Eutyches, and he characteristically amplified that attack in 1543 with one of his explicit invocations of Chalcedon.[26]

For Calvin, then, the signs of bread and wine become an instrument of God's grace in uniting the believer to Christ: hence Brian Gerrish's characterization of Calvin's views on the symbolism of bread and wine as 'symbolic instrumentalism', in contrast to Zwingli's 'symbolic memorialism' or Heinrich Bullinger's tactful move away from Zwingli to 'symbolic parallelism'.[27] Calvin distinguished himself from Luther by emphasizing that God's grace which unites Eucharistic sign and reality, and which makes that sign an instrument of Christ's presence, is offered not to the whole congregation at a Eucharist, but only to God's elect. The Body of Christ is not ubiquitous on earth in the Eucharist, as Luther said, but in heaven at the right hand of the Father. God's grace, brought by the Holy Spirit, lifts elect believers to Christ's presence in heaven.[28] As Calvin himself repeatedly pointed out, the ancient words of the Mass, 'Lift up your hearts' (*Sursum corda*), beautifully express this idea, although he was not the first doctor in the Reformed tradition to do so.[29] Already in the 1520s Johannes Oecolampadius had found this a poetic and inspiring way of making clear that the elements of bread and wine were not too closely associated with the body and blood of Christ, and Bullinger was happy to quote the ancient liturgical words as well.[30]

So here was a consciously Chalcedonian and Augustinian construction of Eucharistic theology, which carefully avoided approaching the Incarnation through an emphasis on the role of Mary, and which vigorously rejected Luther's view of bread and wine as objectively Christ's body and blood. Heinrich Bullinger and Calvin gradually recognized that more united them on the Eucharist than divided them, and the result was the *Consensus Tigurinus*: a remarkable piece of theological statesmanship and a tribute to both Calvin's and Bullinger's common sense and ability to be gracious when circumstances cried out for it.[31] If anything is evidence for Calvin as Doctor of the Church, it is this. All too rarely in the sixteenth century did theologians acknowledge that they had substantial differences, but then go on to produce a joint statement which both sides could find acceptable. Partisans of both sides could find their favourite expressions or insights carefully laid side by side in the text – the great precedent for such balance was of course the Chalcedonian Definition itself. The achievement of the *Consensus* was to create a broad enough area of agreement on the sacraments for the non-Lutheran Protestant Churches of Europe to regard themselves as a single family. This had profound implications for the future direction of the Reformation from the Atlantic Isles to the Carpathian mountains.

It is hardly necessary to point out that the ultimate symbol of Calvin's Chalcedonian orthodoxy was his destructive relationship with Michael Servetus. Even more surprising than Servetus's eventual fiery death in Geneva was the extraordinary sequence of events by which the Inquisition in Vienne was first supplied with the evidence to condemn Servetus from Calvin's own archive, and was then formally approached by the Genevan authorities to provide them with the Inquisition's trial records for a renewed heresy trial. Calvin had also ensured that there had been careful international soundings among Protestants about the sentence; after all, the legality of Geneva burning someone who had merely been passing through the city was not immediately obvious. On the whole, he found a cautious endorsement, with the famous and unofficial exception of Sebastian Castellio. The fact that Geneva chose to emphasize the charge of blasphemy rather than heresy only revealed Protestant squeamishness about the heresy-word so often employed against themselves.[32] The concept of religious error underlying both crimes was common to both halves of the riven Western Church.

Domestically, the serious crisis in which Calvin had found himself by 1553 came to a head over the next two years, when his very success at widening his support in the civic elite drove the infuriated opposition to open confrontation. Calvin gleefully seized on this as an attempted *coup d'état*, and after the *coup* of 1555 his position in the city was secured. John of Leiden lost Münster, but Calvin won Geneva. And the burning of Servetus strengthened Calvin's position not only in Geneva itself but throughout Europe. It was from this moment that he began widely to be perceived as not one reformer among many, but the major voice in Reformation Protestantism – particularly by Roman Catholics. He had shown his seriousness as the defender of Catholic Christianity: a Latin Doctor indeed.

Of course, it was not simply because of this notorious incident that Calvin may be so styled. The cool, measured Latin and French prose of the *Institutes*, the Commentaries and the surviving sermons are a precise, careful distillation of the Western Christian tradition as it had emerged in the fifth century on the back of Chalcedon and the teachings of Augustine. To that we might add the impact of Genevan psalmody even beyond the boundaries of Reformed Christianity. Calvin may not have created it, but without his creation of Reformed Geneva, its impact would have been far less, and psalmody is a fitting monument to a man who very frequently cast himself in the role of King David the psalmist.[33] This whole legacy is one of the many reasons why historians and theologians should do their best to avoid the terms 'Calvinist' and 'Calvinism' when discussing the Reformed tradition. Such labels demean what Calvin was trying to do, and also what he achieved, which was to provide a very precise delineation of the tradition of the previous fifteen hundred years that calls itself Catholic. There may be other versions of the picture on offer from Rome, Canterbury or Wittenberg, but it is impossible to ignore the monument to Western Christianity provided by the Doctor of Geneva.

Yet the term 'Fifth Latin Doctor' also has its uses in precisely *limiting* Calvin's place in the Christian story. Calvin looked to the Council of Chalcedon as a significant stage in the Church's meditation on its message and purposes. Like most Christians in the Latin West and Orthodox East, he would have seen its role in Christian history in terms of triumph: it synthesized the tradition, provided directions for the future, and offered a climax to the doctrinal work of the previous 150 years. Yet if we stand back from this historiographical tradition, we will see that Chalcedon split the Christian world three ways, between the imperial Christians who accepted what was (to be frank) a Christological formula cobbled together in an attempt at creating unity, and two other sections of the Christian Church who, for contrasting reasons, rejected it – the Miaphysites and Dyophysites of Africa and Asia. The historical chances of the next few centuries, by giving an accidental boost to Chalcedonian Christianity, shifted the whole Christian story westwards towards medieval Europe. That has obscured this greatest of might-have-beens in the Christian story, that of Baghdad becoming the centre of gravity in Christianity rather than Rome. If so, the fifth Latin Doctor could have taken a very different place in the Christian story.

5

The Council of Trent

'I wonder if a single thought that has helped forward the human spirit has ever been conceived or written down in an enormous room.' It's one of the great historical putdowns: a patrician Whig punchline to Kenneth Clark's scrutiny of Counter-Reformation art and architecture in his incomparable TV series *Civilisation*, before he turns from the camera and walks away down the considerable length of the Map Room in the Vatican, an Englishman abroad. His stroll is accompanied by a splendid Monteverdi setting of 'As it was in the beginning, is now, and ever shall be'. Well endowed with a sense of irony, Clark would have enjoyed letting that music make its own comment on the scene – those Venetian grandees who commissioned Monteverdi's Vespers were proud of being good Catholics, but like many good Catholics before or since, they had no time for the pope.

Counter-Reformation Rome had plenty of enormous rooms, its skyline punctuated by brand-new palaces built by cardinals who sailed through the reforms of the Council of Trent serenely unreformed. Certainly 'as it was in the beginning, is now, and ever shall be' for them, it seemed. But one enormous room had meanwhile made a world of difference to the medieval Western Church of the Latin Rite, not least in that section which remained loyal to the Bishop of Rome. John O'Malley illustrates the room in his superb new summary history of the Council of Trent: the nave of Trent's church of Santa Maria Maggiore. In that grand setting, seated on an amphitheatre specially erected for the delegates, the episcopal

Fathers of the Council completed the work of an assembly two decades in the planning and nearly two in its deliberations, punctuated
by noises off such as fears of plague, continent-wide war, assassination and torrential rain, not to mention Protestantism.

Santa Maria Maggiore was the last and best-prepared in a sequence
of stately chambers which formed the backdrop for ill-tempered and
frequently aimless debates between 1545 and 1563 in the imperial city
of Trent. Bishops and their attendant theologians were not immune
from exchanging open abuse. During one argument about justification
by faith, the Bishop of La Cava wrenched at the beard of the Cretan
Bishop of Chironissa, who had commented that he was either a knave
or a fool for sounding a bit like Martin Luther on justification. It is
amazing that anything got done at all, and indeed, more than once, the
whole event nearly ended in disarray. For some of the period covered
by the Council and its gestation, the pope was formally at war with
Europe's other most senior Catholic, the Holy Roman Emperor
Charles V, or with Charles's son Philip II of Spain. Successive popes
included one pontiff whose eldest son, Pierluigi Farnese, was widely
accused of raping a twenty-four-year-old bishop, hastening the unfortunate young man's death (Farnese was subsequently murdered by
subordinates of Charles V), while another Holy Father, former principal papal legate at the Council, on being elected Pope Julius III, made
his teenage rentboy lover a cardinal. It might seem appropriate that the
Council's official physician, Girolamo Fracastoro, was the first person
to name and provide a detailed diagnosis for syphilis; contemporary
senior churchmen would have provided Fracastoro with plenty of case
studies for his epic poem on the subject.

The late medieval and Tridentine Catholic Church is a soft target for
satire, and it is a matter of individual judgement as to whether the
thoughts gathered in the nave of Santa Maria Maggiore in Trent did
much to help forward the human spirit. Now, however, there is a
chance to move out of the confessional slit-trenches which rendered
one-dimensional the story of Trent, love it or hate it. I remember how
dull I found the history of the Counter-Reformation as a student: a
matter of going through the formal decisions of the various sessions at
the Council, the rise of the Jesuits, the formation of a new and more
efficient papal bureaucracy, the rapid hardening of lines of division

with the Protestant world. It was dull because it was only a fraction of the truth. Over the last twenty years we have been afforded a much more exciting picture: a story of near-misses, might-have-beens, characters with much theological baggage to hide (the early Jesuits being prominent among them). Professor Massimo Firpo and other historians have introduced us to an Italy much closer to turning Protestant than anyone had thought, and to a wild Mediterranean proto-Protestantism which owed much to secret Spanish Judaism, fled persecution by the Spanish Inquisition, then fascinated some of the best minds in Catholic Italy (Michelangelo included) before taking refuge in the Protestant plains of eastern Europe. Thanks to John O'Malley, a veteran Jesuit historian of the Counter-Reformation, we can also enjoy a beautifully clear and honest reappraisal of the tangled story of Trent, in all its complexity, paradox, achievement and lost opportunity. It is the first time that English-speaking readers have had this privilege, for all other accounts of Trent have been either too short, or too long for interested non-specialists: in particular, the four-volume German account by Hubert Jedin (in innumerable ways admirable), proved too exhausting after two volumes for anglophone publishers to translate further.

The difference which the Council of Trent made to the history and ethos of the Catholic Church can be gauged by the successive and overlapping careers of three sixteenth-century Scots clergymen called William Chisholm. All three William Chisholms in turn exercised episcopal jurisdiction in the Diocese of Dunblane; no need to ask if they were by any chance related. They were Scottish noblemen, and that's what medieval Scottish noblemen did: pass on large quantities of Church property and offices down the family line. In 1527 the first William succeeded his half-brother James Chisholm as Bishop of Dunblane, having already acted as James's coadjutor (assistant bishop): this William fathered a brood of children, necessarily illegitimate, though that would not greatly have concerned him, any more than it would have done any of the other family men among the medieval Scottish episcopate. His nephew William in turn became his coadjutor, succeeding him in 1561 as bishop amid the maelstrom of the Scottish Reformation, which eventually in 1569 forced this younger William into exile, to become bishop in Vaison-la-Romaine, a sunny hilltop city in Provence.

Yet the second Bishop William Chisholm hesitated in breaking totally with an Established Scottish Church which was now firmly Reformed Protestant; he found a brief period of renewed recognition as Bishop of Dunblane by Protestant James VI, before ending his days in France as a Carthusian, the most austere possible variety of monk. The third William, nephew to the second, spent time at one of the brand-new colleges set up in Rome to give proper Catholic theological training to high-flyers in the Church. He had begun his episcopal career as the second William's coadjutor in Dunblane, but in 1585 he succeeded his uncle as Bishop of Vaison and became a model exponent of the Counter-Reformation, enthusiastic for his duties and very generous to his French cathedral, remembering another exiled Scottish priest there in his will, a century after the first William had succeeded to Dunblane.[1]

This reverse Rake's Progress is instructive: from medieval clerical worldliness, through the doubts and confusions of mid-century to a discovery of a new seriousness, informed theological awareness and commitment, far from home in the case of William Chisholm III, but safe in the bosom of Mother Church. It reminds us that not only Protestants were constructing new identities in the sixteenth century; it is the story of the Counter-Reformation. As individuals, Roman Catholics were transformed by what happened, and collectively their Church, for all its claims of continuity with the medieval Western Church, changed almost as radically as the new European Churches whose adherents had rejected papal obedience. Purely in terms of clerical structure and church discipline, the Tridentine Church was more reformed than the Reformed Protestant Church of England. For instance, Trent set out to institute seminaries – specialist training colleges for all clergy – in every diocese; it was a scheme pioneered by Cardinal Reginald Pole in Mary Tudor's revived Catholic Church in England, but instantly abandoned by Protestant Elizabeth I, and not taken up by Protestants until the nineteenth century.

Granted, there was much more to the innovations in Counter-Reformation Catholicism than Trent got round to discussing: you would not know from its decrees, for instance, that it was in this age, thanks to missionaries in America, Africa and Asia, that Christianity became the first world-encompassing religion, and in a Roman Catholic form.

The Council did little to provide new regulation for the Orders of monks and friars, and its effort to enclose all female religious in nunneries away from the world was creatively frustrated by ingenious female founders of new societies and bishops sympathetic to them. Trent did not seek to reform the confraternities or guilds, those associations of laypeople who were the backbone of activism in the Roman Catholic Church over the next centuries; but in all these three instances, it didn't try to mend things that weren't broke. What it eventually provided was a sense of renewed purpose and recovered morale, necessary to let the faithful flourish in ways which could be worked out to suit particular situations.

The legislation Trent did pass was mostly for clergy and Church structures, but in one vital respect, its decree *Tametsi* altered the lives of every Roman Catholic thereafter. Christians (particularly when they are making categorical statements about Christian marriage) forget that there was no such thing as a church wedding in the first millennium of Church history. In a remarkable development, not in accordance with Early Church tradition, since *Tametsi* was approved by the Council of Trent in 1563, the Church of Rome has recognized no marriage between Catholics as valid unless performed by a priest, even though, untidily, the marriage itself is still created by an act of consent between the couple. Protestant Churches, as worried as Tridentine Churchmen about a breakdown of society, tended to follow suit over the next couple of centuries.

That's just one example of how Christians who think of doctrine as 'As it was in the beginning, is now, and ever shall be' don't know their history. It would be easy to think that the big issue at Trent was how to differentiate and protect the Catholic Church from Protestants. O'Malley points out that in fact German Protestants actually attended some sessions of the Council and were even allowed to speak: unfortunately, these sessions happened at a moment of peculiar futility in the Council's proceedings, in 1547–8, when intra-Catholic squabbles ruined any chance of progress, and the Protestants went away. When they were invited back, in 1561, both Protestants and Catholics had become far more confrontational, and it was too late. In terms of the issues which agitate modern Christians (usually about what human beings do with their genitals), it may come as a disappointment to learn that although *Tametsi* took up quite a bit of the Council's time in its last session, the aggro at Trent concerned an utterly different issue, which now sounds as if there really isn't anything to argue about: whether or not bishops should reside in their dioceses or are entitled to be absentees. In fact the Council nearly imploded over this question of non-residence. That might seem all the more surprising because in 1552 the Council had already pronounced, logically enough, that bishops should indeed reside in their dioceses.

So what was the problem? It lay in the very fact of scrutinizing what a bishop was – had the office of bishop been constituted by Christ, or by the Church in its early development? If the latter, it implied that the authority of bishops came from the pope, successor of Peter, chosen by Christ to be the rock on which he built his Church (Matthew 16:18), rather than the radically different position that every bishop directly represented Christ's authority. Prince-bishops in the Holy Roman Empire were not the only prominent members of the episcopate to feel unenthusiastic about an affirmation of the pope's exclusive position: virtually every Spanish bishop felt the same way. They would say that it was an issue of 'divine law' (*ius divinum*) for bishops to reside in their dioceses, and if so, the pope had no business dispensing bishops to be non-resident, as was clearly still the case ten years after the 1552 decree, when no fewer than 113 bishops of the Western Church were actually living in Rome. And that phrase *ius divinum* had some very sinister overtones for the papacy: King Henry VIII of England had used it to justify his deeply self-righteous claim that he had never married a lady called Catherine of Aragon, and that God was very angry with him, both for having mistakenly thinking that he had done so, and allowing the pope to provide a dispensation for the marriage to take place, against *ius divinum*.

Non-residence was thus fatally linked to the question of whether the pope was supreme in the whole state of Christ's Church militant here on earth or, alternatively, just a rather special bishop among bishops. The question was too explosive to resolve at Trent, and it took some masterly drafting to create a formula which would not definitively place exclusive divine authority in either the papacy or the general body of the episcopate. In presenting the reality of that dispute, at first sight so esoteric, O'Malley reveals an extraordinarily valuable feature of his careful and rather neutrally presented narrative. It has urgent relevance to the present-day travails of the Roman Catholic Church, which has since experienced two further Councils, Vatican I (1870–71) and Vatican II (1962–5).

The first Vatican Council aggressively answered questions which Trent, in order to achieve anything by 1563, had avoided: it concentrated authority in the papal monarchy just at the time when all other monarchs in Europe were beginning to concede power to electorates which in the end would consist of every citizen of the state. In this concentration of power, Vatican I ignored (and assumed that it had consigned to oblivion) centuries of Catholic thought about the independent role of Councils in the Church. The second Vatican Council met in a Western Europe which had now decisively adopted universal democracy as its principle, and to the huge surprise and alarm of the central Vatican bureaucracy, Pope John XXIII himself opened up discussions about authority which threatened to reverse the decisions of Vatican I and give (restore?) power not merely to bishops but to the entire faithful. The outcome of those discussions is still fiercely contested. In the minds of the last two popes, John Paul II and Benedict XVI, they never really happened, and nothing much has changed.

John O'Malley, I suspect, does not agree with these successive Supreme Pontiffs. He is of the generation which found Vatican II to be a liberation and a new programme for the future. Indeed, he points out, in examining a particularly fraught stage of discussions on bishops in 1563, that the unruly Spanish bishops demanded a statement which 'was close to that ratified in Vatican Council II in the mid-twentieth century'.[2] In previous books, echoed here, he has spoken eloquently of the scholasticism which unhelpfully dominated the thinking of theologians and bishops at Trent and contrasted it with the different mood at Vatican II, at which a humanistic culture of poetry and rhetoric flourished, sensitive to the worlds beyond Christian dogma, to produce a Council which in contrast to Trent, 'defined nothing'.[3] In the eyes of John Paul II and Benedict, scholasticism still rules OK as the means by which the Church analyses the world. Perhaps O'Malley is being unfair to Trent in saying that its lack of openness to Renaissance humanist scholarship was the reason that its grasp of Church history was so poor: try seeing what sixteenth-century humanist scholars, both Catholic and Protestant, made of early Church history, and they really don't do much better.

The great impression left by this excellent book is that Trent settled much less than people think. On clerical marriage and the use of the vernacular in liturgy, its statements were distinctly guarded and undogmatic. In the end, that was not intended to please Protestants, whom Rome had written off by the time of the third Council session in the 1560s, but to act as a gentle lure to the Orthodox, who cherished both clerical marriage and vernacular liturgy. That strategy was triumphantly successful in the next two centuries, as large swathes of Orthodox Christians in eastern Europe and significant numbers in the Middle East became reconciled to Roman obedience; but it has borne new fruit in the modern age too in relation to worship, and clerical marriage will no doubt come next. Trent left open the question of where power in the Church would lie in future; it was not the fault of the Tridentine delegates that in default of any independent body to keep a brief on developing its work, the papacy and its officials in the Curia stepped in to take the next initiatives, such as providing a universal catechism, a worldwide norm in liturgy and a revised edition of St Jerome's Latin Bible. The same seizure of the reins happened after Vatican II, though O'Malley is too tactful to point that out here. Two grouches: he doesn't provide enough year-dates in the text, so you forget whether some row or decree happened in May 1545 or May 1546, and have to flip back through pages to work it out. And it's a pity that even in the hands of a great historian, American English has decided to amalgate two useful but distinct words, 'episcopacy' (government by bishops) and the 'episcopate' (whole group of individual bishops, or term of office of a bishop). 'Episcopacy' shouldn't be doing the work for both. To those who say it can, let them be anathema.

6

The Italian Inquisition

This is one of Christopher Black's verdicts on the work of the Roman Inquisition:

> The human casualties among major thinkers were fewer than might have been expected; Bruno might have been saved, Galileo could have suffered worse; Campanella endured lengthy imprisonment; Giannone and Crudeli were partly just unlucky.

Yes, Pietro Giannone and Tommaso Crudeli were indeed 'unlucky', since they both died as a result of their experience of the Inquisition's prisons. So that's all right, then: just unlucky. Back in the 1980s, one of the more memorable sketches of *Not the Nine O'Clock News* was a solemn mini-documentary entitled 'The Devil: is he all bad?', featuring the liberal opinions of a trendy vicar and careful explanations by a nice suburban couple about the mitigating features of their sacrifice of virgins. There is a reminiscence of that wonderful parody of fair-mindedness in the historical judgements provided by Black during his absorbing account of Inquisitions in the Italian peninsula between the sixteenth and eighteenth centuries. It is reassuring to know from Black that the Roman Inquisition helped discourage 'undesirable superstitious beliefs and practices'. On the subject of the respective merits of torture by fire applied to feet coated in pork fat or by suspension by the arms tied behind one's back, Inquisition suspects facing torture would no doubt nod sagely at Black's opinion that 'a fire that scalded the feet might be less harmful for a man likely to be sentenced as an oarsman to the galleys than injury to the shoulders'.

A religion claiming to be based on precepts of love and forgiveness cannot but hang its head in shame at the record of inquisitions in the Western Church of the Latin Rite. Maybe inquisitions didn't achieve such a high percentage of executions as contemporary secular courts among those they indicted, and maybe they didn't torture people so often; maybe fewer witches died at the hands of Italian and Spanish inquisitions than elsewhere in Europe, because inquisitors were much more professional than other judges in their assessment of evidence. But still, it won't do. In the twentieth century, the Roman Catholic Church obliquely acknowledged that it wouldn't do, by twice re-naming the Roman Inquisition, latterly as the Congregation for the Doctrine of the Faith. One Josef Ratzinger was head of this organiza-tion before he became Pope Benedict XVI. The outlook of an inquisitor has been likened to that of officials in the Cheka, Bolshevik Russia's first secret police, where the aim was not merely to repress, but to change society for the better. There is often a fine line between idealism and sadism, but it does no favours to idealism, whether reli-gious or secular, to use too much historical empathy in excusing those who have crossed the line.

Inquisitors would no doubt retort that they did their work accord-ing to good biblical principles, and that their first effort was always to persuade and reconcile the erring. It was not their fault if the erring obstinately continued to err (that is, after all, the strict definition of a heretic); in fact it was their duty to rid society of such pollutants. Inquisitors could point, for instance, to Acts 19:19–20 to justify book-burning, since in the course of what the writer of Acts presents as a spectacularly successful missionary visit to Ephesus, St Paul the Apostle presided over a holocaust of books of magic arts, worth in total 50,000 pieces of silver. 'So the word of the Lord grew and pre-vailed mightily.' More than one painter of the Counter-Reformation, or his ecclesiastical patron, found this an edifying subject for art, and Christopher Black has chosen one example for his book-jacket: a dramatic version by the Flemish artist Maerten de Vos, with an over-excited St Paul having to be restrained in his zeal. De Vos entirely transposed this first-century destruction of learning to the Counter-Reformation Europe that he knew, complete with modern-style books (codices) being consigned to the flames, rather than the scrolls of the ancient world, and a large excited crowd in attendance around the scaffolding in the marketplace – an unlikely setting for Church activity in the small-scale and powerless beginnings of the Christian faith.

Certainly, medieval inquisitors did not invent the concept of heresy, which is embedded in the later layers of New Testament literature in a series of bilious references to 'sects' and went on to flourish richly as Christianity elaborated boundaries around its beliefs from the second century CE. Nor did medieval Western inquisitions invent that terrible death for heretics, burning them alive. Christianity borrowed burning at the stake from its great third-century enemy the Emperor Diocletian, who decreed burning for the new synthesis of monotheistic belief known as Manicheism, a dualist religion whose answer to the problem of the existence of evil has not been bettered: evil just is, and that's all there is to it. Christian leaders were just as offended as Diocletian by Manicheism and other dualist religious systems, and once bishops came to share in the power of Roman Emperors, they noted the precedent. Burning alive for beliefs similar to Manicheism was intermittently used in the Christianized Byzantine Empire from the seventh century, although not very often, and the Byzantine burnings ceased, soon after Western Latin Christianity took up the burning of heretics in the eleventh century. In fact there was a long tradition in the Orthodox Church of leading churchmen criticizing burnings at the stake, which has little or no parallel in medieval Western Catholicism. In later centuries, burnings resumed in Orthodox Muscovy – apparently thanks at first to prompting from Western Latin envoys of the Holy Roman Emperor in 1490. Once the Orthodox Churches of the East and the Balkans were in the hands of the Ottoman Turks, persecuting Christian heretics was in any case no longer a practical proposition for Orthodox Christians, who were thus saved from themselves by their own state of subjection to another religion.

Another outbreak of dualist belief occurred in southern France in the twelfth century, probably inspired by the Eastern dualism which the Byzantines had fought: these heretics were known as the pure – *Cathari* – or 'people of Albi', Albigensians. It took decades of crusading to wipe out their power, and there remained a neurosis about whether they would return from concealment, biding their time and meanwhile concealing their heresies. A Spanish Augustinian canon, Dominic, formulated one response to the situation: he gathered preachers who would lead a life so simple and apostolic in poverty as to outdo the austere Cathar leadership, and thus convince people that the official Church was a worthy vehicle for a message of love and forgiveness. Not only that, but Dominic's 'brothers' (*fratres* or friars) would have the best education that he could devise to make even their simplest message intellectually tough. Alongside the coming of the friars, the Church authorities devised tribunals of inquiry to investigate the beliefs of folk in the former Cathar regions: these were the first inquisitions, proceeding along guidelines drawn up by a great Council of the Church called to the pope's Lateran Palace in 1215. Over the next centuries, such tribunals proliferated, because they were useful against other forms of deviant belief, particularly in Spain, as Christianity clawed back territories from Muslim rulers and faced the problem of people who converted suspiciously quickly from Islam or Judaism. And all the while, the Dominicans continued their association with the institution which had emerged from the same Albigensian crisis as themselves. These highly skilled communicators soon dominated inquisitions, just as they dominated medieval Europe's universities. In a rueful division of their Latin name, some came to call them *Domini canes*, 'hounds of the Lord'. The other major grouping among the friars, the followers of Francis, also staffed inquisitions, but as Christopher Black points out, Franciscans rapidly lost their already minority share of the inquisitor market during the sixteenth century.

So there were inquisitions long before there was the Inquisition. And in fact there never was 'the Inquisition'. There was the Spanish Inquisition, an organization created in the 1470s under the control of the peninsular monarchs Fernando of Aragon and Isabella of Castile, in a cession of power to temporal rulers which the papacy soon bitterly regretted. This novel organization's main concern was to create a 'purified' and strong Latin Christianity free from heresy or non-Christian deviation, and indeed to spread this Christian monoculture throughout the Spanish Empire which in the next decades emerged across the oceans. So the Spanish Inquisition principally targeted secret Jews or Muslims, seeking to discipline the outburst of spiritual energy which the destruction of multicultural Spain had released in the late fifteenth century. Among the victims was a courtier from the

Basque Country, Ignatius Loyola, who had to flee the Inquisition to study at the University of Paris, with momentous consequences for the Catholic Church through his founding of the Society of Jesus. Mindful of his own encounter with the Spanish Inquisition, Loyola saw to it that his Jesuits never followed the Dominicans into staffing inquisitions, a highly significant statement of principle which I did not see noted in Black's narrative.

Another spiritual guru of interestingly creative opinions, Juan de Valdés, whose brother Alfonso was no less a figure than Secretary to the Holy Roman Emperor, and whose uncle had been burned by the Inquisition for secret Jewish practices, did better than Loyola; he got out of Spain before the Inquisition could finger him. He escaped to Italy, to the kingdom of Naples, a Spanish possession covering nearly half the Italian peninsula, which was spared the attentions of the Spanish Inquisition because, in a pleasing clash of jurisdictions, the pope refused to authorize its presence there. In Naples, Valdés spent a fruitful decade developing a new vision of Christianity whose adherents might be described as Valdesians, or in allusion to the role of the Holy Spirit in his thinking, *Spirituali*. Valdesianism was generous, exploratory, and not a little sympathetic to the purer monotheisms of Judaism and Islam, now so repressed in his native country. Valdés entranced some of the noblest names in Italy, with popes and cardinals in their pedigrees – Gonzaga, Colonna – and some of the best minds, including Michelangelo Buonarroti. Even a thoughtful, nuanced and cultured English cardinal in exile from his native land, Reginald Pole, who had a better claim than Henry VIII to be King of England, became a not uncritical admirer of the ambiguous Spaniard. In the 1530s, it looked as if Valdesianism might shape the future of the Western Latin Church.

That it did not was largely thanks to the institution which is the main focus of Christopher Black's book: the Roman Inquisition, newly founded in 1542 as one solution to the crisis which engulfed the Western Church after its mishandling of the Augustinian Eremite academic Martin Luther. Behind this deliberate imitation of the Spanish Inquisition placed firmly under the control of the papacy was a Neapolitan nobleman and career cleric, Gian Pietro Carafa. He became the nemesis of the Valdesian movement, and anyone that he suspected might be part of it, even unto the third generation. Black does not indulge in character-sketches, and so his readers are left to construct their own. Only gradually does it become apparent that Carafa, later Pope Paul IV, was one of the nastiest men of the sixteenth century, even by the exacting standards of Reformation and Counter-Reformation nastiness. Cardinal Pole privately called the Roman Inquisition masterminded by Carafa 'satanic'. Paul IV was a good hater, and his hatreds ranged from the trivial to the profoundly important. He hated nudity in art. He hated Jews, and confined the Jewish communities of the Papal States for the first time in ghettos and made them wear distinctive yellow hats. He hated the independent spirit of the Jesuits, and once they had lost the temporizing skills of their founder Ignatius on his death in 1556, Pope Paul forced them to surrender much of their freedom of decision-making and began remodelling them into a more conventional religious order. He also hated senior clergy like Reginald Pole, who had fostered the *Spirituali*. He never had the satisfaction of burning Juan de Valdés at the stake, since Valdés had the sense to die the year before the Roman Inquisition was founded, and he never caught up with Cardinal Pole, much to his annoyance. But he and his faithful acolyte in inquisitioning Michele Ghislieri (who later became Pope St Pius V) devoted much of their considerable energy to eliminating any trace of Valdesianism from the whole Church of Rome. On the way, they took in the confusingly similar-sounding medieval heresy of Waldensianism (not to mention, of course, Protestantism), and it is therefore not surprising that the Roman Inquisition had little interest in extending its persecuting skills to witches, given these very considerable items on its menu. Its finest hour was the persecution, torture and execution in 1567 of an Italian nobleman called Pietro Carnesecchi, a friend of Gonzaga, Colonna and Pole, whose wretched fate Black describes in detail. After that, Valdesianism and the *Spirituali* were cowed out of the devotional life of Italy, and Tridentine Catholicism was the poorer for it (some exiles from the movement became imaginative and innovative Protestant Christians, which of course Carafa would have seen as proving his case). Only the Jesuits, who had originated as part of that murky world, but who were remarkably adroit in disguising that fact later, carried on something of the spirit of these lost energies.

One of the consolations of the fascinating and depressing story which Black has to tell is the alternative tale which emerges from his diligent array of evidence: contemporary contempt and hatred for the work of inquisitions. Some may regard it as poetic justice that the Dominican patron saint of inquisitors (yes, there is one: Peter Martyr by name) ended his days hacked down with an axe by an angry Cathar in 1252. Among the necessary expenses for Paolo Costabili, the inquisitor of Ferrara in the 1560s, were extra guards to protect him, since a series of executions (burnings and beheadings) had, as Black puts it, 'rendered Costabili unpopular'. And hurrah for the mobs of Rome, whose jubilant reaction to the death of their Holy Father Paul IV in 1559 was to burst into the offices of the Inquisition and wreck its archives (a bad setback for the hounding of Pietro Carnesecchi). And how one's heart does not bleed for the complaint of the Mantuan inquisitor Domenico Istriani da Pesaro, who in 1596 lamented the difficulty of providing enough copies of the new papal Index of prohibited books, which had in any case 'disgusted many people in the city and surrounding area . . . How could he publish his Index without the means to implement it, and cope with the whispering against it?' Hurrah also for the enterprising publishers of Europe, who looked eagerly to the latest edition of the Index and used it as a library-list for advertising their wares to good Protestants and not-so-good Catholics. Perhaps the final word should go to Black's quotation of a pious and also clear-sighted nobleman of Brescia called Elia Capriolo, angrily reproaching the Dominican inquisitors of his city in a sensibly anonymous pamphlet of 1505:

> you seize from the Valcamonica certain old women who are stupid and frozen in a kind of mental daze, and you interrogate them about their faith, the Trinity, and other such topics. You bring in scribes and drag out proceedings; you conduct examinations under torture so that, by inflicting pain and torment on women who are admittedly little different from brutish beasts, you may appear as guardians of the Christian faith.

PART II
The English Reformation

7

Tudor Royal Image-Making

The considerable fuss in 2009 over the fifth centenary of Henry VIII's Coronation concealed the real surprise in the Tudor achievement: rebranding a failed cross-channel state as an island kingdom. In 1485 Henry's father, Henry VII, seized power in what had once been an example to all Europe of how to centralize government in a monarchy. The example was set by the Anglo-Saxon monarchs of Wessex, who, with the help of the Church, had manufactured a national idea called England, only to have their achievement hijacked by a shrewd representative of Scandinavian carpet-baggers, named William of Normandy. William's Angevin successors then created a power of continent-wide importance, an Anglo-French polity which represented these islands' best effort yet at European integration, but it had thrice fallen apart: successively in the thirteenth, fourteenth and fifteenth centuries. On the two occasions that competent and ruthless kings rebuilt it (Edward III, then Henry V), infuriatingly self-indulgent kings lost it (Richard II, then Henry VI). The uselessness of the two latter monarchs had led to their murder by ambitious would-be replacements, and their nobility had been so unimpressed by the victims' performance on the throne that they had mostly stood aside and let the assassinations happen. Henry VI did rather better after death than Richard II, because ordinary English folk were perplexed by Henry's frequent insanity (and utter wetness when occasionally sane), and then shocked at his unnecessarily sticky end. They decided that all this could only be explained if he was a saint. St Henry was an asset that the Tudors were not slow to exploit when they succeeded the two Yorkist brothers whose family were responsible for Henry's murder. Tudors rather than Henry VI gave us that incomparable monument of late medieval English Gothic, King's College Chapel in Cambridge, but the Protestant Reformation made it difficult to exploit a royal saintly cult. After some spirited ceremonial experiments in the opening months of the reign of Henry VIII's son Edward, another boy-king who was the sixth of his name, St Henry was allowed to fade away, remembered only in the grateful public prayers of his beneficiaries on King's Parade.

What remained was a dynasty with as ridiculously weak a claim to the throne of England as any monarch since William the Norman. The root of it was a marriage which was a love-match between King Henry V's French widow, Catherine of Valois, and her Welsh servant Owen Tudor – a marriage certainly valid in the eyes of God, but in English law made illegal by an Act of Parliament, since it had not obtained the royal permission which the Act required. Not surprisingly, this piece of legislation disappeared from public view sometime around 1485, only to be recovered in the twentieth century from its lurking-place in the borough archives of Leicester, whose Tudor mayors might have been highly alarmed if they had known of the explosive document they were harbouring. Henry VII's victory at Bosworth Field was one of the most astonishing political reverses in English history, the culmination of long-term plotting spearheaded by his formidable mother, Lady Margaret Beaufort, the most successful politician in fifteenth-century England. Her role, largely forgotten for centuries and thrillingly rediscovered by Michael K. Jones and Malcolm G. Underwood (*The King's Mother*, 1992), might usefully have played a greater part in Kevin Sharpe's admittedly already massive study of Tudor spin-doctoring.

Sharpe's subject is the considerable range of devices which the Tudor family employed as a distraction from their unconvincing genealogy: public pronouncements such as proclamations and preambles to parliamentary legislation, literature, architecture, painting and artefacts of all sorts. Many of their subjects proved anxious to help, and in the process, over more than a century turned England from a dowdy, unfashionable outlier on the European cultural scene into the country of Shakespeare and William Byrd. Byrd is indeed an exemplar of Tudor success: a Roman Catholic who in his religious outlook represented that diminishing but always significant minority which did not buy into the Protestant project of the last of the Tudors, and yet still remained the chief ornament of Elizabeth I's Chapel Royal.[1] Sharpe is as concerned to represent those disloyal to the dynasty as he is its supporters.

In reality, as C. S. L. Davies usefully reminded us,[2] sixteenth-century people did not normally think of 'the Tudors' or 'the Tudor Age'. They thought of Henry VIII and his children. They did not think all that much of Henry VII because they did not think much about him at all, despite his best efforts to bludgeon his image into the national consciousness with his megalomaniac chantry foundation, stapled ostentatiously onto the eastern extremity of Westminster Abbey. Consciously or unconsciously, Sharpe emphasizes this point on the dust-jacket of his book, which is dominated by Lucas de Heere's painting from the 1570s, now at Sudeley Castle, its subject precisely Henry VIII's family (see Plate 4). It is a portrait with no sense of chronology. The old king sits in full vigour on his throne, handing over his sword to an Edward who is well into his teens. On the king's right hand is his elder daughter Mary, with the husband who by the 1570s was something of an embarrassing national memory, Philip II of Spain. While Philip and Mary are depicted with perfect fairness, and in what might be considered the position of honour, they yield in size and in body language to the star of the picture, Queen Elizabeth I, who upstages everyone else. The only figure as big as her is the lady whom she appears to be introducing to the gratified company, the personification of Peace. The message is clear: after all the upsets caused by her jovial but terrifying parent and her unsatisfactory siblings, Elizabeth is complacently pointing (literally) to her own achievement, a nation united in harmony.

Of course it was not that simple, but Elizabeth's embrace of peace, a stance which came naturally to a lady combining nuance with extrovert theatricality, was an adroit disguise of her father's massive failure. Central to Henry VIII's vision for his reign was his attempt to fight his way back into the major league in Europe. Manifestly, his real position was inferior to the Big Three in continental power: the Holy

Roman Emperor and the Kings of France and Poland-Lithuania. Consistently, Henry tried to act as if he was their equal, and apart from
humiliating reverses like the total waste of money which was the Field
of the Cloth of Gold (a celebration of Anglo-French amity which led
nowhere), he never succeeded in being another Edward III or Henry
V. He was obsessed with giving reality to his empty claim to be King
of France, a claim that took up 50 per cent of the royal heraldry of the
realm. For the sake of paying for French victories, he made a vast and
easy profit at his subjects' expense, debasing the English sterling currency, previously one of the most respected in Europe, with which
none of the equally selfish and unscrupulous monarchs of the fifteenth
century had tampered. To gain even more cash for a series of up-to-
date coastal defences against French invasion, in 1538–9 he turned
the selective closure and reform of monasteries into wholesale dissolution without exception, a policy of which there had been no sign
even a year before. And all for what? Maybe the French were indeed
deterred from invasion by St Mawes or Walmer Castles (such forts
did not stop the Spaniards landing and causing mayhem in west Cornwall in 1595). But despite his posturing in various campaigns across
the Channel, Henry scored one net gain of a French city – Boulogne
– which the Privy Council had the sense to give back to the French
only three years after his death. After that, there was only Calais,
which the incompetence and neglect of his daughter Mary's government delivered into French hands in 1558 after two English centuries.
Now England's mainland empire was gone for ever, despite occasional
plaintive squawks to Paris from Queen Elizabeth about Calais. It took
the Hanoverians to bring back substantial mainland territory to the
English, and then only by means of dynastic alliance, which was broken in 1837. The loss was thanks to bluff King Harry, who did not
have the realism forced on his successors to confine his French Crown
to his coat of arms. His subjects might have been spared much misery
if he had contented himself with what he had got.

A clear narrative emerges from Sharpe's account. Henry VIII put a
good deal of effort into persuading, manipulating or bullying his
people into accepting policies which most of them did not like: the
annulment of a marriage to a popular and conscientious royal spouse;
marriage to another who was dismayingly clever and a bit flash; a

breach with a reassuringly distant Holy Father in Rome and the rebranding of him as the Antichrist; the closure of the monasteries; and monetary debasement. Henry's success against very considerable apparent odds was a tribute to his personal magnetism, still powerful enough to make plays about him saleable a century after his death. The successive groups of evangelical politicians who helped Henry's son Edward VI travel towards manhood put much of their propaganda efforts into showing how a boy could lead a national religious revolution from above, and why boys could be as good kings as men. They had the Bible to help them in their task. The Old Testament told with relish the story of a boy-king who was an undoubted Good Thing: Josiah of Judah. This precocious youth had caused the books of God's law to be discovered in his temple, and had then put his energies to destroying all the idols which offended God throughout his kingdom. God had been duly pleased. Go figure, as Protestants all over Europe were soon saying with gleeful frequency about Edward, though usually in Latin. Sharpe quotes an unjustly celebrated text purporting to be Archbishop Cranmer's address to King Edward VI at his Coronation in Westminster Abbey in 1547, in which the young king is duly styled a second Josiah – and many historians have cited it before him, including myself. But alas, we must all subtract this supposed sermon from our databases on the Edwardian regime; it is an unscrupulous ultra-Protestant forgery from the 1670s and it has beguiled us for too long.[3]

The Edwardian show was going well until the principal actor had abruptly to leave the cast, indisposed. His Catholic half-sister Mary started with some adroit expenditure from her father's deposit account in the national memory, which won her an extraordinary triumph against Queen Jane Grey in July 1553. It is one of the finest achievements of Tudor image-manipulation to make Jane Grey 'the nine days queen', in line with a proverbial expression for brevity which must then already have been well established, when in fact she reigned for a fortnight. We have forgotten the wider reality of this event: a rebellion and *coup d'état* by the Lady Mary against Queen Jane, whose claim to the throne was not at all weak, but whose drawback was not being Henry VIII's daughter (this perspective now appears very clearly in a recent study of those extraordinary events by the late Eric Ives).[4]

The turnaround in monarchs was a tribute to the old monster, still enduing his offspring with his mana. Yet Queen Mary then had something of a problem in establishing an image which would avoid her royal prestige being absorbed into the far more formidable power of the Habsburg imperial regime. Poor lady, she was torn between wanting just such absorption, as a dutiful wife and mother to the son and heir who would perpetuate her Catholicism, and her family urge to self-assertion as Henry VIII's daughter. The contradictions are exemplified in her refusal to give up the title 'Queen of Ireland', a kingly claim which her father had unilaterally created to emphasize his defiance of the pope and replace the 'Lordship of Ireland' supposedly granted by the twelfth-century papacy.

Elizabeth, the most controversial Protestant monarch in Europe at her accession, and subsequently the only monarch to be declared deposed by the Vatican, had a daunting task in maintaining her position and prestige. But she emerges in Sharpe's story in rather traditional fashion as the heroine: Good Queen Bess, possessed of keen emotional intelligence and highly developed acting skills. Monuments were spontaneously erected to her around the country after her death, with no pressure from national government, rather like local war memorials after 1919. Moreover, and most significantly, Sharpe shows how the nature of the paraphernalia selling monarchy changed during Elizabeth's reign. Most of what he describes in the time of the earlier Tudors stemmed from royal initiative, from action by the narrow political elite around the monarch, or from efforts by literary chancers hoping to gain royal attention and favour. By 1603, there was a much wider royal souvenir industry, to gladden the heart of any stall-holder in modern Whitehall: medals, miniature portraits of the queen, commemorative pottery, wall-posters – even for the first time, a pack of national-themed playing cards, with the picture and heraldry of the queen diplomatically placed on introductory cards additional to the set, so that no one would actually cheapen the royal image by gambling with it.

This was the small change of a 'public sphere' in English politics a century and more before Jürgen Habermas detected it in central Europe: the outward and visible expression of a national society which had a much more ancient consciousness of being a single, centralized unit than anywhere else of similar size in Europe. Paradoxically, in an age when many monarchs were trying to achieve a polity at least as integrated as the Tudors had inherited from their predecessors, the very longevity of the English monarchical machine made it difficult for the successors of the Tudors to build up new power in the fashion of their European contemporaries; centralized English institutions were too complex and well established to make drastic change easy. The ruler who achieved most in the short term was Oliver Cromwell, who brought radical change indeed, to the extent of creating a single British Isles for the first time in the history of the Atlantic archipelago. The trouble was that his triumph was bought with the backing of a large army which most of the English detested, and no amount of spin would alter that. Cromwell proved a much less successful pater-familias to the nation than Henry VIII: the ignominious sidelining of his harmless and agreeable son in favour of another Stuart – Mary's *coup d'état* of 1553 played as farce – showed the advantages of the glamour which royal families enjoyed, just as Charles I's fate had demonstrated the pitfalls.

8

Henry VIII: pious king

Two provinces of the Western Church Catholic happened to coincide with the frontiers of the medieval kingdom of England: Canterbury and York. There were clear contrasts between them. York was much smaller than Canterbury, with only three dioceses to Canterbury's fourteen; it was remoter from the centre of national affairs, and it was a poorer region overall. Either province had its own clerical parliament, Convocation, but the Convocation of Canterbury met while the national Parliament was assembled and had real significance as a law-making body; York more or less rubber-stamped decisions from the south. After long and bitter disputes over three centuries from the Norman Conquest, the Archbishop of Canterbury had emerged with a subtly adjusted title of precedence over the Archbishop of York: 'Primate of All England', as against York's 'Primate of England'.[1]

This relationship reflected the realities of power in the medieval kingdom of England and Wales, which, more than any other major European state, was a unit under centralized direction. In ordinary conditions, power lay in the south-east and around the capital city in the Thames valley; Lambeth Palace near London, the Archbishop of Canterbury's headquarters, looked directly across the Thames to the ancient seat of government in the Palace of Westminster. This tradition would be one of Henry VIII's chief assets in his idiosyncratic Reformation: more an act of state than any other major break with the old Church in sixteenth-century Europe. Out of his head came a Church which puzzled observers at the time, yet which briefly in the 1540s embraced a wider spectrum of religious opinion than any version of the Church in England since.

Compared with other provinces elsewhere in Europe, Canterbury and York were in satisfactory condition in 1509. In Henry VIII's other Tudor territory, Ireland, the Church was in a state of extreme confusion because of the country's political fragmentation; on the other hand, from the 1470s it was being swept by a religious revival led by friars, which had no parallel elsewhere in the British Isles. The late medieval Scottish Church was the victim of much greater diversions of finances for the benefit of the nobility than in England: profitable monastic offices were colonized by non-monastic protégés and members of noble families, and parish revenues were siphoned off for the foundation of collegiate churches, whose main function was the uphill struggle to pray for the salvation of Scottish aristocrats.[2] England's church government was far more orderly than administration in either Scotland or Ireland, and there were none of the scandals of central church government in Rome. Looking at the English Church, one could see much that was good, much that was indifferent, but little that was disastrous.

If the Church in England had problems in 1509, they were the problems of complacency born of success. In the late fourteenth and early fifteenth centuries, the Church had faced a real challenge from the Lollards, a movement of theological and devotional dissent which initially attracted some powerful political backing and some of the best minds in the English universities. The Lollards had then chosen the wrong side in politics, and they had been rooted out of polite society. They survived in defensive and occasionally persecuted communities scattered through lowland England; although we have realized in recent years that Lollard leaders were slightly higher up the social scale than we thought, and that Lollardy was at least sustaining itself on the eve of the Reformation, the movement as a whole was not showing any dramatic signs of expansion. For all the fears of some bishops, it was not going to overturn the old order single-handed.

The Church had won, and as part of its victory, in 1407 it had even banned the unlicensed use or independent translation of the Bible in English, a highly unusual ban in Europe and a deliberate triumphalist reaction to the Lollard stress on Bible-reading. Every new king in the unstable politics of fifteenth-century England had hastened to bolster his position by buying the support of the Church, funding lavish building projects and courting leading churchmen, who generally backed whatever regime had captured the throne. Henry VII put some curbs on the Church's legal independence, but these did not greatly change its relationship to the kingdom.[3] The English Church remained a pair of independent provinces, with their own parliaments, courts and legal system; working hand in glove with the monarchy, but confident of their own ultimate integrity.

Into this rather stuffy world came the man who would blow the system apart. Henry's religious policy won few unqualified admirers within the Protestant Church of England before the nineteenth century, when the Oxford Movement influenced a new breed of church historian. They wanted to find a suitable ancestry for their view that their Church was the true heir of the pre-Reformation Western Catholic Church, and not the residue of a Protestant revolt against it; they therefore lovingly excavated the Henrician Reformation as being reassuringly Catholic without the pope. One Anglo-Catholic, writing anonymously in 1891, summed up their attitude in extreme form: 'It has been well said that almost the only real reform that remained to be carried out at the death of Henry VIII, was the translation of the new services into English.'[4]

This was a deliberately comprehensive put-down for the Reformation carried out under Edward VI which, as fossilized in Elizabeth I's church settlement of 1559, in reality created the Anglican Church's liturgy and official statement of doctrine still in place at the present day. The comment also conveniently ignored some features of the Henrician Reformation which did not fit the Anglo-Catholic bill: Henry had eliminated the monastic life, destroyed all the shrines of England and Wales, and struck a mortal blow at a complex of beliefs about the afterlife centring on purgatory, which had been at the heart of late medieval religion in northern Europe. Other Anglo-Catholics could be as virulent as any Roman Catholic about Henry. At a modern stronghold of Anglo-Catholicism, the Shrine of Our Lady near the site of Walsingham Priory in Norfolk (dissolved by Henry in 1538), Anglican pilgrims process to a twentieth-century hymn containing a swift pen-portrait of the founder of the Church of England:

> But at last came a King who had greed in his eyes,
> And he lusted for treasure with fraud and with lies.[5]

Henry's was a strange sort of Catholicism, even after one has sub-tracted the pope. Yet as far as the king himself was concerned, his Reformation also proceeded without Luther or Zwingli, let alone the obscure young French exile Jean Calvin. Luther and Henry detested each other, and it was actually the more thoroughgoing Reformation of Switzerland which made the first important Reformation contacts with the king. The first of the only two major names among the con-tinental reformers ever to meet King Henry face to face was Simon Grynaeus, a south German humanist academic who became first col-league and then successor to Johannes Oecolampadius, the radical theologian at Basel University in Switzerland.[6] Grynaeus visited Eng-land from Basel in spring and early summer 1531; he came over supposedly to look for Greek manuscripts in English libraries, but in reality to see whether the evangelical Reformers could mastermind a better deal than the pope had been prepared to countenance for Henry to rid himself of Catherine of Aragon.

Grynaeus was enthusiastic for Henry VIII's theological arguments about his marriage, and for a few months in 1531 he cherished a vision of England poised on the springboard of a dramatic reforma-tion. However, he was unable to persuade the great names of the continental reform to present a united front on the divorce: hardly surprisingly, since they had failed to do so on the more basic issue of what the Christian Church believed about the Eucharist. Henry's fleeting encounter with the Swiss Reformation seems to have left no impression on the king, although it would have great significance for Thomas Cranmer in the long term. Henry could be politely apprecia-tive when continental reformers later sent him their works to augment his impressive library, but there is no evidence that their writings directly affected his thinking.[7]

Catholicism without the pope: Reformation without reformers. It is easy to mock Henry's religious policies, as the whims of a man who flattened a village church and churchyard to build his fantasy palace at Nonsuch, and who redeployed the church windows of Rewley Abbey outside Oxford to light his bowling alley at Hampton Court.[8] Yet Henry took his special relationship with God very seriously. The 1485 Act of Parliament which had recognized the fait accompli of his father's accession after the Battle of Bosworth could find no stronger

97

justification for the event than it was 'to the pleasure of Almighty God', ignoring the somewhat embarrassing question of hereditary right; the Tudor dynasty knew that it had been put in place by God's peculiar favour, and not much else.[9]

Moreover, Henry took time off from the pleasures of hunting and war, not only to read theology voraciously, but to write it. Unlike his great-great-nephew King James I, he put his name to the title-page of only one printed book, the *Assertio Septem Sacramentorum* of 1521, and even then most of the donkey-work was done by a committee of experts. However, this represents a fraction of the king's output in the 1520s, most of which remained in manuscript.[10] Later, throughout the years of the Reformation, the king was an assiduous corrector of others' theological drafts, and an improver in the margins of others' ideas – a practice not dissimilar to his approach to musical composition. He meditated, for instance, on the Coronation oath which he himself had sworn, and toyed with the idea of making some significant changes for the future to emphasize royal control over ecclesiastical affairs, speaking of 'imperial jurisdiction'.[11] From autumn 1537, now recognized by Parliament as enjoying just such imperial rights in all the institutions of his kingdom, he revealed an extraordinary will to rush in where theological professionals feared to tread: when revising his bishops' published statement of doctrine (the *Bishops' Book* of 1537), the king made bids to improve on the divinely authored text of the Ten Commandments, attempting, for instance, to tone down the biblical text's condemnation of image-worship. His editorial work earned him a schoolmasterly rebuke from Archbishop Cranmer: 'all the long sentence before . . . is the very words of God in Deuteronomy, which would be recited sincerely without any addition'. Later on in the same notes, a royal effort to tinker with that perennially difficult phrase in the Lord's Prayer, 'lead us not into temptation', was successfully torpedoed by the archbishop: 'we should not alter any word in the scripture . . . although it shall appear to us in many places to signify much absurdity'.[12]

The king indeed turned to theological activity for comfort in successive great crises of his life, crises which were associated with his tangled matrimonial affairs. His efforts to rid himself of the Aragon marriage were fatally complicated from the beginning by his obstinate refusal to see the question as anything else than theological: a confrontation between his own sin and an angry God. Likewise in his grief at the loss of Jane Seymour (for whom a natural death in 1537 intervened before royal boredom), Henry turned to revision of the *Bishops' Book*. Humiliated and betrayed by his fifth wife Catherine Howard, he took solace during 1542 in reading and moodily annotating newly delivered devotional manuscripts, and his continued theological musings culminated in a fusillade of ecclesiastical activity during the first half of 1543, including the final published version of a revised doctrinal statement for his Church, appropriately named the *King's Book*.[13]

Henry's vision of his relationship with God changed over time. As a young man, he was the conventionally pious son of a king who had imitated the devotion of his medieval predecessors. Henry VII sought an easy passage through purgatory with foundations designed to pour out prayers to God for him from grateful clergy and the poor and sick: the Savoy Hospital in London, and a mammoth chantry to serve his tomb in Westminster Abbey. The tone of the royal household was set by the intense devotional life of Henry VIII's grandmother Lady Margaret Beaufort, a woman whose turbulent political career had left her with much to be grateful for, but also with an intense and frequently tearful consciousness of the changeability of human affairs. More prepared to experiment than her son the king, Lady Margaret had been guided by her close associate Bishop John Fisher into financing new ventures in humanist higher education, alongside her investment in the purgatory industry: the intimate weave between the two aspects of her benevolence was symbolized by her foundation of university chairs of theology (with Fisher as first occupant at Cambridge) which were to be funded as part of the new royal chantry foundation at Westminster Abbey.[14]

In the grounds of Henry VIII's principal homes at Richmond and Greenwich were brand-new convents of the reformed order of Observant Friars, whose church buildings would loom over the two palaces' gardens until the beginning of Elizabeth's reign, ruinous and baleful reminders of the past, more than two decades after Henry had destroyed their communities for opposing his wishes.[15] Near Richmond were the Carthusian monks of Sheen, and a mile across the river from the palace stood the unique community of Bridgettine sisters and brothers at Syon Abbey. Syon, with its witness to the mystical intensity of the fourteenth-century St Bridget of Sweden, was an aristocratic convent with wide influence among the elite of London and the English nobility generally: it was 'the virtues[t] house of religion that was in England', said the London chronicler Charles Wriothesley at its suppression in 1539. The royal family, Wolsey and Syon between them accounted for half the dedications of printed books in the first two decades of Henry VIII's reign.[16]

Altogether, this complex of royal monastic foundations built within the previous century was intimidating proof of the continuing liveliness and creativity of the Church's devotion. William Tyndale, with no friendly intent, described the constant tolling of bells between Syon and Sheen in Richmond's royal enclave around the river Thames, sounds with which the young king would have grown up: 'when the friars of Sion ring out, the nuns begin; and when the nuns ring out of service, the monks on the other side [at Sheen] begin; and when they ring out, the friars begin again, and vex themselves night and day, and take pain for God's sake.'[17] It is noticeable that all these communities were deeply involved in the resistance to Henry's plans to annul his first marriage and break with the Bishop of Rome. Henry must have felt a beleaguered man when those indefatigable bells turned hostile: one should appreciate the personal dimension of his later enmity to clerical power, with these constant reminders of the devotional claustrophobia of his youth so near to hand.

From his early years, the king showed himself torn in his attitude to the power represented by the bells of Syon and Sheen. He did the things expected of him with enthusiasm, going on pilgrimage to Walsingham and hearing several masses a day at the variety of altars available to him in his palaces. He was instinctively a loyal son of Rome; when in 1512 he entered his first war, against Louis XII of France, his main declared reason was his horror at Louis's rebellion against the pope's authority.[18] However, there was another side to Henry even in the early years. He was already attacking the legal privileges of sanctuary and benefit of clergy, and he was unsympathetic to the Church hierarchy's inept attempts at self-assertion in the controversy over whether a London merchant called Richard Hunne had died an heretical suicide or an innocent murder victim of a church official. In the final act of this prolonged drama at Baynard's Castle in November 1515, Henry was provoked to declare before the assembled notables of the kingdom that 'by the ordinance and sufferance of God we are King of England, and the kings of England in time past have never had any superior but God alone'.[19] Even the result of the first French war, that supposed crusade for the pope, resulted in a similar declaration. One of the war's meagre gains was the city of Tournai, which the English occupied for six years up to 1519. A row developed over who would be bishop there: Henry's chief minister Thomas Wolsey or a French nominee. The French candidate appealed to Rome, and the subsequent dispute produced a claim from Henry in late 1516 that he now had 'supreme power as lord and king in the regality of Tournai without recognition of any superior'; furious at an oblique threat of excommunication from Pope Leo, Henry also issued dark threats.[20]

In this instance, the conflict led nowhere; Leo chose to defuse the situation with a conciliatory letter to the king, and by February 1517 peace had broken out. Soon Tournai was French again, and in the meantime, a far more serious threat had arisen to trouble the Holy Father: Martin Luther. Henry's rebuke to Luther, the *Assertio Septem Sacramentorum*, was both a vigorous and a remarkably concise and effective defence of traditional religion, which would seem incongruous in later years. Indeed, Sir Thomas More mischievously reminisced in the 1530s that he had vainly tried to persuade the king to tone down passages in the *Assertio* which acclaimed papal supremacy, particularly in its second chapter, 'Of the Pope's Authority'.[21] Famously, the work won Henry the papal grant of a title to rank alongside those of the Holy Roman Emperor and the Most Christian King of France: Defender of the Faith. He would obstinately cherish this honour, and hand it down to his successors.

Yet the faith which Henry was defending radically shifted in the crisis of his first marriage. The fiasco of the Blackfriars trial in 1529, cheating the king of his confidently anticipated papal marriage annulment, propelled him away from his fitfully intense acceptance of the Church's authority. The king who always had to be right was forced to admit that he had been wrong, that he had been deceived by clergymen: he had been wrong to fight France for the pope in 1512, wrong to write the *Assertio*. He must reconstruct his mental world, with no coherent set of instructions as to how to do this. The results were unpredictable, confused observers at the time, and have gone on confusing. The immediate result in 1529 was to propel Henry away from Thomas Wolsey towards the aristocrats at court who were uninhibited in their suspicion of clerical power. Such magnates as the Dukes of Norfolk and Suffolk had no sympathy for the continental Reformation (although Suffolk's few brain-cells would later suffer successful assault by the evangelical beliefs of his remarkable fourth wife, Catherine Willoughby).[22] To call their views anticlerical is inaccurate. They were anti-prelatical, suspicious of the pretensions of higher clergy to equality with aristocrats and (worse still) to an independent and superior jurisdiction within the realm: in particular, they saw such prelatical arrogance personified in Cardinal Wolsey. Their hostility to higher Church authority was paralleled in another anti-prelatical group: leading figures among the London common lawyers. Christopher St German, a barrister of the Inner Temple who was equally conservative in his general religious outlook, expressed in his writings an intense pride in the English common law, a system unique in Europe which had bred one of the few professional groups independent of the clerical profession. St German consistently argued for common law's superiority within England to the provisions of the Church's own canon law.[23] One man who knew this legal circle well, Wolsey's servant Thomas Cromwell, would soon mastermind the moves which decisively and permanently asserted that superiority.

In summer 1529 the aristocratic clique around Suffolk and Norfolk drew up a programme which was not simply intended to complete the personal and political ruin of Cardinal Wolsey, but also proposed an attack on the power of the church hierarchy generally, by giving the king the power to reform abuses in the Church, drastically pruning the Church's wealth and even considering the dissolution of all English monasteries. King Henry expressed in extreme form the anti-prelatical stance of this group when in October 1529 he said to the imperial ambassador Chapuys that the only power which the clergy had over laymen was absolution from sin.[24] This was a vision of the universal Church as little more than a trade union of confessors: if authority was to be provided for such a shapeless body, it would best come from the anointed monarch of the realm. Attacks on the absolute power of the papacy could claim medieval precedents, although they had rarely proved as subversive of papal monarchy in practice as in theory; even Henry's break with Rome might have left him a doctrinal traditionalist in all other respects. What was different from the past was that Henry's assertion of his unique place in the English Church (so conducive to his natural arrogance) might now gather to itself some of the flotsam of the theological upheavals taking place at the same time on the Continent.

For Henry said more to Chapuys, in a conversation which must have electrified the ambassador, quickly accustomed though he was becoming to Henry's efforts to shock him. The king now thought that his old enemy Luther had written many truths as well as much heresy in his attacks on the Church. Here we can detect another influence on him more radical than that of the aristocratic leadership: Anne Boleyn. Despite doubts expressed by George Bernard, there is little reason to dismiss the genuine interest in church reform which Anne was showing by the late 1520s, bringing her to read a wide range of reformist works. Through her, they reached the king. Anne introduced Henry to the writings of William Tyndale, and possibly also to those of the stridently anticlerical common lawyer Simon Fish; these put into words Henry's resentments against clergymen, and reinforced his growing conviction of his own absolute power over cleric and layman alike in the realm.[25]

It is important to decide what label we should give radical reformist opinion around Henry VIII, because the obvious description 'Protestant' presents serious problems for discussion of the Henrician Reformation. It was a label only created in 1529, the same year as Henry's great disappointment at the Blackfriars marriage hearing, and it was invented in a foreign country to describe a foreign situation: the crisis in the Imperial Diet at Speyer. In 1530s and 1540s England, therefore, it was as alien and awkward as were *perestroika* and *glasnost* in 1980s England, and the first signs of it becoming naturalized in English discourse only appear tentatively in the bitter polarizations of Mary's reign, after 1553.[26] 'Lutheran' is nearly as bad, not least because traditionalist Catholics like Ambassador Chapuys applied the label without discrimination to anyone whose religious views they disliked. During the 1520s, Luther had a major influence on English enthusiasts for religious change, but I have argued elsewhere that his variety of reformism was already beginning to give ground in England to the more radical theological influences of Strassburg and Switzerland in the 1530s. This was probably because of the pre-existing native dissent of Lollardy, which was much closer to the theology of Strassburg and Switzerland than to that of Luther.[27] There was also the unpredictable effect in the two universities of enthusiasm for Erasmus and other humanists, which could lead to radical scepticism about the claims and structures of the old Church, and there was the equally unpredictable effect of common law studies on those who practised them. Besides this, the independently developing strand of reformism in France was particularly significant for Anne Boleyn herself, because of her personal links with groups around the French court in which reformism was strong.

All these labels have a tendency to give a premature precision to people's outlooks at a time when new religious identities were only painfully and gradually being created out of a myriad individual rebellions against and unhappinesses with medieval Catholic theology. The vague label 'evangelical' is perhaps the best solution to the problem of description, precisely because it is vague. What it conveys is a necessary distinction from at least three groups of religious conservatives in politics who, like the evangelicals, supported the royal campaign for the divorce in the late 1520s and early 1530s: first, the anti-prelatical aristocratic circle at court; second, lawyers like St German, whose prime quarrel with the medieval Western Church was over jurisdiction; third, humanist academics who did not choose to leave the Catholic fold.

For the evangelicals, the major rallying point was the need to reconstruct religion out of the scriptural text of the Good News, the *evangelion*: what is so useful about this criterion is that it relates to that major phenomenon in the pre-Reformation English Church, its ban on the vernacular Bible. Richard Rex has convincingly shown that on the eve of the break with Rome, orthodox senior English churchmen like John Fisher were openly admitting that it would be a good thing if the Bible were in English; also undeniable, however, is that in the middle of many other worries and struggles, they did nothing about Bible translation. Cuthbert Tunstall, Bishop of London, indeed rejected the approaches of William Tyndale in the 1520s, and in the 1530s and 1540s non-evangelical bishops of previously impeccable humanist credentials like John Stokesley and Stephen Gardiner deliberately dragged their heels against initiatives of translation.[28] The Roman Catholic Church would have to wait until the 1580s before it acquired an English version of scripture without a health warning attached. By contrast, the evangelicals consistently emphasized the priority of creating direct access to scripture, and the publication of an official version of the Bible would be the lasting positive achievement of the 1530s.

There is plenty of evidence for Anne Boleyn's patronage of Bible production and Bible reading; likewise Anne also proved to be the earliest significant patron of a group of clergy who were to emerge as the leaders of the movement to disseminate evangelical opinions during the 1530s and later. She showed a marked preference for Cambridge graduates and dons; Cambridge men would take the lead in the early Reformation over Oxford, despite the powerful counter-influence at Cambridge of John Fisher. One can point as a minimum list of Boleyn protégés to William Bettes, Thomas Cranmer, Edward Crome, Nicholas Heath, Hugh and William Latimer, Matthew Parker, Nicholas Shaxton and John Skip: admittedly, not all would remain evangelicals for their entire careers. Three of these men (Crome, Shaxton and Skip) were from Gonville Hall in Cambridge, where Anne's great-great-uncle had been Master; a Gonville layman who also had close connections with Anne was Dr William Butts, and he would have an important role in promoting the evangelical cause at court after Anne's death because of his continuing closeness to the king. One of Anne's most significant evangelical protégés has been neglected probably thanks to male chauvinism: the royal silkwoman Jane Wilkinson (sister to the civil servant and future peer Edward North) was to be one of the chief financial and moral mainstays of the Protestant Marian exiles two decades later.[29]

Alongside Anne, Thomas Cromwell and Thomas Cranmer emerged as the great patrons of evangelicals when the two men became prominent in the king's counsels during 1531, and they both managed to survive her fall in 1536. The evolution of Cromwell's religious opinions remains mysterious: he may have followed a similar development to Cranmer, who apparently remained a conservative humanist until 1531, but who then rapidly developed sympathy for and understanding of German Lutheran belief – Cranmer indeed sealed his Lutheran allegiance with the extraordinary step of breaking his clerical vows of celibacy, when he married Margarete, the niece of Andreas Osiander, a German theologian. Thereafter Cranmer can be adequately defined as Lutheran in his evangelicalism throughout Henry's reign, retaining a belief like Luther in Christ's real and corporal presence in the Eucharistic elements of bread and wine; his abandonment of real presence belief some time after 1546 was a useful peg on which his Catholic enemies could later hang charges of inconsistency. Cromwell's beliefs cannot be so closely examined, and analysis is muddied by the accusations of sacramentarian heresy (that is, denial of the real presence in the Eucharist) with which he was destroyed in 1540. However, it is clear that from the moment of the archbishop's consecration in spring 1533, Cromwell and Cranmer worked closely together to push an evangelical agenda of change on the Church; it was Cromwell who was most responsible for achieving that key item on the evangelical agenda, the official authorization of an English Bible. A topsy-turvy scrap of evidence for their close cooperation is that the stray surviving letter-book of Cranmer's outgoing correspondence for 1533–5 contains no copies of his letters to Cromwell; clearly they were preserved in a separate administrative file, a testimony to a special relationship.[30]

Cromwell's partnership with Cranmer was an unequal one, and Cromwell's dominance in it was formalized thanks to Henry's grant to him of a unique status in the Church: Vicar-General and Vice-Gerent in Spirituals. The grant of the Vice-Gerency became necessary because of the humiliating failure of Cranmer's first major excursion into reform: an archiepiscopal visitation of the Province of Canterbury during summer 1534. A trio of conservative bishops, Longland of Lincoln, Stokesley of London and Nix of Norwich, disrupted the proceedings by protesting against Cranmer's exercise of his jurisdiction, Stokesley and Longland using the highly damaging argument that Cranmer's powers to visit were derived from the pope; Corpus Christi College, Oxford, later followed suit, perhaps inspired by hints from the College Visitor, Stephen Gardiner.

It was clear after this that change in the Church would have to be engineered in other ways. The passage of the Act of Supremacy in November 1534 specifically confirmed the king in rights of visitation as Supreme Head of the Church, and this was followed by the granting of the commission which created Cromwell's Vice-Gerency, probably on 21 January 1535. Henceforth Cromwell's jurisdiction, deputed from that of Henry as Supreme Head, outranked Cranmer's, just as, after 1518, Cardinal Wolsey's authority as legate delegated from the Pope had outranked Archbishop Warham's powers as Primate.[31] Cranmer, however, showed no sign of resentment at the erosion of the ancient powers of his office. It is clear that he felt out of his depth in politics, and he consistently took his lead from Cromwell. On one occasion it would have been better if Cromwell had listened to him: during 1538 or 1539 Cranmer tentatively advised Cromwell that the widowed king should remarry someone within the realm, since 'it would be very strange to be married with her that he could not talk withal'. Cranmer, with his German wife, spoke from experience! Yet Cromwell, clearly appalled at the thought of the promotion of one family from among his aristocratic rivals, brusquely pushed aside the suggestion, saying that 'there was none meet for [Henry] within this realm'; and the stage was set for the Anne of Cleves debacle which destroyed the Vice-Gerent.[32]

Evangelicals might disagree among themselves about such political matters and about how far they wished to push religious change, yet two external factors forced on them a unity of purpose and outlook. First was their nervousness about religious radicalism beyond the pale, the assorted reassessments of mainstream Christianity which were crudely summed up as Anabaptism. Such radicalism was a continental phenomenon which only marginally affected Henry's England, mostly as continental Anabaptists escaped to England to seek a slightly less hostile atmosphere. Only a small minority of English people were influenced by these immigrants, and there are no traceable Anabaptists within the political nation of Henrician England, in contrast with the sympathy which the radicals initially found among aristocrats and civic leaders in the Low Countries. Cranmer, for instance, was involved in the persecution against Anabaptism right from the first English campaign against them in spring 1535; he then personally examined and disputed with some of them, and he would remain at the centre of official efforts to combat their doctrines, including the only three burnings for heresy to take place in the reign of Edward VI.[33]

Perhaps still more significant in uniting the evangelicals was the consistent hostility and danger of attack which they experienced from the various conservative groupings, symbolized by the abusive phrase which traditionalist Catholics quickly coined in the 1520s, 'the New Learning'. At the time this term was never applied to humanism, as has misleadingly become common in modern historical writing, but always to those of evangelical outlook; the phrase much annoyed evangelicals, prompting them in turn defensively to accuse tradition-alists of being the real innovators. Conservatives may not have known much about theology, but they knew what they disliked.[34]

However, conservatives were divided in politics as evangelicals were not, in ways which proved fatal to any attempt to put up effec-tive resistance to the gradual spread of evangelicalism within the Church during the 1530s and 1540s. Fundamental to their divisions was the crisis over Henry VIII's campaign for annulment of his first marriage. This was not a contest between the Old and the New Learn-ing: Luther was as consistent in his hostility to the annulment and in his sympathy for Catherine of Aragon as were the Holy Roman Emperor and the pope. The big fight about the annulment between 1527 and 1529 was among religious conservatives. The chief actors in the drive to get the king the theological arguments that he wanted included John Stokesley, Stephen Gardiner, Richard Croke, Robert Wakefield and the Duke of Norfolk, while many others who became sucked into this royal research industry did not enter it as evangeli-cals: witness Thomas Cranmer. Championing Queen Catherine were John Fisher and (much more discreetly) Thomas More, together with the great names in the complex of convents around the royal palaces. The chief researchers in the king's camp had previously been part of the same world of devout, refined humanist Catholicism.[35] This breach among conservatives would never be healed. Moreover, the natural supporters of the old Church had been split during the 1520s in a dif-ferent way, by their attitude to Wolsey: either loyalty to a provider of lavish patronage, or principled detestation, often connected with the cardinal's high-handed attempts to redirect monastic wealth for his own collegiate foundations. Wolsey, for instance, signally humiliated Richard Nix of Norwich, the model of a conscientious traditionalist bishop, and an anonymous chronicler of Butley Priory in Suffolk described the cardinal's monastic dissolutions as being to the shame, scandal, destruction and ruin of all the monks and nuns of England.[36]

A sign of what might have been possible for conservatives against evangelicals is the changing political stance of Thomas, Lord Darcy of Templehurst. Darcy, a veteran royal servant particularly on the northern English border, had actually been the scribe for the radical programme for attacking the power and wealth of the Church put forward by the anti-prelatical aristocrats in summer 1529. By 1535, increasingly alarmed at the direction taken by the Church with Thomas Cromwell as Vicar-General and Vice-Gerent, and in particular at the rapidly developing attack on the monasteries, he was in regular treasonable communication with Eustace Chapuys, discussing rebellion against the king; in 1536 he joined the rebels in the Pilgrimage of Grace, surrendering his charge of Pontefract Castle to them. If other prominent conservatives had followed suit, notably the leader of the expeditionary force against the rebels, Thomas, Duke of Norfolk, then the evangelicals would have been doomed. But Darcy remained the most prominent traditionalist nobleman to rally to the Pilgrims' banner. The defenders of traditional religion had hesitated, and their cause was ultimately lost.

Throughout the 1530s the problem for conservatives was to decide when enough was enough, and when to make a stand. This is best exemplified by the dissolution of the monasteries, an operation of remarkable efficiency which within eight years extinguished all monasteries, nunneries and friaries within England and Wales. At no time during this process did the government officially condemn the principle of the monastic life (a fact which would be of use to those Anglicans who revived it by private enterprise in the nineteenth century); indeed, on the only occasion that Parliament was consulted about an extension of the dissolution, in spring 1536, the plan was presented in the preamble of the Act as an effort to strengthen the greater monasteries, even though the government simultaneously blackened the reputations of the monks as much as it could. Richard Hoyle has underlined the clever strategy of this measure: it contained an escape clause for the preservation of worthy smaller monasteries, which allowed any Member of Parliament who knew that accusations of depravity did not apply to his own local house, to vote for the measure without too much struggle of conscience. Hoyle interprets this as a tacit admission by the government that it could never secure conscious Parliamentary assent to a radical strategy of dissolution. Gradualism was the key.[37]

The final parliamentary dissolution legislation of 1539 merely recognized a fait accompli without further explanation: what else could it do, after the approving noises about greater monasteries in the 1536 preamble? Hoyle, indeed, argues for a consistent strategy of wholesale dissolution from the beginning of the operation. It is possible, however, to look for consistent differences of vision even among those involved in planning the dissolution. We tend to see the process through the office papers of Thomas Cromwell, since that is the archive which has happened to survive; how would it look if the archives of Framlingham Castle and Kenninghall Palace were intact, and we could hear the conversations around the conservative leader, the Duke of Norfolk, who was equally intimately involved in the monastic dissolutions? If there was indeed no unified vision of what would happen to the monasteries, then it was all the harder for the conservatives to construct a unified opposition.

In this as in all the major steps of religious change, we need to consider the man at the centre of politics: the king himself. From the mid-1530s, Henry was deliberately presenting a policy of balance, of Janus-like impartiality, in his religious strategy. One can see this in his successive attempts in the 1530s and 1540s to take a leaf out of the Reformers' book and issue statements about what his Church actually believed: the subtly adjusted three-way balances between Catholic tradition, Catholic humanist reform and evangelical innovation within the Ten Articles (1536), *Bishops' Book* (1537) and *King's Book* (1543) remain both confusing to the novice student and flashpoints for controversy among scholars. Even the Six Articles of 1539, at first sight a savagely uncompromising traditionalist document, made one major concession to evangelicals in the Articles' description of auricular confession: they said that this sacrament is merely 'expedient and necessary to be retained and continued . . . in the Church of God', a departure from medieval doctrine which infuriated the conservative Bishop of

Durham, Cuthbert Tunstall. Remarkably and surely significantly, they also opened with a repeated reference to the 'Church and Congregation of England'. '*Congregatio*' was a word which Erasmus had suggested as an alternative translation to 'church' for the Greek '*ekklesia*', but it had become more than a piece of humanist pedantry; it was taken up by such alarming evangelicals as the Bible translator William Tyndale. In the Articles, the source was probably the Lutheran Augsburg Confession of 1530, where Philip Melanchthon had defined the Church as the '*congregatio sanctorum*'.[38]

The strategy of balance was repeatedly announced by both Henry and his Primate of All England, Cranmer; it was clearly something which much impressed Cranmer about the king's religious policy. Henry, for instance, in a major speech to Parliament in December 1545, denounced both those who 'be too stiff in their old mumpsimus' and those who were 'too busy and curious in their new sumpsimus', and he reduced himself to tears as he pleaded for unity in his realm.[39] What is interesting about this speech is that it echoes a major public text by Cranmer of five years before, his Preface to the official Great Bible. Henry picked up not only Cranmer's description of the Bible as a 'most precious jewel', but also Cranmer's general strategy in his Preface, which echoed Henry's Janus-like outlook in being a twofold sermon addressed both to those 'that be too slow, and need the spur', and those who 'seem too quick, and need more of the bridle'.[40] When Cranmer chose six preachers for the reorganized Canterbury Cathedral foundation in 1540, he 'set in Christchurch [Cathedral] . . . three of the Old Learning and three of the New . . . and said that he had showed the King's Grace what he had done in that matter, and that the King's pleasure was that it should be so'.[41] It was no coincidence that the only major reformer whom the king made strenuous efforts (ultimately in vain) to tempt into an English visit was that habitual seeker after the middle way and moderator of Luther's angular faith, Philip Melanchthon.

The strategy of balance was not mere empty rhetoric. From time to time we can catch fleeting glimpses of the furious rows and backroom fudges which produced the successive statements of official doctrine: for instance, the exasperated remarks by Hugh Latimer (not a man born to compromise) about the painful creation of the *Bishops' Book* in July 1537:

As for myself, I can nothing else but pray God that when it is done it be well and sufficiently done, so that we shall not need to have any more such doings. For verily, for my part, I had liever be poor parson of poor [*West*] Kington again, than to continue thus Bishop of Worcester ... forsooth it is a troublous thing to agree upon a doctrine in things of such controversy, with judgements of such diversity, every man (I trust) meaning well, and yet not all meaning one way.[42]

Occasionally also the working papers behind statements survive, vividly illustrating the continual process of compromise forced by the king. One such set consists of a pair of drafts for the 1536 Ten Articles, trying to construct what would become Articles 6, 7 and 8 on images, honouring of saints and praying to saints. The second of the two drafts is consistently evangelical in flavour, giving only a grudging role to images and saints, and only one phrase from it appears in the eventual text of Article 7. More was used from the first of the drafts, and corrections on it reveal an interesting tussle between Cranmer and Cuthbert Tunstall. Tunstall adds to the secretary's text an affirmation that 'we may pray to our blessed Lady and John Baptist, the Apostles or any other saint particularly as our devotion doth serve us, without any superstition'; Cranmer sharply corrects the end phrase to 'so that [i.e. as long as] it be done without any vain superstition'. The combination of the two bishops' alterations arrives in the finished text. Noticeably, the elements of the first draft which were cut out include a long meandering introductory discussion of the limitations of images as poor men's substitutes for books, together with a rather silly list by Cranmer ridiculing the more esoteric calls of devotees on saints' time, including 'St Apollonia for toothache ... St Barbara for thunder and gunshot, and such other'. The final product is a far less discursive, far more focused and dignified piece of prose; above all, it contains something to please both evangelicals and traditionalists, and something to annoy them both.[43]

The royal strategy of balance was not just arbitrary political expediency; it reflected the deep rift within the king's own theological outlook which had opened up fully by the beginning of the 1540s. In many ways, the king jettisoned the past in his last decade. Most importantly, the idea of purgatory, central to the faith of northern Europe for centuries, lost its grip on him. In 1536 he was still prepared to put up a vigorous and rather effective attack on a paper compiled by Hugh Latimer against purgatory. For instance, he gleefully knocked down Latimer's unwise use of the argument from silence on the subject in selected early Church writings: 'Must the saints take occasion to write where you think place is for them, or where they think it meetest?'[44] However, already in his proposed revisions of the *Bishops' Book*, in late 1537 or early 1538, Henry showed that he was drifting away from any lively belief in purgatory. The *King's Book*, which was the eventual fruit in 1543 of this process of revision, generally made changes in a conservative direction, but significantly this was not so on purgatory. Even the name was now declared suspect: 'we should therefore abstain from the name of Purgatory and no more dispute or reason thereof.' The *King's Book* still commended masses for the dead, yet not to deliver people from purgatory pain but merely out of charity because the dead are part of the body of Christ, like us. Now purgatory's ancient power over human destiny was reduced to the vaguest of assertions, and as the most recent historian of the chantries' destruction has said, this 'effectively cut the ground from beneath the chantry system'.[45]

There are other signs of Henry's changing ideas. His suspicion of clerical pretension encouraged him in the *King's Book* to downgrade the sacraments of confirmation, and extreme unction and to reject the full traditional mystique of priestly ordination.[46] He also changed his mind on the character of individual confession to a priest; in the *Assertio* in 1521 he and his tame academics had put the traditional view that it had been instituted by God himself. By 1539, when the king was in other respects backing an extreme conservative religious reaction, he had changed his mind on confession; it was not instituted by God. He got very angry when Bishop Tunstall argued the traditionalist case, and he tore Tunstall off a strip in one of the longest letters he ever wrote: especially remarkable since Henry hated putting pen to paper. As already noted, this was the only significant point which the king allowed the evangelicals to win in the Six Articles.[47] We can also get an insight into Henry's mind from his rather complacent annotations to his personal psalter which date from the 1540s. These reveal that he remained proud of his achievement in destroying shrines and sacred images, which he completed in 1542: he repeatedly noted

God's anger against false worship and idols, and singled out a mention of Phineas, an Old Testament judge who rescued Israel from the consequences of idolatry.[48]

Alongside this was the king who remained a conservative to his dying day. He never accepted the central Protestant doctrine of justification by faith, despite all Cranmer's efforts to persuade him, especially in the revision of the *Bishops' Book*; so he had lost his hold on purgatory while not finding his way to a coherent replacement doctrine on salvation.[49] To see this is to make some sense at last of the apparently baffling twists of policy and inconsistencies in the king: he was caught between his lack of full belief in two mutually opposed ways of seeing the road to salvation. What did he have instead? A ragbag of emotional preferences. He cherished his beautiful personal rosary, which still exists; he maintained the mass in all its ancient Latin splendour and he left instructions in his will for a generous supply of requiems, in line with his new rationale for them in the *King's Book*.

Henry was at his most reactionary and obstinate on the subject of marriage – understandably – since this had lain at the heart of his recurrent personal crises. He insisted (against the facts of scripture and Church history) that marriage was one of the basic scriptural sacraments like baptism and the Eucharist, and his bishops obediently pandered to his prejudices when they were compiling the *Bishops' Book*: there marriage managed to pull rank on the sacraments of baptism and the Eucharist by having been 'instituted by God and consecrated by his word and dignified by his laws, even from the beginning of the world'. The king liked the bishops' work on marriage so much that it was preserved virtually unaltered in the *King's Book*.[50] Henry also upheld the ancient ban on clerical marriage, additionally refusing to release from their celibate vows the monks and nuns whose lives he had shattered and whose communities he had destroyed. He added a special personal provision to the Act of Six Articles that people who had taken vows of widowhood should be treated as severely as other celibates under the Act if they broke their vows; that exposed them to the threat of execution as felons. Yet even in his obstinate traditionalism on marriage, his anticlericalism asserted itself; he said that married clergy would form dynasties which would be even more of a threat to royal power than the celibates![51]

Henry VIII once described 'the law of every man's conscience' to be 'the highest and supreme court for judgement or justice'.[52] He was afforded the luxury of erecting his private conscience into the guiding religious teaching of an entire kingdom, and it was a luxury which he often abused. His prized theory of balance could turn to murderous paranoia, most notably in the incident in which three prominent evangelical clergy and three prominent papalist Catholics were executed on the same day (30 July 1540), but also all through the 1540s, when more evangelicals and papalists died for not fitting the king's conscience. His last year of life was particularly full of abrupt swings of mood. In January 1546 Cranmer was eagerly presenting him with plans for further liturgical change, acting on signals from the king himself, but nothing came of them; in spring and early summer Henry allowed a murderous campaign against the evangelicals by conservatives, yet by August he was suggesting to the French ambassador the abolition of the Mass in both England and France. In December, the Duke of Norfolk and the house of Howard, aristocratic backbone of traditionalist religion, were brought low and the duke was packed off to the Tower of London because of the dying king's fury and fear when Norfolk's heir, the Earl of Surrey (ironically himself a favourer of evangelical reform), rashly stressed Howard royal blood; Bishop Gardiner was then also in disgrace, and the future of the realm was in the hands of evangelicals.[53]

Amid these swings of fortune, all through the 1540s, the key people close to the king's person were evangelicals: notably his long-trusted doctor William Butts (d. 1545), Sir Anthony Denny, the Chief Gentleman of his Privy Chamber, quiet compliant Archbishop Cranmer and the king's last wife from 1543, Catherine Parr. His son's education – so vital for the future of England's religion – was in the hands of evangelicals from Cambridge, although it would have been perfectly possible to have chosen orthodox Catholic academics.[54] However much Henry was in his lifetime balancing change, he was stacking the odds after his death in favour of the evangelicals. It is worth noting a reminiscence of Martin Bucer, the reformer of Strassburg, who, like Philip Melanchthon, always sought consensus and the middle way among evangelicals. Only a year after Henry's death, Bucer claimed that he had recently offered the king a book attacking compulsory clerical celibacy against the writings of Bishop Gardiner of Winchester and others; however, Henry replied

> that he had rather I should defer for a season the publishing abroad
> thereof, for he trusted to come to pass that I should speak of this and
> other controversies in religion at some time peaceably with Winchester,
> and other learned of his realm, to the intent a godly concord and unity
> in religion might be sought forth, and a further instauration [i.e. reno-
> vation] of the churches, which his purpose I might have hindered, if
> Winchester (whose bitterness in writing he did in no manner wise
> allow) should have been provoked to write any more openly against us
> [the evangelical reformers].[55]

Bucer's words add some weight to the possibility that Henry, confident both of his abilities as theological referee and of his own survival
on this earth, was planning further to alter his Church's balancing act,
and move England in an evangelical direction.

What united the diverse strands of Henry's religious policy? Apparently it was Henry's conviction of his unique relationship with God as
his anointed deputy on earth, a conviction strong enough to be shared
by his devoted but not uncritical admirer Cranmer. Once or twice
Henry half-heartedly entered negotiations which implied some surrender of his Royal Supremacy: first at the Imperial Diet at Regensburg
(Ratisbon) in 1541, when in diplomatic isolation he was eagerly
courting the emperor's favour, and second in that fevered summer of
1546, in response to a quixotic mission from an ultra-Anglophile
papal envoy, Gurone Bertano. Yet it is difficult to believe that Henry
would ever seriously have contemplated surrendering the Supremacy.
Increasingly in the decoration of his palaces and personal possessions,
he identified himself with the Old Testament hero-king David, who in
his youth had slain Goliath as Henry had slain the Goliath of the
papacy. In his last years, the king turned for comfort to the songs of
David in the Psalms and to the thoughts of David's son Solomon in
Proverbs; who better, after all, than his fellow-monarchs to speak to
the private thoughts of a king? We still have his personal copies of
both books.[56] Henry's illustrated psalter makes the point straight
away (see Plate 6). Psalm 1 begins 'Blessed is the man who does not
walk in the counsel of the ungodly ... his delight is in the law of the

Lord, and on his law he meditates day and night': against this verse, Henry scrawled 'note who is blessed'. Above is the picture of a royal bedroom, with a king meditating day and night on a book: a king who is both the Old Testament king who wrote the psalm, and the Tudor king, dressed in the clothes familiar to us from Holbein portraits. After a career in which he had discovered the full meaning of an English king's supremacy in the Church, Henry had no doubts that he was that blessed man of whom his royal predecessor had spoken.

9

Tolerant Cranmer?

It matters to use words precisely, so let us linger over words before seeing how they apply to Thomas Cranmer. Two scholars of French history, Mario Turchetti and Malcolm Smith, considered how they might discuss toleration amid the murderous religious divisions of sixteenth-century France, and their friendly argument has a more general application.[1] Turchetti draws a distinction between concord and tolerance: that is, refusing diversity, in order to create 'concord', versus acceptance of diversity. Smith refines this distinction, by identifying two sorts of concord or refusal of diversity:

– one can enforce concord and overcome diversity by coercion, prohibition and ultimately violence;
– or one can seek concord by discussion and persuasion, the spinning of formulae and the cultivation of generous vagueness in definition.[2]

Naturally, it is possible to slide from one to the other: a famous example, one indeed much quoted in the Reformation, would be Augustine of Hippo's change of stance on his Donatist opponents in North Africa to 'compel them to come in', once conferences had failed. More happily, on occasion, coercion can move to discussion in the search for true concord.

Moving on from concord to tolerance: as Turchetti points out, tolerance implies the recognition of something which is forbidden and which remains forbidden. It involves concessions by an authority which remains in a superior position, in a society which has not fundamentally adjusted its structures or the ideologies which legitimize them, even though it is putting up for the time being with an alternative set of ideas. There is a stage beyond this tolerance: religious freedom – what Smith calls 'the right of individuals and of groups to hold any belief and express that belief publicly', or what that great historian of Reformation Germany Bob Scribner called 'indifference to difference'.[3] So we can consider a fourfold range of possibilities in any society which takes religious practice seriously: concord by coercion, concord by discussion, by tolerance or by religious freedom.

How does this set of definitions apply to Thomas Cranmer, Primate of All England for twenty-three years from 1533? Straight away we can narrow down our discussion by removing the last of our fourfold categories from consideration. Cranmer had no interest in religious freedom. His mind was alert and outstandingly well furnished, on the basis of what was probably the best scholarly library in the England of his day, but he was rarely an original thinker; it would have taken bold original thought in early Tudor England to conceive of publicly expressed freedom of belief. One original English mind, Thomas More, had indeed made the toleration of 'varied and manifold forms of worship' one of the founding principles of the commonwealth of Utopia. Yet Utopia was precisely that – nowhere – and More's persecuting practice while he held political power made it clear that he thought that the best place for religious freedom was nowhere.[4] Small wonder that a cautious, well-read humanist like Thomas Cranmer had no time for the idea. The most generous reflection which he made on the subject came in his 1549 adaptation of a medieval prayer for the conversion of non-Christians, derived from the Sarum Rite for use on Good Friday. Here he asked God to 'have mercy upon all Jews, Turks, infidels and heretics, and take from them all ignorance, hardness of heart and contempt of thy word'. His description was marginally more courteous than Sarum's 'pro hereticis . . . et pro perfidis iudeis . . . et pro paganis', but in the end the sentiment was the same.[5]

So Cranmer had three options for the English Church: concord by coercion, concord by discussion or concord by tolerance. He was not the inspired, charismatic leader of a 'Reformation from below', as Luther was at first, as Thomas Müntzer was for a moment, and as John Knox remained; he was not even the inspired, charismatic leader of a 'Reformation from above', as Zwingli and Calvin discovered that they were. He was an agent, not an initiator, and that is how he wished it to be. Cranmer had a profound belief in the supposedly ancient truth which Henry VIII and Thomas Cromwell had discovered in the 1530s: the best form of government in the Church was through the sole authority of the anointed godly prince. From about 1531 until literally the last morning of his life, this remained Cranmer's guiding principle, even if on occasion he could feel deeply frustrated that God's anointed had not yet grasped the point of what God wanted.[6]

Cranmer took this belief to a remarkable extreme. In 1540, as a member of one of Henry VIII's interminable series of doctrinal commit-tees, the archbishop answered a set of questions about the sacraments and the nature of the Church. One of these questions was 'whether the apostles lacking a higher power, as in not having a Christian king among them, made bishops by that necessity, or by authority given them by God'.[7] In the course of a lengthy answer, Cranmer pointed out that the apostles of the first century AD had lacked 'remedy then for the correction of vice, or appointing of ministers' and had to make do with 'the consent of christian multitude among themselves'. There is an unmistakeable distaste in his use of the word 'multitude'; Cranmer would have sympathized with the dictum attributed to the Rev. Dr Jabez Bunting, a great autocrat of nineteenth-century Wesleyanism, that Methodism was 'as opposed to democracy as it is to sin'.[8] Far from holding any doctrine of apostolic succession, Cranmer viewed the first Christians as casting around to create makeshift structures of authority: 'they were constrained of necessity to take such curates and priests as either they knew themselves to be meet thereunto, or else as were commended unto them by other that were so replete with the Spirit of God . . . that they ought even of very conscience to give credit unto them'.

This view of Church history is a consequence of a view of royal supremacy as the natural condition of the Church. It puts an interest-ing question-mark against a common assumption among humanist reformers: that the Apostolic Church of the first generation should be the ultimate court of appeal in all disputes about the nature of the contemporary Church. In this respect at least, Cranmer did show a certain originality among leaders of the Reformation: in his eyes, the Apostolic Church was an imperfect, incomplete model for the Church of the sixteenth century. One can express this in terms of one variant on the common Protestant Reformation sport of defining the marks of the true Church. If one takes three marks – first, true preaching of the Gospel, second, right administration of the sacraments, and third, discipline – Cranmer considered that the early Church was only normative for the first two: preaching and the sacraments, not for discipline. This view was liable to create a gulf between Cranmer and those reformers, both English and continental, who took apostolicity as their criterion for discipline as well. From the early 1530s, the archbishop was familiar with the publications of Martin Bucer, who became his admiring correspondent, and he also quickly bought the first edition of Calvin's *Institutes* of 1536. Already Bucer and Calvin were wrestling with notions about church polity which would lead to Bucer's attempts to restructure the Church at Strassburg on scriptural lines; later, Calvin would make an even more thorough-going claim that the Church of the New Testament was a clear and unequivocal guide to the perfect form of any Church of Christ.

Cranmer could not and would not go down the same path. What probably weighed more with him than the developing theories of these eminently respectable figures was his wish to defend the true Church of which Henry was Supreme Head against a double threat: papistry and evangelical radicalism of many varieties. Between 1531 and 1533, Cranmer abandoned what had been a very conventional late medieval piety, not simply for a new belief in the royal supremacy, but also for a fairly complete identification with Lutheran theology.[9] During the course of the 1540s, he would drastically modify his Lutheranism, particularly under Bucer's influence, but this would not affect his sense of standing between two extremes which were both enemies of truth.

After 1531, perhaps at an even faster pace than Henry VIII, Cranmer came to have a deep hatred for the papacy. By early 1536, he was publicly preaching that the pope was the Antichrist: a remarkable statement for a cautious, gentle theologian who was also Primate of All England. The only prominent English commentator previously to say the same thing was William Tyndale, and he was then lying in a Low Countries gaol awaiting death, with the connivance of Henry VIII.[10] At the other extreme from papistry was the multiform threat of continental Anabaptism, which first seems to have caused the English authorities alarm in 1534–5. From the start, Cranmer was involved in the suppression of the Anabaptists.[11] We can point to his persistent hatred for the Anabaptists and other radical reformers, an echo of which we have heard in his fastidious choice of the word 'multitude'.

Cranmer and his circle had a useful rhetorical device for linking the two extremes: they referred to both of them as 'sects'. Papistry and the radicals had 'divided, rent and torn in pieces the quiet unity and friendly concord of thy holy religion', as Cranmer's chaplain Thomas Becon informed God in 1550.[12] The various orders of monks and friars which were the chief source of the worst features of papistry could be listed in their diversity alongside the diversity of the radicals. Thomas Becon, for example, produced a splendid list of sects ten lines long, which begins with St Benedict and his Rule and ends with sacramentaries and libertines – a combination which would not have pleased either end of this spectrum.[13] Cranmer's old friend Hugh Latimer, preaching two years later in 1552, picked up another supposed common feature of the monastic orders and the Anabaptists: neither of them could 'abide the company of men' and so they forgot the 'commandment of love and charity' by quitting normal society.[14] Very precisely, then, papists and evangelical radicals broke concord in the Church.

If we return to Cranmer's distinctive historical relativism about the early Church, we may now appreciate how it was encouraged by his wish to defend the Church against the twofold sectarian threat. With this aim in mind, he would be deaf to the attractions of Bucer's and Calvin's developing ecclesiology and their emphasis on recovering the structural forms of the Apostolic Church. The radicals' constant cry was for a return to the Church of the Apostles; they perceived (in fact, perfectly correctly) that the Apostolic Church had been ambiguous in its attitude to civil government, and they were frankly hostile to what the Emperor Constantine the Great had done to Western Christianity. At the same time, opposing the other flank, Cranmer wanted to repudiate the false claims to authority by the traditional Church, with its constant defence of error by reference to 'unwritten verities', against the authority of scripture.

The neat solution was to kill these two birds with one stone, by denying any independent authority or identity at all to the Church, and this is what Cranmer did in his responses to those questions posed in 1540. Once this had been done, one was left with the authority of the Christian prince, who could be persuaded and educated in the right use of Holy Scripture in order to govern his kingdom correctly. Now, it was no doubt apparent to Cranmer even in 1540 that there might be theoretical drawbacks to this scheme; he had just witnessed with deep distress Henry VIII's wrong turn in backing the passage of the traditionalist provisions in the Act of Six Articles in 1539, including the personal trauma of having to send off his clandestine wife Margaret to refuge in Germany. The drawbacks of the Supremacy would become even more painfully apparent with Mary's accession in 1553. It is likely, too, that the archbishop was later influenced by Martin Bucer's arrival in England in the reign of Edward VI, and by the face-to-face conversations which the two men were then able to have about the nature of the Church; this would give the archbishop cause to modify the stark version of Erastian belief which he had presented for the boisterous approval of Henry VIII at the beginning of the 1540s. Yet his basic trust in the royal supremacy in the Church remained.

The royal supremacy in England under all three sovereigns – Henry, Edward and Mary – involved concord by coercion, and there was little that Cranmer could do to stop this, even if he had wanted to. Once more, remember that he was an agent, not an initiator. Very precisely, he was an adviser: chaplain to Henry VIII, godfather to Edward VI. Henry VIII executed religious dissidents from both ends of the spectrum, famously illustrating the nature of his murderous ecumenism on 30 July 1540 when he killed three papalists and three evangelicals – the papalists for treason and the evangelicals for heresy. These executions revealed both the similarities and differences between the outlooks of the king and his archbishop. What they had in common was a passionately held view of the English Church as possessing a middle ground of truth which needed to be defended from two extremes of error, and they both frequently articulated this view, often in the same language.

However, Cranmer and Henry VIII never came to agreement on what made up the content of this middle ground; both men constructed their own package of truth, in Henry's case a weird jackdaw's nest containing a jumble of theological ideas from traditionalist and evangelical sources.[15] Cranmer would never have considered Barnes, Garrett and Jerome, the evangelicals who died in 1540, as heretics; they were in fact his colleagues, representatives of the evangelical mainstream, Robert Barnes in particular being the most self-conscious Lutheran among leading English clergy. Their deaths came at a moment of unusual political mayhem and danger for the archbishop, who with a small change in the political equation at that moment might have shared their fate. To criticize Cranmer for standing aside while Barnes, Jerome and Garrett died is to be unrealistic about the brutal business of politics.[16]

Cranmer's uneasy relationship to other Henrician executions has often been criticized. In particular, his attitude to the death of his friends and patrons Queen Anne Boleyn and Thomas Cromwell has been the source of much ill-directed sarcasm.[17] More relevant is to note that there were two executions of apparently mainstream evangelicals on heresy charges during the 1530s in which he was directly involved: one was the death of John Frith in 1533; the other, the death of John Lambert in 1538. Both died primarily because of the views which they had expressed on the Eucharistic presence, views which were similar to those which Cranmer came to hold after 1546–7. This irony was already gleefully exploited at Cranmer's trial for heresy in 1555, and we need to consider these two cases carefully.[18]

First is the case of John Frith. In his first few months as archbishop, Cranmer inherited this from his predecessor. Cranmer reported on the proceedings to his friend and successor as ambassador to the Emperor (Charles V), Nicholas Hawkins; he was quite clear that Frith was in serious error on the Eucharist:

whose opinion was so notably erroneous, that we could not dispatch him . . . His said opinion is of such nature, that he thought it not necessary to be believed as an article of our faith, that there is the very corporal presence of Christ within the host and sacrament of the altar, and holdeth of this point most after the opinion of Oecolampadius. And surely I myself sent for him three or four times to persuade him to leave that his imagination; but for all that we could do therein, he would not apply to any counsel.[19]

Martin Luther would have said no less. Cranmer already knew exactly what he was talking about when discussing variants on Swiss theology, and he was evidently prepared to spend a good deal of time to argue Frith out of his views; but when he failed, the law must proceed. He saw no problem in moving from the concord of persuasion to the concord of coercion, and as he told Hawkins without especial drama, Frith now 'looketh every day to go unto the fire'. However, one notes that the archbishop had given the Basel reformer Oecolampadius his Latinized academic surname, so he recognized his status as an evangelical fellow scholar. Most hostile Catholic English commentators referred to Oecolampadius (if they knew of him at all) only by his original German surname, Hussgen. It may also be significant that in this account written to an intimate friend, Cranmer did not use the word 'heretic' about Frith, a word which by contrast he habitually used about traditionalists of whom he particularly disapproved. Luther and Lutherans, having been so often called heretics themselves, tended to avoid this term as being tainted, and Cranmer, after his experience of Lutheran Germany, may have felt the same way.[20]

Frith was burned on 4 July 1533. His death was not of Cranmer's making; the situation was one which he had inherited, and he can hardly be blamed for not knowing in 1533 that he would change his mind on the question of the Eucharist thirteen years later. One also has to consider the politics of the Frith case against the general political background in the Church. It occurred in the course of a long-standing row about the preaching of Cranmer's close associate Hugh Latimer, which by summer 1533 was being gradually resolved in Latimer's favour. It would be a gift to Latimer's enemies if someone like Frith, who could be associated with Latimer's evangelical circle, and who had gone so grievously off the rails in Eucharistic theology, was seen to be let off the hook. As the breach with Rome widened, it was important to be firm against such 'sacramentaries' as Frith in order that Henry's regime did not lose the loyalty of conservative leaders like Bishop Stokesley of London, who continued to detest Latimer to the extent of forbidding him to preach in his diocese during autumn 1533.[21]

Nevertheless, the Frith affair is not a happy story, particularly since Frith's reputation remained high among evangelicals, and his writings and Catholic refutations of them continued to be printed right into the reign of Edward VI. John Foxe clearly found the whole business embarrassing; first he minimized Cranmer's role and later seized gratefully on a circumstantial account of one of Cranmer's household gentlemen vainly giving Frith the chance to escape in the woods around Brixton while they escorted him to Cranmer's palace at Croydon. However, honesty compelled Foxe to narrate the story in a way which made it clear that Cranmer was not involved in this abortive act of mercy to Frith. Foxe also tried to make the best of a bad job by suggesting that much later, in Cranmer's published *Answer* to Stephen Gardiner of 1551, Frith was the chief source of ammunition for the archbishop's assault on 'Wily Winchester's Eucharistic theology: 'I doubt much whether the archbishop ever gave any more credit unto any author of that doctrine, than unto this aforesaid Frith,' he said.[22] It may be so, and in terms of common outlook, Cranmer's Eucharistic theology did eventually settle down to be much like Frith's, but unless Foxe had information otherwise lost to us, Cranmer kept his revised opinion of Frith to himself.

The disaster which befell John Lambert in 1538 also well illustrates the English evangelical establishment's continuing hard line on the corporal presence of Christ in the Eucharist. What is evident from the embarrassed account in Foxe's narrative on Lambert is that it was the evangelicals who caused his downfall. Lambert began by arguing about the Eucharist with John Taylor (who would become Bishop of Lincoln under Edward VI); Taylor called on Robert Barnes to back him up in confuting Lambert, and Barnes in turn decided that Cranmer ought to be brought in; after the archbishop had examined him, Lambert was confined in Lambeth Palace. Lambert is then said to have appealed to the king: a highly unwise move in autumn 1538 because Henry was then taking one of his occasional fitful but intense bursts of interest in his religious policy. The king decided to single out Lambert for destruction, by summoning a special heresy tribunal to Westminster, over which he would preside in person as Supreme Head of the Church.[23]

Since all the leading bishops were present at the tribunal, it was only natural that the king should ask Cranmer to take up the questioning when he himself had finished. Cranmer concentrated on putting arguments that the body of Christ could be in two places at once, on the analogy of Christ's appearance to Paul on the road to Damascus, an approach which would have drawn the approval of Martin Luther. There is one aspect of the subsequent discussions which is surely significant: their avoidance of the technical language of transubstantiation. If Foxe's summary of the proceedings is to be trusted, none of the first four interrogators – Henry, Cranmer, Bishops Gardiner and Tunstall – used the word 'substance' in their arguments against him; it was only the ultra-conservative Bishop Stokesley, speaking fifth, who is recorded as bringing in this term and using it in a scholastic sense. Nor, perhaps even more significantly, had the word 'substance' appeared in the otherwise stridently conservative language about the sacrament of the altar in the king's proclamation against heresy issued that day; this was all the more remarkable because Lambert himself had used the scholastic language of substance fairly freely in previous arguments and in a Eucharistic treatise which he had addressed to the king from prison at Lambeth.[24]

The primary Eucharistic argument in the trial itself, therefore, could be regarded as being about presence and not about the scholastic definition of the Eucharistic miracle as transubstantiation. Lambert's case was not like that of Adam Damplip of Calais earlier that same year: Cranmer had successfully defended Damplip, although he denied transubstantiation, because he still upheld the 'truth' in the Eucharistic presence.[25] The analogy for Lambert was rather the examination of John Frith in 1533; Lambert was going to die for his error in denying the truth of the presence, and that must have been some consolation for Cranmer as the king pronounced sentence. More straightforwardly, it may be that John Foxe's account has suppressed other more unpalatable opinions of Lambert's which put him squarely in the radical camp, and which any evangelical would regard with horror: the chronicler Charles Wriothesley records Lambert facing charges of denying infant baptism and of affirming that Christ took no human flesh of the Virgin Mary.

In the cases of both Frith and Lambert, then, Cranmer was being true to himself. A man should not be condemned for changing his mind at a later date. Indeed, when in 1546 there are signs that he had indeed begun to change his mind on the nature of Eucharistic

presence, he kept severely away from the persecutions of sacramentarian evangelicals which then took place, and which in fact was
intended to endanger himself.[26] Nevertheless, one must admit that in
the cases which we have just examined, we have had to tread carefully
in order to guide Cranmer away from charges of hypocrisy and cow-
ardice. Cranmer's record in relation to his conservative opponents is
more straightforward.

The archbishop exhibited a remarkable forbearance towards
intransigent Catholics; he hated the sin but loved the sinner. In fact, he
was frequently criticized by his friends for doing so; no less a person
than Henry VIII lost his temper with Cranmer when he asked a favour
for a Kentish gentleman who had just been one of the ringleaders in
the conservative plot of 1543 to destroy the archbishop and all his
evangelical associates.[27] His attitude is well illustrated by the case of
two monks who were indeed executed for treason in 1535 for denying the royal supremacy: the Carthusian prior of Axholme and the
Bridgettine monk of Syon, Richard Reynolds. Even after their condemnation, Cranmer felt that they should not die for their initial
resistance to instruction; he had a particular admiration for the scholarship and therefore for the possible convertibility of his old
Cambridge acquaintance Reynolds. He pleaded that the two should
be spared, to encourage 'the conversion of the fautors hereof' (i.e.
papalists), and also so 'that their consciences may be clearly averted
from the same by communication of sincere doctrine'; he offered to
undertake the task of persuasion himself.[28]

There was only one exception to this general advocacy of concord
by persuasion, though admittedly it is a very considerable exception:
Cranmer bitterly hated the Observant Franciscans, and he was not
merely a passive conniver at their destruction by Henry VIII. He
played a major part in the horrible death of Friar John Forest, who
was roasted alive in chains in 1538, and he personally hounded Friar
Hugh Payne into a gaol where he died of illness in 1539; Cranmer
recorded Payne's death with what can only be termed righteous relish.[29] This was hardly surprising. The Observants were the most
effective and respected exponents of what the archbishop regarded as
devilish error, not simply on questions of systematic theology, but in
their opposition to his cherished royal supremacy. To adapt his phrase

about a different aspect of Romish doctrine, they were 'the roots of the weeds'.[30]

Otherwise, those of a more coercive bent than Cranmer were bewildered by his mildness towards his enemies, as was recorded by his long-term servant and admirer Ralph Morice. Morice's elder brother William, a fervently evangelical courtier, tackled the archbishop because 'he alwaies bare a good face and countenance unto the papistes, and wolde both in worde and dede do very moche for theym, pardonyng thair offences ... encoraging therby the papistes, and also therby ... discoraging the protestants'. However William Morice also realized that this was 'not to be don but apon some purpose': it was a strategy, not simply a temperamental inclination to woolly liberalism. Cranmer explained his rationale at length, in relation both to traditionalists and to evangelicals. Let us consider what he had to say about the first category:[31]

> What will ye have a man do to hym that ys not yet come to the knowledge of the trueth of the gospell, nor peradventure as yet callid, and whose vocation ys to me uncerteyne? Shall we perhapps, in his jorney comyng towards us, by severities and cruell behaviour overthrowe hym, and as it were in his viage stoppe hym? I take not this the way to alleure men to enbrace the doctrine of the gospell. And if it be a true rule of our Saviour Christe to do good for evill, than lett suche as are not yet come to favour our religion, lerne to folowe the doctrine of the gospell by our example in using them frendlie and charitablie.

The terms in which Cranmer discussed this problem reveal what is also apparent from recent research into his private notebooks: he was a convinced predestinarian.[32] For him, unenlightened conservatives still enmired among papist sects might well be part of the elect, who were simply awaiting the call of God in faithful preaching of the word: the only exception to this general principle would be the obviously incorrigible agents of Satan like the sect of Franciscan Observants. This being so, the imposition of concord by coercion could actually be an obstacle to the pilgrimage of the elect towards their consciousness of election.

Let us turn now to Cranmer's opinion of radical evangelicals:

On thother side, such as have tasted of syncere religion, and as it were taken holde of the gospell, and seme in wourdes to maynteyne the true doctrine therof, and than by the evill example of thair lyves moste pernitiously become stombeling blockes unto suche as are weake, and not attall as yet enterid into this voiage, what wolde you have me do with them? beare with them and wyncke at their faultes, and so willinglie suffer the gospell (by thair outeragious doinges) to be troden under our feete? neglecting herwith an other notable saying of our Saviour oute of our memorie, whiche saieth, 'The servante knowing his Lorde and Master's pleasure and comandement, yf he regardith not the same, is (as a man might say, of all other) wourthie of many plagues.'

Here, once again, the problem was election, but now an added dimension was justification. Justification, as Luther and Cranmer understood it, was a once-for-all act of God, but that was not to say that the elect could not temporarily stumble and fall away in this life from the subsequent process of sanctification. They needed sharp correction for this reason alone, for their own spiritual health; once justified, they were servants who knew their master's commands, and were therefore particularly worthy of punishment when they disobeyed, as Cranmer's quotation from Luke 12:47 made clear. Moreover, by the bad example of their sin, the elect could hinder the elect among the traditionalists who were making their painful journey towards consciousness of the truth. Committed evangelicals therefore bore a double responsibility in their errors: a much heavier responsibility than traditionalists.

With this clarification of Cranmer's position in mind, it is interesting to note how it was mirrored in official policy in the reign of Edward VI. To begin with, no Catholic was executed solely for his or her belief by Edward's governments; indeed, even among the political executions, far more convinced evangelicals than Catholics were put to death. Even more to the point, there were three burnings at the stake for heresy of radicals or Anabaptists who had proclaimed Unitarian views on christology. This and other Edwardian trials of Anabaptists took place in spite of the government's ostentatious repeal of all previous heresy legislation; the use of coercion reflected acute alarm at the rapid growth of radicalism in south-east England after Henry VIII's death.[33] There was little controversy about the principle of what happened. The blueprint for the reform of England written by Cranmer's friend Martin Bucer just before his death, *De Regno Christi*, defended the death penalty for heretics, and it was also proposed in the abortive reform of English canon law in 1553, the so-called *Reformatio Legum*.[34]

One of those who died was a long-standing spokeswoman of English radicals, Joan Bocher (1550), and another was a Fleming, George van Parris (1551). To begin with Joan: she had been a noisy member of Cranmer's diocesan flock for a decade when she died, and she had more than a decade of evangelical activism elsewhere before that.[35] Her nickname 'the Maid of Kent' instantly recalls another strong-minded female who, ten years before, had also been called the Maid of Kent, the traditionalist visionary Elizabeth Barton: this is an example of the way in which the two extremes were given similar labels and could thus be yoked together by mainstream evangelicals. Cranmer's treatment of Joan aroused the indignation of John Foxe, who was very unusual among English evangelicals in deploring all executions, even of those who were clearly in error. Foxe made his disapproval clear at length in the 1559 Latin edition of *Acts and Monuments*, in a passage reflecting on Cranmer's eventual death at the stake; he then decided that this was too controversial and deleted it from subsequent editions.

Even so, Foxe remained so upset by the Bocher affair that most uncharacteristically he continued to tell a disapproving story of his hero Cranmer: he said that the archbishop had bullied a reluctant Edward VI into signing Joan's death warrant. Moreover this story has subsequently been proved to be much exaggerated.[36] Yet even when one has corrected Foxe's facts, his main point remains: the fate of Joan Bocher was a perfect example of concord by persuasion moving Augustine-like to concord by coercion. Cranmer's diocesan officials had examined Bocher in the early 1540s, but had protected her from serious consequences; however, instead of returning to the central ground of the evangelical fold, she had become more radical, and by 1548 she was under arrest again. After that she showed herself a resourceful and sophisticated opponent, not scrupling to sneer at her principal judges' recent change of mind on the nature of the Eucharist; unlike the other Anabaptists put on trial by the Edwardian government in 1549, she would not give way. She was kept alive for a year before her imperviousness to argument led to the sentence being carried out on her. Cranmer would indeed have been the obvious person in persuading the young king of his duty to burn his first heretic in 1550.

Finally, the question of tolerance. Did Cranmer show any signs of enthusiasm for allowing religious diversity in the commonwealth of England? We can dismiss the case of the Lady Mary, the king's half-sister, who under Edward VI was granted a very temporary, grudging and sometimes interrupted permission to hear the traditional Latin Mass, on account of her rank, and under extreme diplomatic pressure from the Holy Roman Emperor. More pertinent is the remarkable opportunity provided by the Edwardian regime for the establishment in London of a grouping of autonomous foreign congregations, collectively known as the Stranger Church; another specialized French congregation was set up at Glastonbury in Somerset. The London Stranger Church was a congregational organization whose ministry and decision-making were organized on a different principle from the threefold order of bishop, priest and deacon: that order had been officially reaffirmed for the Church of England in the same year by the issue of the Ordinal. The Strangers' anomalous status in relation to the royal supremacy was formalized by a royal grant of letters patent in July 1550.

There can be no doubt of Cranmer's direct involvement in the London initiative. The first general superintendent of the London church was the Polish evangelical Jan Łaski (Johannes à Lasco), who stayed with Cranmer at Lambeth Palace all through the period in which the royal grant establishing the Church was in preparation.[37] Yet from the start there were tensions between the English evangelical establishment and Łaski and his followers. It was clear that the model for the Stranger enterprise was the Church of Zürich, and it was equally clear that many English evangelical activists regarded the new congregations as models for a more drastic restructuring of the Church of England than Cranmer had countenanced. Only a few months after the granting of the letters patent to the Stranger Church, Cranmer was already showing himself unhappy about its usage of sitting to receive communion and its rejection of English clerical dress, and a tense correspondence began between him and Łaski.[38] Worse still, Łaski was quickly drawn into an internal power struggle in the English Church. In 1550–51 John Hooper tried to defy Cranmer and Bishop Ridley of London by refusing to wear distinctive episcopal vestments when he was consecrated Bishop of Gloucester; Łaski proved to be Hooper's most prominent foreign supporter before Cranmer and Ridley forced Hooper to yield. Partly because of this row, Bishop Ridley was consistently more hostile than Cranmer to the Stranger Church, and he was still harassing it and trying to assert his jurisdiction over it when mutual disaster overtook them with the accession of Queen Mary in 1553.

The tensions between the Stranger Church and Cranmer and Ridley are easy to explain, given their commitment to uniformity in the practice of the English Church; one remembers that the essence of concord as defined by Turchetti is the refusal of diversity. What needs some explanation, therefore, is the tolerance which the Stranger Church initiative apparently represents. One motive for Cranmer in backing it will have been precisely the achievement of concord by discussion: the risky idealism of the hope that close contact between churches of different nationalities would promote useful dialogue, and that differences could thereby be reduced to unimportance. It is highly relevant that Cranmer was a lifelong enthusiast for councils of the worldwide Church to agree on doctrine. Even in the 1520s, when his theology was fully within the orbit of the traditional Church, he had shown a particular enthusiasm for the ideal of the General Council, and a particular detestation of Martin Luther because he felt that Luther had denigrated the authority of General Councils.[39] Later, as we have seen, his favourite continental theologians would be successively Philipp Melanchthon and Martin Bucer, the two arch-exponents of the spinning of formulae designed to unite conferences of diverse theologians. After the Hooper vestments row was safely buried, Cranmer would put a good deal of vain effort in 1551–2 to secure a European-wide ecumenical conference of evangelicals to rival the false General Council of Trent.[40]

However, there was more to the Stranger Church initiative than this. In his private journal, King Edward recorded that the motive for making what was a very generous financial grant of premises as well as legal status to the Strangers, was for 'avoiding all sects of Anabaptists and suchlike'.[41] Joan Bocher had been executed only two months before the royal letters patent; there was an obvious advantage to be gained in setting up a structure of authority and discipline to control radicals who could otherwise flourish in the middle of London protected by their alien languages and private support systems. The Stranger Church itself was anxious to please in this respect; it was so nervous about Anabaptists that it even included a polemical defence of infant baptism in its baptismal liturgy – not a happy setting for *odium theologicum*![42] Indeed, the burning of George van Parris for heresy to take place under Edward VI shows that the mechanism of the Stranger Church could work effectively for the suppression of radicalism. Van Parris was a member of the Stranger congregation, and he was excommunicated by them for his Unitarianism. It is most likely that the Strangers themselves denounced him to Cranmer, who tried him under a royal commission for investigating heresy, before activating the traditional mechanism to hand him over to the secular power for burning. There is a notable silence in sources from the Strangers' Church itself on van Parris, no doubt reflecting their unease about what they had done. Heretic he might have been, but it did not reflect well on a Church which consisted of refugees from persecution, itself to initiate persecution.[43] The only convincing justification was that offered by Cranmer to William Morice: evangelicals in error did far more harm to God's purposes than traditionalists in error.

So even the one initiative of tolerance in which Cranmer played a definite part was directed rather to concord: both concord by persuasion and concord by coercion. Noticeably, when Cranmer found himself at the mercy of Mary's Catholic government which was determined to destroy him, he never challenged the government's right to treat him as it did; he made a careful distinction between Mary's legitimate powers as Supreme Head which she happened to be using in a bad cause, and the wholly illegitimate powers of the pope.[44] His belief in the royal supremacy was so strong that in 1556 it combined with his sense of guilt at having betrayed Mary for Queen Jane, almost to shipwreck his evangelical faith in a series of steadily more abject recantations. Only on the last morning of his life did he finally reject more than two decades of obedience, and join the defiant martyrs whose deaths he had watched during his years as archbishop. The effect of this new departure on his views on concord and tolerance can be known only to the inhabitants of Paradise.

Forty years later, the great Jesuit conspirator Robert Parsons produced a proposal for the aftermath of a Catholic victory in England. He was envisaging a situation in which English Catholicism would be in much the same position as the evangelicals of the reign of Edward VI: an active and victorious minority, facing a broad swathe of the confused and indifferent, and a committed minority of enemies. In this situation, he advocated dealing with obstinate Protestants by a cautious 'connivance or toleration of magistrates only for a certain time'. Superficially, this sounds more generous than Cranmer, but Parsons went on to emphasize the very temporary nature of such 'toleration' (in my terms, tolerance). Once more, his aim was concord by persuasion, or if necessary by coercion:

> I do give notice that my meaning is not in any way to persuade hereby that liberty of religion, to live how a man will, should be permitted to any person in any Christian commonwealth, for any cause or respect whatsoever; from which I am so far off in my judgment and affection as I think no one thing to be so dangerous, dishonourable or more offensive to Almighty God in the world than that any prince should permit the Ark of Israel and Dagon, God and the Devil, to stand and be honoured together, within his realm or country.[45]

In this respect at least, Archbishop Cranmer would have been happy to echo the words of a member of the Jesuit sect.

10

The Making of the Prayer Book

Here is the first trivia quiz question on the Book of Common Prayer (BCP): who was the only layperson not of royal blood ever prayed for by name in the Prayer Book? Answer: Sir James Croft, Lord Deputy of Ireland, in the Dublin edition of 1551, and the fact that Sir James died in his bed three decades later, despite a risky career of double-dealing and his son's execution for witchcraft, suggests that the prayers of the Irish faithful did him a bit of good. Second trivia question: who is St Enurchus? Answer: no one, because he is a misprint, and his original, the massively obscure St Evurtius, Bishop of Orleans, crept into the Prayer Book's Calendar obliquely and entirely without authorization in 1604, almost certainly because his feast of 7 September happened to be the birthday of the lately deceased Queen Elizabeth I – it was some learned printer's joke, and perhaps a little cock of the snook at the newly arrived King James I. Brian Cummings evidently relishes the evanescent saint, as he dates the Preface of his magnificent edition of the Prayer Book on the feast-day of Enurchus.

Those of us – a diminishing band – who grew up with the BCP as the staple of their hours in church sustained our mixture of attempted reverence and youthful boredom with such incidental delights as these, as we leafed surreptitiously through the little black book in front of us, perhaps a presentation copy from our proud parents, which resembled no other book in our experience – often (and this is something I never actually noticed in all those hours) the only book we knew without any page numbers. Equally, its language resembled nothing else that a child might hear, with the exception of occasional exposure to Shakespeare, and it defeated many adults too. I looked forward to the occasions when my father's venerable churchwarden took Evensong, because he habitually prayed to an evidently long-suffering yet still benevolent Almighty on behalf of the queen to 'endure her plenteously with heavenly gifts'. I savoured journeying through the book as far as 'the Ministration of Baptism to such as are of riper years', imagining a cheerful occasion involving an ex-chorus girl of majestic proportions, who, in the aftermath of a colourful career, had at last turned to the Church.

English society is diminished as the Prayer Book fades from popular consciousness, but this definitive publication may do something to stem the process. It heralds a significant anniversary – 350 years since the final version of the book was authorized by Parliament in 1662 – that comes hard on the heels of the quatercentenary celebrations during 2011 for another milestone of Stuart English prose composition, the King James Bible. I was frankly surprised by the large amount of public interest shown in that commemoration – all credit to the heroic planning of the King James Bible Trust – but the Prayer Book did not have such an impact. It did, after all, have formidable competition during 2012 from Charles Dickens. There were many who regarded this simply as a tribal occasion for a particular Christian denomination, and so they chose, like the Priest and the Levite in the Gospel for the Thirteenth Sunday after Trinity, to pass by on the other side.

That was a mistake. The modern Church of England might look like and often behave like a 'denomination', but from the sixteenth century to at least 1800, it was not: it was in fact as well as in name the national Church, enjoying the allegiance of the great majority of the population in both England and Wales. Its liturgy was not a denominational artefact; it was the literary text most thoroughly known by most people in this country, and one should include the Bible among its lesser rivals. This was because the English and the Welsh were active participants in the BCP, as they made their liturgical replies to the person leading worship in the thousands of churches throughout the realm: they were actors week by week in a drama whose cast included and united most of the nation, and which therefore was a much more significant play, and more culturally central, than anything by Shakespeare. The year 1662 was a decisive date in the history of the BCP, as it was then that a century of argument about its form and content was settled, and indeed that form remained unchallenged until 1927–8 when proposals to alter it engendered a nationwide controversy played out in Parliament which, to the astonishment and fury of the Church's bishops, rejected the innovations.

It was also a significant year because the freezing of the BCP at that moment prompted the departure of two thousand clergy from the parishes who refused to sign up to the new book, and formed what became Old Dissent, whereas before the mid-century civil wars most of them would have served in the Church of England with reasonable good grace. This was a major reformulation of national life, ensuring that thereafter the Established Church was never so overwhelmingly hegemonic in England as were Scandinavian Lutheranism or Mediterranean Catholicism in their respective cultural spheres. English and Welsh Protestantism remained divided between church and chapel, with the vital consequence that religious and then political pluralism became embedded in national identity. All this was the fault of the Prayer Book's return in 1662. Yet even when in the eighteenth century an increasingly powerful 'New Dissent' appeared in the form of Methodism, the dominant Wesleyan Methodism was as ambivalent towards the Prayer Book as it was towards the Established Church itself. I was archivist for many years of English Methodism's then oldest surviving theological college, Wesley College, Bristol, and had in my custody the two quarto copies of the BCP used in the College's original chapel from its opening in Manchester in 1842: they were worn to fragility with regular use in leading the community's communal worship.

Even so, if the BCP had remained what it was to begin with, a vehicle for national worship in a marginal and second-rank kingdom in Europe, then its significance would have remained limited. But instead, the English created two successive world empires beyond the archipelago they inhabit, the second of which is still with us in the ghostly form of the Commonwealth. Where Anglicans went, so did their Prayer Book. A heroic work of chronological listings, published by Archdeacon David Griffiths in 2002,[1] rounded up about 4,800 editions of the Prayer Book or of liturgies stemming from its Scottish and American derivatives; around 1,200 of these are in 199 other languages, ranging from the Acholi of Uganda to Zulu. Griffiths demonstrated that the peak year for production of versions of the Prayer Book was in 1850, at the height of the second British Empire's vigour and self-confidence and, despite predictable subsequent decline, around 1,000 editions still appeared in the twentieth century (I myself was partly responsible for one of them).[2] Brian Cummings's version has a certain memorial quality, partly because it answers so many questions about the book and partly because of the classic splendour of the Oxford University Press production, but it is unlikely to be the last.

What a babble of voices those translations represented across the globe. Archbishop Cranmer's work in presiding over the creation of the first English BCP in 1549 had been designed to replace the Latin liturgy of the Western Church, because he and his fellow Protestants felt that Latin excluded uneducated laity from the proper praise of God. Yet Cranmer had absolutely no objection to Latin as such; it was the international language of his era, and in the right circumstances it might be just as much a vehicle for godly Protestant worship as it had been an ally of popery. Such was the prospect in Ireland, the other realm of the Tudor monarchs. In 1560 Cranmer's former publisher and posthumous relative by marriage, the Dutch printer Reyner Wolfe, brought out the first proper Latin version of the BCP, specifically for use in the Gaelic-speaking parts of Ireland, which were then far more extensive than the embattled anglophone zone around Dublin called the Pale. The fact that the English Church authorities thought this Latin translation to be worth the effort is a tribute to the scale and sophistication of Irish Gaelic culture at the time. By contrast, no one had listened in 1549 to the plea of Cornish rebels, protesting against the introduction of the first English Prayer Book, that some of them spoke no English. That was probably hardly true even then, and the government of Edward VI had no hesitation in massacring them for their linguistic obduracy.

Early translations into major modern European languages followed, for diplomatic purposes, to demonstrate to potential Roman Catholic royal brides or their anxious advisers that the English Protestant liturgy was a respectable route to God: a French translation in 1616 and one in Spanish in 1623 were both connected to proposed Catholic royal marriages. An Italian version had already been commissioned in 1607 by the scholarly diplomat Sir Henry Wotton as English ambassador in Venice, in an optimistic bid to cash in on a bitter stand-off between the Serene Republic and the pope, by converting the Venetians to the Church of England. Portuguese came later, in 1695, and that translation was significantly sponsored by the East India Company, as the British Empire was beginning to make inroads on the decaying Iberian overseas possessions in Asia and elsewhere. In 1821 the Wesleyan Methodists were still close enough to their Anglican roots to feel it worthwhile to translate the Prayer Book into Portuguese pidgin-Creole for their work in what is now Sri Lanka. The Polish BCP had to wait until 1836, in an effort at an Anglican mission among Jews in eastern Europe even more quixotic than Sir Henry Wotton's wooing of Venice. This translation was suppressed by the Russian authorities, predictably without any signs of regret in the Polish Roman Catholic Church; interesting questions arise as to how different history would have been if the shtetls had come to resound to Stanford in B flat. And who would have expected the King of the Sandwich Islands personally to have undertaken the translation of the Prayer Book into Hawaiian?

Those who arrive fresh to the Prayer Book may wonder why Brian Cummings has crammed three books into one set of covers, particularly considering that so many of the words in the three books are remarkably similar, and that the end result is just short of 900 pages. If they read his generously detailed Introduction or, even better, delve into the voracious and sprightly learning of his explanatory endnotes to the text, they will understand. His story goes back more than a century before 1662. The first essays in translating parts of the Latin liturgy into English were done during the 1530s by a variety of enthusiasts for Reformation, in the teeth of murderous disapproval from Henry VIII, a fierce conservative in liturgical matters despite his own break with the Bishop of Rome. His watchful and scholarly chaplain Thomas Cranmer did not share the king's prejudices. On Cranmer's first encounter with Protestantism in mainland Europe, on embassy in Lutheran Nuremberg, he took a keen interest in the innovative liturgy he saw there, but also in Margarete, niece of the pastor presiding at worship in the church of St Lorenz; he married the lady just before Henry VIII chose him as Archbishop of Canterbury, and she eventually joined him in his archiepiscopal palaces. That gesture by itself showed that Cranmer had embraced the Reformation in more than one sense: medieval priests might commonly take mistresses, but Protestant clergy were quick to show their contempt for compulsory clerical celibacy by making respectable and public marriages. When Cranmer came to compose a new version of the marriage service, which has stood the test of centuries remarkably well, this first married Archbishop of Canterbury said for the first time in Christian liturgical history that one of the reasons for getting married was that it was good for you, and also quite fun: 'for the mutual society, help, and comfort, that the one ought have of the other'.

While Henry's religious moods and diplomatic priorities continued to sway between old mumpsimus and new sumpsimus, Cranmer squirrelled away in his luxuriously large library at Croydon Palace the many liturgical experiments both of English evangelicals and the emerging Reformations of the mainland. Like all mainstream Protestant Reformers, he shared with his popish enemies the conviction that a crowd of ordinary Christians left to themselves were incapable of spontaneously finding appropriate words to approach God in corporate prayer; many might still agree. The archbishop began his own efforts to meld a multitude of new experiments and old forms with the main tradition of medieval Western liturgy popular in the English Church, which took its cue from practices devised for Salisbury Cathedral in previous centuries – the Sarum Use. Various initiatives in Henry's lifetime produced nothing more than a vernacular processional rite (a litany) pestering God to back the king in his last major war against the French, but matters changed rapidly from 1547, once Henry's young son Edward was on the throne and his advisers were determined on a real religious revolution. By 1549, Cranmer's first English vernacular liturgy was in place, authorized by Parliament to be universally observed on Whitsunday, an appropriate festival, since it celebrated the occasion on which the apostles had been heard to speak in many languages. No one, not just the Cornish rebels, much liked this book at the time; it was a compromise with one eye on the formidable phalanx of traditionalists among Cranmer's episcopal colleagues, and few among his evangelical soulmates appreciated its nuanced presentation of Protestant theology under traditional forms. Once some of the less cooperative English bishops were safely locked up for various demonstrations of opposition to the accelerating religious changes, Cranmer got something more like what he actually wanted, a liturgy whose sole use came into force in autumn 1552. There was less than a year for it to bed down (and in Ireland, virtually no time) before Edward VI was dead and Catholic Mary on the throne, but in 1559 the BCP was brought back almost unaltered by a Protestant government much less disposed to compromise with Catholics than Edward's government had been ten years earlier. It was this production of Cranmer's unbuttoned Protestant Indian summer which remained in place until the wars of the 1640s, and then in 1662, after the unexpected return of both monarchy and episcopally governed Church in Charles II's Restoration, the Prayer Book took on its final form.

The early fortunes of the Prayer Book sound complicated enough set out like that, but its peculiar nature renders it more complex still. In 1552 it embodied Protestant religious revolution, but less than ninety years later it provoked Protestant religious revolution in its turn in Scotland, and then by domino effect in England too. Because of that, the historical logic of its recall and revision in 1662 signalled an end to revolution in the kingdom. That tangled story embodied a great argument about what sort of Protestantism English Protestantism was. At the beginning of it all was Cranmer, chief architect of the BCP, whose theology shifted during his clerical career from conventional late medieval piety into Protestantism, and not once but twice. Cranmer ended up aligning himself with the more thoroughgoing form of Protestantism in central Europe, which came to call itself Reformed, as opposed to the developing 'Lutheran' bloc, which was the more conservative Protestantism he had first experienced in Nuremberg. The great issue beginning the separation between these two sorts of Protestants was their understanding of what happened in the Lord's Supper, the Eucharist. Did bread and wine become in some physical or corporal form the body and blood of Christ during this service? The pope said yes – and so did Martin Luther. The Reformed said no: bread and wine were symbols of body and blood, and symbols they remained in this service. There was still much to discuss if one took this line, but the great gulf was clear between the Reformed on the one hand, and both Lutherans and Roman Catholics on the other.

Cranmer, like most early English Protestants, dawdled for a while in Lutheran pastures, then jumped over the waters onto the Reformed bank. He presided over both versions of the Edwardian Prayer Book with that Reformed conviction in mind, but one would have needed to be as subtle and scholarly as the archbishop himself to notice it the first time round in 1549. There are still certain medieval vestments specified in the book, together with choral singing, which could presumably be completely traditional; there are crosses actually printed in the text to signify where the priest should make manual signs of blessing, both in the Eucharistic service and at other moments of clerical blessing in the book, such as in marriage or baptism. No wonder so many Protestant leaders fumed when they saw the truculently Catholic Bishop Bonner of London performing the 1549 rite 'sadly and discreetly', which in the Tudor language of the approving traditionalist commentator who recorded the occasion meant the exact opposite of what it means today. Bonner, who was not a fool, gleefully celebrated the new Eucharist with as much medieval pomp and dignified ceremony as he could squeeze into it, for 'sadly' means 'with solemnity', and 'discreetly' means 'with due judgement'.

Something had to give, and there was a great deal of frenzied revision of the rite before its reissue in 1552. In the new 1552 service of Eucharist, there is the emphatic feeling of a Reformed Lord's Supper – not even a Lutheran rite. Not only does it repeatedly shy away from any potentially dramatic liturgical climax until all those present have actually received the bread and wine – something which already puzzled me when I was in the congregation as a boy – but appended to the service is a stage direction (a rubric, in ecclesiastical jargon), which is an absolute killer to any idea that a priest has created the body and blood of Christ on a table. The rubric deals with what should happen to any bread and wine remaining unconsumed: 'the curate shall have it to his own use', it says. In other words, take it home for his tea. You don't do that to God, but you do do it to bread and wine. This instruction survived through 1559, and then significantly disappeared in 1662.

If that is a remarkably brutal transformation, Cranmer could be nuanced in his deployment of language in realigning the nature of this drama which so divided Christians in the Reformation. He was unhappily conscious in 1549 that his traditionalist colleagues in the

House of Lords loathed his new liturgical proposals, and the mark of the resulting clash is there in the actual title of the service during which the people of England would take bread and wine. The 1549 BCP calls it 'The Supper of the Lord, and the Holy Communion, commonly called the Mass'. That sounds like three things, but it is in fact only two, the second of which is the addition of 'the Mass', in a fashion which might politely be described as grudging. I have little doubt that the word is there only because members of the Lords insisted in debate that it should be thrust into the draft BCP, otherwise they would scupper the passage of the entire book. Cranmer's apparent first intention was that the whole Eucharistic service should henceforth be called the Lord's Supper, but into the structure of the new English service he placed a short English rite for communicants to receive the bread and wine, the 'Order for Communion', which he had already published a year before the BCP. Clergy had been ordered in 1548 to insert this 'Order for Communion' rather incongruously into the traditional Latin service: it was the first time that there had been any official tinkering with the Mass. That interloper 'Communion' was then a word without much English back-story, but it has proved one of Cranmer's most resonant coinages, for it has become the normal Anglican word for the whole service. This is largely the result of one of Cranmer's most subtle shifts in a lifetime of verbal subtlety. When he came to give a title to the same service in his revised book of 1552, the word 'Mass', which he despised, was of course ruthlessly removed, but Cranmer also changed the balance between 'Lord's Supper' and 'Communion'. The latter word might then have seemed redundant, with memories of its separate appearance in 1548 fading; instead, it was promoted. No longer were these concepts a single unit, a liturgical Russian doll with the 'Supper' containing the 'Communion', because 'OR' replaced 'AND THE': the title became 'The Lord's Supper OR holy Communion', as if any fool would know that these were two alternative names for the same thing. And curiously, it was the second of these labels, 'Communion', which in the long term seized the Church of England's imagination, separating out English Protestants from both German Lutherans and German Reformed, who have stuck with 'Supper' or *Abendmahl*, as have francophone Reformed Protestants with their *Cène*.

It is unlikely that Cranmer anticipated this outcome, still less intended it; within a year he was a prisoner in the Tower at the mercy of Bloody Mary, unable to influence events except by his eventual martyrdom, and it was the Church after 1559 which established 'Communion' as the norm. There's a nice little doctoral project awaiting someone to trace out how 'Communion' won the battle against 'Lord's Supper'; I would make a preliminary guess that it was not until 1662.

The likely explanation for that move away from the 'Supper' usage, which if it had survived would have gone on happily uniting the English Church with the best Reformed Churches of Europe, lies in a shift in the nature of the English Church itself, a shift which Cranmer himself would probably have deplored. The C of E has become 'Anglican', a word which came into common use only in the nineteenth century, and which was originally the property of a faction within the Church which self-consciously saw itself as 'Catholic'. Cranmer would also of course have called the Church of England 'Catholic', but in the sense that John Calvin of Geneva or Heinrich Bullinger of Zürich would likewise have called their Churches Catholic: they were all parts of the Universal Church which had rejected the medieval corruptions of the Church of Rome in order to regain an authentic Catholicity. Many Anglicans, however, have come to see Anglicanism as a 'middle way' between Rome and Protestantism, a position which would have bewildered Cranmer: how can one have a 'middle way' between Antichrist and truth? How might this have happened? he would have asked.

The answer lies in the Prayer Book that he himself had created. Probably Cranmer would have revised and simplified it further, had his time as Primate of All England been prolonged for another ten or twenty years; certainly that was what people who had known him said he had intended. Instead, his effort of 1552 was fossilized in its revival in 1559, and it remained the most elaborate liturgy of any Reformed Church in Europe, its observance of the traditional festival shape of the Church's year more conservative than any other. Even the Lutherans of mainland Europe did not go on observing Lent with the punctiliousness demanded both by the English Prayer Book and by English legislation enforcing fasting during those forty days. Scotland went so far as to abolish Christmas; by contrast, Cranmer gave the day a special little prayer or collect which he specified should be used in services every day until New Year's Eve. And his four-score collects for particular days of the Church's year are one of the glories of his liturgical work, sometimes composed brand new, but more often a sparkling brooch of tiny verbal gems culled from the worship of the Universal Church as far back as the fifth century and crafted together in his own sonorous English. Even those who are not natural fans of set liturgy (or of brief prayers) can grudgingly concede the worth of Cranmer's collects.

The liturgical peculiarity of the English Church coincided with its other unique feature: its great cathedral churches survived as institutions with virtually all their medieval infrastructure. It is a puzzle: no other Protestant Church in Europe was like this. Chantries and all the apparatus of purgatory were abolished, certainly, but an Elizabethan cathedral still had its surrounding close like a miniature town, populated not just by a dean and chapter as might survive in attenuated legal form in Lutheran Germany or Scandinavia, but also by minor canons, choristers, organists, vergers – a formidable machine for worship. The worship could only be that of Cranmer's BCP, but cathedrals performed it, as Bishop Bonner might have recognized with sarcastic amusement, 'sadly and discreetly', with the benefit of choir and organ, even some vestments – a totally different approach to the way in which the Prayer Book was used in England's thousands of parish churches, with their services largely said, and the only music the psalms sung metrically in the fashion of Geneva. In Cranmer's last months of power, cathedral organs were being demolished and the choirs set to singing metrical psalms, but when Queen Elizabeth ascended the throne, she ignored that trajectory and her own Chapel Royal set a standard of musical elaboration and beauty which the Church of England has never forgotten. Westminster Abbey, across the road from the Palace of Whitehall, was frequently infuriated when Elizabeth's Chapel Royal hijacked its best singers, but the dean and chapter might have been consoled if they had known that these royal kidnappings were safeguarding the future of the English choral tradition.

There was more to this unexpected turn in the English Reformation than merely good music. The cathedrals and the Chapel Royal fostered an attitude to the sacred which strayed far from the normal Protestant emphasis on communal praise by the people and the Word of God interpreted by the minister from the pulpit. English cathedrals preserved a sense that regular prayer and the contemplation of the divine through beauty constituted an equally valid road to divinity. In counterpoint to Cranmer's evangelicalism, they erected a fabric of sacramental – yes, Catholic – devotion. This made the Church of England theologically Janus-faced, and in the time of Queen Elizabeth's Stuart successors, the tension tore the nation apart. That was how Thomas Cranmer's attempt to turn Reformation truths into set liturgy ended up being seen by many of the English as a symbol of popery, an insult to God's pure service. Worse still, in 1638 the English court tried imposing a version of the BCP on the proudly Reformed Church of Scotland, and even more seriously than that, theirs was a version revised away from the English Book and 'backwards' towards 1549. It was hardly an advertisement for the beauty of holiness when the Bishop of Brechin led worship from the new service book in Brechin Cathedral glaring at his mutinous congregation over a pair of loaded pistols, just in case they tried to drag him out of his prayer-desk.

Such was the trigger of the Scottish revolt against the government of Charles I which led to the Wars of the Three Kingdoms. And when the episcopally governed Church of England was set up again in 1660, it did very little to conciliate the party which had so objected to the Prayer Book: one or two small concessions, and otherwise a book which sorted out a few angularities in Cranmer's old text, added some useful afterthoughts to deal with new pastoral situations, such as the existence of a much enlarged Royal Navy, and then delicately tiptoed slightly further from the Reformed European mainstream. Hence the disappearance of that howling affirmation that left-over bread and wine were not body and blood, because they could be consumed for the parson's dinner, from among the rubrics at the end of Holy Communion. Anglicanism was born.

The Prayer Book is by no means simply an historical document; it lives as Shakespeare lives, and often therefore in translation or adaptation. Its presence or its memory is the main thing which unites that not especially united family of Churches which now calls itself the Anglican Communion. Parts of the book are unquestionably as much past history as the Thirty-Nine Articles of Religion, which are still the theoretical doctrinal norm of the Church of England, yet which have their eyes unhelpfully fixed on the concerns of the mid-sixteenth century. For instance, the service for 'Thanksgiving of women after child-birth, commonly called . . . Churching' was still in regular use in my father's rural parish in the 1960s, but its overtones of purification from ritual uncleanness could hardly survive the revolution in gender relations which then occurred, and the epitaph for Churching can be found in the adroit title of Margaret Houlbrooke's charming recent study of its twentieth-century history, *Rite Out of Time*.[3] Indeed, during the 1960s and 1970s, it seemed that most of the Church hierarchy were content to let the whole book die, as they became preoccupied with revisions and extensions of liturgy, some of which were admittedly long overdue. It was the heroically grumpy efforts of the Prayer Book Society which then shamed Anglicans into arresting the decline. In one respect the BCP flourishes as never before: in the popularity of Choral Evensong, gloriously performed with an aesthetic care which Archbishop Cranmer would have deplored, in great churches like cathedrals for which he had no perceptible affection. Nor would he have approved of what makes Evensong so attractive to so many who now crowd cathedrals and choral foundations as extras in its musical drama. For those who view a well-signposted theological motorway, straight as an arrow, as an unconvincing route to divinity, or who are repelled by the bleak certainties and bullying self-righteousness of much organized religion, Choral Evensong according to the Prayer Book affords understated hospitality, of that gentle, accepting sort described by one who loved the 1559 BCP, lived his life by it, and wrote much verse about how to use it:

> Love bade me welcome: yet my soul drew back,
>> Guilty of dust and sin.
> But quick-ey'd Love, observing me grow slack
>> From my first entrance in,
> Drew nearer to me, sweetly questioning,
>> If I lack'd any thing . . .
> . . . You must sit down, says Love, and taste my meat:
>> So I did sit and eat.[4]

II

Tudor Queens: Mary and Elizabeth

King Henry VIII's daughters, Mary and Elizabeth, were respectively the daughters of Catherine of Aragon and Anne Boleyn. To understand someone, meet their mother – and so it was with these Tudor princesses. Mary, the subject of David Loades's succinct biography, was straightforward, pious, brave in a crisis and not especially bright. Her whole life was shaped by her mother's straightforwardness and bravery in a crisis: when Henry wanted Catherine of Aragon to accept that she had never been married to him, Catherine refused to do so, leading to England's break with the Roman obedience. By her unchanging refusal, she gave her daughter an example of how to behave which Mary never forgot. Mary spent her whole life trying to undo the wrong done to her mother and her mother's world which Henry's first annulment crisis represented.

Elizabeth's mother Anne Boleyn was equal to Catherine in stubbornness and her definite superior in intelligence: the only one of Henry's six wives whose marriage to the king was regularly called her 'reign' by contemporaries. She had a mind of her own and was not afraid to use it – the most plausible explanation of her eventual downfall in 1536. Eric Ives's biography of Anne[1] revealed her as a major player in the early English Reformation, the beginning of a Reformation unique in Europe in having two women as leading architects: Anne Boleyn and her daughter. The uncharitable (including most English historians since John Foxe) would probably add Elizabeth's half-sister to make up a formative trio. Bloody Mary inadvertently brought back heroism to English Protestantism after some rather unfortunate hiccups during and after the reign of Edward VI.

There is a further striking contrast in the early lives of the princesses. Mary's early years were spent as the centre of attention, the heir apparent to the English throne. In 1525, at the age of nine, she was sent off to be the figurehead of Cardinal Wolsey's revived experiment of government, a Council in the Marches of Wales. The Princess of Wales had her own court at Ludlow Castle, and went on her own mini-royal progresses. It was a year or two, as a young teenager, before she became aware of the threat to her mother's marriage and to her own position; but after 1533, aged seventeen, she could not avoid isolation and humiliation. In 1536 she was declared illegitimate since Catherine's marriage was claimed never to have taken place; after her mother's death, she was forced to acknowledge her position and was then an outcast for almost a decade. Catherine Parr improved the situation when from 1543 she brought together her three royal stepchildren, and Mary's position in the succession was regularized by an Act of Parliament in 1544.

Mary's experience was of a childhood of privilege and honour, followed by total loss and humiliation. Elizabeth's was the other way round. She would have been too young to remember her three years as heir to the throne: she went through the next seven years in a highly ambiguous and probably uncomfortable position as a bastard daughter of the king. Just at the age when Mary's world had begun collapsing, things began getting better for Elizabeth: when Catherine Parr rebuilt the king's family, she saw to Elizabeth's education. So Mary's youth was one of bitter disappointment: a feeling that all that there was in life was to hang on and be true to oneself. For Elizabeth, it was the opposite experience: if you kept quiet, played your cards right, or let other people play a convenient hand on your behalf, things might get better. There is much to be gained by keeping in mind this contrast when considering their successive reigns.

The main point of royal daughters was as saleable breeding stock. From an early age, Mary would have been conscious that she was a prime piece of property. At the age of two she was already signed up for a marriage to the King of France's son; at five, diplomacy changed, and she was to marry her cousin, the Holy Roman Emperor Charles

V, at that time twenty-one years old. Unlikely as it would seem in 1521, this was one of the most important relationships in Mary's life, though she and Charles met only once. When Mary was swept into her mother's marriage crisis, the emperor was their chief friend. More than any other English monarch between Henry II and Charles II, Mary was preoccupied with a country beyond the sea, or rather a dynasty beyond the sea, the Habsburgs. She married Charles's son Philip, and once she was married she was desperate to secure a Catholic future by having his child. That child might with the right quirks of genealogy have ruled half the known world, and a good deal of it not then known – an empire combining the Spanish and Portuguese Empires and the old British Empire, nearly the whole of north and south America, and much more besides. So the baby which Mary never had is one of the great might-have-beens of history. Mary's biological failure is perhaps the saddest and most pitiable aspect of her life – certainly she would have thought so – and that is clearly the point in the mock-Tudor title of Loades's biography. Mary's failure dealt a permanent blow to England's long-standing alignment with the Habsburgs and their Burgundian predecessors.

Both Mary and Elizabeth had a capacity for inspiring loyalty from close friends who formed their households. Both profited a great deal by using this household circle when they came to power, so that both their reigns had a strong start. Mary's arrival was indeed much more spectacular than Elizabeth's: she replaced Queen Jane Grey, and because Queen Jane lost, we forget what an astonishing achievement Mary's accession was. Jane had a good claim to the throne, not just because the previous king, Edward VI, had ordered that she should succeed, but because her royal blood was convincing, as the granddaughter of a sister of Henry VIII; in other words, she had the same sort of claim which brought James VI to the throne of England in 1603 (he was a great-grandson of a sister of Henry VIII). By contrast, both Mary and Elizabeth had been officially declared bastards by their father; that had not changed by 1553. So it was perfectly plausible for Protestants to see Jane as the best legitimate heir. Both the Archbishop of Canterbury, Thomas Cranmer, and the Bishop of London, Nicholas Ridley, said openly and precisely that Mary and Elizabeth were bastards, embarrassing admirers later when they became Protestant martyrs and Protestant Queen Elizabeth was on the throne.

Mary's remarkable initial success came by single-mindedly stressing the one asset which she possessed: bastard or no bastard, she was flesh of Henry VIII's flesh. What she did not say, and in fact deliberately avoided saying all through her bid for the throne, was that she was going to restore fully the Catholic faith: she made no official statement about religion at all until she was safely in control of London. Hence she managed to unite virtually the whole East Anglian political establishment, Catholic and Protestant alike, creating a critical mass to overthrow the government in Westminster. It was the only time after 1485 when the provinces brought the Westminster government to military defeat: it was one of very few successful rebellions of the Tudor age. The silence on religion is so unlike Mary's normal nononsense Catholicism that she must have received strong advice to keep her mouth shut; and that counsel must have come from the tight little group of household officers steering her *coup d'état*. To a man they were Catholics, like her, but they had the political sense to see that they would only narrow their potential support if they talked about religion. Mary's loyal advisers got her to power in 1553 against all the odds.

Once Mary and Elizabeth were on the throne, they differed in their capacity to reach beyond the people they trusted and broaden their government; Mary was not nearly as adroit as Elizabeth proved to be. Both women started out with the same problem: how to combine the close friends who had helped to put them in place with a set of politicians who were there simply because they had been around for a long time. Particularly difficult for Mary was uniting her real friends with those who had been part of the government of Henry VIII and Edward VI and had made her life miserable for her since the 1530s. In this she was not wholly successful. Recently some historians have tended to downplay the divisions in her Council, pointing out that much of the evidence about these divisions came from foreign ambassadors who were often being fed lines by councillors for their own purposes, or who wanted to emphasize that they had their own special access to Mary's inner circle.[2] But even if true, that cannot disguise real problems in Mary's government. Bishop Stephen Gardiner and William, Lord

Paget, hated each other, all the more because Paget had been Gardiner's favourite student at Cambridge, and then for years on end during
King Henry's reign Gardiner had not noticed that Paget had been
working against him. Even though Paget was on the Privy Council, in
1554 he wrecked two pieces of government legislation in the House
of Lords, bringing about the destruction of a bill against heresy and a
bill extending the treason laws to protect Philip, Mary's husband. Furthermore, there was a curious incoherence in Mary's government: one
of her most trusted advisers and a major sponsor of religious change,
Cardinal Reginald Pole, was not even a member of her Privy Council.

For exactly half a century from 1553, for the first time in English
history England was ruled by two women in succession. Women
rulers were not at all unusual in sixteenth-century Europe: they were
familiar from contemporary Scotland and the Low Countries, and
later also from France. But such women were not expected to take
initiatives, to start wars or conquer territory. They acted as caretakers
for their dominions, usually literally, so that successive sisters of the
ruling male Habsburg monarch were in charge in the Low Countries,
and in both Scotland and France the widowed mothers of the young
monarchs ruled in their stead. Stability in the situation came from the
status of the women – sister, widow – that automatically limited their
role in relation to their brother or young son or daughter. However,
for Mary and Elizabeth, there was uncertainty as to what would happen when normality was restored and these queens regnant married:
the expectation was that their regimes would cease to be in the hands
of caretakers and would be taken over by their husbands. English
politicians tried to avoid that eventuality with Mary's marriage to
Philip of Spain, first by opposing it, then seeking to tie Philip down
with as many conditions as possible. They were quite successful in
this second aim, but only at the cost of permanent ill will between
themselves and Philip and his Spanish politicians. Elizabeth tackled
the same problem in the end by the radical solution of avoiding all
husbands.

Female caretakers did not take initiatives, but they could react to
situations which they inherited, playing their role as mother of the
realm in seeking to reconcile or solve problems. Both Mary and Elizabeth were living after a period of creativity in government and

immense upheaval in the Church. The two women had diametrically opposed reactions to what Henry and Edward had done. If anything, Marian Catholicism was more creative than Elizabethan Protestantism, both in religion and other policies. Professor Loades remains firmly fixed on biography, giving only a few side-glances at much recent fascinating reassessment of Mary's religious policies: where A. G. Dickens half a century ago described a Marian 'reaction', a posse of historians led by Eamon Duffy, Christopher Haigh, John Edwards and to a considerable extent Loades himself, have found a Reformation as full of potential as anything that Protestants did, indeed the largest-scale attempt to restore Catholicism up until then in all Europe.[3] We ought to forget A. G. Dickens's uncharacteristically obtuse remark that Mary 'failed to discover the Counter-Reformation'.[4] She could hardly succeed in finding something which had not yet happened: many of the most important decisions of the Council of Trent which put the Counter-Reformation into practice came after her death, while decisions in Mary's England anticipated the outcome of Trent. As papal legate, her Archbishop of Canterbury Cardinal Pole drew up proposals for clergy training schools (seminaries) in every English diocese, before Trent had got round to this most important of initiatives to transform the Catholic Church worldwide. Pole ordered that the consecrated bread of the Mass which was the Body of the Lord should be placed for veneration in a tabernacle placed on a church's principal altar: a new devotional arrangement which soon became standard in Counter-Reformation churches throughout Europe. Moreover, the Marian Church and clergy were proving as creative and imaginative in their instructional literature as their later Counter-Reformation colleagues, before Mary's death transformed the situation.

If Mary had had forty-five years on the throne instead of five, England could have become a bastion of the Counter-Reformation. The Jesuits would have arrived in force, as they could not in Mary's reign. What would have been the point that early? There were as yet no Jesuits who had completed their training who spoke that peculiar offshore tongue, English, and there was little point in sending Jesuits who could only communicate in Latin, Spanish or French to an audience at court or universities, when King Philip had already imported top-class Spanish Dominicans to do the job just as well. Jesuits might consider hacking through the jungles of the Americas or encountering the great civilizations of the Far East rather more glamorous than anything they could do in a country with a tediously reliable Catholic queen. Not surprising, therefore, that only two ever arrived, with hardly time to unpack and repack their bags before Queen Mary's death.

An essential skill of a successful sixteenth-century monarch was image-building and public relations. Once more, contrast the two mothers: Catherine – conscientious, correct, aware of the importance of proper splendour, but not notable for any apparent initiatives or innovation; Anne Boleyn – fond of modish French-style magnificence, high-spirited and extrovert. The court of Queen Mary and the court of Queen Elizabeth revealed a similar contrast. Neither queen lacked personal courage. Mary was clearly splendid in moments of acute crisis: she rallied and enthused the gentlemen of East Anglia in 1553; she steadied the nerve of her government and won London to her side in Wyatt's rebellion in 1554. These were the equivalents of Elizabeth's Tilbury speech of 1588. Mary enjoyed a good laugh: one of her closest and most valued companions was Jane the Fool. But she was W. C. Sellar's and R. J. Yeatman's 'Broody Mary' in more senses than one: frequently ill in adult life, and after her marriage miserably preoccupied with her failure to have children, believing in her false pregnancies with an intensity which thoroughly embarrassed those around her. She seems to have had little idea of making a show. One of the few buildings still standing to proclaim her patronage is the chapel of Trinity College, Cambridge, one of the dullest major religious buildings put up in England during the sixteenth century. Her court equally had the reputation of being the dullest in Europe, middle-aged to elderly, being full of earnestly pious Catholic admirers who tended to be figures of her own generation or older. Mary never went on any major nationwide progress, partly because of her health, partly because the government was worried about the unrest which had affected the country each summer since 1548. That contrasts with Elizabeth, who from early in her reign used the progress as one of her chief methods of self-publicity, and went further afield to show herself to her subjects than her father had normally done. Monarchs who went on regular progress were usually the success stories of that period.

It is Elizabeth that we remember as the Virgin Queen, but this was not an unusual image – in fact it was essential for an unmarried female monarch, for obvious reasons. All the Tudors came to the throne officially as virgins and, to begin with, Mary could and did play on the image of the Virgin Queen just as much as Elizabeth. An example all the more telling for its pedestrian clumsiness is an extended poem by one of her Catholic admirers, George Cavendish (Wolsey's biographer). Celebrating Mary's succession to Edward VI, he said:

> For the loss of a king which was a virgin clean,
> [God] hath restored us a maiden queen.

Cavendish even tried drastically to rewrite history with regard to the Spanish marriage:

> To a virgin life, which liked the best,
> Profest was thine heart: when, moved with zeal
> And tears of subjects expressing request
> For no lust, but love of the common weal
> Virginity's vow thou diddest repel.[5]

Elizabeth's achievement was to take up an image of permanent virginity foisted on her in mid-reign by politicians who opposed her prospective marriage to a Catholic, then turn it to her own triumphant use. That illustrates why Elizabeth was always likely to be more successful than Mary, even if they had been granted an equal number of regnal years. She knew how to make the best of a situation: how to give way, how to transform events to her best advantage. She could be stubborn and tactless, but also superb in her efforts to repair the damage. However much we try to be revisionist about Mary and write down Elizabeth, the personalities of the two monarchs laid on the dissecting table show Elizabeth's advantage. She seized opportunities offered; Mary grimly continued burning Protestants long after the policy had become a public relations disaster and has suffered the consequences in historical memory. Both women started with success – in Mary's case, extraordinary success. But Elizabeth from the outset of her reign steadily built on advantage; Mary did not. Forty-five years of her religious policies, even if successful, were likely to have caused as much division and disaster in the realm as did the French monarchy's efforts to contain France's Reformation. Professor Loades, in this latest admirably up-to-date offering after his lifelong study of the broody queen, gives plenty of reasons to see Mary's lost opportunity as England's long-term gain.

12

William Byrd

We know a gratifying amount about William Byrd, partly thanks to quite recent archival rediscoveries; and Kerry McCarthy splendidly and concisely presents it all in this intelligent and affectionate biography. Alas, the one thing we don't have is a contemporary portrait, not even anything as clumsy as the dome-headed icon of Shakespeare so universally recognizable: the portrait-image of Byrd adorning CD sleeves or scores is an unimaginative Georgian-Tudor pastiche. That presents a problem to designers of dust-jackets for Byrd biographies: how to symbolize him? McCarthy has opted for a picture which, although an initially baffling choice, nails down one half of his identity very well (see Plate 5). It is a pioneering equivalent of those group photos taken at the end of G20 Summits and the like: world statesmen exhibiting false bonhomie to camera, although the conventions of oil portraiture make unnecessary the wide smiles of the twenty-first century, which the deficiencies of Tudor dentistry would also render unwise. These were the English and Spanish/Flemish delegates at one of the most important peace conferences of the Tudor age, which took place a year after Elizabeth I's death, at Somerset House in London. They had succeeded in ending three decades of cold and hot war between Reformed Protestant powers and the Spanish Habsburgs, confirming in the process the independence of the Protestant northern Netherlands, and offering the possibility that Roman Catholicism might not always be seen as the inevitable enemy of the Elizabethan way of life.

Remarkably, all five English politicians portrayed on one side of the Somerset House table in 1604 were linked to William Byrd. The most powerful, the great Protestant statesman Robert Cecil, Earl of Salisbury, was the dedicatee of one of Byrd's last and most haunting keyboard ensembles of pavan and galliard, so popular that they remained admired and adapted through the centuries when most Tudor music had been relegated to the archives. Beside him are Thomas Sackville, Earl of Dorset, and the cousins, Earls Charles and Henry Howard. All three were Byrd's patrons, and to various degrees shared the shifts and ambiguities of his religious convictions; it was odds-on that all of them would have conformed to a restoration of Catholicism in England if it had chanced to take place. The last portrayed, Charles Blount, Earl of Devonshire, would have enjoyed the complimentary references to his scandalously flaunted mistress Lady Penelope Rich in several of Byrd's songs written about this time.

And so Byrd's public life is refracted through the images of these English noblemen. He was the much-honoured and privileged royal servant to Elizabeth and James for over half a century, called 'a father of music' in the records of their Chapel Royal at his death in his eighties; a man of affairs who, when he produced a list of reasons to become proficient in singing, emphasized first its benefits to health and public speaking. To judge from one of his surviving books, Byrd may have been at home in the barbarously archaic Norman-French of the Tudor law courts, which he certainly exploited with enthusiasm in perennial litigation, as any self-respecting Elizabethan gentleman would. It is symbolic of a certain insularity in Byrd that he owned this peculiarly English legal text while his inept word-setting in his one Italian song reveals that he had no idea how that language was spoken. And he never travelled abroad, so never experienced the working out of the Counter-Reformation in mainland Europe which succeeded the end of the Council of Trent in 1563, unlike many young Englishmen of restless spirit and Catholic inclinations.

The Somerset House picture is still only half William Byrd. If McCarthy's publishers had budgeted for a back-cover image, I would have recommended an empty lawn to be found on the fringes of north London: it is the site of the gargantuan Romanesque Abbey Church at Waltham Holy Cross, whose admittedly stately parish church abutting on the west end of the lawn is often mistaken by casual visitors for part of that lost building. The monastery was closed and stripped in 1540, around the time that Byrd was born, Waltham being the last purely monastic house in all England to suffer Henry VIII's dissolutions. So Byrd would never have experienced its echoing acoustic, unlike his collaborator and close friend Thomas Tallis (later godfather to Byrd's youngest son, Thomas), who lost his job as organist when Waltham Abbey was destroyed and who thoughtfully squirrelled away a century-old manuscript on music theory from the Abbey library.

Yet it was Byrd who seemed to mourn that lost world rather than his friend Tallis, who had actually been part of it. McCarthy perceptively remarks,[1] 'his nostalgia was that of a young man for something he had never really known'. It might equally be said that amid his compositional energy, Byrd created an English Catholic musical future which failed to go any further; English Catholics would not have the potential resources or public presence to use his work for another three centuries (and then not many of them did). Byrd delighted in producing choral settings of the innumerable fragments which go to make up the 'proper' of the mass: those sections of text, mostly particles of scripture, which around the unchanging core sections of the service from Kyrie to Agnus Dei (the 'ordinary'), orchestrate in literal sense the mood-music through the intricate shifts of the Catholic liturgical year. His two late printed collections entitled *Gradualia* encompass no fewer than 109 such occasional pieces, mostly no more than two minutes long, but collectively a formidably luxurious provision for a service which, throughout his adult lifetime, was illegal in England and which might result in execution for those who celebrated it or even attended it.

Byrd lived through a period of chaos in English church music without parallel in our history – not even the seventeenth-century civil wars produced such a sequence of rapid reversals of fortune, all the work of four successive Tudor monarchs. The last years of Henry VIII, when Byrd was a child, witnessed a slow leaching of life away from those parts of Catholic devotional practice which the king had allowed to remain after the dissolution of the monasteries. Edward VI presided enthusiastically over a wholesale assault on this Catholic tradition which, if he had not died in his teens, would have probably eliminated all church organs and any liturgical music more elaborate than metrical psalms, together with the cathedrals which had continued to provide shelter for professional church musicians. English religion would have resembled what Reformed Protestant Scotland became in the next few decades. Queen Mary not only restored traditional Catholic liturgy but encouraged new experiments destined to turn into the Counter-Reformation, one tiny symptom of which is a fragment of an Easter Vigil psalm by 'Byrd' (then a teenager, if it is our William) which represents an interesting and unusual collaboration with composers much older than him.

Nevertheless Mary enjoyed even fewer years of power than her half-brother, and the Roman Catholic English establishment died with her. Queen Elizabeth brought back a Reformed Protestantism which in the parliamentary and convocation enactments of 1559–63 suggested a return to the last and most destructive phase of Edward VI's reign, based on a Prayer Book and theological statements virtually identical to those that he had sanctioned in 1552–3. But Elizabeth was not Edward, having her own rather mysterious religious convictions which she usually had the sense to keep to herself, the most effective means of getting her own way by stealth. She confounded the expectations of her subjects, Catholic or Protestant, not by the positive legislation of the Elizabethan settlement, but by what did not happen next. Music was one of her great enthusiasms, and her personal religious amenities provided by the institution of the Chapel Royal included much elaborate choral music (backed up by pipe-organs) which acted as a protection and example for the surviving greater churches. While parish church choirs faded away unless they knuckled under to the nationwide regime of Geneva psalms, the cathedrals and choral establishments were not drastically modified, let alone unroofed like Waltham Abbey. As I have already noted,[2] cathedrals became a subversion of what was otherwise in essence a fairly typical Reformed Protestant Church. The C of E has evolved willy-nilly towards a theological schizophrenia, in which self-consciously 'Catholic' and 'Protestant' identities are paradoxical but indestructible strands of a double helix.

All that was in the future beyond Byrd, but his career remained inseparable from the inbuilt contradictions in the newly Established Protestant Church of England. His first major job came in one of those surviving cathedrals. Francis Mallett, then Dean of Lincoln, had once been Archbishop Cranmer's chaplain, but after Protestant waverings had become one of Queen Mary's most stridently Catholic chaplains: his continued tenure at Lincoln under Elizabeth was an example of her inclination to let Catholics keep their place in her Church as long as they remained sleeping dogs. When Byrd ran into serious trouble for providing over-elaborate music, his woes would have come from the opposite faction among the Cathedral staff – forward Protestants – with Dean Mallett passively fronting their complaints (maybe as a not-so-secret Catholic, he didn't much care what a schismatic cathedral did with its music). Lincoln more happily provided the young composer with a wife, who became a Catholic recusant (refusing to attend services of the Protestant Established Church) long before he did. She may have been the source of his lurch away from Protestantism, for his brothers remained conformist despite early careers as choristers at St Paul's Cathedral.

In 1572 came an accidental drowning of a Gentleman of the Chapel Royal, which vacancy gave Byrd his chance to escape the tensions of Lincoln. The Chapel Royal continued to provide him with the protection of appreciative monarchs until his death, despite his increasingly salient Catholicism. Here his friendship with Tallis blossomed and produced some vigorous musical entrepreneurship centring on a joint royal patent which they secured for music printing, and which long outlived them. After a shaky start during which the public did not feel much need to buy the musical novelties which Byrd and Tallis jointly produced, this became a reliable money-spinner, serving a growing market in which amateur music-making became one of the most respectable as well as enjoyable forms of home entertainment.

Some of this published repertoire is dangerously Catholic, as revealed by even a casual perusal of the collections entitled with careful neutrality *Cantiones sacrae* ('Sacred Songs'), but there was a Protestant etiquette here: musical piety banned in church was considered just about acceptable at home, just as there was a much more generous threshold for sacred domestic art than for religious imagery found in Elizabethan church buildings. Much of the content is in penitential mood – McCarthy calls the 1589 *Cantiones sacrae* 'a musical cycle with few rivals for sustained gloominess until the nineteenth century',[3] but we might think of this as the Tudor domestic equivalent of lolling in our living rooms before a nice gory murder story or *film noir* on the telly. There is no evidence that Byrd acquired a downbeat reputation like his younger contemporary William Dowland, who showed at least some measure of humorous self-deprecation in writing an instrumental piece entitled *Semper Dowland, semper dolens* – dat's Dowland, always doomy. On the contrary, Byrd seems to have been a welcome dinner guest among the great and the not necessarily good, and that must also have helped as he negotiated potentially dangerous confessional shoals over sixty years.

Musicians are in any case inclined to blur ideological boundaries in their fascination with creativity, and the sixteenth-century Reformation was not always as easily pigeon-holed as the tidy-minded on both sides would have liked. There is the fascinating case of *Infelix ego*, Byrd's sumptuous six-part motet from the *Cantiones sacrae*, which sets a century-old deathbed meditation by the Florentine Renaissance reformer Girolamo Savonarola. What was the significance of this anguished text? If you didn't know anything about it, you might use it to stiffen your nerve as a harassed Catholic recusant, yet Thomas Cranmer had plagiarized it for his final speech before being burned at the stake by Mary Tudor in 1556. Previously Savonarola's similar death as a heretic had not stopped his writings becoming firm favourites among ultra-pious pre-Reformation English Catholics. How much would Byrd have known of this twisted history?

In any case, Byrd's hardening resolve to turn his Catholic convictions towards open recusancy in the 1590s did not end his flow of compositions for the Protestant Church. One of the most splendid comes from late in his career, his 'Great Service', written either in Elizabeth's last years or James's first, and only rediscovered in a Durham Cathedral cupboard in 1922: it provides music for Prayer Book Mattins, Evensong and Holy Communion. In its no-expense-spared use of two choirs of five voices, it was surely intended for the Chapel Royal. Up to the nineteenth century, Anglican liturgy very sparingly employed music for Communion, and it was Byrd's Mattins and Evensong settings and a handful of his anthems in English which survived in use (his very cheerful psalm adaptation 'O Lord, make thy servant Elizabeth our Queen to rejoice in thy strength' has enjoyed a recent revival, thanks to time's royal whirligig). Yet behind this Protestant repertoire lurked the plainsong of the old Western Church, simpler parts of which were still used in Elizabethan cathedrals to chant Prayer Book words, in a fashion which was clearly so universally understood and practised that no contemporaries bothered to leave us any description of it. Byrd occasionally let fragments of it protrude more aggressively out of his English music, such as in 'Teach me, O Lord'. This is one of his best-known verse-anthems, a form which he helped to embed in English choral tradition, consisting of an accompanied solo alternating with choral sections. In this example, the choir blatantly sings the 'Tonus Peregrinus', a plainsong psalm-tone rather atypical in its peregrine wanderings; Byrd must have especially liked it, since it also appears in one of his still very frequently used Magnificats.

We forget just how separate were the two confessional halves of Byrd's choral repertoire in his lifetime: not even Queen Elizabeth dared allow the use of Latin in choral pieces in the Church's liturgy. Now in a more ecumenical age, Byrd's Latin music is probably more often performed liturgically by Anglicans than Roman Catholics, his mass settings in particular. At the time, a Catholic composer would have expected to spend most of his liturgical energy on the ordinary of the Mass: in Counter-Reformation Italy, Palestrina wrote about a hundred such settings. Byrd wrote only three, but what a trio they are: in three, four and five parts, all dating from a few years in the 1590s and straightaway put into print by the composer with only minimum discretion, despite the dangers.

These are the last major English Catholic mass settings before the nineteenth century, yet they are not the end of a tradition, and are startling in their lack of deference to what had gone before. Notably, Byrd sets the Kyrie chorally instead of leaving it as plainsong, for the first time in English liturgical practice. Admittedly, choirs who sing his three-part Kyrie are puzzled by its almost apologetic brevity. Surely, in reality, Byrd must have intended its three solemn chordal sequences for alternation with sections of plainsong chant, creating something of a musical bridge to a former age. After that opening element of the three-part Mass's proper, the gloriously athletic ingenuity of the remaining sections gives the illusion of a much denser texture than three voices, but it is easily sustained by an experienced trio of singers, such as might unobtrusively arrive at a recusant country house for a very discreet gathering of the faithful. McCarthy intriguingly points to technical indications in the original published text which suggest that all three of Byrd's Mass settings could have been performed non-stop over a sotto voce spoken celebration of a low Mass, adding solemnity to a sacred occasion which was a brave defiance of Protestant persecution, but which nevertheless needed to be over as quickly as possible.

Byrd's keyboard music was less ideologically freighted, but likewise it represents a new era in English composition for organ or virginals. This was not based on exciting technical innovation. For the next two centuries English organ-builders remained resolutely uninterested in the growing variety of sounds which their mainland competitors were adding to their instruments, so there is little parallel in Byrd to the French romantic drama of Jean Titelouze's meditations on plainsong, or the lushly proliferating sound effects with which Jan Pietersz. Sweelinck entertained Dutch music-gadders. Byrd's keyboard creativity rarely suggests works designed specifically for organ rather than virginals or vice versa, but in more than six decades it still represents a transformation in sound-worlds. At the beginning are Thomas Tallis's longer keyboard compositions weaving variants around the plainsong theme *Felix namque*; though intellectually ingenious, they are frankly desperately dull and po-faced, either to play or to listen to. At the other end is the kaleidoscope of moods in the compositions which Byrd, John Bull and Orlando Gibbons shrewdly assembled in 1612 as a commercially saleable wedding present for James I's daughter Princess Elizabeth, *Parthenia, or the Maydenhead of the first musicke that ever was printed for the Virginalls.* In the intervening decades, a wealth of keyboard compositions moved their centre of gravity from ecclesiastical accompaniment to domestic entertainment. One of the most charming is Byrd's piece simply called *Ut re mi fa sol la,* which he evidently wrote to encourage a child starting out on the keyboard. The little fingers pick out a slow high scale up and down, while underneath the tutor (Mr Byrd, the father?) plays a steadily more vigorous set of variations, ending with the irresistibly jolly dance-rhythms of 'The Woods so Wild', repeated relentlessly enough times to satisfy any six-year-old.

From this delight in the musical instruction of children, a modern parallel leaps out. McCarthy reminds us of Joseph Kerman's judgement that Byrd was to sixteenth-century European music what Arnold Schoenberg was in the twentieth century,[4] but it is Benjamin Britten who makes the more interesting comparison. There is that combination of pugnacity (seen in Byrd's case at Lincoln Cathedral and in his lifetime of litigation) with an extraordinary capacity for deep friendship. Byrd's career, as we have seen, was littered with collaborations with other musicians, so his name is always linked with them as much as is Britten's with so many of his contemporaries among artists and performers, way beyond the obvious partner in Aldeburgh. But more than that, both men are fascinating in their insider/outsider or conformist/nonconformist status. For Byrd, there is confessional religion: the contrasting symbolism of the Somerset House group portrait versus the empty lawn of Waltham Abbey Church. For Britten, it was not Catholicism but homosexuality. Through most of Byrd's adult life in Tudor and early Stuart England, the majority of the population came to regard 'papists' with a similar mixture of repulsion, fear and secret fascination as prevailed in mid-twentieth-century Britain towards 'pansies': the Elizabethan Catholic minority behaved with that mixture of concealment, equivocation, secret pride and clandestine networking recognizable to older gay men and lesbians today. Byrd and Britten (who ended up as peer, OM and CH) both enjoyed a charmed existence amid a world of persecution partly thanks to their personal closeness to a Queen Elizabeth. Without the constant moral and social dilemmas which these twin geniuses experienced, we might not have two such extraordinary and contradictory legacies of musical splendour: England's distinctive gift to the world of music, joining hands over four centuries.

13
The Bible before King James

In the fifteenth century the official Church in England scored a not-able success in destroying the uniquely English dissenting movement known as Lollardy. One of the results of this was that the Church banished the Bible in English; access to the Lollard Bible translation was in theory confined to those who could be trusted to read it with-out ill consequence – a handful of approved scholars and gentry. After that, England's lack of provision for vernacular Bibles stood in stark contrast to their presence in the rest of Western Europe, which was quickly expanding, despite the disapproval of individual prelates, notably Pope Leo X. Between 1466 and 1522 there were twenty-two editions of the Bible in High or Low German; the Bible appeared in Italian in 1471, Dutch in 1477, Spanish in 1478, Czech around the same time and Catalan in 1492. In England, there simply remained the Vulgate, though thanks to printing that was readily available. One hundred and fifty-six complete Latin editions of the Bible had been published across Europe by 1520, and in a well-regulated part of the Western Church like England, it was likely that every priest with any pretence to education would have possessed one.[1] The traditional Latin of the Vulgate was to see off any competitor in Latin even among Protestants: in the latter part of the century, such a militant champion of the new faith as John Knox's friend Anne Vaughan, whose second husband was the brilliant Puritan preacher Edward Dering, made use of it in her pioneering sonnet versions of the psalms.[2]

The biblical scholarship of Desiderius Erasmus represented a dra-matic break with any previous biblical tradition in England: when he translated the New Testament afresh into Latin and published it in 1516, he went back to the original Greek. When he commented on scripture, his emphasis was on the early commentators in the first five Christian centuries (with pride of place going to that most audacious among them, Origen); his work is notable for the absence of much reference to the great medieval commentators. This attitude was fully shared by William Tyndale, the creator of the first and greatest Tudor translation of the Bible, although Tyndale's judicial murder at the hands of the Holy Roman Emperor, and indirectly Henry VIII, prevented his work reaching beyond the New Testament and the Pentateuch. Tyndale came from the remote West Country Forest of Dean on the borders of Wales, and it is not fanciful to see his fascination with translation as springing out of the market days of his childhood, listening to the mixed babble of Welsh and English around him.[3] His is the ancestor of all Bibles in the English language, especially the version of 1611; Tyndale's biographer David Daniell has bluntly pointed out that 'Nine-tenths of the Authorised Version's New Testament is Tyndale's.'[4]

There was no reason why this pioneer should have had the talent of an exceptional writer as well as being an exceptional scholar, but the Forest of Dean man was a gourmet of language: it pleased him to discover as he moved into translating the Old Testament that Hebrew and English were so much more compatible than Hebrew and Greek. He was an admirer of what Luther was achieving in Wittenberg in the 1520s, and visited the town during his years of exile at the end of that decade, but he was also his own man. When creating his New Testament translations, he drew generously on Luther's own introductions to individual books, but as he came to translate the Pentateuch, the Books of the Law, his own estimate of their spiritual worth began to diverge from Luther's strong contrast between the roles of law and gospel, and the plagiarism of Luther's German ceased, to be replaced by his own thoughts.

Surreptitiously read and discussed during the 1520s and 1530s, Tyndale's still incomplete Bible translation worked on the imaginations of those who so far had virtually no access to public evangelical preaching in England. It may be significant that even before King Henry's quarrel with the pope, during the 1520s there was a perceptible nationwide decline in ordinations in England: perhaps the traditional Church was losing its grip on those thinking of a clerical career. By the time of Tyndale's martyrdom in 1536, perhaps 16,000 copies of his translation had passed into England, a country of no more than two and a half million people with, at that stage, a very poorly developed market for books.[5] And this new presence of the vernacular Bible in Henry VIII's England entwined itself in a complex fashion around the king's own eccentric agenda for religious change in his realm, as the monarch, his leading churchmen and secular politicians all puzzled over the meaning of the king's quarrel and break with the pope in Rome, which had begun in matters remote from the passionate theological claims of religious Reformers.

Even though traditionalists loved to sneer at Protestantism as 'the New Learning', many leading figures among those defending traditional religion also wanted to reform the Church in their own way, and they were aware of how anomalous it was that England did not have a good Catholic vernacular version of the Bible. Bishop John Fisher, the prime scholar among the English bishops of the 1520s, made a point in late 1527 of arguing for such a project, and Sir Thomas More, a fierce controversialist with Tyndale, was also very ready to support biblical translation in principle. He claimed that his friends among the bishops were prepared to give their approval to such a translation project, should the Church approve.[6] Yet simultaneously, Bishop Cuthbert Tunstall of London, as cultivated a humanist as Fisher, was buying up Tyndale's New Testaments in order to burn them, an action which has rather outshone in the historical record the initially very tepid efforts, with royal encouragement, to begin work on a replacement which would not be tainted by the 'New Learning'. A royal proclamation inspired by Chancellor More on 22 June 1530 announced that not only should all existing translations be surrendered to the bishops, but that 'having respect to the malignity of this present time', it was better to have scripture expounded in reliable sermons; it was not necessary for the Bible to be in the hands of common people. If Tyndale's Bibles 'and all other books of heresy' were given up, then that would be the time for the king to implement his intention of a translation by 'great, learned and Catholic persons'. This highly conditional offer represented a turning-back from More's earlier agreement that an English vernacular translation was overdue; he had even made proposals for preparing such a project.[7]

This talk of an official Bible translated under the supervision of the existing episcopal hierarchy persisted through the next decade. On 19 December 1534, after the discreet evangelical Thomas Cranmer had become Archbishop of Canterbury, the Convocation of Canterbury put a positive spin on the 1530 proclamation by petitioning the king not only for the suppression of heretical books but also for a new effort of translation.[8] Elizabeth I's Archbishop Matthew Parker later recalled that the arch-traditionalist Stephen Gardiner, Bishop of Winchester, did everything he could to oppose this move, though six months after Convocation's petition, Gardiner claimed to be worn out by his efforts in translating the Gospels of Luke and John which Convocation had assigned to him.[9] Indeed, that summer of 1535, with Henry VIII in one of the sunniest phases of his marriage to Queen Anne Boleyn and with evangelicals in high favour, it was a good time to be seen to favour the English scriptures: 'that same yere beganne the new testament in English' commented one conservative London chronicler who was not greatly enamoured of the new situation.[10] King Henry himself, never predictable in matters religious, achieved a first at the same time by commissioning the first Bible printed in the British Isles – not in English, but a Latin text, with selected edited highlights from the Vulgate Old Testament and the whole of the New Testament. Henry took a keen interest in this project, furnishing it with a very personal Preface which, among other things, commended the typeface he had himself chosen for ease of reading (he was beginning to have trouble with his eyesight and was using spectacles for reading, though he did not confide in his subjects on this matter).[11]

That idiosyncratic royal enterprise proved a dead end in comparison with a march of the vernacular through Henry's kingdom that nevertheless owed little to most of his bishops. The apparent disappearance of all the sections of the Bible allotted to various divines in the 1534 Convocation remains one of the literary mysteries of the English Reformation, and one suspects that these labours were not as complete as their undertakers claimed. Certainly by 1537 Archbishop Cranmer was sarcastically commenting that it would 'not be till a day after doomsday' before the episcopate completed a translation, and he was now enthusiastically commending for public use a rival completed Bible: England's first since the time of the Lollards.[12] Its first version, optimistically dedicated to Henry VIII, had appeared from an Antwerp press in summer 1535, and consisted of a completion of Tyndale's truncated work by the fugitive Augustinian friar Miles Coverdale.[13] Only a year passed before Thomas Cromwell was using his newly acquired powers as Vice-Gerent to issue injunctions which ordered for the provision of a Bible in English and Latin in all churches. So while King Henry's shortened Vulgate would have fitted the bill on the Latin side, Coverdale's was the only English option available. The man who had translated most of it, Tyndale, was that same year trapped and executed as a heretic by the imperial authorities in Brussels, after a plot involving not merely the Bishop of London but the king in whose name Cromwell now acted – one of the many ironies which characterized Henry's convoluted religious policies.

The incongruity deepened when (after what was evidently a good deal of passive resistance to the Vice-Gerential injunctions from traditionalist higher clergy) the order was intensified and repeated during 1537 and 1538. Probably the king never realized that his power was being used to spread the inspired translation of the man whom he had grown to hate and whose destruction he had helped to engineer.[14] Thanks to Cranmer and Cromwell, King Henry was now actually giving his royal licence to a further presentation of the complete Coverdale translation with further prefaces and commentary. The editing had been done by a former associate of Tyndale's called John Rogers, although his work went under the pseudonym of Thomas Matthew – apparently derived from some rather approximate anagram formation around the name of the editor of topical apparatus which Rogers had lifted and translated from the first French Protestant Bible of 1535.[15]

Hot on the heels of the Matthew Bible, Coverdale produced yet another refinement of his completed text which, despite traditionalist attempts to get it revised in Henry's last years, was to remain definitive for more than two decades. It has acquired the nickname of the 'Great Bible'; thanks to a Preface provided in 1541 by the archbishop, it has with little justification often been called 'Cranmer's Bible'. More than any other version of the Henrician period, it gained the aura of an official translation, helped by the coincidence of optimistic preparations for Henry's disastrous marriage to Anne of Cleves in 1540.

The ceiling of the Chapel Royal in St James's Palace, installed exactly at this period, displays the phrase 'VERBUM DEI' five times, the only motif prominent in it apart from royal and dynastic symbols, and the same phrase is much repeated on the famous title-page of the Great Bible, probably not designed by Hans Holbein, as often asserted, but by a French master engraver.[16] Here the king is depicted as the benevolent provider of Bibles to clergy and laity alike, each layer of society in turn delivering them to the order below, all duly signifying their social superiority or inferiority by their covered or bare heads. The picture is a fine diagram of the hierarchy of the kingdom, as is the prison menacingly placed at the bottom right, showing what happens to those who violate the hierarchical rules and reject the good news of divine mercy as interpreted by the royal donor of the text. One of the most remarkable features of its text is that at 2 Chronicles 36:8 it actually amplifies the biblical original by adding a sin to the many committed by King Jehoiakim of Judah: he allowed carved images. Roman Catholics were gleeful when they discovered this gratuitous piece of evangelical spin.[17]

Even after Cromwell's fall and execution in 1540 (his heraldry on the title-page of the Great Bible then became an unexplained oval white blank in the busy design; see Plate 7), Henry himself gave the parishes an effective extra spur to provide Bibles in a proclamation of 1541 which threatened fines if they did not.[18] Alas for his enthusiasm, not all took the hint which the picture of the prison provided. Popular excitement at the Bible was sufficiently noticeable for the king to take fright. Ever since 1539 he had been complaining about unruly public reading of the Bible now to be found in the kingdom's churches, and he was deeply troubled at the possibility that the lower orders might have radical thoughts as a result of irresponsible thumbing through its pages. In 1543 Henry pushed Parliament into ordering that only upper-status groups in society, presumably deemed less excitable, should be allowed to read it at all. Interestingly, in the same year the Scottish Parliament – dominated after King James V's death by a regency regime toying with church reform – passed an Act which for the first time allowed lieges, that is landowners, to possess the Bible; the Scots were thus newly allowed access to the Bible approximately equivalent to its newly restricted access in England. It was a brief moment of concession: for the most part, successive Scottish governments in the 1530s and 1540s remained hostile to the Reformation and did their best to curb its growth, with only short-term success.

The greater evangelical freedom of Edward VI's reign produced new editions of the biblical versions made before the Great Bible. These were kitted out with fresh notes taking notice of new theological departures in the Protestant Churches of Switzerland and Geneva, particularly the agreement on the Eucharist achieved by Bullinger and Calvin in 1549, later termed the *Consensus Tigurinus*. For now, Geneva and its large community of French exiles had emerged as a major force in European Reformation. It was in Geneva that the French Bible publisher Robert Estienne (Stephanus) produced a French New Testament with a system of verse divisions which has survived to the present day, even in Catholic Bibles. It was soon taken up in a new translation produced in the late 1550s by a number of English exiles from Queen Mary Tudor's Catholic England.

Finally published as a whole in 1560 after the death of Mary, this 'Geneva Bible' showed all the enterprise of Geneva's publishing industry, then the city's greatest money-spinner. It was designed deliberately to be a popular edition for the whole anglophone market, not a lectern Bible in folio, with maximum aids to individual study: it contained not just the verse numbering but also attractive features such as maps of the Holy Land and the Garden of Eden, plus a generous marginal commentary. It drew on the considerable biblical scholarship available in a city which boasted such distinguished scholars as Calvin himself and his colleague Theodore Beza; hence its interesting improvements on previous English versions which were not confined to the famous 'Breeches' translation of Genesis 3:7, 'and they sewed fig leaves together, and made themselves breeches'. Frequently editions were bound up with a metrical psalter, much less frequently with a bowdlerized version of the Book of Common Prayer, so that altogether it might be a complete kit for worship and education in the home.

The Geneva Bible got off to a slow start in circulation in the home country, but from its first English printing in 1576 it became a firm favourite with the reading public. The Church of England's establishment had brought out a revision of the Great Bible in 1568, known appropriately as the Bishops' Bible, which became the dignified folio version for use in worship, but one should not see these two versions necessarily as rivals: people would expect to hear one in church and use the other at home. Shakespeare evidently drew on both in his quotation of scripture in his plays. One highly significant feature of the Geneva Bible was its use in the Church of Scotland, which, after its turbulent Reformation in 1560, tended to out-Calvin Calvin in its enthusiasm for Reformed Protestant change. Along with the Genevan-inspired *Book of Common Order*, Scotland's adoption of the Geneva Bible meant that the official English used in the worship of England's neighbour-kingdom was that of London and not the Lowland Scots of Edinburgh. It was the beginning of the binding-in to a common Protestant purpose of the two polities that had been enemies for centuries.

Roman Catholics remained highly suspicious of lay use of the vernacular Bible. Even if they could not ban it outright in northern Europe, as became the case in southern Europe generally (even Queen Mary Tudor confined herself to ordering the Great Bible out of her churches rather than banning vernacular Bible-reading altogether), Catholics saw reading the Bible primarily as a professional necessity in arguing with Protestantism. The result was that when English Roman Catholics created their first English biblical translation in exile at Douai and Reims, it was not for ordinary folk to read, but for priests to use as a polemical weapon – the explicit purpose which the 1582 title-page and Preface of the Reims New Testament proclaimed. Part of the polemic in the Catholic literature which accompanied the publication was in pointing out tendentious readings in the Protestant English Bibles, and in this the Catholic scholars scored some palpable hits. This was one good reason for King James to commission a new translation, and when it was completed, it was possible to see some of the readings of the Douai-Reims version amid all the work of Tyndale, Coverdale and the Geneva translators.

14
The King James Bible

The quatercentenary commemorative King James Bible (KJB) sits on my desk as I write: a satisfying artefact in its chocolate livery enriched by richly gilded top, tail and fore edges, with stout chocolate slipcase to match – impressive in its folio bulk, though not nearly as bulky as the originals of 1611, which needed stout lecterns to bear them, announcing their presence with a swagger equal to the most majestic of England's medieval church buildings. Inside, Oxford University Press thoughtfully provided a sticky-back presentation label, since most of these monuments will no doubt end up as gifts for clergy (I pity the Archbishop of Canterbury in particular). Without question, they will be graceful additions to any study. They give something of the flavour of the original: 1611 spelling, ornamental capitals beginning each chapter, a detailed map of Palestine engraved by John Speed (just like his maps of English counties which were selling so well at the time), a Kalendar of Church of England holy days and lessons for church services and, strangest of all, thirty-four meticulously referenced genealogical tables of biblical characters culminating in Jesus Christ and Paul of Tarsus, to convince the good folk of Jacobean England that the Twelve Tribes of Israel and the notables of the Old Testament were gentry families rather like those who ruled the shires of England in 1611 – or better still, that the whole people of England were like the Twelve Tribes of Israel. Altogether, this array of extras was an encouragement to the English to aspire to the privileged status of Israel in the eyes of a gracious Jehovah, and it hinted that England might even do a bit better than the Israelites under a thoroughly godly Protestant monarch like James I. To hammer home the point, 1611 provided a whole page devoted to the royal arms, just like the big heraldic display which congregations would see proudly affixed to the wall of their parish church as they sat in their pews (in careful hierarchical arrangement), listening to the words of King James's God. Very often those same church walls would themselves bear the emblems of the Twelve Tribes of Israel; one or two examples can be seen still.

Yet any reader familiar with seventeenth-century printing will immediately smell a rat when opening this quasi-facsimile edition: the typeface is patently of two centuries later, and indeed Gordon Campbell comes clean in his appended essay. The Gothic or black-letter type of the original is thought to be too difficult to read easily, even for the sort of people who would enjoy such a volume. That has an unfortunate side effect common to any modern edition of the KJB which keeps the original convention of indicating in italics those words which the 1611 translators added for the reader's comprehension – for example, 'and what if *the sword* contemne euen the rodde? it shall be no *more*, sayth the Lord GOD' (Ezekiel 21:13). Originally, these italicized words would have appeared in discreetly smaller italic type amid the robust black-letter, indicating their auxiliary status: now, because of the different use to which we put italic typeface, these italicized words shout their presence (the radically different visual effect of the original is illustrated in both the doppelgänger books by Campbell and David Norton under review).

It's a pity, but what the change does emphasize is just how remote the modern 'King James' Bible is from its original. It doesn't look the same, it isn't spelled the same, and many of its words are not the same. In fact it is a Disneyfied reconstruction of the original, dating from the eighteenth century, when a Cambridge don called Francis Parris seized the 1611 text by the scruff of the neck and in 1743 published his own Georgian version. This was only slightly modified in 1769 by an

Oxford scholar, Benjamin Blayney, who succeeded in taking most of the credit, and their joint effort is what KJB enthusiasts read today. If they are real KJB completists, they have the benefit of the marginal chronology first added to the Bible in 1679. This is useful in letting us know that Noah's flood happened in 2849 BC, and of course, famously, that the creation of the world took place in 4004 BC (thanks to a misplaced piece of ingenuity by the genuinely learned and original historian James Ussher, Archbishop of Armagh). All this and much more is well told in two books by Gordon Campbell and David Norton. They are respectively published by Oxford and Cambridge University Presses, not always friendly rivals since the seventeenth century in publishing the KJB (in Oxford's case, through a dedicated printing company, whose incorporation in OUP remains a useful source of cash for the University). Like the KJB editions published by the two universities, the two books are beautiful to look at; they are written to the highest standards by two acknowledged experts who, despite their individual insights, end up saying much the same thing, though Norton has a better index. The story of the KJB and its influence has often been told, and we heard it repeated to distraction in the quatercentenary year. If one wonders whether it's worth telling again, well, like the KJB itself, it sells, and good luck to publishers who turn an honest penny by it.

This is the Bible which I was brought up to call the 'Authorized Version' – in my parson's son sophistication, rather looking down on Americans who called it the King James Bible. Yet they were right and I was wrong: the KJB was first called the Authorized Version only as late as the 1820s, and as so often, Americans were preserving an older usage. The KJB nowhere calls itself Authorized. The only Bibles to do so were its Tudor ancestors which were given official status by Henry VIII and Elizabeth I: first, the 'Great Bible' of 1539, making this announcement on the title-page of its 1541 edition, and then belatedly for the fairly light revision of the Great Bible undertaken in the 1560s by the Elizabethan episcopate, in which 'Bishops' Bible' took up the 'authorized' word in 1584. That latter impulse probably arose from some official annoyance at the recent commercial success of another new version which had not bothered to seek any authorization. This translation had been developed in the late 1550s by a group

of Englishmen sheltering in Geneva from Queen Mary Tudor's Romanist persecution, who to a man turned out to be underwhelmed by
the form in which Queen Elizabeth restored a Protestant Church to
their native land in 1559. They considered her C of E not nearly so
godly as their refuge in Geneva, or indeed as the Protestant Established Church which other enthusiasts for Geneva erected in the
neighbouring kingdom of Scotland during the 1560s. Their 'Geneva
Bible' did well because it took up a fashion new in Bibles at the time,
dividing up the whole text not merely into the chapter divisions long
established, but within them into verses, thus making it much easier
to locate and quote biblical fragments. Geneva Bibles also boasted a
mass of marginal commentary around the biblical text, so that everyone might have the luxury of their own personalized Protestant
preacher lurking within the covers, ready with a wise insight for any
occasion. Very often these Bibles were bound up with an extra version
of King David's 150 psalms in strong, simple rhyming verse. These
'metrical' psalms were very different from the Geneva translators'
own translation, but also took their cue from Genevan practice: they
were ready-made to be sung to well-known tunes, and throughout
Europe, in a great array of different languages, they constituted one of
the secret weapons of the Reformed or Calvinist strand of Protestantism.

Small wonder that the English bishops felt a little upstaged by the
Geneva version. Queen Elizabeth herself overcame her distaste for all
things Genevan, apparently appreciating her black-and-silver-thread-
bound presentation Geneva Bible enough to write her own extended
pious commendation of 'the pleasant fields of the holy scriptures'
within the front cover in her fine italic hand – this interesting
rediscovery by John King and Aaron Pratt in Oxford's Bodleian
Library deserves to be better known. In fact, most Elizabethan English folk were probably quite happy to multitask in their experience
of the Bible: they could have a big fat Bishops' Bible read solemnly to
them in their parish church, then communally roar out a metrical
psalm from the back of their Geneva volume at the end of the church
service, before returning home for Sunday dinner and a pleasant postprandial rumination over the Geneva marginal notes. James VI of
Scotland and I of England felt more strongly than Queen Elizabeth

about 'the bitter notes' of Geneva; his strenuous time as King of Scotland left him with little enthusiasm for a preaching minister perching on everyone's shoulder without benefit of royal advice. Accordingly, that shrewd and good-humoured monarch was disposed to seek a new translation, undoubtedly with the subsidiary motive of diverting the energies of his more alarmingly enthusiastic senior clergy into a worthwhile task. He first tried this ploy at a meeting of the General Assembly of the Church of Scotland, which met in 1601 in the appropriately forward-looking Reformed Protestant setting of the recently built parish kirk at Burntisland in Fife. Nothing came of this, apart from a useful outcrop of surprised goodwill towards their king from the Scottish ministers. Only three years later, now King of England, James pursued the theme when facing a potentially difficult informal meeting of English clerical notables at Hampton Court, and this time his project gained momentum. Within seven years, a remarkably efficient and scandalously under-financed set of committees had cooperated to create the revised biblical text which was to prove one of the most lasting commemorations of the first person to rule the entire Atlantic archipelago. Pointedly, it was issued with no marginal notes other than cross references, many of which dated back to the Latin Vulgate (a fact embarrassingly revealed by the system of numbering the Psalms as the Vulgate does, rather than using the numbering in the KJB itself).

Why did the 1611 version have such a lasting effect? Partly because of the good work done in its anglophone predecessors, all of which it cannibalized, explicitly in the case of the Bishops' Bible, but with taciturn ecumenism, also including Geneva and even the translation produced by Roman Catholic scholars who had sought to show the faithful how badly Protestant heretics did the job. There were so many translators on King James's committees that the effect was not cacophony but uniformity: one translator read out his effort at revision of his allotted section to his fellows, and they all joined in criticism and helpful suggestion to smooth out idiosyncrasies – prompting some to suppose that some invisible genius (Shakespeare? Francis Bacon?) was ventriloquizing those owlish dons and clerics. Rather than pursuing such mare's nests, we should note that behind all the earlier English Bibles (which Norton rather mischievously styles 'drafts' of the KJB) there loomed a single early Tudor translator of genius, William Tyndale: the English he created could hardly be bettered. Indeed, the KJB translators did not try very hard to do so, except where (in accordance with the brief which King James gave them) they felt that it needed to sound more like the parish church than the alehouse. For much of the Old Testament and a little of the New, they did not have Tyndale as a guide. He had never finished his self-appointed task, being judicially murdered in 1536 by the Holy Roman Emperor. The main hand among those completing his task was that of Miles Coverdale, who had the all-important task of Eng-lishing the Psalms, not tackled by Tyndale. Such was Coverdale's success that the Book of Common Prayer still employs his Psalter text and not King James's: a curious decision in view of the Prayer Book's thorough revision in 1662, by which time the KJB was well estab-lished. Maybe the Prayer Book revisers simply thought that Coverdale was better.

Once more, that possibility does pose the question of how good the KJB actually was, and is. Undoubtedly it possesses literary merit, but also a great deal of luck. It was produced in a narrow window of opportunity in the 1610s, when the English and Scottish Churches were rather grudgingly moving together under King James's guidance, and before English Protestantism had fragmented irretrievably. This was something of a golden age for the Church of England, before the obtuseness of James's son King Charles nearly ruined it for ever. Pub-lished under the auspices of a king who in retrospect appeared a model of Protestant commitment compared with his untrustworthy offspring, the KJB had the potential to become a uniting symbol for English-speaking Protestantism – and rather against the odds that is precisely what happened. It was not tainted by Charles I; it did not become a totem of royalism, as it might so easily have done, and indeed versions were printed under the aegis of Lord Protector Cromwell. By the time the episcopally governed Church of England came back with Charles II in 1660, even those Protestants who so disapproved of bishops and the Prayer Book that they refused to join the new Established Church, had turned away from the Geneva version which their parents would have preferred, towards the new Bible. Two literary lions that are crucial exemplars of this process, John Bunyan and John Milton, rejected the new Anglican establishment and suffered at its hands. While England's majority population of Anglicans henceforth experienced two books which suffused their prose – the Prayer Book and the Bible – English Protestant Dissenters and the Established Church of Scotland, which in the end also rejected episcopal Church government, became people of a single book, the KJB.

So it was that when England and Scotland jointly stumbled on a 'British' world empire, the one anglophone book which they shared in taking to new lands was the KJB. It is important to realize that its unifying effect was not simply on English Anglicans and Dissenters. The Scots, in their acceptance first of the Geneva Bible, then of King James's, increasingly confined their own centuries-old northern forms of English to private use, since throughout the sixteenth century and thereafter they read the Word of God in the language of London: if anything welded the two ancient enemies together, it was this joint possession of an English Protestant Bible. Now its most ardent defenders are to be found amid the multiple Protestantisms which British emigration has bequeathed to the USA. Some of them, 'King James Only' folk, believe that it possesses an extra dose of the Holy Spirit not granted to any other English version, which is very generous of them, considering that it was commissioned by a monarch whose jovial bisexuality would cause them apoplexy at the present day.

The history of the KJB after it escaped King James's England and Scotland is exhilaratingly explored by the essayists captained by Hannibal Hamlin and Norman W. Jones, who scrutinize it severally from linguistic, historical and literary perspectives. What emerges is the importance of the British Empire in cementing the KJB's reputation. During the later seventeenth century, KJB language, already self-consciously old-fashioned in 1611, seemed almost embarrassing, as a teenager feels embarrassed by Mum and Dad. That mood strengthened in the eighteenth century, and Isabel Rivers's essay explores how influential was the Protestant Dissenter Philip Doddridge with his monumental paraphrase of and commentary on the KJB, so huge that it was only posthumously completed in print two decades after he began issuing parts of it in 1738. Doddridge's work was much plagiarized, and it might well have burst into a flash flood of retranslation, but politics intervened. The French Revolution convinced the British that foreigners were not just irritatingly foreign but a threat to all that was good in our islands' national heritage, so the KJB took on its present iconic status: the same mood canonized Shakespeare. Several of Hamlin's and Jones's essayists show how thereafter, throughout the anglophone world, it is possible to hear echoes of the KJB, simply because it was so important in the basic education of anyone who spoke English. Consequently it still exerts a literary influence which may reflect as much hostility to the religious and political tenets which inspired it as it does reverence for the biblical message. In a variety of guises and moods, one can hear the KJB resonating in the work of Virginia Woolf, William Faulkner and Toni Morrison.

One of the most interesting and perceptive essayists for Hamlin and Jones is R. S. Sugirtharajah, even though his post-colonial scrutiny of the KJB takes surprisingly bitter sideswipes at a rather good recent history of 1611 by Adam Nicolson.[1] Sugirtharajah chronicles how successful a handmaid of empire the KJB proved; its unprecedentedly numerous usages of the word 'nation' as a translation for four different Hebrew words in the Old Testament helped to colour a new vision of Britishness as a nationality with a mission. He also points out what a malign effect supposedly authoritative KJB prose can have, when those formerly colonized by the British retain the simplistic attitudes to its message once peddled to them by the missionaries. Homophobic African bishops had better understand how colonialist they are being in their homophobia, when they accuse European and American Anglican liberals of colonialism or condescension on the subject of sexuality. Ironically, among many conservative Evangelicals in the USA, the KJB has lost its hegemony over the last half-century, as a welter of new translations have appeared, reflecting the diverging agendas of an American Evangelical Protestantism which was once given a certain unity by the cadences of 1611. This story is entertainingly and perceptively outlined by Paul Gutjahr, who takes us on a tour around Bibles rewritten for Busy Moms, Policemen, Extreme Teens, or any special interest group looking for spiritual guidance to suit itself, without the fatigue of having to listen to any of the Bible's multitude of alternative voices. I relish the prospect of opening the *Celebrate Recovery Bible*: it would be pleasing and appropriate if it beguiled its former addicts with the hallucinogenic art of William Blake – but somehow I doubt it.

In our own time, the KJB persists as no other book in its influence on English and English-speakers, mediating to one of the world's greatest language-families the myriad glimpses of God afforded to the ancient Israelites and to the first followers of Jesus Christ who sought to capture the puzzles, joys and drama of his brief earthly life. David Crystal's contribution to its commemoration is quirky and rather original in exploring this continuing background hum of Jacobean sacred text. A superior version of the literature which one helpfully shelves for the studious in the lavatory, this is prime material for enjoyable browsing, though it can produce a surfeit of pleasure if read cover to cover at a sitting. It represents the fruits of much labour, based on a clearly exhaustive journey straight through the KJB text, scrutinizing page after page for familiar phrases to pop up through the thees and thous. Crystal has subjected them to diligent Googling to locate their uses and perversions in English speakers' innumerable efforts at witticisms or arresting newspaper headlines. I do not intend criticism in mentioning the role of Google, for tracking down the ripples from these KJB fragments would hardly have been conceivable without modern search engines, and the exercise does have a serious point. What Crystal has done is to subject to quasi-statistical scrutiny that oft-repeated claim (which by the end of 2011 was even more oft-repeated) that 'No book has had greater influence on the English language' than the KJB. The influence is in fact uneven, being strongest from the more exciting bits of the Old Testament, principally Genesis and Exodus, plus Isaiah (a little help there from Handel's *Messiah*), then a fairly consistent run of the New Testament, which is still in modern anglophone conversation generally treated more reverently than the Old. The English, being Protestants, have not been much affected by the text of the KJB Apocrypha, and being in large numbers nominally C of E, they have looked to the Prayer Book (and so to Coverdale) as much as the KJB's update when they make reference to the Psalms. Thanks to Crystal, we can know, rather as Archbishop Ussher knew that the world had been created in 4004 BC, that there are 257 instances of the KJB being the most likely candidate to have created a phrase in current use in English, although the total reduces to eighteen if we look austerely for exact phrases from the KJB with no known source earlier than the KJB.

This figure of 257 is about three times that which can on similar principles be attributed to the works of Shakespeare, and it by no means exhausts the ramifications of English's still-intimate involvement with the 1611 text, which is knotted up with our love of incongruous verbal juxtapositions. Crystal directs us to the biblical parody song which gives him his title – 'Begat' from *Finian's Rainbow* (1947) – but he does not complete the joke in Adam's preliminary observation to Eve, 'The time has come to begin the begat': a cross-referential pun to Cole Porter's song of twelve years earlier, 'Begin the Beguine'. Crystal's treatment largely leaves aside sustained para-biblical texts – satires and squibs adopting KJB style. This genre can be traced back at least as far as a savage royalist summary narrative of the English Civil War published at the time of Charles I's execution in 1649, which opens 'The Booke of the Generation of JOHN PIM, the sonne of Judas, the sonne of Belzebub'.[2] Less polemical in intent is Brother Maynard's solemn reading from the *Book of Armaments*, which saves Monty Python's King Arthur from slaughter by the fearsome bunny-rabbit, as the text culminates in the vital information 'Once the number three, being the third number, be reached, then lobbest thou thy Holy Hand Grenade of Antioch towards thy foe, who being naughty in My sight, shall snuff it.' And Crystal, though not lacking either a sense of humour or an ability to call a spade a spade, spares us the need to blush at that para-biblical phrase 'Go forth and multiply', which over the last century has become a treasured part of English usage.

15

The Bay Psalm Book

It is the fate of much-loved and much-used books to be worn away in long service, and the first edition of *The Bay Psalm Book* exemplifies this: of around 1,700 copies in that first print run from Boston, Massachusetts, in 1640, we know of only eleven specimens surviving to the present day. The Bodleian Library's copy of this super-rare text, now faithfully published in facsimile,[1] probably owes its survival to having been removed from a sympathetic Puritan environment fairly early in its career, so it quickly became an object of interest rather than use. By the early eighteenth century, it had arrived in England and was in the possession of Thomas Tanner, an eminent Anglican Oxford don and antiquary who ended up as a bishop of the Church of England – a figure who would therefore have been anathema to the stern pioneers of New England, and who is unlikely ever to have attempted singing its rather rebarbative texts. The little book's present remarkably robust state is providential: after having evidently survived the watery rigours of an Atlantic crossing from the colonies, it was among a consignment of books tipped from a barge into the River Thames at Wallingford as Dr Tanner moved his library from Norwich to Oxford in 1731; the distraught scholar's bundles of rarities reputedly lay nearly a day under water. Its subsequent history has been less eventful, thanks to Tanner's generosity in bequeathing his collection to the Bodleian Library, and its state of textual perfection makes it an excellent candidate for facsimile.

The Bay Psalm Book lacks the aesthetic richness of the Gutenberg Bible or the Nuremberg Chronicle: it is for other reasons that the only copy released into the wild in modern times made an unprecedented price for a printed book when, in November 2013, it sold at auction at Sotheby's for $14.2 million, effortlessly outclassing the previous world record of $11.5 million for a much more obviously seductive volume, Audubon's *Birds of America*. This record-breaking edition achieves its unique status not by outward beauty but by being first: the first book printed in North America, in 1640. Its printer had in fact already created two printed texts the previous year: one an almanac, the other a printed form for swearing an oath as a freeman of the colony. But these texts were not books, and in any case they have had the good manners to disappear from sight altogether.

So *The Bay Psalm Book* stands triumphantly first – and it is proudly emblematic of everything that the first English-speaking colonies in America stood for, being a new translation of the 150 psalms of David for public worship. Scattered through initially tiny settlements over more than 500 miles of coastline, the colonies did not all speak with one voice, but from Church of England Virginia through Separatist Plymouth to 'Congregationalist' Boston, they were all variants on a Protestant theme: an English version of the great family of Reformed Protestant Churches which, back home in Europe, stretched from the Outer Hebrides to Transylvania. The Reformed were 'Reformed' because they were not Lutheran, a form of Christianity which they regarded with almost as much loathing as that of the pope in Rome, even though (or probably because) Lutherans also bore the name Protestant. The Reformed were united in their determination to worship God in purity, so (unlike Lutherans) they banned sacred images from their churches and gave a unique importance to the communal singing of the psalms of David.

Martin Luther was the first of many to create beautiful vernacular hymns for his version of the Protestant Reformation. From the 1530s onwards, the Reformed by contrast focused on singing David's poetry in metrical and rhyming form, first in French-speaking Europe, but soon in a multitude of different linguistic cultures. The French origins of this distinctive psalmody were reflected in its common name in English, 'Geneva Psalms', for it was in John Calvin's francophone Geneva that many psalm collections were compiled and printed, including some in English. Commonly one of the most popular collections, compiled by the early English Reformed Protestants Thomas Sternhold and John Hopkins, it was bound up with editions of the

Bible, particularly the unofficially authorized 'Geneva' Bible created in Calvin's stronghold by Englishmen fleeing the papist Queen Mary I. As the editors of the Psalm Book emphasize in their Preface, rhyming metrical verse was the natural mode for English people to use in the psalms, since that was the form of English poetry, and psalms were Hebrew poetry. Even at the time, others would have said that matters might not be that simple, but the *Bay Psalm* folk were not great admirers of religious nuance.

The Reformed were a European-wide family, but they were very good at family quarrels. The Church of England from which the North American colonists came had not satisfied all English Protestants, from the moment that Queen Elizabeth and her Parliament had given it form in 1559. Yes, it was Reformed Protestant in its statements of belief and in the theological outlook of nearly all the new clergy whom Elizabeth appointed to lead it, but it did not discard nearly enough of its idolatrous Roman past, in comparison with the 'best Reformed Churches' of mainland Europe such as those of Zürich or Geneva. One of the first causes for offence was precisely music. English congregations took up metrical psalms with relish, so that it would have been very rare to hear any other music in parish churches within a decade of Elizabeth's settlement. Yet there were English great churches which went on behaving musically and liturgically in a very different fashion: cathedrals (an institution surviving among European Reformed Churches only in England, Wales and Ireland) and a handful of similar special churches, chief of which were the queen's own private chapels. There, by contrast, music was sung by professional choirs, was much more elaborate and included intricate settings of the words of the Book of Common Prayer, itself far more prescriptive and detailed in its liturgy than many of the Reformed thought fit for public worship. In fact, the word 'liturgy' seems to have started its career in English with a sneer attached by its critics.

Such malcontents rapidly acquired the hostile nickname 'Puritans' from Protestants who did not share their frustration at Queen Elizabeth's Church settlement. Puritan grievances widened: as Elizabeth's bishops defended the settlement, some saw them as institutionally tainted and standing in the way of gospel purity, and they increasingly insisted that a godly Church should have no bishops. Reformed

Protestants being Reformed Protestants, they then bitterly disagreed as to what sort of government the Church should have instead. Some, sensationally, rejected a thousand years of tradition and said that Church government should have nothing to do with secular government, and that godly folk should separate their religious life from the magistrate altogether.

This potted history would have been in the heads of virtually all the English who crossed the Atlantic for the new colonies at the beginning of the seventeenth century. It would be naive to suppose that they all set out with the prime motive of worshipping in freedom: many sought the profits and new lives which Spaniards and Portuguese had made in the 'New World' over the previous century, and this was especially true in the southernmost colonies which gathered under the name Virginia. There the official Church was an undemonstrative version of the Established Church back in England, even accepting the authority of the Bishop of London, who was conveniently far distant from them. It was a different story for settlers who sought the northern colonies. They saw the early Stuart Church of England as too flawed to be truly God's Church. Often America was not their first choice when they looked for somewhere to build a purer community. Some migrated to the Protestant United Provinces of the Netherlands, others to Ireland, but neither refuge provided such possibilities of a wholly new start as the land which was christened New England.

Nevertheless, even when they arrived there, Puritan settlers were divided. The first colony in this northern region, Plymouth, in what later became part of Massachusetts, was founded in 1620 by separatists who made no bones about their wish to isolate themselves completely from corrupt English religion. This group, since the nineteenth century commonly given the celebratory title the 'Pilgrim Fathers', had first migrated as a single congregation to the Netherlands, but now they sought a less restricting place, to become a 'civill body politick, for our better ordering & preservation'.[2] For all its subsequent fame in American mythology, the settlement remained small and poor, for not many wished to join the Pilgrims; they made their brave voyage in the years before King Charles I allowed a new group of ceremonialist and Catholic-minded clergy around Bishop William Laud to achieve power in the English Church. Now, in the

1630s, things changed. Reformed Protestants felt unwelcome strangers in a Church which had once seemed a not altogether contemptible member of the Reformed family. Many gentry, clergy and ordinary people resolved to risk the long Atlantic voyage, though they had no inclination to religious separatism and despised the Plymouth experiment. Most sailed to New England and in 1630 founded a new colony sponsored by the Massachusetts Bay Company.

The Company's leaders were less socially prominent than in Virginia or more southerly English Caribbean enterprises, being mostly ministers and minor gentry; moreover they proposed to migrate to the colony themselves rather than stay in England. This was a measure of their commitment to starting England afresh overseas. From the beginning, they were a 'Commonwealth', whose government lay in the hands of the godly adult males who were the investors and colonists. John Winthrop, the first governor chosen by the investors, was an East Anglian gentleman of no great local standing who had survived financial and family crisis in the late 1620s – rather like another East Anglian gentleman, his contemporary, who stayed at home to make his mark, Oliver Cromwell. Winthrop's associates included a number of university-trained ministers ejected from or not prepared to serve in William Laud's Church, and as early as 1636 they founded a university college in Massachusetts to train up new clergy. Significantly, they placed the new college (soon named Harvard after an early benefactor) in a town named Cambridge – back in England over the previous century Cambridge University had been a much firmer centre of Reformation than Oxford.

The new colony contemptuously rejected England's Prayer Book, but they were not rejecting the idea of a Church establishment. The form assumed by the Church of Massachusetts was therefore the paradoxical one of an Established Reformed Church run by local assemblies of the self-selected godly – what John Cotton, one of the first ministers, called a 'Congregationalist' form of Church government.[3] Harvard's precocious foundation meant that Massachusetts was unique among the North American colonies in never being short of ministers to serve its parishes, and that made the task of establishing a single dominant Church all the easier. The clergy ministered to a federation of parishes made up of laity who were devotees of the religion of the book, possibly the most literate society then existing in the world. They felt as keenly as any godly congregations in the worldwide Reformed Protestant family that they must fulfil the hopes of a century of Reformation in the universal Church; they kept in close touch with like-minded congregations in England all through the century and beyond, and were very conscious of their international heritage. Cotton, for forty years minister first of Boston (England) and then of Boston (Massachusetts), was remembered as declaring with rather alarming relish, 'I love to sweeten my mouth with a piece of Calvin before I sleep.'[4] The great reformer of Geneva might have been surprised, but perhaps gratified, to hear himself likened to a toothbrush.

This fresh start of Reformed Protestantism in the New World was in itself an act of cleansing: one of the *Bay Psalm Book*'s recent historians, Dwight Bozeman, feels that the word 'primitivist' best describes its aspirations, going right back to the first generation of the Christian Church.[5] Nowhere would this be more true than in psalm-singing, a central component of Massachusetts worship alongside the minister's sermon and extempore prayer. The old psalm books of the tainted Church of England would not do, and there was no way that Boston was going to use the psalter used down the coast in Plymouth, created for separatist congregations by Henry Ainsworth before they had sailed to America. So within less than a decade, a new enterprise of translation began. The ministers came from a confident English scholarly culture which had just witnessed the best minds of Oxford and Cambridge and the wider Church create a new English Bible by committee, the 'King James' version of 1611. Now they would outdo King James by a much more literal rendering of the 150 psalms, as near as seventeenth-century Englishmen could get to King David's own performance of his sacred ditties. The effect is in its way as seamless as the text of the King James Bible, and we have nothing even as informative as the scrappy surviving committee papers of the Bible translators to give us clues as to which psalms were retranslated by the ministers Richard Mather, Thomas Welde or John Eliot, or the exact role of John Cotton, although some psalms are given in alternative translations which presumably come from different hands. The English Puritan poet Francis Quarles apparently sent over some psalm versions to

Winthrop and Cotton for the enterprise, but the respective psalms in the collection do not resound with his talent.[6]

The second task was to get the translations into print. This required the arrival of a printing press and someone to operate it. The agent was a minister who was joining his fellows in Massachusetts after refusing to make a public reading of that ungodly text, King James I's *Book of Sports*, in his Surrey parish church – Joseph or Josse Glover. From Cambridge (England) Glover recruited a locksmith, Stephen Day (1593/4–1668), to run the press, though, as he died on the voyage, the minister never saw Day operate it in the other Cambridge. Glover's widow married the president of Harvard, Henry Dunster, a year after the publication of the *Bay* Psalter, and henceforth the press was in the control of the College and the Church of the Commonwealth.

Stephen Day bore a proud Protestant printer's name, for John Daye (1521/2–84) had not only printed that archetypal work of English Protestant identity, Foxe's *Book of Martyrs*, but also one of the most influential psalters of the 1560s, which had come to be known as Daye's Psalter. Alas, if that echo influenced Mr Glover's choice of operator for his press, any evidence of a family link between the two printers is lacking, and Stephen Day's career does not suggest a deep-seated vocation for printing. Within a few years he diversified his activities into ironworks, mining and trading, and he became involved in legal action to get back some of his costs in printing the psalter (fortunately for us, for his complaints give us some precious details about the book's production). The Psalm Book itself does not evidence pre-existing skill or experience, for the printer's signatures for binding the pages in order are peppered with anomalies and inconsistencies, and the note of errors in the text on the last leaf rather charmingly encourages the reader to correct further slips 'as you finde them obvious'.

It is hardly surprising that Day did not try the even more difficult task of printing music for his psalms, even though they were intended for singing. We can see from a final note on the page facing the errata that he and his employers expected congregations to have some help on hand for this, such as the major collection of tunes in Thomas Ravenscroft's *The Whole Booke of Psalmes* (1621), or the various tunes 'in our english psalm books' at the back of their Geneva Bibles. This advice notably included recommendations to use tunes from that earlier collection for singing metrical versions of the Ten Commandments and Lord's Prayer, remarkably described in popish fashion as 'the Pater Noster'! For all its claims for primitive purity, the *Bay Psalm Book* was in its early days fated to remain in the debt of its imperfect predecessors.

The literary merits of the *Bay* Psalter have often been dismissed. Some psalms sound well enough in comparison with their predecessors. Take Psalm 148, where the translator has used the unusual metre which had then become traditional for this psalm, known to us from Samuel Crossman's lovely later poem 'My Song is Love Unknown'; it will go pleasingly, if anachronistically, with John Ireland's modern tune setting for that hymn. Admittedly, if one simply reads the texts aloud, many of the false measures and word inversions are grating. Psalm 23 is always a good sample test in biblical translation, and here it opens:

> The Lord to mee a shepheard is
> > want therefore shall not I.
> Hee in the folds of tender-grasse
> > doth cause mee downe to lie:
> To waters calme me gently leads
> > Restore my soule doth hee:
> he doth in paths of righteousness
> > for his names sake leade mee.

However, these texts were not meant to be read, but sung – and sung in a particular manner, very slowly, roared out by a congregation exalting in its common voice, taking comfort from communal purpose amid a wilderness and proud also of the distinctiveness and angular peculiarity of this text. The ministers told these Massachusetts Bay folk, rightly, that their texts had made a particular effort to get closer than earlier paraphrases to the meaning of the original Hebrew. The differences may not seem great enough to us to justify their condescension towards Sternhold, Hopkins and Ainsworth and their fellows, and just as in earlier versions, there are not a few useful particles like 'eke' and 'doth' thrown in to make up the metre. But to the pioneers of Massachusetts, this was the Psalter of 'the Bay', which made them what they were. Congregations in the Commonwealth went on using editions of it well into the eighteenth century, as did their fellow Congregationalists in England and Scotland (so it was America's earliest literary export). And it stood for a particular sacred aesthetic which was both quintessentially Reformed, and as North American as a Shaker chair, spelled out for the godly reader in its vigorously combative Preface:

> If therefore the verses are not always so smooth and elegant as some may desire or expect; let them consider that Gods altar needs not our polishing .... and soe [we] have attended Conscience rather than Elegance, fidelity rather than poetry, in translating the hebrew words into english language, and Davids poetry into english meetre.

Subsequent generations may confuse Massachusetts Puritans with Plymouth Pilgrim Fathers, but if they attend to the message of this book, they will understand much that lies at the origins of one of the world's great Protestant cultures, and may better comprehend its complicated and contested present and future.

PART III

Looking Back on the English Reformation

16
Putting the English Reformation on the Map

I had two agendas in mind in constructing this title. The first is the ongoing task of asserting that England did indeed have a Reformation in the sixteenth century. This might seem superfluous: after all, we have all heard of Henry VIII and his marital troubles, and we have all heard of bloody Mary and good Queen Bess defeating the Spanish Armada with a fine speech and a dose of English bad weather laid on by the Almighty. But the Church of England has over the last two centuries become increasingly adept at covering its tracks and concealing the fact that it springs from a Reformation which was Protestant in tooth and claw.[1] This labour of obfuscation began with the aim of showing that Anglicans were as good if not better Catholics than the followers of the pope. It then continued with the perhaps more worthy aim of finding a road back to unity with Rome, in the series of ecumenical discussions which began in 1970, known by the acronym ARCIC (Anglican-Roman Catholic International Commission). The participants in these discussions have not been anxious to emphasize difference, and very often they have fallen back on the Anglo-Catholic rewriting of English Church history pioneered by John Keble and John Henry Newman in the 1830s, as the Oxford Movement took shape. A good deal of my career has been spent trying to undo the Anglo-Catholic view of history, not because I think that Anglo-Catholics are bad people, but simply because within their ranks over a century and a half, there has been a troupe of historians who have been too clever for their own good.[2]

Yet even before the Anglo-Catholics turned their talents to rewriting the English Reformation, something strange had happened to the

Protestant Church of the Reformation in England. After the Restoration of Charles II in 1660 it became something distinctive, and whatever that was, was in the nineteenth century christened Anglicanism.[3] One of the fascinations of practising English Church history is to see how this unique Anglican synthesis of Western Christianity evolved, and how it relates to the Reformation which went before it. There are still areas within that map on which there are dragons and unknown territories. It has been one of the exciting experiences of my academic career to see Church history become once more a crowded area of exploration, where many young scholars without any confessional axes to grind feel that it is worthwhile to become familiar with the theological jargon and the agonies and ecstasies of early modern religion.

Perhaps after two decades of plugging away at this theme, I might feel (and others might feel still more strongly) that the point has been made, if not done to death. But then my second mapping task becomes important. So often, even those who were not inhibited in talking about a Reformation in England took up that peculiar English assumption that England is by definition different and special and that therefore, even if it did have a Reformation, an English Reformation could not have all that much to do with the noises off across the English Channel, let alone whatever noises filtered southwards over the border with Scotland or across the Irish Sea. This attitude is a reflection of that English habit of talking about the rest of Europe as 'the Continent', something which the English have even persuaded Americans to do, in a thoroughly illogical way. That will not do. England's Reformation was remarkably barren of original theologians, at least until the coming of that quietly wayward figure, Richard Hooker. The insularity of the English story might be said to begin with Hooker, and not just because of his own cooling attitudes to the Reformations of the rest of Europe. What is remarkable about Hooker was that none of his writings were translated into Latin. In other words, no one in any other European region could be bothered to read him, so Hooker was left languishing in that baffling and marginal European language, English (which, it must be said, is particularly baffling when Hooker writes it).[4] Otherwise, the flow of ideas in the Reformation seems at least at first sight to be a matter of imports from abroad, with an emphatically unfavourable English balance of payments.

If England had a Reformation, and an emphatically Protestant Reformation, and apparently it borrowed most of its ideas from elsewhere, what sort of Reformation was it? How should we relate it to the Reformations which sprang from Martin Luther's fury over indulgences in 1517 and Huldrych Zwingli's championing of Lenten sausage-eating in 1522? Can we apply labels like 'Lutheran' or 'Reformed' in an English context, and what might they mean here? When I was telling myself the story of the whole European Reformation so that I could write a big fat book on the subject, this issue was always on my mind, and it is that on which I propose to concentrate today – with just a few kicks at the twitching corpse of High Church Anglican history.

We will start our mapping in royal palaces: the Reformations of kings and queens both English and overseas. First, let us meet Henry VIII. Henry was a king fascinated by theology, because he was convinced that his crown brought him a unique relationship with God. God had put his family on the throne, even though (as Henry knew full well but would never admit) they had a remarkably weak claim by blood to be Kings of England. His father had won the Crown by God's favour in a battle at Bosworth in 1485. So it mattered what God thought of his actions, and all his life Henry was determined to get this right. His first instinct in the Reformation was that it was a blasphemy against God. He read Martin Luther, another man who felt he had a one-to-one relationship with God and was passionately determined to get the relationship right. Henry's reaction to Luther's encounter with God was, however, wholly negative, and expressed in his ghost-written *Assertio Septem Sacramentorum*, earning both papal gratitude and a riposte from Luther which was rightly taken as *lèse-majesté*.

Luther and Henry never laid aside their mutual loathing through their remaining quarter-century of life, particularly since Luther disapproved of Henry's repudiation of Catherine of Aragon with a good deal more genuine moral fervour than Pope Clement VII. Yet Henry was still the first king in Europe fully to declare against Rome; all those rulers who had previously done so were mere princes or city councils. Not even the newly minted King Gustav Vasa of

Sweden made such a clean break with the Holy See when he set up his untidy alliance with the Reformation from the late 1520s. Inevitably Henry must decide what this break had to do with the Reformations in progress in central Europe. There is much that is puzzling about the decisions which Henry made, and one can easily catalogue the puzzles.[5]

Henry VIII made his Reformation a complicated matter. His Church has often been called 'Catholicism without the Pope' – recent scholars have seen it more as 'Lutheranism without justification by faith', for the king never accepted this central doctrine of the Reformation.[6] Henry was part of the old religious world and the new. Throughout the king's reign, the Latin Mass remained in all its splendour and all his clergy had to remain celibate, as did the monks and nuns whose lives he had ruined. On the other hand, Henry ceased to pay much attention to the doctrine of purgatory, he destroyed all monasteries and nunneries in England and Wales (and, where he could, in Ireland), and he was positively proud of closing and destroying all the shrines in England and Wales.

It is worth seeing this mixture in a wider context, in a way that classically Anglican historians are rarely inclined to do. Several northern European monarchs were not necessarily enthused by Luther and Wittenberg, yet still made their own pick-and-mix Reformations, sometimes without breaking with Rome. I have already mentioned Gustav Vasa of Sweden, but an equally interesting case is the Elector of Brandenburg, Joachim II, who had a Lutheran brother-in-law but also a Catholic father-in-law, the King of Poland. Joachim's uncle was Luther's enemy, the indulgence-peddling Cardinal Albrecht of Mainz, so it is perhaps not surprising that the Elector had no excessive reverence for the old Church hierarchy. He took it upon himself to enact his own religious settlement for Brandenburg. He specifically declared the settlement to be temporary until there could be a general settlement throughout the Empire. The Elector made no break with Rome, but he confiscated much of the Church's lands and dissolved monasteries, just as Henry VIII was doing at the same time in England, and with almost as much lack of concern to reinvest his winnings in good causes.[7]

Equally interesting were the policies of Johann III, Duke of the

United Duchies of Jülich-Cleves-Berg. In 1532–3 he enacted a Church Ordinance without consulting his clergy, and yet equally without breaking with Rome. Johann's son succeeded as Wilhelm V in 1539: he was not only the brother-in-law of Luther's protector, the Elector of Saxony, but, more importantly for England, he was Anne of Cleves's brother. So the English political and religious leadership would be particularly aware of what was going on in Jülich-Cleves at the end of the 1530s, when for instance Henry VIII pushed a new doctrinal statement through Parliament, the Six Articles of 1539.[8] Just as in the changes in Cleves, these reaffirmed the traditional liturgical ceremonies of the Church, and yet they did not reverse any of the changes that had so far occurred in England.

Yet equally a keynote of the Cleves changes, as embodied in Duke Johann's 1532/3 *Kirchenordnung*, was that preaching should be based on scripture and the early Fathers and should be free of polemics. This was of course also the constant cliché of the Henrician Reformation. Many will be familiar with its encapsulation in the great pictorial title-page of the Great Bible of 1539, which shows Henry handing down the Bible to his grateful subjects, but historians have neglected an exactly contemporary artefact associated with the king. This was a literal witness to the Anne of Cleves marriage, and also a fascinating witness to the official mood on the eve of that disastrous marital adventure: the ceiling of the chapel of St James's Palace, installed at the time of Anne of Cleves's arrival in 1540. What is noticeable about this emphatic statement of Henry's religious policy is that the only motif apart from royal emblems and the initials of Anne of Cleves is the repeated motto *Verbum Dei* – 'the Word of God'. There is not a trace of any traditional Catholic symbolism.[9]

As always, Henry VIII managed to confuse his subjects about his views on the Bible. In 1543 he forced an Act through Parliament which overlooked King Canute's lesson to his courtiers and tried to limit Bible-reading on the basis of social hierarchy. It is not always remembered that, exactly at that time in Scotland, there was very similar legislation about Bible-reading in the Scottish Parliament, but this Scottish legislation was not restrictive but permissive in its effect. An Act of 1543 for the first time allowed lieges, that is landowners, to possess the Bible.[10] What we are seeing in Brandenburg, Jülich-Cleves,

England and the Scotland of 1543 is a whole series of attempts to find a 'middle way' – that phrase which meant so much to King Henry, let alone to others like Archbishop Cranmer who often radically disagreed with him as to precisely what it might mean.[11]

This was because Henry VIII's own personal Reformation was not the only Reformation on the map of Henry's England: there were at least two others. First, let us note the Reformation from below, which was also a Reformation before the Reformation – that of Lollardy. Without saying too much about the Lollards, I would reaffirm, against some of my colleagues, that in terms of the theological future of the Church of England, they mattered a great deal.[12] Admittedly Lollardy was never a unified force, and in the fifteenth and sixteenth centuries it was certainly not identical with the views of John Wyclif: given the way that it had been so effectively persecuted out of the universities and positions of power, that was hardly surprising. Nevertheless, on the eve of the Reformation, one can assemble an array of core beliefs which were common to most of those who would have thought of themselves (and who were recognized by neighbours and the old Church authorities) as having a distinctive and dissident identity or outlook within English religion: the identity which their detractors labelled Lollardy.[13] Equally, when a definite shape emerged for the Protestant Church of England's thought in the reign of Elizabeth, it had three major characteristics: a distrust of assertions of the real presence in the Eucharist, a deep animus against images and shrines, and a reassertion of the value of law and moral systems within the Reformation structure of salvation. All three points were also characteristic of mainstream early Tudor Lollardy, and all three clashed with Luther's style of Protestantism. I am not saying anything as silly or as simple as to assert that the English Reformation was home-grown, or nothing but Lollardy writ large. Nevertheless, the Lollard inheritance cannot be ignored when seeing the choices which the English Reformers now made, constrained as they were by the existence of Henry VIII and of competing Reformations on the other side of the North Sea.[14]

There was then yet another English Reformation: the programme sought and put into effect as far as they dared by the group of politicians and senior clergy who had been rallied by Queen Anne Boleyn,

Thomas Cromwell and Thomas Cranmer. I have labelled them evangelicals in previous writings, and I will not labour the point as to why I think this a better word than Protestant in the conditions of early Tudor England.[15] Thanks to Boleyn, Cromwell and Cranmer, there was something of an evangelical establishment in Church and royal court, with constant if precarious access to power from 1531 right up to the old king's death. This group started close to the beliefs of Martin Luther, because to begin with, as news of the Reformation filtered into England in the early 1520s, Luther seemed to be the only act in town. There were always anomalies, such as the marked hostility of the English evangelicals to imagery in church: that was apparent already in the 1530s when the evangelicals tortuously smuggled their views on various matters of doctrine into the Church's official doctrinal statements. They made sure that Henry VIII's Church renumbered the Ten Commandments in such a way as to stress the command against graven images, something which Luther did not do, any more than did the pope, but which had been newly revived in Zürich. It is too simple to see this momentous little change simply as a borrowing from the Swiss Reformation. It suggests the tug of a Lollard agenda already at work even on those who were now bishops and politicians.[16]

However, the Lutheranism of these establishment evangelicals remained strong on the vital matter of the Eucharist throughout the 1530s. It began weakening after a symbolic moment in 1540 when King Henry burned England's most prominent and self-conscious Lutheran spokesman, Robert Barnes – Barnes was one of the very few major magisterial Reformers to be executed anywhere in the European Reformation and, in one of history's great ironies, he was executed by the pope's chief enemy in Europe.[17] Now the future of England's Protestantism turned out to lie not with Wittenberg, but somewhere else. To find out where this future lay and what it turned out to be, we must meet some more European rulers trying to find a middle way.

One of the most important is Hermann von Wied, Archbishop of Cologne. After gradually moving from Roman obedience, von Wied tried to create an autonomous Protestant Church in the Lower Rhineland, but he was evicted by Charles V in 1546 after vigorous opposition to his plans from the canons of his own cathedral. Von Wied has often been casually characterized in English-speaking historiography as a Lutheran in his later years, but he did not at all conform to Lutheran doctrinal tramlines (particularly on the matter of images), and he became an inspiration for theologians who equally kept outside the Lutheran fold. One of them was his fellow archbishop, Thomas Cranmer, who seems to have kept in touch, even in von Wied's years of retirement in the 1550s.[18] Von Wied's proposals to reform the liturgy were highly influential on the construction of the Book of Common Prayer. He represented one possible future direction for the European Reformation, snuffed out on the mainland by the Holy Roman Emperor's action against him.

Besides von Wied, there is the story of the little imperial territory of East Friesland. This tiny corner of Europe has a disproportionate significance for the course of northern European Reformations in many ways, not least for the early Reformation in England. When its ruler Count Enno II died in 1540, he left his widow Anna von Oldenburg with three young sons. Countess Anna was a resourceful and cultured woman: she brushed aside opposition and assumed regency power on behalf of her children, planning to build them a secure and well-governed inheritance in East Friesland which might form the basis of greater things for the dynasty. It was not her fault that none of her sons proved her equal in capability or strategic vision. In politics she sought out alliances with rulers who, like herself, wanted to keep out of religious or diplomatic entanglements.[19]

In her own domestic religious policy, Countess Anna likewise sought to avoid total identification with either Lutherans or papalist Catholics, just as Henry VIII generally did after his break with Rome. When she began her efforts in East Friesland, she chose as principal pastor in her little port-capital at Emden an exotic and cosmopolitan figure from the Polish noble caste, Jan Łaski (usually known in his international travels as Johannes à Lasco by non-Polish Latin-speakers trying to get their tongues around Polish pronunciation). Łaski was a humanist scholar, friend and benefactor of Erasmus. When he broke with the old Church in the late 1530s, he remained an admirer of Archbishop von Wied of Cologne. Łaski was also in friendly contact with Swiss Reformers, and he had views on the Eucharist diametrically opposed to Luther – the sort of views which Cranmer was about to develop for himself in England. The remarkable career of this cosmopolitan Pole is a symbol of how effortlessly the non-Lutheran Reformation crossed cultural and linguistic boundaries. It is arguable that by the end of his life in 1560, he had become more influential in the geographical spread of Reformed Protestantism than John Calvin. The two men were in any case never soulmates.[20]

How might we label the theology which Łaski represented? In the 1540s it is anachronistic to call this movement Reformed Protestantism, though that is what it became. What we are seeing in these beginnings is the conscious creation (in a variety of different contexts and shapes) of what might be termed a 'third way', avoiding Wittenberg and Rome. In doing so, enthusiasts for a 'third way' were naturally drawn to various other great reforming centres, which in the 1540s meant Zürich, Basel and Strassburg. And it was this triangle which chiefly influenced what happened next in England, the decisive moment in shaping the actual structures of the English Reformation. No longer was Wittenberg the chief inspiration for England's evangelical religious changes.

In 1547 Henry's Reformation was swept away when his son Edward inherited the throne. Little legacy of that first Henrician Reformation remains in the Church of England with three very considerable exceptions: the break with Rome, the royal supremacy and the cathedrals which he had either preserved, refounded or founded for the first time (a matter to which this collection of essays of necessity frequently returns). Edward was the figurehead for the evangelical-minded clique of politicians both lay and clerical, including the now veteran evangelical Archbishop Cranmer as a prominent member. This clique, now freed from the watchful eye of the old king, immediately began accelerating religious changes.

All this was against the background of the subtle shift in theological stance among the English evangelical leadership which we have begun exploring. To recapitulate: in general in Henry VIII's time they had been broadly Lutheran in sympathy, mostly, for instance, continuing to accept the real presence in the Eucharist (one has to point out that this made their relations with the king a good deal less dangerous than otherwise might have been the case). Around the time of the old king's death in 1547, Archbishop Cranmer became convinced that Luther was wrong in affirming Eucharistic real presence. One might cynically call this a convenient moment to change his convictions, but we should never underestimate the psychological effect of suddenly being released from the hypnotic power of Henry's extraordinary personality.

The king's death came at a crucial moment in another way: a military and political disaster for central European Protestants. In 1547, Emperor Charles V defeated leading Protestant German princes in the Schmalkaldic Wars. England was suddenly poised to act as a refuge for prominent European Protestants – but not Lutherans – who generally either accepted the compromise imposed by the emperor or stayed and fought it (and each other) from comparatively safe refuges like Magdeburg. Accordingly, from late 1547 Cranmer welcomed to England many overseas Reformers displaced by the Catholic victories. The refugees whom he found most congenial were now non-Lutherans; indeed, some of the most important were from the then vanishing Reformation of Italy, which was for the most part now finding refuge in non-Lutheran strongholds, especially Zürich and Strassburg. Two of the refugees, the great Italian preacher Peter Martyr Vermigli and some time later the leader of the Strassburg Reformation Martin Bucer, were given the leading professorial chairs in Oxford and Cambridge respectively. In their wake came hundreds of lesser asylum-seekers.

In 1550 came a significant step: the official foundation of a London 'Stranger Church' intended to embrace all those various refugees, whatever their cultural or linguistic background. Its superintendent – in effect, its bishop – was none other than Jan Łaski, who had likewise eventually been forced out of East Friesland in the wake of the 'Interim' settlement imposed on the Holy Roman Empire by Charles V in 1548. The English government was anxious to use his leadership skills to curb religious radicalism among the refugees, so they gave him a handsome salary and one of the largest churches in the city, Austin Friars. Łaski administered his congregation to show how England might gain a pure Reformed Church (this was clearly the intention of several leading English politicians).[21] So Edward's Reformation was marked both by its awareness of being part of international Protestantism, and by its now open move towards the Churches which were consciously not Lutheran – those which would soon come to be called Reformed. The English break with Lutheranism was destined to be permanent. At the very end of Edward's reign, the English government tried to entice Philipp Melanchthon from Wittenberg to succeed Martin Bucer as Regius Professor at Cambridge. Indeed, they got to the point where they sent him his travel expenses and had set a date for him to arrive, in late June 1553 – but the young king's death intervened, and Melanchthon had enough warning so that he could quietly drop the whole idea (what happened to the English money is not clear). But it is unlikely that Melanchthon would have brought a Lutheran future with him to England. It is more probable that Cambridge would have proved the escape-route from hard-line Lutheranism which he sought for much of his career, and that he would have found a new home in Reformed Protestantism.[22]

Before this melancholy coda, the short reign of Edward VI had created many of the institutions of the Church of England which survive to the present day. Cranmer transformed the liturgy by masterminding two successive versions of a Prayer Book in English, the first in 1549. He was generally cautious in orchestrating the pace of change, and his caution was justified when a major rebellion in western England in summer 1549 targeted the religious revolution, specifically his first Prayer Book. Not just Catholics objected to the book: no one liked it. It was too full of traditional survivals for Protestants, and it was probably only ever intended to be a stopgap until Cranmer thought it safe to produce something more radical.[23] In dialogue with Peter Martyr and Martin Bucer, Cranmer produced a second Prayer Book in 1552 far more radical than that of 1549; the theology of the Eucharist which its liturgy expressed was close to the *Consensus Tigurinus*. The creation of the *Consensus* between Zürich and Geneva was a crucial moment in the European Reformation. It provided a rallying point for non-Lutherans and also a point of attack for hard-line Lutherans such as Joachim Westphal of Hamburg, thus making permanent the division between the Lutherans and the Reformed. When England aligned with the *Consensus Tigurinus*, it was clear that the English evangelical establishment was by now fully ready to reject openly conscious Lutheran stances in theology.

Cranmer also presided over the formulation of a statement of doctrine (the Forty-Two Articles) and the drafting of a complete revision of canon law. This scheme was a remarkable witness to Cranmer's vision of England as leader of Reformation throughout Europe: Peter Martyr and Łaski were both active members of the working party which drafted the law reform, even though Łaski had often been vocal in his disapproval of the slow pace at which England was implementing religious change. With this combination of authors, it is not surprising that the draft scheme of canon law was hostile to Lutheran belief on the Eucharist as well as to Roman Catholicism and to radical sectaries like Anabaptists.[24]

The canon law reform is admittedly one of the great might-have-beens of English history. It was defeated in Parliament out of sheer spite, because the secular politicians in the regime had fallen out badly with leading Protestant clergy, who accused them of plundering the Church, not for the sake of the Reformation but for themselves. So in spring 1553, the Duke of Northumberland blocked a procedural motion which would have extended the life of the law reform commission and would therefore have allowed its work to be considered for parliamentary enactment.[25] As a result, the carefully drafted scheme fell into oblivion – Elizabeth I never revived it when she restored Protestantism. In one of the great untidinesses of the Reformation, the Protestant Church courts of England went on using the pope's canon law. There was an effort to tidy it up fifty years later to remove its worst popish features, but the next great push did not come until the time of Archbishop Geoffrey Fisher in the 1950s. And crucially, the lost legislation had provided for the introduction of procedures for divorce. Because those provisions fell, the Church of England was left as the only Protestant Church in Europe not to make any provision for divorce – for no more elevated theological reasons than a politician's malice and Elizabethan inertia. This was the first respect in which the English Reformation diverged from the European-wide norm.

Let us lay aside the interval of Mary's reign, despite the major significance which historians now realize that it had for the Counter-Reformation throughout Europe.[26] We need to note only that Mary made her own vital contribution to the Protestant Reformation by restoring the heresy laws, and burning Cranmer and his various colleagues. That bitter experience became a central part of English consciousness in succeeding Protestant centuries. It tied Protestant England into an active and deeply felt anti-Catholicism which was the particular forte of Reformed Protestant Christians. If anything was the glue which fixed the kingdom into a Reformed Protestant rather than a Lutheran mould, this was it.

Those later centuries proved to be Protestant because Mary's greatest contribution to the English Reformation was to die after only five years. Yet never again did the kingdom of England play the captaining role which Cranmer had planned for it among the Reformed Churches, and that was thanks to the next queen on the throne, Mary's younger half-sister Elizabeth. Indeed, it is worth noting that the shape of the English Reformation was unique in Europe, because it owed so much to two women, Henry VIII's Queen Anne Boleyn and her daughter Queen Elizabeth. Mischievously, one might say it owed a good deal to a third, Queen Mary I, as well.

The young Queen Elizabeth was marked out in 1558 as a Protestant, not least because she was her mother's daughter. She faced a formidable array of Catholic power in Europe, and she had to make careful choices about how to structure the religion of her traumatized and rudderless kingdoms of England and Ireland. She did so in a Settlement steered through her Parliament in 1559, which has formed the basis of the Church of England (and therefore of worldwide Anglicanism) to the present day. It has been the subject of much argument, which is of course an argument about the nature of Anglicanism. In much traditional historical writing about English religion, the emphasis has been on the religious compromises which Elizabeth made in this 1559 religious Settlement. It would be more sensible to note how little compromise the queen made in swiftly and decisively setting up an unmistakeably Protestant regime in Westminster.

The new queen proved expert at making soothing noises to ambassadors from dangerous Catholic foreign powers, but few people could be deceived about the nature of her programme. There was no question of offering the Settlement for the inspection or approval of the overwhelmingly Catholic clerical assemblies, the Convocations of Canterbury and York. Its enactment in parliamentary legislation faced stiff opposition from the Catholic majority in the House of Lords.

This meant a delay in implementing it until April 1559, when two Catholic bishops were arrested on trumped-up charges, and the loss of their parliamentary votes resulted in a tiny majority for the government's bills in the Lords. It could be said that the 1559 Settlement was based on ruthless politicking and a complete disregard for the opinions of the senior clergy who were then in post. Revolutions usually cut corners, and this was a revolution, however much it was finessed.[27]

The shape of the resulting parliamentary Settlement was in fact a snapshot of Edward VI's Church as it had been in doctrine and liturgy in autumn 1552.[28] That meant bringing back the 1552 Prayer Book, not the 1549 Book, which enjoyed virtually no support from anyone, and which not even the queen attempted to revive.[29] The 1559 legislation made a number of small modifications in the 1552 Prayer Book and associated liturgical provisions, centring on liturgical dress and the Eucharist. Traditionally in Anglican history, these were called concessions to Catholics. That is absurd. How would these little verbal and visual adjustments mollify Catholic-minded clergy and laity, whom the Settlement simultaneously deprived of the Latin Mass, monasteries, chantries, shrines, guilds and a compulsorily celibate priesthood? Clearly they did have a purpose and significance: the alterations were probably aimed at conciliating Lutheran Protestants either at home or abroad. At home, Elizabeth had no way of knowing the theological temperature of her Protestant subjects in 1559, while over the North Sea, the Lutheran rulers of northern Europe were watching anxiously to see whether the new English regime would be as offensively Reformed as had been the government of Edward VI.[30] It was worthwhile for Elizabeth's government to throw the Lutherans a few theological scraps, and the change also chimed with the queen's personal inclination to Lutheran views on Eucharistic presence.

Nevertheless, the new Church of England was different in tone and style from the Edwardian Church. Edward's regime had wanted to lead militant international Protestantism in a forward-moving revolution. Many Edwardian leaders had gone into exile under Mary to parts of Europe where they saw such militant change in action, and they expected to carry on the good work now that God had given them the chance to come home. Elizabeth begged to differ. She took particular exception to returning exiles associated with Geneva: she excluded them from high office in the new Church, because she was furious with the Scottish Edwardian activist and Genevan enthusiast John Knox – he had written the famously titled *First Blast of the Trumpet against the Monstrous Regiment of Women*, claiming that it was unnatural (monstrous) for a woman to rule. Knox had intended it against Elizabeth's predecessor Mary, then found that, unfortunately, the arguments applied to Elizabeth as well.[31]

Elizabeth's own brand of Protestantism was peculiarly conservative. And in one respect, the new queen gathered around her like-minded people as she planned the religious future. Neither she nor any of her leading advisers (including her new Archbishop of Canterbury, Matthew Parker, and her first nominee for Archbishop of York, William May) had gone abroad under Mary. They had conformed outwardly to the traditional Catholic Church; in other words, they were what John Calvin sneeringly called 'Nicodemites' – like the cowardly Nicodemus, who only came to Jesus Christ under cover of darkness. Elizabeth and her advisers knew the specialized heroism of making choices about concealing opinions and compromising in dangerous times, rather than the luxury of proclaiming their convictions in unsullied purity. No other Protestant Church in Europe had such a beginning. It meant that the queen had a sympathy for traditionalist Catholics whose religious convictions she detested but who kept similarly quiet in her own Church.

Elizabeth was a subtle and reflective woman who had learnt about politics the hard way. She showed no enthusiasm for high-temperature religion, despite the private depth and quiet intensity of her own devotional life. Many of her Protestant subjects, including many of her bishops, found this extremely frustrating, particularly when it became clear in the 1560s that she would permit no change in the 1559 Settlement. There were idiosyncratic features of this Settlement which were randomly preserved in her fossilization of the Edwardian Church. Notable were the traditionally shaped threefold ministry of bishop, priest and deacon, together with the preservation of the devotional life and endowments of cathedrals. Neither at the time bore much ideological freight.

As far as the threefold ministry was concerned, Archbishop Cranmer had preserved separate ordination services for the three orders of ministry in constructing his Ordinal of 1550, despite advice to the contrary from his friend Martin Bucer, but it is difficult to discern in Cranmer any sense of apostolic succession of the ministry or any idea that ministers of God's word and sacraments differed materially from other servants of the Tudor monarchy.[32] On 17 December 1559, Matthew Parker was consecrated Archbishop of Canterbury by four colleagues in episcopal orders: William Barlow, John Scory, Miles Coverdale and John Hodgkin. These bishops represented a certain spectrum of Protestant theological perspectives, indicated by the interesting variety of clerical garments which they chose to don at various moments of the ceremony, but it is unlikely that anyone regarded any of the quartet as more significant than another: the common factor was that they had all been bishops in the reign of King Edward VI.

Victorian Anglo-Catholics became very excited by the fact that, back in 1536, Barlow had been consecrated under the pre-Reformation Catholic Ordinal, albeit after the Roman schism, and they devoted an inordinate amount of ink to investigating this, because of a frustrating lack of exact documentary corroboration of the original consecration (which certainly had taken place). It is likely that Barlow would have told them not to bother: it was not a matter which he would have regarded as of any importance in 1559. His ministry was validated by its discreet witness to evangelical reform under Henry VIII and its more ample exercise under Edward VI. Neither did anyone else make an issue of Barlow's consecration at the time, despite the bitter controversies between Catholics and Protestants which were already raging around Parker's consecration from the later years of Elizabeth I.[33] The notion of apostolic succession dependent on a line of bishops was not something which appealed to early Elizabethan bishops, although by the early seventeenth century the situation was changing, as we will see.

The other fossils from Edward's interrupted Reformation, the cathedrals, were particularly important in the unexpected developments of the English Church in subsequent generations. Cathedrals were a hangover from King Henry's Reformation which had no parallel anywhere else in Protestant Europe. Most northern European Protestant cathedrals survived (where they survived at all) simply as

1–3. The west-front of Bath Cathedral Priory, featuring Jacob's Ladder, commissioned by Oliver King, Bishop of Bath and Wells, *c.* 1500. With engaging literalism, some of its angels descend to earth headfirst, while others more fortunate ascend to heaven (see Ch. 2).

4. Lucas de Heere, 'Allegory of the Tudor Succession', *c.* 1572 (see Ch. 7).

5. A commemorative group portrait of delegates at the Somerset House Conference, 1604, by an unknown artist. Spanish delegates sit on the left, English on the right (see Ch. 12).

6. The opening of Psalm 1 in Henry VIII's Psalter, annotated by the King (see Ch. 8).

7. The Great Bible, authorized by Henry VIII. In this 1541 edition, the blank oval to the right represents the Stalinesque removal of Thomas Cromwell's heraldry after his execution; Archbishop Cranmer's arms opposite remain untouched (see Ch. 8).

8. Thomas Cranmer, *c.* 1545, in a portrait by Gerlach Flicke.

9. A portrait of Cranmer derived from Flicke, in Gilbert Burnet's *History of the Reformation* (1679–82).

10. A bearded Thomas Cranmer, *c.* 1550, at Lambeth Palace, by an unknown artist (see Ch. 19).

11. Cranmer at the stake, from John Foxe's *Rerum in ecclesia gestarum* (1559).

12. Henry VIII and his bishops (Cranmer, bearded, is centre left), from Christopher Lever's *History of the Defendors of the Catholique Faith* (1627) (see Ch. 19).

The Holy Bible

THE HISTORY
of the
REFORMATION
of the
Church of England
The Second Part

Bp. Ridley.   Bp. Latimer.   Arch. Bp. Cranmer.

Printed for Rich: Chiswell at the Rose and Crowne in St. Pauls Church yard.

13. Edward VI receiving communion paired with the Oxford Martyrs (unhistorically grouped together, and unhistorically observed by Queen Mary), on the title page of Burnet's *History of the Reformation* (see Ch. 19).

In Bib: Colmans
I got this
memorand on
the 6th of octor
1657

Part of Sr Henry Spelmey's Memoyers Anno
1554 1558 in Matters Ecclesiastical
touching reformation in the Church
of England

Anno 1679 Luthers writings spreading abroad and working on the
minds and hearts of subiets, in several Principalities
and Kings territoryes, King Henry the 8th in Case he
did not writt against Luther as some writters suppose he
did not, yett he furthered or owned that book Supposed
to be his, for which the Pope Anno 1521 Calld him
(fidei defensor) yett not withstanding all his honour
or Credit of Rome, within some few years after
uzt Annis, 1530, and 1531 he begun to fall from her
usurped Authority. Then Comparing of Records and
Searching into them, he found how his Predecessours had
bin lashed with Papal stripes, and How they had
drained the wealth of his Relmes and Confined of
same into their Romish Coffers. King Henry and
his Councell Argued together touching the title
(fidei defensor) Thomas Cranmore Arch Bishop
of Canterbury, Anno 1554, Shewed unto the Kings
Highness and his Councell the Historyes of Gildas
shewing the Antiquity of the Cristian faith in
the Realme of Britany Before Eluthrius his days
also other ould Cronacles and Historys shewing there
in how Eluthrias himself Confessed Lucius to be
Chief vicar within the Realme. Then saying if
these things were wrote before yr highness
Questioned the Bishop of Rome Authority, as your
Grace see they do, And that none hitherto have
Contradicted them, doubtless your highness have a
still the same prerogatives where upon they
were Confirmed by Parliament.

The Kings Highness about this time being resolved
to demolish the Abbyes prioryes and Monasteryes of
the Church of Rome within his Realm of England
The franciscan Monastry of London (with others)
being about this dayes to be dissolved the pryors
sent their agent unto yr Kings Highness to speak
in their Behalf, Intimating unto his Highness
what

14. Notices of Henry VIII's reign in Robert Ware's hand, with a marginal note for Bishop Jones to contact Gilbert Burnet (see Ch. 21).

big churches, sometimes retaining a rather vestigial chapter of canons in Lutheran territories. Why the English cathedrals were not dissolved like the monasteries is not clear, but it has a lot to do with the personal preferences of Queen Elizabeth. In any case, dissolved they were not, and that made the Church of England unique in the European Reformation. Within their walls, they made of Cranmer's Prayer Book something which he had not intended: it became the basis for a regular (ideally, daily) presentation of a liturgy in musical and ceremonial form.

Other than in the cathedrals, this choral exploitation of the Prayer Book was practised very rarely in Elizabethan and Jacobean England. It was to be found in Westminster Abbey and in Queen Elizabeth's Chapel Royal (plus the little brother of the Chapel Royal at Ludlow, headquarters of the Council in the Marches of Wales).[34] Otherwise only a minority of Oxbridge college chapels adopted this tradition, perhaps accompanied (and probably in attenuated form during Elizabeth's reign) by a small clutch of churches which had come through the Reformation still collegiate, through one or other accident of history. The parish churches of England, all 9,000 of them, would hear very little music at all, beyond the enormously popular congregationally sung metrical psalms created in the mid-Tudor period by a variety of hands: these were part of the great outpouring of metrical psalmody which was the common property of the European-wide Reformed Protestant family. That remained the case down to the late seventeenth century, and then the replacement psalmody collection of 1696, popularly known as 'Tate and Brady', only marginally extended the parochial musical repertoire, until the coming of Methodism set new standards of popular hymnody for its mother Church in the eighteenth century.[35]

The cathedrals, those great and glorious churches, were an ideological subversion of the Church of England as re-established in 1559. Otherwise it was Reformed Protestant in sympathy. If it was Catholic, it was Catholic in the same sense that John Calvin was Catholic, and up to the mid-seventeenth century it thought of itself as a part (although a slightly peculiar part) of the international Reformed Protestant family of churches, alongside the Netherlands, Geneva, the Rhineland, Scotland or Transylvania. It had long left Lutheranism behind. Lutherans had not helped their cause by some egregious examples of harassment of Protestant exiles from England in Mary's reign. For example, marked inhospitality had been shown in Scandinavia to Jan Łaski's Stranger Church exiles, and the little English exile congregation suffered expulsion from the town of Wesel in 1556 because of their Reformed Eucharistic beliefs: in the latter case, Switzerland offered the twice-exiled English from Wesel a safe refuge at Aarau, thanks to the good offices of the government of Bern. The Elizabethan episcopal hierarchy, so many of whom had themselves been Marian exiles, would not forget that Lutheran inhospitality.[36]

Back in the 1970s and 1980s, historians spent a lot of time arguing about whether there was a 'Calvinist consensus' in the Elizabethan Church.[37] That was a necessary debate which produced much fruitful thinking, but it was the wrong question to ask. John Calvin had virtually no effect on the Church of Edward VI: in no sense had it been Calvinist, although that description is still sometimes misleadingly found in textbooks. Cranmer, Łaski, Bullinger, Bucer and Martyr were the great names of that Edwardian Church, and Calvin's hour had not yet come; he was not well informed about affairs in England.[38] By 1558, however, times had changed. What about Elizabeth's Church of England? It was certainly a Reformed Protestant Church, and it was certainly also the case that Calvin's emergence on the English scene was important.

But we have to remember that Calvin never became a Reformed pope. The effect of his example and his writings was greatest in those Churches created during the popular upheavals of the 1560s – in Scotland, France and the Netherlands – as well as in the attempted Reformations by certain princes and civic corporations in Germany's 'Second Reformation' later in the century and into the following one. Even in such settings, the other great non-Lutheran Reformers were read and honoured, and their thought was influential. Everywhere there was nuance and eclecticism – a spectrum. Just as in England, everywhere in Europe Heinrich Bullinger, Peter Martyr, Jan Łaski and also Luther's former colleague Philipp Melanchthon had as much shaping effect as Calvin. What emerges from detailed scrutiny of the Elizabethan Church of England is a Church on this European-wide spectrum of Reformed Protestantism, with a tendency to sympathize with Zürich rather than with Geneva – where Bullinger's *Decades* were made compulsory reading for the less-educated clergy of the Province of Canterbury by Archbishop Whitgift, and where the sort of sacramental theology espoused in Geneva was regarded as rather over-sacramentalist by the majority of English divines.[39]

Then, around 1600, some English theologians, such as Richard Hooker, or his friend and admirer, Lancelot Andrewes, began questioning various aspects of the theological package which I have described. Hooker remained very individual in what he chose to criticize or defend, and it was Andrewes who was the chief shaper of the theological sea-change which now began taking shape in the English Church. Andrewes and his associates felt distressed by the Reformed assertion of predestination, and they listened sympathetically to the objections to it which were being vigorously voiced by self-consciously Lutheran theologians in Germany and Scandinavia.[40] As they formulated a new approach to the problem of grace and salvation, they began feeling that there must be more to God's sacramental gift of the Eucharist than the carefully balanced formulations of the Reformed theologians in the *Consensus Tigurinus*, and so they began to look again at how to describe the nature of Eucharistic presence. Often in parallel with their new thoughts on predestination, they initially took their cue from Lutheran writers on the real presence, though this explicit interest in Lutheranism gradually lessened among them and their successors: the name of Luther was too much part of the Reformation.[41] Unlike Luther, these English 'revisionists' began valuing bishops to the extent that they asserted episcopal government as the only divinely approved form of church government. They even valued cathedrals and their elaborate devotional life.[42]

All these ideas came together in what one might call a second revolutionary theology. This was a theology increasingly important to one party within the Church of England: those who have been variously labelled Arminians, Laudians, 'avant-garde conformists', call them what you will. In the early seventeenth century, that party, a sacramentalist, hierarchically minded party, gradually gained power in the Church, thanks in particular to some nimble political footwork on the part of Lancelot Andrewes, and a subsequent alliance with King Charles I.[43] The party eventually included the Archbishops of Canterbury and

York, William Laud and Richard Neile. In the seventeenth century, few of them were prepared to reject the word Protestant – that would be the achievement of the later Non-Jurors and the Oxford Movement – but the more mischievous of them were certainly prepared to borrow a Roman Catholic joke and call the Reformation a 'Deformation'.[44] In terms of the wider Reformation, they came to see their Church of England as more and more separate from the general story of the Reformations through the rest of the European continent, and so they anticipated the younger Pitt in deciding that it was time to roll up the map of Europe as far as English religion was concerned. Most telling was the campaign of conformity which Archbishop Laud waged in the 1630s against the Stranger Churches – those same Churches which under Jan Łaski had once been a template for a future Church of England.[45]

The immediate result was that many central theologians of the Reformed Protestant English tradition became increasingly unhappy and angry. The same anger motivated many during the 1630s to flee across the Atlantic, to form a true Church of England in New England.[46] One might argue that the subsequent history of the Church of England in the old country is an unpredictable deviation from this story – that the real story of the English Reformation was to be told in New England, and not in Lambeth Palace. That is one reason why, in order to understand the dynamic of the English Reformation, it is so important to keep an eye on a still wider map: the patterns which English people created when they travelled across the Atlantic. Even in southern American colonies like Virginia, the version of the episcopal Church of England which southern colonists had established by the end of the seventeenth century was not quite that which was to be found in the Old Country.[47]

The Church of England has never decisively settled the question of who owns its history, and therefore of what its colour might be on the world map of Christianity. Within it remain two worlds: one, the sacramental world of theologians like Lancelot Andrewes and William Laud, the world that still values real presence, bishops and beauty; and the other, the world of the Elizabethan Reformation, which rejects shrines and images, which rejects real presence, which values law and moral regulation based on both Old and New Testament precept.

These two worlds contend for mastery within English tradition, and they have created that fascinating dialogue about the sacred which the world calls Anglicanism. Long may the fight continue. It will be better for the sanity of the Anglican tradition if neither side manages to win.

17

The Latitude of the Church
of England

The word 'latitude' has a useful ambiguity, reflecting two tasks in this essay. One is to continue my efforts to place the pre-Restoration Church of England in its theological latitude in Protestant Europe up to the late seventeenth century.[1] The other is to note just how much latitude was possible within this structure, and to consider why that might be. On the first point, the historiography has been complicated by the battles of Church parties which started in the seventeenth century, the aim of which was very precisely to shift the latitude of the C of E. Sometimes the aim has been to tow the Church firmly into the latitude of sixteenth-century Geneva or seventeenth-century Boston. Sometimes the ship has been tugged into the Tiber and moored against the Trastevere bank within sight of the Vatican. A more generally popular course has been to head for a theological Bermuda Triangle and label the location 'Anglicanism', well out of reach of any foreign pollution and not susceptible to ready identification with any other 'ism'. The implication of this is that Anglicanism is *sui generis,* and that in some mysterious or mystical way this was the intention of the Tudor monarchs, churchmen and statesmen who founded it in the first place.

This Anglican latitude certainly does represent something essential and undeniable about the modern Church of England and its sister Churches of Wales, Scotland and Ireland and their worldwide offshoots; but the Anglican identity is extremely problematic if applied to the pre-1662 C of E. I have consistently discouraged students from using the word at all in that earlier context, though I still constantly notice the usage in places distressingly beyond my influence or control.[2]

It cannot be emphasized too often that the Anglican word is comparatively recent as a usage. It may well have been invented by King James VI of Scotland, and if so, it was meant as a term of abuse: in 1598, he assured a suspicious Church of Scotland that his proposed strengthening of episcopacy would not take Scotland down a path to 'papistical or Anglican' bishops.[3] After that, the word was hardly used at all until the nineteenth century, when it was found convenient for describing a Church now spreading throughout the world – in the case of the Protestant Episcopal Church of the United States and its missions, developing beyond the British Empire and therefore without the benefit of a Supreme Governor. As this sudden vast expansion of the Church was already taking place at a time of internal party strife, Anglicanism was a convenient concept to bridge the Church's theological divisions. For High Churchmen turning a wistful eye towards Roman Catholicism, it also had the convenient echo of a respectably antique movement of sturdy independence within the Catholic fold, Gallicanism. So, in a nice historical irony, the word Anglicanism took a new lease of life as a result of the American Revolution, just as Gallicanism was eviscerated by the French Revolution.

The prehistory of the 1559 Settlement which created the present-day Church of England lay in the reigns of Henry VIII and Edward VI. I have suggested elsewhere that in the actions of such monarchs as King Henry we are witnessing an effort to create a European 'third way' in religion which was neither in thrall to Luther or the pope.[4] The early English Reformation represents a march away from an initial Lutheran mould, at a much earlier stage than the same process in Scotland. There was more to what Alec Ryrie has termed 'the strange death of Lutheran England' than the familiar story of King Henry's mood-swings.[5] Thomas Cranmer, at the heart of the Henrician and Edwardian Reformations, was in close touch with Martin Bucer and the Strassburg Reformation as early as 1531, and any theological pundit worth his salt in the 1530s would have seen Strassburg as the future of any united Protestant Reformation. So Cranmer veered away from Luther towards Strassburg and therefore further south, towards the like-minded theologians of Zürich led by Heinrich Bullinger, on the important question of the admissibility of images in worship. This matter was reflected in the basic question of how one

numbers the Ten Commandments. Already in the *Bishops' Book* of
1537, the English Church was numbering the Commandments in the
manner of Strassburg and Zürich, to make a separate commandment
of the order to destroy images, in contrast to Luther's loyalty to the
Western Church's traditional numbering.

The other big divide among evangelicals was on the Eucharist.
Throughout Henry's life, England did remain officially aloof from the
Eucharistic theology of Strassburg and Switzerland, and not simply
because of King Henry's obstinate refusal to alter the liturgical form
of the Mass: establishment evangelicals like Cranmer were just as
committed to the defence of real Eucharistic presence as Luther or the
king, and in 1538 they even actively engineered the downfall and
eventual burning for heresy of their wayward colleague John Lambert, who had denied the real presence.[6] Yet even in the late 1530s,
there are interesting counter-indications. Between the years 1536 and
1538 successive young Englishmen, including young evangelical
Oxford dons from Magdalen College, travelled to Zürich, and in
return Heinrich Bullinger's foster-son Rudolph Gwalther paid a visit
to southern England and Oxford in 1537.[7] He never forgot his warm
welcome there, and it had consequences for the rest of the century, as
we will see.

Now it is clear that Cranmer was prominent in the actual organization of the initial visit to Zürich and he continued to take an interest
in the English 'exchange students'. But as I have looked closely at
those involved and their backgrounds, what has struck me forcibly is,
on the one hand, how few traceable links they had to Cranmer and his
Cambridge-educated clerical circle, and on the other, how many they
had to Thomas Cromwell and the court circle of the Greys, Mar-
quesses of Dorset. I suggest that while political proprieties dictated
that the clergyman Bullinger should deal with the clergyman Cranmer
rather than with politicians, Thomas Cromwell was the driving force
behind the Zürich initiative. During 1537 and 1538 Cranmer made it
clear that he strongly disapproved of the Eucharistic theology of his
Strassburg and Zürich contacts. That makes it all the more interesting
that Cromwell should be so heavily and consistently involved with
the English friends of Zürich, and it makes it all the more clear why
Henry VIII was prepared to listen to those who called Cromwell a

sacramentarian. Perhaps Cromwell's accusers were right, and Cromwell died for what Henry VIII would have considered the right reason. Cromwell has often been called a Lutheran; perhaps he was actually Zürich's best friend in Henry's England.[8]

The Eucharistic gap separating the English evangelical establishment from Strassburg and Zürich was abruptly reversed in 1546–7, when Cranmer and his circle jettisoned their views on the real presence. This may be explained by the liberating effect of Henry VIII's death,[9] but one must also take into account the devastating psychological effect on Cranmer, Latimer and others of the final round of vicious conservative heresy-hunting in spring and summer 1546, when they saw ever closer colleagues burned at the stake for denying the real presence. Real presence Eucharistic doctrine had sustained them even when they rejected transubstantiation as a way of explaining it, but now it must have seemed severely contaminated in what had become literally a fight to the death between traditionalists and evangelicals.[10] So, after 1547, on both images and the Eucharist, the two greatest points of distinction between Lutheran and non-Lutheran Protestants, those in charge of England's religious destiny, had made a decisive break with Wittenberg.

While Henry was the first monarch to break with the pope, and Edward VI's regimes undertook the largest-scale effort at Reformation so far in all Europe, their failures and imperfections ought to be perceived in that light; the same applies to the failures and imperfections of Mary's effort at Catholic Reformation. One essential aspect was the opening of Edwardian England to the possibility of international leadership of the Reformation: particularly after the crushing defeat of the Schmalkaldic League at Mühlberg in spring 1547, there was not much alternative to England. Hence the piecemeal relocation of many of the brightest stars in the Strassburg Reformation to England between 1547 and 1549 and the setting up of the London Stranger Church under Jan Łaski from 1550. Hence also the great caution with which the regime approached making any public statement about the nature of the Eucharist, until Heinrich Bullinger and John Calvin reached a satisfactory compromise in spring 1549 in the *Consensus Tigurinus*. For instance, there was no sermon on the Eucharist among the twelve Homilies issued in 1547, while the doctrines of justification and works were clearly and indeed classically set out in Reformation patterns. A Eucharistic homily promised in 1547 was not delivered until Elizabeth's reign, and Archbishop Cranmer delayed publishing his own extensive treatise on the Eucharist until 1550, when the *Consensus* had been safely agreed and published.

So the Edwardian Reformation was emphatically non-Lutheran: might it still be called simply part of a 'third way'? Such a mediate position became increasingly difficult in the early 1550s, when the fierce ultra-Lutheran attacks on the *Consensus Tigurinus* meant that increasingly one had to make a decision on the Eucharistic issue: Lutheran intransigence was creating a rival bloc, which soon had the label 'Reformed' wished on it. Theologians of the 'third way', who in the 1540s would have included such luminaries of Edwardian England as Martin Bucer, Peter Martyr Vermigli and Łaski, were now clearly part of the new confessional bloc, and their host country with them.

With Strassburg no longer a reforming centre, the chief alternative left was Zürich. English contacts with Zürich do not seem to have been close during the Protectorate of the Duke of Somerset, but when his colleagues overthrew him in autumn 1549, the new regime included the leaders of the Grey family, who had been so prominent in the Zürich exchange visits of the 1530s.[11] Bullinger became a good friend of the English Reformation, commending it as the best hope for convening a true General Council, and seeing it as a bulwark against Anabaptism: from 1550, he dedicated parts of his classic collection of sermons, the *Decades*, successively to King Edward and Henry Grey, Marquess of Dorset. Bullinger had already become a best-selling English author in the 1540s, although generally anonymously because of English versions of his treatise on marriage sponsored by Miles Coverdale.[12] By contrast, John Calvin had few close friends in Edwardian England and kept an obstinate attachment to the fortunes of the Duke of Somerset, a stance which became an embarrassment to those who knew England better.[13] An England ruled by Lady Jane Grey would have been an England increasingly tied in with far-distant Zürich, and far-distant Geneva would not have enjoyed much benefit.

That was a might-have-been, thanks not merely to Queen Jane's defeat by the Lady Mary in 1553, but by the rapid movement of the

Reformation in Europe as a whole over the next decade. Geneva's burning of Miguel Servetus in 1553 established Calvin as a theologian to be treated with respect throughout Protestant Europe. The caucus of English and Scottish exiles from Mary's regime in Geneva for the first time gave the Atlantic Isles a body of churchmen who had experienced Genevan systems at first hand. The extraordinary series of popular Protestant convulsions in the 1560s, which produced such great upheavals successively in Scotland, France and the Netherlands, looked to Geneva rather than Zürich. Zürich's European-wide influence began steadily diminishing at least in Western Europe, particularly in matters of church government, as embodied in the defeat of Zürich partisans in the debates sparked by Thomas Erastus about excommunication in the Palatinate from 1568.

And in the middle of it all was a Reformation established in England in 1559, with virtually no popular convulsion, but through the will of a monarch operating in close cooperation with a close-knit circle of advisers and a strong body of opinion in the secular political nation. Elizabeth created a settlement of religion on the basis of decisions made in negotiation between herself, her Privy Council, a small group of clergy and the House of Commons – obtaining not a whisker of consent from overwhelmingly hostile legislative bodies or the hierarchy of the English Church, and fighting past some formidable opposition in the House of Lords. Only when that opposition had been disposed of did the government activate newly purged Convocations of Canterbury and York to assent to Articles of Religion for the new Church in 1563.[14]

Elizabeth's Settlement of 1559–63 was the subject of much ingenious analysis in the nineteenth century by representatives of the Oxford Movement, analysis designed to obscure its true nature and impose an anachronistic version of 'Catholicity' on it. In fact the parliamentary package of 1559 did something quite simple: restore the structure and liturgy of the Edwardian Church to the point where Parliament had last been able to have a say in it, in other words autumn 1552 and the publication of the previous Prayer Book authorized by Parliament. There was a little tinkering: some small modifications were made to the Prayer Book designed to appeal to the ultra-sensitive Eucharistic antennae of Lutherans abroad and perhaps at home (there proved to be virtually none of the latter).[15] One clause of the Act of Uniformity about 'ornaments' restored the options in relation to clerical apparel which had prevailed in the first English Prayer Book of 1549.[16] No doubt this was intended to appeal to Lutherans equally, with their increasingly militant defence of much of the range of liturgical vestments. Despite its apparent authorization of the traditional chasuble as an alternative to the cope at the Eucharist, there is not a scrap of evidence that any clergyman of Elizabeth's Church habitually used the chasuble when using Cranmer's Book of Common Prayer, and even the use of the cope soon became distinctly suspect in English parishes.[17] Nevertheless, the ham-fisted wording of this clause proved a happy hunting-ground for Anglo-Catholics in the nineteenth century, supposedly allowing them to wear or use at pleasure any variety of liturgical garment or liturgical equipment which Rome had developed before or since.

So, in essence what was restored was a Reformed Church, but, it will be noted, a Reformed Church which in Edward's time had been developed in dialogue with theologians of Strassburg and Zürich, not of Geneva. By 1559 Strassburg was out of the picture, no longer a point of reference for Protestant Europe but an increasingly conventional part of the Lutheran world. Zürich stood firm in its theology, and its influence was now reinforced by its generous hospitality to a small group of exiled English clergy many of whom now became bishops in Elizabeth's Church of England. But before exploring the consequences of that, we need to note ways in which the atmosphere had changed even while the structures of Edward VI's Church were put back into place. First, the Edwardian Reformation had been a dynamic revolution, constantly moving on, constantly changing, modifying and then destroying more and more aspects of the religious past. The Elizabethan Settlement proved remarkably static in its structures, and thanks to the queen deliberately so: as Elizabeth's conservative favourite Sir Christopher Hatton said approvingly three decades after the 1559 legislation, the queen had at the beginning of her reign 'placed her Reformation as upon a square stone to remain constant'.[18] That meant that it was indeed a snapshot of Reformation at one moment in time – autumn 1552 – keeping everything that survived from the pre-Reformation past at that moment.

Most significant of such survivals were the cathedrals, with their unique position in England among European Protestant Churches. Nowhere else was there anything like the continuing life of the English cathedral close. Nothing of that seemed at the time of the Settlement to have much relevance to a Protestant Church. One illustration of that comes from the first English-language edition of Bishop Jewel's official defence or *Apology of the Church of England* published in 1564, which had an added appendix describing the structures of the Church to show how excellent they were. It is significant that the cathedrals were indeed given honourable and extended mention in this description, together with the collegiate churches of Westminster, Windsor, Eton and Winchester, but there was absolutely no mention of music in either case. The cathedrals on this account were centres of preaching and Eton and Winchester were centres of scholarship feeding the universities; a discreet veil was drawn over what the use of Westminster and Windsor might be.[19]

At the heart of this survival against the odds was Elizabeth's stubborn love of church choral music. She kept her choir in the Chapel Royal singing and her composers went on producing music of the finest quality, then the cathedrals were emboldened to follow suit as far as they could. This music had virtually no effect on musical and devotional life in the average English parish church down to the time of the Oxford Movement. So this was not so much a latitude of practice as a polarity, without parallel elsewhere in the Protestant world.[20] The preservation of the cathedral tradition had huge significance for the future of Anglicanism, and it may be Queen Elizabeth's chief original contribution to her Church. Elsewhere I have called the ethos which developed out of this the Westminster Movement, by deliberate analogy with the Oxford Movement. That is because it had much to do with the practice of Westminster Abbey, which behaved more like a cathedral than most cathedrals. The outlook was embodied in the conservative, ceremonialist and anti-Puritan outlooks of the dean, Gabriel Goodman, and the celebrated antiquary and headmaster of Westminster School, William Camden.[21] Admittedly, the new ethos also owed a very great deal to a churchman who only arrived in a Westminster prebendal stall in 1597 and then succeeded Goodman as dean in 1601 – Lancelot Andrewes. Already in the early 1590s,

Andrewes as Rector of St Giles Cripplegate was preaching views from the pulpit which would have sounded astonishing in virtually any other parochial pulpit in the kingdom. The texts in *Apospasmatia sacra*, eventually published in 1657, show a churchman steeped in the liturgical year, criticizing strict predestination and constantly emphasizing the celebration of the Eucharist.[22] Nicholas Tyacke has shown how Andrewes's campaign to change hearts and minds came to be reflected in his administration of his Cripplegate parish, particularly in its liturgical reordering at the end of the 1590s.[23]

Andrewes can be regarded as the first and most important ideologue of the movement which became Arminianism, and his transformation from an establishment Cambridge Reformed Protestant during the late 1580s remains as mysterious as the analogous, though not identical, shift in Richard Hooker at Oxford at much the same time. From the 1590s Andrewes proved to be the critic of Reformed Protestant soteriology with the most effectiveness and long-term influence; moreover, he was prepared to speak about predestination outside the universities when others would only speak inside their cordon sanitaire. The noisiest Cambridge anti-predestinarian, William Barrett, fell by the wayside, crushed by the hostile official reaction to his 1595 sermon, and subsequently became a convert to Rome; other anti-predestinarians kept quiet and waited for better times.[24]

Besides the new stasis of the 1559 Settlement, and its preservation of cathedrals, a further dimension to Elizabeth's Settlement differentiated it from the Edwardian Church. It was a settlement created by Nicodemites. Neither Elizabeth nor any of her leading advisers (including William Cecil and Nicholas Bacon, Matthew Parker, her first Archbishop of Canterbury, and William May, her first nominee for Archbishop of York) had gone abroad under Mary. Although unmistakeably Protestant by conviction, they had all conformed to Catholicism to a greater or lesser extent, even if some of them had covertly worked to help the Protestant cause, as was the case with Elizabeth's quiet political scheming and, as we now know, was also the case with Cecil.[25] Nicodemite, too, was Elizabeth's first Dean of the Chapel Royal, George Carew. The queen's remark, reported by Francis Bacon, that she did not seek to make windows into men's hearts, is often misquoted as referring to men's souls, and I wonder whether the difference is significant. The heart is not the seat of salvation as is the soul. It would not be inconsistent with Protestantism for the queen to care less about feelings or opinions than about salvation.[26]

We could simply regard Elizabeth as the last of the 'third way' monarchs of Europe, deliberately avoiding identification with either of the two great Protestant groupings which had emerged, and achieving uniqueness for herself and her Church by living so long, surviving such determined followers of a 'third way' as Countess Anna von Oldenburg of East Friesland or the veteran champion of non-aligned Reformation, Landgraf Philipp von Hessen.[27] But there may be something more about Queen Elizabeth, making for an official Settlement which enjoyed unusual latitude and showed itself distinctly cool towards forward Protestantism, and which provides at the very least another example of her lack of enthusiasm for opening casements on to the heart. It arises from her long-acknowledged personal contacts with members of that ultimate Nicodemite grouping, the Family of Love, that peculiar quietist and spiritualist sect which established a discreet foothold in Elizabethan elite life, just as it did in the Netherlands.

Great was the consternation in 1580 when some of the queen's Yeomen of the Guard turned out to be 'Familists' – adherents of the Family of Love. Puritans, familiar with the Familists' activities in East Anglia and leading the fight against them there, were enraged: Elizabeth did nothing to oust these personal servants. When in 1581 Puritans sponsored a bill in the Commons to punish the Family, it was quashed by a committee handpicked from among the Privy Council.[28] That was a stonewalling reaction with which Puritans were familiar from their other efforts to reform or extend the Elizabethan Settlement: as they well knew, such obstructions were directly thanks to the queen. Moreover, after a burst of publicity for their cause in a series of tracts during the 1570s, the English Familists went quiet from 1581 until a petition to James I in 1604. It is as if they had adhered to some sort of deal to fall silent until the old monarch was no longer around. There were still Familists among the court officials of her successor James I, including the keeper of the lions in the Tower of London.[29] All this does make one wonder about the queen's own private religious views, although a fascinating suggestion by David Wootton that she was the author of a French poem voicing Familist sentiments remains as yet controversial.[30]

If I were to name names further, I would also finger Dr Andrew Perne, Master of Peterhouse and Rector of the Cambridgeshire village Familist stronghold Balsham, as a major protector of the Familists. If you like conspiracy theories, Perne spent his last years at Lambeth Palace with his old friend and protégé Archbishop Whitgift, who, besides being accused by the muck-raking pseudonymous Puritan Martin Marprelate of having formerly been Perne's homosexual lover, was the patron of both Lancelot Andrewes and Richard Hooker.[31] Moreover, Perne was also patron of the French exile Peter Baro, who was the mentor of another notorious anti-predestinarian, William Barrett, and who was himself accused of Familism.[32] The Familists' constant emphasis on obedience would certainly be music to the ears of both Whitgift and his royal mistress. But all this may be considered to stretch the latitude of my speculations to *Da Vinci Code* levels.

The Family of Love were not the only anomalous adherents of Elizabeth's Church. Lancelot Andrewes did have one or two predecessors in openly opposing predestination, the most colourful and puzzling of whom was the Spanish exile Antonio del Corro. Del Corro was a rare example in England of a type more familiar in eastern Europe, a talented maverick theologian from Southern Europe, who had passed from the world of the Spanish *alumbrados* through evangelical leadership in France, then to something which did not at all fit conventional northern Protestant moulds.[33] This was a man who, as minister of the Spanish exile congregation in London in the late 1560s, was prepared to officiate at the burial of someone he knew to be a crypto-Jew, who was prepared to say that not only Jews but Turks could be saved, and who for some time in the early 1570s refused to join any congregation, refugee or parish. He then gained lecturing positions first in the Temple and then at Oxford, both of which were conveniently marginal and comfortably paid, and finally in 1582 won a prebend at St Paul's (for three years he was a colleague of Lancelot Andrewes there).

All this was despite the fact that, from at least 1570, Corro began openly attacking the doctrine of predestination, and that also by 1570

he had moved towards cautious but unmistakeable statements of unitarianism which put him on the same trajectory as the developing
Socinianism of eastern Europe, encouraged by similar Southern European refugees.[34] He was on at least one occasion accused, alongside
Whitgift's anti-predestinarian protégé Peter Baro, of being a member
of the Family of Love.[35] What is most baffling, and still needs to be
explained, is that Corro's chief patron in his stormy London and
Oxford career was the doyen of Puritan patrons, Robert, Earl of
Leicester. Leicester may have simply found it useful to have a Spaniard to deal with other Iberian refugees, notably the Portuguese
pretender Don Antonio, but if Corro was useful on those grounds, he
must have been very useful to make up for everything else.[36]

Corro also gained a good deal of support from William Cecil, and
more predictably later on, Sir Christopher Hatton.[37] He also addressed
one edition of his printed vindication of his views in 1570 as a New
Year's Gift to the queen, and he issued another edition with a dedication to her confidante, Lady Dorothy Stafford, wife of a former
Marian exile in Geneva – Calvin had been godfather to Lady Stafford's son, but there was no love lost between her and the great
Genevan reformer, and she might be expected to warm to a man who
relished a good scrap with partisans of Geneva. As Corro's biographer
comments of his two dedications, 'only a man convinced of the righteousness of his cause and sure of the support of powerful personages
in the realm could have done so with impunity'.[38] And William Barlow, son of one of the earliest evangelical English bishops, was not far
wrong when he commented in perplexity to the Zürich pastor Josiah
Simler in 1575 that Corro's presence in the English Church was one
of its mysteries 'which I cannot yet fathom'.[39]

So we have a Supreme Governor presiding rather uncomfortably
over a frozen tableau of her brother's Church, a Church officially
Reformed Protestant but not Genevan, with various remarkable
undercurrents permissible beneath her jealous but idiosyncratic gaze.
The Zürich flavour continued in the upper reaches of the Church
throughout the reign to an extent which has often not been fully
appreciated. Let us return to Queen Mary's death and Elizabeth's
accession in 1558. Several of the clergy exiled in Zürich became
bishops in major dioceses. Virtually all the leading former exiles kept

in close touch with Zürich. Interestingly, some former exiles also chose to join the circus of English correspondence with Zürich even though they had never met the Zürich leadership, notably Edmund Grindal and Richard Cox. Grindal's and Cox's initiative makes it all the more surprising that there is a complete silence from Matthew Parker, the first Elizabethan Archbishop of Canterbury. Parker was one of the clergy around the queen who had shared her experience of being a Nicodemite in Queen Mary's Church. Perhaps that made it more difficult for him to join those who had undergone the very different experience of exile in those testing years. Perhaps Zürich also felt the difficulty.

Any initial anxieties in Zürich about what Elizabeth might do with her Church were soon quelled: their main worries were either that there would be major concessions to traditionalist Catholics or a tilt towards the Lutherans. Neither materialized, and there was every reason to suppose that the imperfections already apparent in Edward's unfinished programme of reformation would be remedied over time.[40] That was as much the expectation of the newly appointed English bishops as it was of their friends in Zürich. Moreover, the Zürich leadership were aware of another circumstance about which they would necessarily have to be more reticent in public, but which might give them a certain private satisfaction: it was soon common knowledge that Queen Elizabeth was furious with the Genevan leadership because of their involuntary association with the ghastly faux pas of John Knox in 1558, his *First Blast of the Trumpet against the Monstrous Regiment of Women*. However much Geneva and Zürich might seek to cooperate, and however friendly relations might be between their leaders, there was now a discreet power struggle between the two great reforming cities for dominance in the Reformed world. In England, Geneva's embarrassment over Knox was Zürich's opportunity.[41] It is interesting that Bishop Jewel's *Apology*, such a classic defence of the Settlement as first conceived in the early 1560s, nowhere mentions Calvin: when it speaks of a rift within Protestantism, admittedly in an effort to minimize it to scornful papalist Catholics, the rift is presented as between Luther and Zwingli, despite the bitterness of the 'Supper-strife' between Calvin and Lutherans in the 1550s.[42]

In the next few years, Bullinger and Gwalther's tensions with Geneva inevitably affected their attitude to the developing disagreements in England, into which they found themselves being drawn by their former guests in exile. Friends of Zürich chosen as bishops gradually found themselves defending a static settlement in which they had little emotional investment.[43] The approval or disapproval of Zürich was a valuable prize for those involved in conflicts about the pace of reform, and so increasingly Zürich came to be a touchstone for measuring the imperfectly Reformed Church of England. It was a two-way process: the warring factions in England sought support from an honest broker, and that role suited Zürich very well in its continuing efforts to maintain its position among Reformed Churches.

Broadly speaking, Bullinger and Gwalther acted in the Elizabethan disputes as they had done in earlier clashes about how fast the English should make changes – in King Edward's reign involving John Hooper, and during the Marian exile, the English congregation in Frankfurt: they recommended further reformation, but they did not press uniformity on another Church, and they supported those placed in positions of authority by the civil power.[44] They were annoyed and embarrassed when a consortium of bishops at the height of their clash with Puritans in 1566 published an English translation of what the Zürich leadership had intended to remain private expressions of opinion to old friends. Yet they were even more annoyed when an angry young Puritan, George Withers, visited Zürich with Theodore Beza's backing, and so misrepresented the situation in England that the Zürich leadership wrote more strongly to their English friends than they later felt it warranted.[45]

Bullinger and Gwalther were all too conscious that that same young Puritan had intervened in the dispute over Thomas Erastus's views on excommunication in the Palatinate which ultimately represented a defeat for Zürich's ecclesiology at the hands of Geneva.[46] When they met Withers, they also met a variety of Reformed Protestants who rejected the model of ecclesiastical superintendency uniting such Reformed Churches as Zürich, England, Hungary and Transylvania. Such people also rejected the model of close union between the authority of the civil magistrate and the administration and discipline of the Church which, in very different settings and with very different origins, united England, Zürich and the advocacy of Thomas Erastus in Heidelberg.[47] So when Bullinger and Gwalther encountered English Puritans, they felt themselves drawn closer to the bishops of England, to whom they sent a steady stream of warm book dedications during the 1560s. And their ultimate seal of approval on England's polity in Church and State was Bullinger's vigorous riposte in 1571 to the papal bull excommunicating the queen, rapidly put into an English translation within a few months of its arrival in England.[48]

Ultimately the issue which made Bullinger and Gwalther support the English bishops was more profound simply than considerations of ecclesiastical politics. Bullinger's natural conservatism as a leader of Reformation was sealed from the 1550s by his fraught dealings with anti-Trinitarian radicals in eastern Europe, whom he saw as threatening all the Reformation's gains. In constructing their revisions of the Christology of the fourth and fifth centuries, the radicals maintained that whatever was not taught specifically in Holy Scripture should be repudiated. Bullinger and Zürich steadily maintained the opposite principle, that that which cannot be shown to contradict scripture may be retained even if it is not prescribed by scripture.[49]

By contrast to eastern Europe, few such radicals strayed to England – of course, one who did was the Earl of Leicester's Spanish exile protégé Antonio del Corro, and it was not surprising that when he wrote to Bullinger from London pleading for help against Calvinist attacks on his criticisms of predestination, he did not meet with a sympathetic hearing.[50] Instead, a different group on the English theological scene might be portrayed as raising an echo of Bullinger's foes in Hungary and Poland. The principle of the eastern anti-Trinitarians could with a certain justice be represented as that of Elizabethan Puritans on matters ranging from clerical dress to the office of a bishop; indeed, it could even be represented as that of John Hooper in his intransigence back in 1550. It was a very shrewd hit of Bishop Horne of Winchester when he wrote to Bullinger in 1573 that the English Church was in less danger from papists than from 'false brethren, who seem to be sliding into Anabaptism', by which he meant the Puritans. That provoked one of Bullinger's last interventions in English ecclesiastical politics before his death in 1575: in his reply to Horne he expressed his disapproval of disruptive behaviour from those 'that will seem most evangelical', and he reminisced ruefully about the beginnings of

Anabaptism in Zürich, back at the beginning of his long career in the 1520s.[51] In sixteenth-century terms, Puritans would feel that equating them with Anabaptists was the ultimate insult.

It is no accident that Bullinger's swansong letter to England was preserved and published in both Latin and an English translation in a polemical work against Puritanism by John Whitgift, the future Archbishop of Canterbury. Whitgift represents a third generation of leaders in the English Church who drew on the work of Heinrich Bullinger. The relationship in this generation was completely different from earlier days, or, to be more precise, non-existent. Whitgift never seems to have made any direct approach to the Zürich ministers, and his attitude to them might well be described as utilitarian. Take Whitgift's exploitation of Bullinger in his massive literary war with Thomas Cartwright, the so-called *Admonition* controversy in the years after 1572. Whitgift makes much use of the trope of equating Anabaptism with Puritanism, given colour by quotations from Bullinger's anti-radical writings, and otherwise he makes a good deal of fairly selective use of Bullinger (his tactical quotations of Calvin are necessarily even more selective). Bullinger is drafted in chiefly to illustrate Whitgift's favourite ecclesiological theme, 'I find no one certain and perfect kind of government prescribed or commanded in the scriptures to the church of Christ; which no doubt should have been done, if it had been a matter necessary unto the salvation of the church.' That was the essence of Whitgift's quarrel with the presbyterians, and it must be admitted that Bullinger would certainly have echoed the general sentiment.[52]

At this stage in the early 1570s, Whitgift made no use of Bullinger's *Decades,* which would certainly have provided him with similar material; yet only a few years later he became involved in an enterprise which posthumously naturalized the former Antistes of Zürich as one of the doyens of English theologians. Remarkably, Bullinger was now cast as the defender of England's episcopal system, and his *Decades* was to be a main bulwark of that defence.[53] This was the background to the first complete publication of the *Decades* in English in 1577. With that enterprise, once more we are taken back to Magdalen College Oxford and Gwalther's visit in 1537, for the moving spirit in promoting the *Decades* was an equally anti-Puritan colleague of Whitgift on the episcopal bench, Thomas Cooper, by now

Bishop of Lincoln, who had been associated with Magdalen since 1531.[54]

The Preface to the new complete English edition of the *Decades* places the work firmly on the side of the conformist bishops. It plunges quickly into a defence of the ministry as at present constituted in England, before remembering that one of the tasks of a translator's Preface is to praise the author. Even that manages to incorporate a sneer at the 'obscurity' of Calvin in comparison with Bullinger. And the most striking phrase in the Preface, one to infuriate any Puritan, is the justification for using the *Decades*: 'Better is a good sermon read than none at all.'[55] With this we have a major clue to the purpose of the new edition of the *Decades*. Turning the work to use as a clergy textbook, as was now ordered by Cooper and then other anti-Puritan bishops, Middleton of St David's and Chaderton of Chester, was to provide a means of clergy training and instruction to substitute for the structure of prophesyings, the gatherings which between 1574 and 1576 Queen Elizabeth had decided to suppress as unacceptably Puritan.[56]

There is irony here. The prophesyings now suppressed as the excesses of Puritan zealots were derived from the *Prophezei* of Zürich set up by Bullinger's predecessor Zwingli and so central to its clergy training. Grindal, who had made it his business to become an admiring correspondent of Bullinger even though they had never met, ruined his career defending the prophesyings, and he was not the only bishop from the exile generation who thoroughly approved of them in the face of Elizabeth's hostility. Now a new generation of bishops were exploiting the Antistes of Zürich in a way unthinkable in the days of Edward VI – but there was a certain logic in what they were doing, because their agenda was to combat Geneva's influence in the English Church: to create an alternative Reformed Protestantism which would owe little to Calvin or Beza. The confrontation between conformists and Puritans escalated through the 1580s.[57] Archbishop Whitgift's response to all this was twofold: he summoned up forces of repression, but he also took the positive step of canonizing Bullinger still further as the agent of improving clerical education. In 1586 the archbishop extended throughout the whole Province of Canterbury the order for lower clergy to read Bullinger's *Decades* and be examined on it.

The regular use of the *Decades* in this fashion says something important about the official Elizabethan Church, which distinguished it from the Arminianism which became part of the Church's identity in the next century. It was a Church still fully part of the Reformed Protestant world, and it was able to claim this identity because it drew on Bullinger as an alternative to Calvin and Beza. By canonizing the *Decades*, and getting their clergy to read this book as a statement of the Church of England's own theology, Cooper and Whitgift had still committed themselves to unmistakeably Reformed Protestant theological positions: they maintained a moderate and nuanced predestinarianism, they thought that there was nothing normative or universal about the institution of episcopacy, they saw the leading role of the civil magistrate in the Church as a positive virtue, and they maintained a spiritual presence view of the Eucharist within the broad latitude offered by the *Consensus Tigurinus*, firmly differentiated from confessional Lutheranism. The parallel canonization of the English translation of the adopted Züricher Peter Martyr Vermigli's *Common Places* had the same effect.

As late as 1600, therefore, the official Church of England was marching to rhythms partly set in Zürich between the 1530s and 1550s, even though much of its theological life was set in different patterns decided by Churches and theologians with a greater allegiance to Geneva and its heirs. England was not unique in this: later still, in the early seventeenth century, the Reformed Churches of Hungary and Transylvania were still troubled by tussles between the traditions of Zürich and Geneva.[58] That element of the ambiguity of English divinity, a tension within the Reformed Protestant tradition, has largely been forgotten in the concentration of later party strife in the great fault-lines between Arminians and anti-Arminians, Restoration conformity and Dissent, and Evangelicals and Anglo-Catholics. Undoubtedly the English future turned in other directions, set by Richard Hooker's *Of the Laws of Ecclesiastical Polity*. But even in Hooker, that delicate subverter of the Reformed tradition, the theologian of the Elizabethan Church who most resonates with the idiosyncrasies and strong opinions of Queen Elizabeth I, there is generous quotation from Bullinger, with rather more eclectic reference than Whitgift had made of him. Moreover, one can find emphases which Bullinger would have recognized and of which he would have approved: Hooker's emphatic affirmation of the place of the civil magistrate in the Church, his relativistic discussion of episcopacy and his maintenance of a Reformed view of the Eucharist, still firmly distanced from Lutherans – even his turning away from Calvinistic harshness on predestination would not raise eyebrows in Bullinger's Zürich. The *Ecclesiastical Polity* was much more in the spirit of the *Decades* than has often been realized.

As I have argued elsewhere, Hooker is too protean a figure to be appropriated as uncompromisingly as he later was by the Oxford Movement.[59] In an important and perceptive article, Mark Perrott has argued that the argumentative strategy against Puritans which distinguishes Hooker from his patron Whitgift is not merely his new stress on reason, but through it, an appeal to probability. Whitgift stressed obedience, and saw his Puritan opponents as perversely disobedient, showing themselves no better than Anabaptists. That is why he had used Bullinger as he did. Hooker shifted the ground to recognize that Puritans had genuine scruples of conscience, and he did his best to resolve them. In doing so, he made reason a foil for what he saw as an excessively scripturalist mentality.[60] If the judgement of reason is a major criterion of authority in deciding on matters of controversy, then 'of some things we may very well retaine an opinion that they are probable and not unlikely to be true as when we hold that men have their soules rather by creation then propagation, or that the mother of our Lorde lived alwaies in the state of virginitie as well after his birth as before'. Equally, Hooker could assert of some elements of the presbyterian case from scripture 'That some thinges which they maintaine, as far as some men can probably conjecture, do seeme to have bene out of scripture not absurdly gathered.'[61]

In this death by a thousand probabilities, so infuriating to modern journalists seeking snappy quotations from Anglican theologians, we glimpse the taproot of a tradition. Where might it have travelled next, as the Church of England experienced what Patrick Collinson saw as 'the greatest calamity ever visited upon [it]' – Archbishop Laud?[62] Certainly to William Chillingworth, a particular sort of fellow traveller with Laud and the Arminians. But I suggest that one of the most distinguished representatives of the tradition was Richard Baxter, friend and admirer of that most Elizabethan of Stuart churchmen, Archbishop Ussher, and himself once nearly a bishop at the hands of Charles II. Baxter was a man who, despite that offer, spent most of his career shunted off the main line of the Established Church after the Restoration Settlement, by what he called 'the new Prelatical Way', but he was proud to say of himself something that sounds remarkably like the comfortable confusion of modern mainstream Anglicanism: 'You could not (except a Catholick Christian) have truelier called me than an Episcopal-Presbyterian-Independent.'[63]

Baxter knew his Hooker. Like Hooker, logic and metaphysics were his favourite academic study, and consequently he read the medieval Schoolmen as attentively and perhaps more attentively than any Protestant Scholastic.[64] The consequence sounded like Hooker too: 'And yet, after all, I was glad of probabilities instead of full undoubted certainties.'[65] Baxter, so often seen as a doyen of late Puritanism, went so far as to quote Hooker writing against the classic Elizabethan Puritan Walter Travers: 'that whatever men may pretend, the subjective certainty cannot go beyond the objective evidence; for it is caused thereby as the print on the wax is caused by that on the seal'. Controverting the priorities of the signatories of the Westminster Confession, who followed the innovation of the 1615 Irish Articles among anglophone confessional statements in making the doctrine of scripture the starting-point of their text, he produced a personal hierarchy of certainties which would bear interesting comparison with Descartes: 'My certainty that I am a man is before my certainty that there is a God, for *Quod facit notum est magis notum*; my certainty that there is a God is greater than my certainty that he requireth love and holiness of his creature,' and so on.[66]

No one has ever said that Richard Baxter was a simple or easily defined character, but I would be prepared to try out one title on him. Reginald Askew, in an engagingly quirky series of essays on Bishop Jeremy Taylor, placed his hero among 'the last of the Anglicans'.[67] I would rather suggest that Taylor's ejected contemporary Richard Baxter was the first of the Anglicans. His problem was that the Restoration Church had altered its latitude in both senses in order to exclude the likes of him. It shifted its centre of gravity away from its particular brand of Reformed Protestantism to something more sacramental, and in one sense more insular. It had also destroyed the latitude which had made it possible for Lancelot Andrewes, Antonio del Corro, Elizabeth I and Walter Travers more or less to coexist in the same Church. Anglicanism has been asking questions about latitude ever since; but perhaps it has been hiding from some of the answers.

18

Modern Historians on the English Reformation

In 1971 and early 1972, as a final-year Cambridge undergraduate, I turned to the study of the English Reformation, under the able supervision of Felicity Heal, while attending the lectures of a wonderfully rackety and quirkily learned Fellow of Selwyn, the late and much-lamented patron of the Cambridge Footlights, Harry Porter. The course was entitled 'Thought and Religion in England 1500 to 1650', and it was fairly cutting-edge by the standards of its day: a genuine effort to reach across the divide then standard between the History and Divinity Faculties. It also tried to integrate England with mainland Europe – what in those days we would routinely call, with sublime and literal insularity, 'the Continent'.[1]

It helped that one of the great figures in Cambridge's Divinity Faculty was Gordon Rupp, a historian of the Reformation who had long taken seriously the integration of England's Reformation history with the rest of Europe, witness his little compilation of his essays in 1947, still well worth reading, *Studies in the Making of the English Protestant Tradition*. Indeed, it was perhaps a major factor in delaying an update in English Reformation studies that Rupp turned away from writing about the English Reformation after 1947. Rupp had wide-ranging interests which produced a perceptive study of Martin Luther's theology and a superb volume on English religion in the eighteenth century,[2] but there was one particularly important element in his broad vision: he was a Methodist minister, and thus existentially at one remove from the prevailing narrative of what the English Reformation had been about.

What was this hegemonic narrative? It was, of course, Anglican –

and not just Anglican, but High Church Anglican. There had once been a rival, the Evangelical Anglican hegemonic story, which could look back to the pioneering primary source research of two very clever seventeenth-century bishops, John Williams of Lincoln and York and Gilbert Burnet of Salisbury (Burnet being perhaps the greatest of Anglican historians), plus the decidedly less stellar but extremely hard-working perpetual curate of Low Leyton, Essex, John Strype. Williams, Burnet and Strype had created a narrative of the Reformation which was robust and actually resembled its reality.[3] But Victorian Evangelicals had largely abandoned their interest in high culture, which had once been considerable, and they shunned the 'Humanities' sector in higher education just as it was developing in the 1880s.[4] By and large, they had not concerned themselves with the newly established and godless History departments of late Victorian universities, or with university Theology departments which they would have regarded as even more pernicious in their teachings.

As a result, adherents of the Oxford Movement, or the wider world of Anglo-Catholicism, were dominant in the practice of religious history at university level, and they continued to be, well into the twentieth century. There is still a ghost of this in the undergraduate History syllabus of my own Theology Faculty. A theology undergraduate interested in Church history can study the Early Church, the medieval Church, the Reformation and the nineteenth century. Note no eighteenth century, so that you can't find out about the Enlightenment, at least if you want to be examined on it in Finals. The medieval Church has until recent years been a bit of an afterthought, so the three big beast periods are those which Anglicans have always been supposed to know about: the early Church, to study the Fathers on which Anglicanism likes to think itself as based; the nineteenth century, because that is when the Oxford Movement happened; and the Reformation, in order to wrestle with the embarrassment that the Reformation happened at all.

Anglo-Catholics found the English Reformation embarrassing or distasteful. Much of their research and analysis minimized its revolutionary character and stressed how different it was from the Reformation on the 'Continent'. Self-confident heirs of the Oxford Movement felt somewhat nonplussed when they were ushered into its company. Unaccountably it failed to share many of their passionately held beliefs, and yet it had created the Church of England in which their beliefs were now expressed and put into practice. Such historians played down, deplored or ignored the reign of Edward VI, the most obviously militant phase of change; they looked for 'Catholic' tendencies in the Elizabethan Settlement, and thereafter they saw the coming of Arminianism or Laudianism as a natural product of earlier, Tudor phases of a Church of the *via media*. They treated Puritans as outsiders to and opponents of the Established Church, closely allied with post-1662 'Dissent' or Nonconformity. It was a useful polemical strategy which a priori relegated the Puritans to the margins, doing their best up to 1642 to rock the boat from the inside, but leaving for the lifeboats after 1662, allowing 'Anglicanism' to sail serenely on its way.

The agenda for this was set in the mid-seventeenth century in the deeply polemical writings of Peter Heylyn, Archbishop Laud's chaplain. Heylyn's narrative was opposed vigorously (and I would judge, very successfully) by Gilbert Burnet, but it was continued by the Non-Juror historians of the late seventeenth and early eighteenth centuries, and it was then perpetuated by the Oxford Movement.[5] It can be encountered red in tooth and claw in the monumental work by Canon R. W. Dixon, *History of the Church of England from the Abolition of the Roman Jurisdiction* (6 volumes, 1884–1910), whose very title stressed a break with the medieval past which was jurisdictional rather than theological. The standard reference work to which I would have turned in my undergraduate years was the *Oxford Dictionary of the Christian Church*, edited by a canon of Christ Church, F. L. Cross. It was then in its first edition, published in 1957 but first conceived before the Second World War. That first edition well exemplified the Anglo-Catholic dominance of historiography, to the point of downright misrepresentation of the English Reformation: latterly, under the rigorous editorship of Dr Elizabeth Livingstone, its treatments of that subject steadily moved away from the initial emphases to more inclusive and balanced perspectives.[6]

In other words, at the end of the 1960s the English Reformation was still shackled by instrumental history: the story of the past told in order to justify the present. We have already recalled the work of

Gordon Rupp; it is more than coincidence that before the Second World War another Cambridge Methodist, Herbert Butterfield, had rumbled the same instrumental strategy more widely applied in English historiography, and called it the 'Whig' interpretation of history.[7] It may seem historically inept to align Anglo-Catholic historiography with Whiggery, an association which would have infuriated Tractarians fighting the Whigs in the 1830s, but the principle is the same: the past is used to justify the present, and to explain how it was inevitable that we got to where we are today. It is the historiography of a complacent Establishment in every age.

Still, much of the reading to which my undergraduate supervisor perfectly properly directed me in 1972 was from that tradition. I remember perhaps the least satisfactory essay which I produced for her, and the one which produced more tactful comments from her about its drawbacks than any other in the sequence, was one entitled 'What contribution did the first generation of English reformers make to Protestant theology?' I was frankly puzzled, as well as bored, by much of what I read, and I now realize that it was boring because it was not true. It was indeed making strenuous and elaborate efforts to avoid the truth. Among my reading was Clifford Dugmore's *The Mass and the English Reformers*, a misconceived work devoted to proving that Thomas Cranmer was not really a Protestant and that he, Ridley and the like were trying to synthesize the work of Catholics and Reformers.[8] At least I did not buy that theory even then. Another book which bored me a great deal was volume 1 of Horton Davies's *Worship and Theology in England*. Davies (1916–2005) was a Welsh Congregationalist, who spent most of his teaching career in the USA at Princeton. Despite this Reformed Protestant consciousness, in the first part of what eventually became a six-volume work, published only two years before I wrote my essay, he had apparently completely swallowed the Anglo-Catholic view of the English Reformation.

At the root of the problem with volume 1 was Davies's decision to describe a mainstream tradition in the Tudor Church as 'Anglican'. Davies never really explained where this tradition came from, except that it seemed to have emerged fully armed at the break with Rome in 1534. Thereafter it contended with a rival Protestant tradition which Davies described as 'Puritan', and these traditions appeared to be sufficiently identifiable as to warrant a detailed analysis listing their differences. Strange, then, that the sixteenth-century individuals who belonged particularly to the 'Anglican' tradition seemed so indeterminate. Thomas Cranmer appeared to be one of them at one point, but on the basis of a wholly misleading citation of his homilies;[9] otherwise, Anglicans in the flesh seemed suspiciously anonymous before Richard Hooker, and this first volume culminated in a case-study which enlisted in their ranks John Bruen of Stapleford Bruen (Cheshire) – 'a devout Anglican layman'. Bruen, the archetypal Puritan, who named his son Calvin, would have been baffled by this unwanted compliment, and furious if Davies had explained to him what it meant.

Earlier in the volume, a list of Elizabethan 'Anglican' preachers consisted of those elsewhere described as Calvinists and Puritans, which seemed rather to overturn the possibility of distinguishing Anglicanism in the sixteenth century.[10] Most remarkable was Davies's account of Thomas Cranmer's two Prayer Books, in which he described the first of 1549 as 'the norm' for the nature of Anglican worship.[11] It is odd that Davies should take as a norm a book which within three years was discarded and replaced by one which has survived barely modified at the centre of the Church of England's liturgy ever since.

Having shaken our heads in sorrow at volume 1, we can observe that Davies's volume 2 began unobtrusively to correct the balance. Dealing with the seventeenth rather than the sixteenth century, this was published in 1975 as the last in his sequence of five, and by 1975 he seemed to have picked up a change in the zeitgeist. A technical theological term which appeared to be quite important in the Eucharistic discussion of Book I, 'virtualism', occurred only once in the whole span of volume 2: a welcome absence, since it appears to have been invented by Victorian High Churchmen in order to make sixteenth-century Reformed Protestant Eucharistic thought sound more like their own.[12] Moreover, Davies's general framework of interpretation became less contentious or tendentious as it dealt with the aftermath of 1662, for there it represented realistically the great fault-line which opened up within English Protestantism between the Established Church and Dissent after the Restoration of Charles II. Davies was now describing the tradition from which he himself had sprung.

This characteristic of Davies's work conveniently illuminates a further instrumentalism in the traditional tale of the English Reformation. Alongside the Anglican narrative were other, parallel stories of the Reformation which were equally denominational, and which flanked it in triptych fashion. One was Roman Catholic, the other Free Church. To that extent, this triptych of independent religious historiographies paralleled the way that a very different variety of Reformation was taught in Germany and, indeed, with notable and honourable exceptions, often still is: in German historical writing on the Reformation, there is a Lutheran story, a Reformed story, a Catholic story, and the practitioners of those histories rarely cross the boundaries.[13] There is an institutional difference, however, between England and Germany: in Germany, each historiography can be practised in a university, in Theological Faculties established for Catholics or Protestants. In England, though not in Ireland, there have been virtually no university-level institutions or Theological Faculties specifically devoted to cultivating the non-Anglican stories. The exceptions were institutions significantly placed in institutional terms on the edge of the major universities: in the case of Oxford, the Permanent Private Halls, such as St Benet's Hall for the Benedictines, Mansfield for the Congregationalists, or Regent's Park for the Baptists.

Because of this, the Roman Catholic narrative, which had begun within the Established Church of Mary Tudor by the clients of Cardinal Pole and persisted through many trials ever since, was until very recent years sustained by writers outside the academy, like Cardinal Aidan Gasquet at the end of the nineteenth century. It was tribal history, particularly tribal when Gasquet lost the scholarly assistance of his very able literary collaborator Edmund Bishop, a convert from Anglicanism. The culmination of the tradition was the three-volume *The Reformation in England* by Fr Philip Hughes.[14] In many ways, this is a fine work of synthesis, based on a remarkable sweep of the available primary source material. I was directed in my 'Thought and Religion' course to the section in Hughes's second volume on Mary Tudor's England, and at the time this was undoubtedly the best account of the period available, looking past the traditional Protestant picture of it as failure twinned with cruelty and ineptitude. Hughes anticipated the picture of Marian England so ably delineated by Eamon Duffy in *The Stripping of the Altars* and *Fires of Faith*.[15] But you could not mistake it for anything other than history written by a Roman Catholic, with an apologetic aim: most notably, that section which I read and assiduously noted on Marian England.

The shining exception to this generally polemical character of Catholic historiography on the Reformation appeared in the same decade as Hughes's work: it was the great trilogy by David Knowles, which projected beyond his normal medieval field into the Reformation, in his magnificent *The Monastic Order in England*.[16] If anything, Knowles was not celebratory enough of early Tudor monasticism, famously suggesting that his readers might see his account as 'the description of a falling day and lengthening shades' after 'the splendours of the dawn and noonday'.[17] James Clark has shown us in recent years more life and creativity in the period than we had suspected.[18] But Knowles's willingness to criticize while retaining a deep empathy with his fellow regulars was a mark of the particular position of the man: a monk who had created a delicate distance between himself and his community life, and whose creative genius benefited accordingly.[19]

Like their Roman Catholic mirror-images, the Free Church narratives were largely tribal, speaking to their own various Free Church constituencies and telling them stories about themselves. It was significant that, after spending some years at Mansfield College Oxford, the Congregationalist Horton Davies found his eventual home for half a century in a great American university which did have an institutional Reformed Protestant tradition – Princeton. Often, in an unacknowledged collaboration with the High Church Anglicans, the Free Church historians, especially Presbyterians, Congregationalists and Baptists, annexed the story of Elizabethan and early Stuart Puritans to their own narratives. That was, of course, the strategy behind Horton Davies's narrative, which had led directly to his unholy collusion with the Anglican myth in volume 1 of his history. His book admittedly did illustrate something else more positive and admirable. Although often just as interested in structures and institutions as the Anglicans, Roman Catholics and Free Churchmen had something of a tendency to take investigations of historical theology more seriously; after all, it was their attention to theology which compelled them not to be Anglicans.

All this had begun to break down in the years when I was an under-graduate. The Ecumenical Movement and the relaxation around the Second Vatican Council had encouraged churchmen (they were then indeed practically all men) to talk to each other across the denomina-tional boundaries. There was a certain amount of comparing notes on denominational stories. Instrumentalist, tribal history might at least be questioned more, in the name of a new instrumentalism: breaking down the barriers – though actually the High Church Anglican hegemonic narrative was rather useful for these ecumenists since its aim had always been to minimize the differences between Rome and Canterbury. One of its strongholds has remained the history presented in ecumenical documents produced by the Anglican-Roman Catholic International Commission (ARCIC).[20]

But quite separate developments were beginning to impinge on the practice of Reformation history which had been building up else-where for decades. The focus of religious history had long been on national affairs, which had been reinforced in the nineteenth century by the new availability of primary source material concentrated mainly in London, the records of Westminster government and the antiquarian collections in the British Museum, exemplified for instance in the monumental collections published by J. S. Brewer and his successors as *Letters and Papers, Foreign and Domestic, of the reign of Henry VIII*. Only gradually during the twentieth century did it become clear that equally rich archival material lay in the provinces, as local record offices began to open: the first was in Bedfordshire in the 1920s, but it was followed by many more county record offices from the 1950s. Alongside the Bedfordshire initiative came stirrings in the universities: the establishment of a Research Fellowship in local history at Reading as early as 1908 (though it proved short-lived), while a full-scale department of local history at the University of Leicester opened in 1947.

Suddenly, what had for centuries been antiquarianism became some-thing else. But what? In 1950 G. M. Trevelyan, in a supremely patronizing retrospective on A. L. Rowse's best book *Tudor Cornwall*, saw local history as an apprenticeship for real historians; he 'believed that Mr A. L. Rowse had it in him to become an historian of high rank if he would lay aside lesser activities and bend himself to the production of history on the grand scale'.[21] I more than suspect that my own doctoral supervisor Sir Geoffrey Elton took a similar attitude to my doctoral project on Suffolk in 1973. That particular enterprise was given at least a certain respectability in his eyes because of the fact that I spent most of my time viewing Suffolk through the proper primary sources, in other words, those to be found in the Public Record Office, thanks to peculiar local poverties in my local county record office sources. In fact, one distinguished practitioner of local and indeed East Anglian history, Victor Morgan, tried to discourage me from trying Suffolk; he said that the sources simply weren't up to it.

Others were more fortunate than me as they sifted through what the local record offices were beginning to accumulate. The county archivists came just in time to save many country-house collections, which were then being dispersed, though virtually too late for my own choice of county, Suffolk. They gradually gathered in the parish records and lastly they acquired the diocesan and cathedral archives from previously rather possessive ecclesiastical custodians. It was these ecclesiastical records which turned local history into a serious investigation of the English Reformation: an alternative to the hegemonic narrative. In the year of my graduation, 1972, Felicity Heal, Claire Cross, Stephen Lander and their friends began turning local Reformation history into an industry led by an annual conference which was as central to the movement as the early Socialist Internationals were to Marxism: the Colloquium for Local Reformation Studies. Was it a coincidence that some of the giants in the land in those days were women, Dorothy Owen and Margaret Bowker in particular? Perhaps they were doing the history which the boys disdained.[22]

Nevertheless, the pioneer from the 1930s in such studies had been a man, and an Anglican too: A. G. Dickens. Dickens, despite an affection for High Church liturgy in later life, broke with the Anglo-Catholic consensus on the *Sonderweg* of England in the sixteenth century. With his deep love and first-hand knowledge of Germany, and his zest for the resources of the emerging local record offices, his perspective was both wider and more concentrated than the kingdom of England, as much international as local. While recognizing the crucial role of the Tudor monarchy in religious change, Dickens laid emphasis on the popular elements which worked alongside official change, and there was much for him to say in his classic textbook analysis of the mid-1960s, *The English Reformation*.[23] And so did Patrick Collinson, whose first major publication soon after that, *The Elizabethan Puritan Movement,* started to reposition the Puritans within the structures of the Established Church of England, and thus simultaneously struck a blow at the Anglican and Free Church narratives of the English Reformation. Once more, this new perspective was the work of an outsider to the English ecclesiastical establishment, a product of an astonishingly various experience of interdenominational English Free Church Protestantism, which Collinson lovingly recreated in his memoirs.[24]

One feature nevertheless remained constant within this brave new world of counties and dioceses: the new local history was resolutely uninterested in ideas. A. G. Dickens was perhaps a shining exception here, for as much as Gordon Rupp he was familiar with German Reformation history, where ideas were taken very seriously. But one does not find too many theological disputes even in Dickens's local work. For him as for others, the avoidance was to a great extent because of the sort of sources we used: they were primarily administrative or legal, and it was easy to be satisfied with the extraordinary wealth of new perspectives which this threw up. In my case, the avoidance of ideas was actively encouraged by Sir Geoffrey Elton, whose experience of the horrors of mid-twentieth-century Europe inspired by ideologies made him contemptuous of anything which could be classified as an ideology.

But given that the Reformation had been inspired by a big idea, this was a mistake, and the sources magnified the effect of that mistake. Administrators produce more paper on the subject of conflict and failure than they do on anything else, while legal papers are almost by definition the products of conflict and failure. This became the picture of the English Reformation which began emerging from the sources, most notably in the hugely influential picture of Lancashire painted by Christopher Haigh which was published in 1975.[25] This was a perspective which permeated my own first book on Tudor Suffolk in the mid-1980s. By then this stance had been christened 'revisionism', and no more so than in the collected essays which Haigh published with the significant title *The English Reformation Revised.*[26] A. G.

Dickens was not among the contributors. It became difficult to see why there had been a Reformation at all, given how few people seemed to have wanted it. The conclusion might be rather like that of the old Anglican and hegemonic narratives; it was all down to the Tudors wanting an institutional change, and getting their way, because the Tudors usually did.

A fresh ingredient to the mix of revisionism, which had not been a prominent feature of the first wave of local studies, was a newly assertive Roman Catholicism. That it was a separate ingredient is neatly demonstrated by the fact that the organizers of the Local Reformation Studies Colloquium seriously debated in the mid-1970s whether they should include researchers on recusant history among their invitees: their conclusion was in favour.[27] Now that Roman Catholics had moved into the centre of national life, not least into the centre of university history and theology departments, this was hardly surprising. J. J. Scarisbrick's Ford Lectures given in 1982 and published soon afterwards were a beautifully concentrated distillation of what the local historians had brought home from the fields, and a powerful affirmation of the vitality of late medieval English Catholicism.[28] To that would soon be added the works of Eamon Duffy, and so a trinity was born of Haigh, Scarisbrick and Duffy, names which soon tripped off sixth-form and undergraduate tongues as easily as an earlier generation might have spoken of Wilson, Keppel and Betty or Groucho, Chico and Harpo. These *hypostaseis* were never in as Chalcedonian a relationship as novices might fantasize; and we have all moved on over the decades, as historians do, constantly revising our revisions – we do not always destroy, but we always enrich. But these days we might not unquestioningly sign up to the famous formulation now two decades old, 'The English Reformation: a premature birth, a difficult labour and a sickly child' – maybe not even its author?[29]

So although local studies and revisionism did much to shift the interests of historians, local historians did not have the materials in their preferred primary sources to tackle the theological sleight of hand represented by the old hegemonic narratives exemplified in Dugmore and Davies. That work of theological revision was going on for a long time rather separately from the local history revolution, although one or two personalities had a foot in both camps. One lone voice early on in the 1960s could be heard in an incisive little study by Peter Newman Brooks on Cranmer's Eucharistic theology, which cut through much obfuscation to reveal three phases in his sacramental thinking, the last of which was unquestionably Reformed Protestant, after what amounted in the second phase to Lutheranism.[30] It is no coincidence that Brooks's first mentor was Gordon Rupp, who contributed a Foreword to the original edition (Pat Collinson did the honours for the second). After that, it was yet another student of Rupp, Peter Lake, who, through his doctoral work and subsequent publication of it, revealed that there were people in Elizabethan Cambridge who actually had a coherent theological position which was both Puritan and yet not determinedly subversive of the Church of England. Why should that have been a puzzle? The Church of England, despite many features of which these 'moderate Puritans' disapproved, was a Reformed Protestant Church to set alongside the Churches of Scotland, Geneva, the Northern Netherlands, Hungary or Poland.[31]

This was the dirty little secret which High Church Anglicans had been trying to hide since the time of Peter Heylyn. And it was that which had eluded me in my undergraduate essay on early English Protestants. I had spotted that they had not said anything especially original, but I had not yet been able to form a narrative of how their thoughts were being pulled away from an initial Lutheranism towards the Reformed, as part of the periphery of a wider Protestant story. And this process was not the work of John Calvin, but predated any influence he might have had.[32] So it became more and more apparent in the 1990s and 2000s that the word 'Calvinist' was nearly as redundant as 'Anglican' during the whole period of the English Reformation, and that the label 'Reformed Protestant' did the job much better.

And so Divinity Faculties and History Faculties began to talk to each other fruitfully about the Reformation; and English Faculties began doing so at much the same time. One could explore what that meant in terms of plays, poetry and prose, but I will pursue the theological theme.[33] I offer three crucial works of the new theological eye on the English Reformation which clinch the arguments I have laid out. One is the brilliant essay by my former student Alec Ryrie, 'The strange death of Lutheran England', which encapsulates the argument in the monograph based on his doctoral thesis.[34] A second is a superb account of the Reformed Protestantism of Transylvania by Graeme Murdock, which shows just how intimately enmeshed with the theology of early Stuart England the religious politics of that faraway place became. Who could forget the sad story of the eager Hungarian student who tried to use his Latin in the London docks to find his way to Cambridge University, and ended up not in *Cantabrigia* but in Canterbury? Nothing insular about him, or the university at which he eventually and ruefully arrived.[35]

The last exhibit is a beautifully forensic account of English Reformation Eucharistic theology by Bryan Spinks. By juxtaposing the soteriology and sacramental theology of Richard Hooker and William Perkins, Spinks not only underscores their common Reformed Protestant heritage, but he also makes the point that Perkins, the archetypal 'Puritan' in the Anglican hegemonic narrative, was more representative of the pre-Civil War Church of England than was Hooker. Spinks's last chapter describes the circumstances in which this order was reversed after 1660: then, a remodelled Hooker took his place in the subtly rewritten story of an Anglicanism which hardly existed before Charles II's Restoration. The agent of that particular realignment was the docufiction of Izaak Walton's 'Life of Hooker'.[36]

Yet Hooker's new role in the Church's historiography and identity was also part of a wider story, much of which we hardly suspected at all until recent years. The extraordinary comeback of an episcopal Church of England with a refurbished version of the Book of Common Prayer after 1660 was not just a matter of high politics, but was fuelled by a groundswell of popular support. Evidence for this lies in the steady build-up before the Civil Wars of a persistent affection for the Prayer Book, but even more surprising, during the Interregnum itself (as we now know thanks to the great digital project of the Church of England Clergy Database), there was a quite unexpected clandestine commitment by very many clergy to seek out the episcopal ordination which the Commonwealth's religious settlement had abrogated.[37] After that, the *Reformed* Church of England really did steadily become the *Anglican* Church of England, though it would have to wait until the nineteenth century before anyone unselfconsciously called it by that name.

So with this theological work added to the revolution in local studies, the stage was set for an overarching interpretation of the English Reformation which includes this new and more soundly evidenced Anglican historiography, and which could tritely be called post-Revisionist. It was significant that the Local Reformation Studies Colloquium has become simply the Reformation Studies Colloquium, and it was one of the main instigators of that conference who created the first extended statement in print of that new reality: Felicity Heal's volume in the Oxford History of the Christian Church, *Reformation in Britain and Ireland*.[38] What the local Reformation studies industry freed us to do was to get beyond the idea of the kingdom, still less the nation, as the only natural stage on which our investigations should take place, and go to stages both greater and smaller. We could indeed look at smaller units, as we had done from the 1960s. At first, we were probably too preoccupied with counties and dioceses (because those were the boundaries within which Tudor bureaucrats and judges worked and created archives), rather than thinking of the geographical or economic areas which actually shaped most people's lives. But we could also expand beyond one kingdom to think of larger units, and see how they interacted. So Heal's *Reformation in Britain and Ireland* took its title seriously and treated properly what I have termed, not without opposition, the 'Atlantic Isles' dimension. Regardless of the name, this is essential to understanding the dramatic changes of the sixteenth century. Scotland provides a Reformed Protestant Reformation in purer and more clearly articulated form than England, while Ireland affords the unique spectacle in Europe of a Counter-Reformation coming to fruition despite the efforts of the central government, an achievement of resistance more generally associated with Protestantism.

And then we can run kingdoms together, as the Stuart monarchs tried to do before us, to see what consequences might follow. I think particularly of Haigh's ground-breaking study of Tudor Lancashire, which book exemplifies the religious story for a region which remained peculiar in its religious practice in terms of the rest of England, not just in the sixteenth but into the twentieth century. What happens if we lay Lancashire not against what might be happening in Suffolk or Kent, but against its real neighbours, the Pale of Dublin and North

Wales? This was a region of sea coasts, bordering the Irish Sea, and that might have been as great a reality as any Tudor administrative units which sought to impose their will on these regions. Given the problems or opportunities of transport in the sixteenth century, it would have been less trouble in 1541, when the diocese of Chester was founded, to get from Chester to Dublin than from Chester to York. Do we see these three societies acting in similar ways? Yes, we do: three anglophone elites who mostly refused to accept the Reformation, to the largely impotent annoyance of the English government in Westminster. And we might think of ways in which we might try to reconstruct this society of the Irish Sea and test its foibles.

Here I draw your attention to another way in which that which was once merely antiquarian is now part of a newly holistic approach to the Reformation and what went before it. Now we are free to draw on the lessons of material culture. Andrew Spicer and Alexandra Walsham have made mainstream the study of parish churches and of sacred places, when before these were merely guilty pleasures for some of us. I think of my own youthful enthusiasm for monumental brasses and sepulchral monuments: I did sneak some references to them into my doctoral thesis, though I don't think that Sir Geoffrey approved. To start a line of enquiry on the society of the Irish Sea, I would note the enthusiasm for monumental brasses in lowland England, but also in Yorkshire; contrast that with their striking virtual absence in the Pale of Dublin and North Wales and their significant rarity in Lancashire. These regions commemorated their dead monumentally, certainly, but they did so in other mediums, some of which, such as the alabaster tombs of the English Midlands which can be found in Wales, would have been just as inconvenient to import there as the products of London marblers.[39] What other commonalities might we find in the region, once we start thinking in this lateral way?

Those of us who have explored the importance of material culture have also inevitably been drawn to absences, in other words, the vigorous efforts made in the Reformation to smash up other people's material culture. Here our patron saint is Margaret Aston, who first rescued iconoclasm from the misrepresentations in parish church guidebooks, which habitually presented it as perpetrated by a roving gang of mindless thugs called the Puritans, led by a thug called Oliver

Cromwell. Suddenly we found that bishops and churchwardens had done a lot of it after all. In many cases, the iconoclasts were far from mindless, but deliberately left fragments half-destroyed in their original place as 'monuments of . . . indignation and detestation against them': in other words, symbols of victory over the Catholic past.[40]

Even more dramatic symbols are abbey ruins, and one out of many complex reasons is that we still have abbey ruins from four centuries ago is that Protestants liked to keep them there to gloat. I think of a fascinating if adventurously speculative paper from Paul Everson and David Stocker on the building activity in Lincolnshire by Charles Brandon, Duke of Suffolk, a favourite of Henry VIII, who in 1537 set Brandon up as an informal lieutenant in that recently rebellious county. Brandon's grand new Lincolnshire houses contain some clear visual statements that he was a viceroy for Henry VIII's new religious dispensation, but Everson and Stocker note that at two of these houses at Kirkstead and Barlings, Brandon seems deliberately to have left substantial monastic ruins standing explicitly as ruins in the new ensemble – even as 'ruin gardens' – as a symbol of godly victory: an ideological statement which one could parallel in other Tudor rebuildings to provide great houses for gentlemen at Hailes Abbey (Glos.) and Newstead Abbey (Notts.).[41]

To return to that frequent theme in these essays, the Anglo-Catholic manipulation of the Church of England's past, I will point out for you a beautiful piece of applied Reformation archaeology by Niall Oakey, which shows that some of the biggest iconoclasts were Victorian Anglo-Catholics. Oakey took a sample set of counties to see exactly when medieval rood screens were destroyed in parish churches. It turned out that 30 to 40 per cent of surviving medieval screenwork disappeared in Norfolk churches during the nineteenth century, and no less than 40 to 50 per cent in Dorset. A high proportion of this was the work of Anglican High Churchmen who convinced themselves that their church 'restorations' were undoing the harm of the Reformation by concentrating the eyes of congregations on Eucharistic consecration at the high altar. How about that for the myth of the English Reformation?[42]

Felicity Heal was constrained by the plan of the Oxford History to end her story of the Reformations in the Atlantic Isles around 1600, and she was thus perforce unable to survey what it has become fashionable to see as a 'Long Reformation' stretching into the seventeenth or even the eighteenth century. Yet she was able to make a virtue of this necessity, arguing that by the end of the sixteenth century, after much variety, adjustment and growing self-definition, there was finally 'little cultural space' anywhere in the islands to be anything else but Romanist or Protestant, and so there is some point to making an end at this juncture.[43] This makes sense: 1600 was a watershed moment, a prelude to the greatest proof of the effectiveness of the English Reformation. When 1642 brought civil war to England, and Englishmen were prepared to fight and kill fellow Englishmen, it was not another War of the Roses, when Catholic had fought Catholic just to propel into power a different upper-class twit from the royal family tree. Now Protestant fought Protestant for the future shape of the Protestant Church in England, and to decide the most effective means of defending the realm from popery. That is the measure of how much the English Reformation was a howling success.

So one of the great results of half a century of development in Reformation Studies has been one of liberation, both to look closely and to look broadly. We have not forgotten or laid aside national stories, ours or others, but we also see the context of microcosm and macrocosm, region and continent. We have pluralized Reformations, as Christopher Haigh has taught us to do, in the interests of more intelligently discussing Reformation. We have identified urban Reformations and rural Reformations next door to each other, and seen their differences – and understood better how different Reformations link to each other. We have listened to humble people arguing about Reformation, tried to understand the objects and the landscape which they would have known. We have also remembered that clever people said significant things about Reformation, and were perfectly capable of getting across their messages to those without an Oxbridge education.[44] And we have tried above all to see the Reformation in its own terms and not what people in our own age would like it to have been. The end result is that Reformation history and religious history generally are taken much more seriously by other historians than they were fifty years ago – and that is something to celebrate.

19

Thomas Cranmer's Biographers

As the bonfire grew cold in Oxford's Broad Street on a wet March Saturday in 1556, two ghosts stepped out of the ashes: one a hero, the other a villain. They were both called Thomas Cranmer, and there have been sightings of their contrasting apparitions ever since. One would expect Roman Catholics who had just burned Archbishop Cranmer as a heretic to regard him as a villain. Equally, Reformation commentators should admire Cranmer's heroism. Yet surprisingly, the biographical perception of Thomas Cranmer is not merely a matter of Rome versus Canterbury. Cranmer's role is unexpectedly complex in the history of the Church of England: from hero and father-figure to someone often more like a villain – indeed, often no less than that. Even now, my own effort at biography, intended as part of the modern professional historical enterprise, has become a weapon of contention in ongoing religious debates.

Cranmer is ambiguous because the Church of the English Reformation has come to face in two opposite directions. Many members of that Church have wished to emphasize its links with the Reformations of mainland Europe, as Cranmer himself would have done. However, since the seventeenth century, as we have repeatedly seen in the essays in this book, others have become embarrassed by the Reformation, asserted the Catholic continuity of the post-Reformation English Church with the institutional Church placed there before, and sought to downplay the level of traumatic change which took place. The dialogue between these two poles has produced Anglicanism, which has come to take pride in a theological position in Western Christianity capable of being a 'middle way'.

The earliest biography of Cranmer, probably conceived within a few hours of his death, began the villain narrative: *Bishop Cranmer's Recantacyons* by Cardinal Pole's Archdeacon of Canterbury and diocesan official Nicholas Harpsfield.[1] Written in Latin for an international audience, it effectively invents a new genre, anti-martyrology: its purpose, as in other works of Harpsfield, was to shift the confusing narrative of Cranmer's last months towards his discredit, and make it difficult for Harpsfield's Protestant contemporaries to add him to the growing toll of their Marian martyrs.[2] In pursuit of this agenda, Harpsfield first used the famous story that Cranmer carried his German wife around in a box, which he repeated in subsequent writings, and later became a favourite in the villain-narrative of Cranmer – 'like a huckster he carried his wares in secret, so that at each separation, a box was at hand with the luggage'.[3] This later needed refutation from writers in the hero-narrative tradition.[4] In Harpsfield's English work *A treatise on the pretended divorce*, he not only amplifies the tale of Mrs Cranmer's box, but casts Cranmer as the evil genius behind the dissolution of the monasteries, an aspect of Henry VIII's policy with which in reality he had remarkably little involvement. By contrast, Harpsfield hardly mentions the undoubted *éminence grise* of the dissolution, Thomas Cromwell.[5]

Harpsfield's works had great influence on the English recusant community – particularly important was the transmission of his outlook through younger and much livelier Elizabethan propagandists, Nicholas Sander and the Jesuit Robert Parsons. He set the tone for his portrayal all through subsequent Roman Catholic historiography of the English Reformation. Catholic commentators delighted in pointing up Cranmer's inconsistencies: Bossuet, for instance, commenting on Bishop Burnet's history of the Reformation (of which more below), pithily described 'A Lutheran, a married man, a concealer of his marriage, an archbishop according to the Roman Pontifical subject to the Pope, whose power he detested in his heart, saying Mass which he did not believe in, and giving power to say it.'[6] The abuse was updated to the latest symbol of repulsiveness. So the late seventeenth-century Oxford don and Catholic convert Abraham Woodhead gave Cranmer the chief blame for the religious changes of Edward VI's reign, 'who for flattery, lust, inconstancy, ingratitude, treason, and most damnable Hobbism, utterly pernicious to the being of a Church, deserves the invectives and execrations of all Posterity'.[7] In taking up the Hobbist theme, Woodhead in fact borrowed from another Catholic convert, the formerly Protestant Dean of Derry, Peter Manby, who said that Cranmer had emulated (or rather anticipated) 'the spirit of Hobbes of Malmesbury' in diminishing the status and authority of the Catholic Church.[8]

Not surprisingly, no Roman Catholic bothered to write the life of so odious a figure for three centuries; it was enough to let him take his place in the devilish story of English Protestantism generally.[9] In 1931 the awesomely prolific Hilaire Belloc created a full-scale biography of Cranmer (but he also ran to biographies of Oliver Cromwell, Danton and Robespierre). Belloc still stands in a tradition recognizably descended from Harpsfield, but he is to some extent shackled by his main source of information, the then recently published major biography of Cranmer by A. F. Pollard, which he rather unfairly says 'treats of Cranmer as a "Hero of the Reformation"'.[10] Perhaps as a result his work is a reasonably subtle performance, ending just as Cranmer is dying in the flames, without any further comment or moralizing (Pollard had done the same thing). Belloc, who genuinely admired Cranmer's liturgical prose, could even afford to write more in sorrow than in anger; in a shorter study of Cranmer he expressed a certain personal regret that the Catholic Church authorities had seen fit to persist in burning Cranmer after he had produced written recantations.[11] We need say little more about the post-Harpsfield Roman Catholic villain-narrative of the archbishop; but we have not left Cranmer the villain behind.

Naturally Protestants quickly sought to establish an alternative hero tradition to Harpsfield. The earliest effort in this tradition, possibly written by one of Cranmer's former estate officials, Dr Stephen Nevinson, concentrates on Cranmer's coming to his archbishopric under Henry VIII, his part in the Lady Jane fiasco, his imprisonment by Mary and then the events of his last day on earth – in other words, the areas of Cranmer's career most vulnerable to being successfully presented in a negative fashion.[12] Its manuscript is now to be found in the working papers of the great codifier of the Church of England's martyr tradition, John Foxe. Foxe already used it in the first Latin version of his work published at Basel in 1559, well known from its first English edition of 1563 as Foxe's *Book of Martyrs*. That was a book which Nicholas Harpsfield devoted much of his energy to criticizing and belittling, often to some effect.[13]

In his 1559 work, Foxe actually made Cranmer's martyrdom the culmination of his main text. In subsequent expansions and rearrangements, he added much first-hand material deriving from Cranmer's secretary Ralph Morice, mainly in the section forming a large-scale biography of the archbishop. This was placed in Foxe's customary arrangement under the year of Cranmer's martyrdom, and its general shape was decided in his 1563 revision.[14] Such a long and complicated story as Cranmer's needed careful managing. Foxe decided to subdivide his account into three, the threefold nature being accurately described in its title, 'The life, state, and storie of the Reuerend Pastour and Prelate, Thomas Cranmer Archbishop of Caunterburie, Martyr'. The 'life' element was an 'early life' prelude, before Cranmer became archbishop (much indebted to 'Nevinson'); the third part, the 'storie', was of course the story of the martyrdom, much extended to Cranmer's arrest, trial and death under Mary from 1553. However, that left much to tell from Cranmer's twenty active years as archbishop, that is his 'state' or 'estate'; some of this tale was difficult. Like 'Nevinson' before him, Foxe decided to say virtually nothing about Cranmer's activities under King Edward at this point; Cranmer featured in generous measure in other parts of Foxe's book, but the good things the archbishop had done for the Edwardian Reformation could here almost be taken for granted. All Foxe included was a relatively brief reference to Cranmer's Edwardian writings against the Mass, neutralizing Foxe's admission both here and elsewhere that the archbishop had earlier held unsound Lutheran-style views on the real presence in the Eucharist.[15] That was all that was said before dealing with the Lady Jane Grey episode and Cranmer's Marian troubles, so Edwardian Cranmer formed the prelude to the 'storie'.

Now, for the bulk of the 'state' came the considerable problem of Cranmer's activities under Henry VIII, much of which consisted of collaborating with the old king's often deplorably conservative agenda. How could this be turned into something edifying? Foxe made a bold and creative counter-stroke against his difficulty: he turned much of Cranmer's rather confusing and nuanced career as Henry VIII's archbishop into a paradigm for the perfect apostolic bishop or Reformed Church leader. He used the checklist to be found in Paul's first Epistle to Timothy (3:2–7) and his Epistle to Titus (1:7–9), describing the character demanded of a bishop, and arranging miscellaneous anecdotes of Cranmer's life under the headings which he constructed from successive verses in Titus to throw the best light possible on them. Thus was the 'state' element of 'life, state, and storie' made manageable. As always, Foxe was torn between telling an exemplary tale and facing up to documents and evidence, so he put a suitable health warning on his exercise: 'which exemplare it shall be harde in these straunge daies to finde the image of any Bishop correspondent; yet for example sake let us take thys Archbishop of Canterburie, and trie him by the rule thereof, to see either howe neere hee commeth to the description of S. Paule; or else howe farre off he swarveth from the common course of other in hys time, of his calling'.[16]

So Cranmer was given a head start. He lived in bad times and could take whatever credit his actions permitted for being less like his unsatisfactory contemporaries on the episcopal bench and more like St Paul's ideal. The heading derived from Titus 1:7, 'a Bishop ought not to be stubberne', shows how this might work. Here Foxe gratefully fitted in a brief account of Cranmer's less than stubborn capitulation to the infamous Six Articles, emphasizing his 'humble behavioure in woordes towardes hys Prince', while pointing out the protests which Cranmer had undoubtedly made, and the heavy pressure from heavyweight politicians to which he had been subjected. He then immediately jumped to a quick reminder that in the end Cranmer had suffered a 'bitter death in the fire', before turning back to a small and historically slightly confused fragment of Cranmer's Edwardian career, his resistance to the Edwardian government's proposals to dissolve chantries.

This might seem to an impartial reader an example of stubbornness (although certainly an example of unsuccessful resistance, since the chantries had indeed been dissolved), but Foxe turned it to reinforce the positive message from Cranmer's conduct around the Six Articles. In 1539, the archbishop had capitulated to the Articles to be loyal to his prince, but in this second instance he had also tried to block the dissolution measure to demonstrate his loyalty. He had said, according to Foxe, that action on the chantries should wait for Edward VI to attain his legal majority, so that the king could fully benefit from the financial windfall. Of these contrasting instances, Foxe drew a moral accentuating the positive in both cases: 'So deare was to him the cause of God, and of hys Prince, that for the one he would not keepe his conscience clogged, nor for the other lurke or hide his head.' The reader might be forgiven for trying to work out which virtue applied to which authority, or wondering whether these were the most important lessons to be learned from Foxe's two examples. However, in a final balanced judgement, Foxe regained his poise and his clarity: he not only gave Cranmer full marks on the particular Pauline criterion, but also pointed out the downside: 'he was altogether voide of the vice of stubbernnesse, and rather culpable of over muche facilitie and gentlenesse'.[17]

Foxe's life of Cranmer shared in the success of his great work. His topos of taking the criteria for episcopal ministry in the Epistles to Timothy and Titus was imitated in biographical celebrations of various seventeenth-century bishops and ministers – mostly less problematic subjects than Cranmer.[18] Foxe's work was European in effect, taking its place in its 1559 Latin version alongside the classic Reformed martyrologies of Jean Crespin and Adrian Haemstaede. One commentator, Henry Pantaleon, indeed felt compelled to complete Foxe's 1559 *Commentarii* with a second volume of examples from mainland Europe entitled *Martyrum historia*, published in Basel only four years later explicitly as 'pars secunda' of Foxe.[19] Even by themselves, in their 1559 Latin, Foxe's English tales inspired overseas readers who saw the English martyrs' troubles as their own; there was a German translation of Cranmer's story in 1561 by Augustinus Jonas.[20] More far flung still was the inspiration which Foxe's account of Cranmer gave to the Hungarian Reformed Protestant churchman, humanist and poet Mihály Sztárai. After a perusal of Foxe in his 1559 Latin version, only a year after its publication in Basel, Sztárai was inspired to write a Hungarian narrative poem celebrating the life and martyrdom of Cranmer; this was eventually published posthumously in Debrecen in 1582.[21] Clearly this was an attempt to use a heroic example from far-away England to inspire the Hungarian Protestant Church which was taking institutional shape in the 1560s: this developing Church owed a great deal to the reformers of Switzerland. Foxe's book had travelled very quickly from Basel to the ravaged plains of Ottoman-occupied Hungary, where the population knew a great deal about martyrdom.

Foxe's essay in its various editions was so influential that it also proved the last large-scale life of Cranmer until the late seventeenth century, and for a century English Protestant comment on Cranmer was really a comment on Foxe's biography. Foxe's only rival in print was a substantial contemporary life of Cranmer, also produced as part of a much larger-scale but very different enterprise: Archbishop Matthew Parker's *De antiquitate Britannicae ecclesiae* of 1572. Parker had known Cranmer well, much better than had Foxe, and he used an overlapping but distinct range of sources in writing that were equally a celebration of a leading hero of the Reformation. However, the emphasis was different, because Parker placed his admiring life of Cranmer sixty-eighth in a biographical sequence of sixty-nine Arch-bishops of Canterbury right back to Augustine. Himself the seventieth archbishop, Parker saw God's struggle with Antichrist during Cran-mer's time in primarily institutional terms: indeed, before introducing Cranmer's birth and education, he wrote a long account of the royal manoeuvres leading to the break with Rome, Henry VIII's marriage to Anne Boleyn, and the birth of Elizabeth I. He also followed his bio-graphy with the life of Cranmer's nemesis Cardinal Pole as sixty-ninth archbishop, and even tried to be fair to the cardinal despite Pole's part in Cranmer's destruction.

This historical scrupulousness did Parker's work no favours with the reading public, especially since *De antiquitate* was in elegant humanist Latin rather than Foxe's colourful English.[22] Parker's work was damagingly ridiculed in print two years after its publication. A Puritan surreptitiously obtained and pirated an English translation of Parker's own Latin autobiography intended to form the seventieth essay in his sequence: the editor (probably the sprightly lawyer John Stubbs, later deprived of his right hand for denouncing Queen Eliza-beth's marriage plans) sarcastically annotated his edition of Parker's autobiographical essay and followed it by a lengthy denunciation of the unfortunate archbishop and his history of popish bishops, dis-missed as 'a legend off Canterbury tales' (that was one of the more polite descriptions). He specifically exempted Parker's life of 'that onely most trueli gracious bishope and blessed martyr holy Cranmor', but otherwise mockingly wondered if the reader might ask whether Parker's autobiography might be 'wished dead and buried never to rise againe with 68 off those 69 Canterburie tales'.[23] It was not surprising that Parker's biography of Cranmer in his *De antiquitate* was tainted with guilt by association and did not prove to be nearly as influential as that of Foxe.

The prime thesis for John Foxe was that Cranmer's life was validated by his martyrdom. That was in any case the theme of the whole of Foxe's work, but for him it was genuinely much more important than Cranmer's actual achievements in life, particularly that for which he is largely remembered today: the creation of the Book of Common Prayer. There was good reason for this: Foxe regarded the Prayer Book as an imperfect work in progress, urgently needing revision in the light of lessons learnt by international Protestantism in the years since Cranmer had produced the second version in 1552. In his introduction of 1571 to the published text of the canon law revision prepared under Cranmer's chairmanship but never enacted for the Edwardian Church, Foxe felt compelled to point out the one serious flaw in this document prepared by his hero: it ordered the exclusive use of the Prayer Book.[24]

Yet even Archbishop Parker, who spent much of his time being goaded by Queen Elizabeth into harassing the Church of England into conformity with her wishes, said no more than a sentence about the Prayer Book in his life of Cranmer. His portrait was of a prelate like himself, conscientiously adopting ancient popish ecclesiastical institutions for godly purposes.[25] For Parker, there was nothing particularly sacred about the form of the Prayer Book, which he too may well have privately regarded as ripe for further development in a godly direction. But there was more to his neglect than that. For a century and more after the Prayer Book's composition, both friends and foes of Cranmer regarded it not so much as a work of his individual genius as the product of a royally appointed committee of senior churchmen, whose reputations were collectively bound up with it: it is very rare to find any reference to 'Cranmer's Prayer Book'.[26] Formally, of course, they were right. Since everyone was then interested in the Book primarily as a vehicle for liturgy or the expression of theological principles, they had little interest in its literary qualities, which can now be ascribed to the particular talents of Thomas Cranmer and admired for their own sake.

Elizabeth's 1559 Settlement began the Church of England's long march away from Cranmer's Eucharistic theology and his international Reformed Protestant enthusiasm, to the angry bewilderment of many of the Church's members. Thanks to this unexpected turn of events, the memory of the Oxford martyrs became as much the property of those who deplored the Elizabethan Church's half-reformed polity as of senior churchmen who were Cranmer's former colleagues; a tussle took place for the honour of being the heirs of Cranmer, Latimer and Ridley between Puritans and conformists in the Church. Both sides claimed the myth-making biography of Foxe's *Book of Martyrs* for their own; both sides emphasized the importance of the martyrdom at the centre of the myth, but equally both sides began making of it what they wanted. For conformists, the martyrdom of the bishops at Oxford validated the English Prayer Book, whatever its small faults, so that they symbolized defence of the liturgy against Puritans, just as they had done in disputes among the Marian exiles about how the 1552 Book should be used.[27] For Puritans, this distorted the Cranmer legacy – the drive to reform a popishly corrupted Church, the project tragically cut off before it could be completed. Even some separatists, who had gone one stage further than the Puritans and had broken with Cranmer's Church, used Cranmer and his fellow martyrs as portrayed by Foxe as sticks to beat Elizabethan bishops.[28] The way to avoid the seeming contradiction of attacking Cranmer's Prayer Book while regarding him as an example to all good Protestants was the quite reasonable supposition that his work had been interrupted: already in the early 1570s there was a confident Puritan assertion that in time he would have 'drawn up a book of prayer a hundred times more perfect than this that we now have'.[29]

A less positive view of Cranmer emerged from the 1580s in a different quarter – among the first sacramentalists or 'High Churchmen', labelled 'Arminians' from the 1610s. Above all, these sacramentalists wished to restore the notion of real presence in the Eucharist to what they regarded as its rightful key place in Christian doctrine – a doctrine which Cranmer had devoted much of his literary energy to attacking and, arguably, for denying which he had died at the stake.

Cranmer's 1552 Prayer Book, only lightly revised in 1559, was not promising territory for them; nor did they enjoy contemplating the Edwardian Church as portrayed by John Foxe. For most of them, there was no question of open criticism; Arminians, after all, made much of their loyalty to the Established Church. Rather, their disapproval manifested itself in a discreet lack of comment about the virtues of the Edwardian Church, and also an increasing interest in Cranmer's first vernacular Prayer Book of 1549. This interest sprang from the very reason that Cranmer had drastically reshaped it in 1552, because it offered more possibilities of reinstating a more extrovert Catholic practice and devotion than the 1559 rite. When in 1637 the sacramentalists had the chance to create an entire new liturgy for the kingdom of Scotland, they looked for a model to 1549 and not to 1559.[30]

Matters were made worse when the Arminians' growing ascendancy in the early Stuart Church met with opposition from the older Church establishment. Frequently Cranmer was called in from the pages of Foxe or from his own writings to witness against Arminianism.[31] If Cranmer had such friends, then it is not surprising that Archbishop William Laud and other Arminians thought little of him. They did their best to put their own positive gloss on Foxe's picture of the English martyrs, but one gets the feeling that this was because they felt it politic to do so, rather than out of any genuine enthusiasm.[32] More revealing were Laud's words when he had nothing more to lose, making his final speech facing death on the scaffold at the hands of the Westminster Parliament in 1645. His thoughts on this very public opportunity for self-fashioning turned to two previous medieval Archbishops of Canterbury likewise killed in office, Alphege and Simon Sudbury, together with ancient martyrs from John the Baptist to Bishop Cyprian of Carthage. Astonishingly, while still protesting his Protestant credentials, he preferred Roman Catholic primates to a Protestant martyr of less than a century before whom he did not name: his predecessor Cranmer. At least he had the decency also to remain silent on the Reformers' bête noire – Thomas Becket.[33]

Laud's execution was one episode in twenty years of warfare and religious experiment, leaving English Protestantism now decisively polarized between supporters and opponents of episcopacy. During the Interregnum, love for episcopacy was increasingly associated with a more positive view of sacramental presence in the Eucharist which Laud would have recognized, drawing away from the international Reformed Protestantism characterizing the English Church from Edward VI's reign to the rise of Arminianism. This introduced something which can be unequivocally styled Anglicanism. When Charles II's Restoration Settlement of 1660–62 produced a startling triumph of militant Anglicanism, Cranmer naturally had a rhetorical part in the return. He would have been unlikely to be happy that the new, more narrowly drawn identity of Anglicanism in 1662 excluded many Protestants who had a home in the pre-Laudian Church: almost single-handed, the triumphalist Anglicanism of the Restoration created that phenomenon so distinctive in English religious tradition, large-scale Protestant Nonconformity or Dissent. Within the Anglican Church there were still two wings: intransigent High Churchmen glad to see Dissenters sent packing, and moderates who regretted the split and sought ways to reunite English Protestantism. They were conscious of a growing threat from Roman Catholicism, including the heir to the throne, James, Duke of York. They sought to recall England to a consciousness of its Reformation heritage.

Accordingly, opponents of High Churchmen turned to writing Reformation history. The outstanding example was from Bishop Gilbert Burnet, an episcopal recruit from the Church of Scotland. His *History of the Reformation*, first published in 1679–81 amid the exclusion crisis which sought to remove James from the royal succession, was based on a wealth of unpublished documentation and careful judgement, despite its clear commitment to the Protestant cause.[34] He was conscious of contradicting wrong impressions from two directions, first Roman Catholic historiography, but now also the Arminian historiography chiefly promoted by William Laud's former chaplain Peter Heylyn, author of a major history of the Reformation published in 1662, which was extremely queasy about the Reformation changes and decidedly unfriendly to Cranmer. Burnet, by contrast, made much of Cranmer, climaxing his Preface to the Reader in the 1679 volume of his work with a two-page meditation sympathetically acknowledging Cranmer's faults and placing them in the circumstances of the time. Not without justification did Bishop Bossuet describe Cranmer as Burnet's 'Hero'.[35] Burnet's work was not a life of Cranmer, but the archbishop haunted the pages of the two volumes spanning his years as Primate, his imprisonment and death.

Burnet was followed as champion of the moderate Anglican view of history by John Strype, a clergyman who shared if not surpassed his scholarly diligence, while lacking his creative talent. Strype's first published work in 1694 was his *Memorials of . . . Thomas Cranmer*, the first life of Cranmer to be put independently into print, the first major effort of any sort since Foxe and Parker, and the first of Strype's series of studies of worthies of the mid-Tudor and Elizabethan periods, mostly archbishops.[36] Burnet and Strype were not soulmates. Strype had come to feel a passionate hatred of Protestant Noncon-formity. He was critical of Burnet both as historian and as activist Whig before and during the 1688 Glorious Revolution, an event which Strype himself accepted with the gingerly passivity of many Anglicans, in contrast to Burnet's active role in the proceedings which overthrew King James. Strype's work therefore trod a fine line between celebrating heroic militancy in the English Reformation and deploring the militant disloyalty of Dissenters to the Established Church of English Protestantism; he was much more inclined than Burnet to smooth out rough edges in the story. Strype celebrated what he saw as Cranmer's chief virtues in his dedication of the biography to the post-revolutionary Archbishop of Canterbury John Tillotson. The qualities to which 'both the Kings and People of this Realm owe their Deliverance from the Long and cruel Bondage of Rome' turned out to be 'solid Learning, Deliberation, and indefatigable Pains', by which Strype clearly did not mean anything as dramatic as martyr-dom, just the everyday slog of being an archbishop. To dwell too much on martyrdom for conscience might raise embarrassing paral-lels with Tillotson's immediate predecessor William Sancroft, who, although not martyred for his loyalty to his Coronation oath to James II, had given up his primatial see for conscience rather than swear loyalty to William III. Interestingly, despite Strype's emphasis on scholarship and hard work, he still said little about Cranmer in rela-tion to the Prayer Book: it featured only briefly in the body of his text, and not at all in his dedication to Archbishop Tillotson. The scholar-ship of which he spoke was presumably Cranmer's books on the

Eucharist, plus general busyness in the legislation and reforms of the Henrician and Edwardian years.

With Burnet and Strype we find a turning point for one of the most fascinating symbolic divisions in perceiving the life of Cranmer: the battle of the beard (see Plates 8–13). Two surviving contemporary portraits of Cranmer look radically different, because one Cranmer is clean-shaven and the other is lavishly bearded. They represent two different phases of his life. The first, by Gerlach Flicke (undoubtedly the better painting, and often in the past attributed to Holbein), is now in the National Portrait Gallery. It shows a clean-shaven Henrician Primate in 1545. The second, anonymous, is in Lambeth Palace. It dates from some time after Cranmer first grew his beard at the beginning of Edward VI's reign. Cranmer died at the stake wearing a long beard, and is thus dramatically depicted in Foxe's *Acts and Monuments*, in more than one version through various editions. Foxe even took the trouble in 1563 to commission a new version of an engraving from the first year of Edward VI's reign, where the boy-king is shown giving the Bible to his bishops: in the original of 1548, they were clean-shaven and Henrician, now they had beards.[37] At the time, everyone realized the significance of this: throughout northern Europe, clergymen wearing beards equated with Protestantism (Renaissance popes and Cardinal Pole being the exceptions to prove the rule). When Cranmer grew his beard in 1547, he was making an emphatic rejection of the old Church.[38]

So whichever of the two portraits was chosen as the image of Cranmer decided how he was perceived: Henry's obedient archbishop, or participant in the international revolution alongside majestically hirsute Heinrich Bullinger, Peter Martyr or Jan Łaski. In late sixteenth-century Europe, Cranmer was invariably the bearded Reformer, particularly thanks to the influential collection of portraits by Jean-Jacques Boissard, first published in 1597. The bearded image, for instance, is seen (though now alas badly damaged) in Oxford's Bodleian Library, in the Upper Reading Room's frieze of great theologians and reformers painted in 1618–20.[39] In a survey of the English Reformation of 1627, slavishly derived from Foxe's *Acts and Monuments* by a quintessentially Reformed Protestant English clergyman Christopher Lever, the illustrated title-page changes history by showing Cranmer in the presence of Henry VIII as a bearded archbishop (Thomas Cromwell is also awarded this hairy tribute to his Protestantism); the distraught defeated Catholic clerics and the pope himself remain, as always, clean-shaven (see Plate 12).[40] However, after the trauma of the English Civil Wars and the emergence of Anglicanism, the balance of Cranmer's portraiture began to change.

Burnet is as usual scrupulously historical. From the first edition of his *History of the Reformation* onwards, he reproduces a reversed version of the Flicke portrait, placed appropriately amid his account of Henry's reign in the first volume.[41] His second volume deals with the later Reformation from Edward VI to Elizabeth I, and each volume has an appropriate engraved title-page. Volume 1's title-page shows the destruction of superstition and the building of true religion, flanked by the chief actors, Henry VIII and Cranmer. Henry is derived from the famous Holbein standing image and Cranmer once more from Flicke's clean-shaven portrait. That is as it should be in terms of the progress of the Reformation, for through his two volumes, Burnet is making a positive point about the development of a truly godly Church. His title-page in volume 2 takes as its image of Edward's reign, young king Edward kneeling to receive communion from a now bearded prelate (decently attired in rochet, chimere and skull-cap, as a late Stuart bishop would be). This is probably intended for Cranmer, but even if we cannot be certain of that, Mary's reign is symbolized by a picture of the three Oxford martyrs, all explicitly labelled (history is telescoped to get them all at the stake at the same time). Cranmer, of course, has the longest beard of all of them, as yet untouched by the flames (see Plates 9, 13).

It was Strype who abandoned bearded images and made the decisive move from beard to smooth chin. He did not have an illustrated title-page to his 1694 *Memorials of . . . Cranmer*, contenting himself with a frontispiece portrait of his hero. His publisher, Richard Chiswell, had also published Burnet's *History of the Reformation*, and to begin with Chiswell simply reused his existing full-page version of the Flicke Cranmer portrait from Burnet's work, not even changing the reference to Burnet's page-number at the foot. Clearly this would not do for Strype, and so most copies of Strype's *Memorials* contain a completely re-engraved version of the Flicke portrait, a rather more accurate reproduction, as well as reversed to face in the right direction.[42] Now Cranmer's beardlessness stood unmodified, in contrast to the handful of Strype's further images of Cranmer's mainland European colleagues – Łaski, Bucer, Martyr, Melanchthon – plus Bishop Latimer: they all kept their beards. Strype's Cranmer is exclusively Flicke's beardless Primate, because his book contains no images of the archbishop in his latter days and at his martyrdom to counteract Flicke.

Cranmer was thus made safe for Anglicanism, a tidily grave divine decorously quarantined from the alarming facial bushiness of the Protestants across the Channel: the bearded portrait was sidelined, though still well known and on display at Lambeth Palace. Foxe's dramatic last scenes of the archbishop's life could never be fully expunged, but even when an emphatically Protestant Georgian version of Foxe's *Acts and Monuments* was produced and repeatedly reprinted for monthly subscribers, it was noticeable that the new illustrations showed a Cranmer whose beard was a good deal more trim than before, and he even acquired a neat moustache.[43] With the Flicke portrait image fixed in his first independent biography, Cranmer invariably remained in Flicke's version right down to the twentieth century, in all the histories which featured him prominently, and in all the biographies of him before my own.

Only six years before Strype's publication, the Glorious Revolution of 1688 represented a crisis for High Church Anglicans, resulting in the Non-Juror schism. Non-Jurors regarded themselves as the true Church of England, but as time went on, some began to profit from their separation, glorying in the unsullied purity of their Church and vaunting its Catholicity against the tainted established body which successively adhered to William and Mary and the Hanoverians; they made the intoxicating discovery that there was no necessary link between Church and State. That had more than one consequence: first, they no longer felt inhibited as early seventeenth-century Arminians had generally been in criticizing leaders of the English Reformation. Second, they intensified the abuse of Cranmer as Erastian betrayer of the Catholic Church, a theme then fashionably styled 'Hobbism': as we have already seen, this was introduced by Roman Catholic polemicists such as Woodhead and Manby in James II's reign. Ironically Woodhead and Manby were in turn drawing on the

High Church Anglican Heylyn, so there was a cross-fertilization of poisons going on here across confessional boundaries.[44] Non-Jurors set the tone for a new and more intense abuse of what had happened in England particularly in the reign of Edward VI: they regarded Cranmer and his colleagues as rogues or fools deceived by evil continental Protestants, pawns of greedy secular politicians, and the ruin of the Catholic Church of England.

The Non-Juror movement faded in the eighteenth century, particularly after the failure of the 'Forty-Five rebellion, but its rhetoric survived among more eccentric High Churchmen within the Established Church, particularly on the subject of Erastianism. That rhetoric flourished again in the nineteenth century with the coming of the Oxford Movement, which often shared the Non-Jurors' contempt for Church establishment in a fashion unthinkable to Archbishop Laud. A good illustration of this unbridled abuse in the wake of the Non-Jurors comes from a copy of Strype's *Memorials of . . . Thomas Cranmer* first owned by the Cambridge don and antiquary William Cole (1714–82) and now in Oxford's Bodleian Library. Cole was an extreme High Churchman who on more than one occasion contemplated converting to Roman Catholicism; he was also fascinated by his copy of Strype, annotating it extensively and even providing an elaborate index to it.[45]

Some representative samples of Cole's marginalia will suffice. Reading accusations of heresy against Cranmer made by Bishop Gardiner of Winchester and Canterbury Prebendaries in 1543 (Strype, *Memorials of . . . Thomas Cranmer*, p. 117), he clearly believed popish Gardiner rather than Cranmer: 'It is hardly probable that Bp. Gardiner and Bonner and these Prebendaries shd. thus article agst. the ArchBp. had not his Grace either openly or privately endeavoured to introduce his beloved German and Calvinistical Doctrines into this Church.' Later (ibid., p. 123) he mused apropos of Cranmer's uncle by marriage, Andreas Osiander of Nuremberg, 'It is a pity that Master Osiander and his Germans had not Interest enough to have made him a Superintendent among them, that this Church might not have had such a Wretch for an Archbishop.' Finally, a clear restatement of Arminian doubts about the 1552 Prayer Book, against Strype's description of the help the foreign divines gave in the liturgical revision (ibid., p. 210):

'The more the Pity. It shew'd a wonderful sagacity in this great English Primate not to be able to manage his own Reformation, but must introduce a Mess or Medley of all sorts of foreign Divines to correct it. What they altered in the old and first and best Book of Common Prayer, has much depreciated the Value of it.'

The final element in criticism of Cranmer is to see him as a persecutor of conscience. Under Henry he was involved in burning mainstream evangelicals like John Frith and John Lambert, who died for holding opinions on the Eucharist which in later years he came to hold himself. He was also involved in Henry VIII's horrific execution by roasting in chains of Friar John Forest for being a champion of traditional Catholicism, and in Edward's reign he presided over the burning of at least two Unitarian radicals. This theme can be found from the earliest days of his biographies, because rather surprisingly it is to be found in John Foxe.[46] Later radicals in Elizabeth's reign, conscious heirs of the Unitarians martyred under Edward VI, consistently showed no admiration for the Oxford martyrs, having scorned them even amid the common suffering of prelates and radicals under Queen Mary.[47] Their attitudes were subsequently picked up by remarkably diverse commentators who lacked their radical religious enthusiasms. The seventeenth-century Tacitean historian Sir John Hayward noted Foxe's story about Bocher, pointed out Cranmer's own fiery end and said tartly of him, 'it may be that by his importunity for bloud, hee did offend, for a good thing is not good if it be immoderatlie desired or done'.[48] Later Edward Gibbon pointed out with slight geographical inaccuracy that 'the flames of Smithfield, in which he was afterwards consumed, had been kindled for the Anabaptists by the zeal of Cranmer'. Equally lurid in the nineteenth century was the language of William Cobbett, who as a non-Catholic radical journalist was one of the more unexpected by-products of the Harpsfield tradition. Seeing the English Reformation as a huge confidence trick played on the English people, he made Cranmer into its chief villain in rather similar terms to Abraham Woodhead – 'a name which deserves to be held in everlasting execration'. The main reason was Cranmer's part in persecution.[49] Cobbett derived his comment from Catholics like Bishop John Milner who had decided that, on the matter of persecution, attack was the best form of defence, and so vilified Cranmer for his treatment of Catholics. For Cobbett, Cranmer's name could not be pronounced 'without almost doubting of the justice of God, were it not for our knowledge of the fact, that the cold-blooded, most perfidious man expired at last amidst those flames which he himself had been the chief cause of kindling'.[50]

Thus Cranmer came under assault from a bizarre alliance of Anglican High Churchmen, religious and political radicals, Roman Catholics, and those who simply deplored religious leaders wielding political power. As the archbishop entered the nineteenth century, Roman Catholics like John Milner and John Lingard persisted with the villain-narrative, cheered on from the radical sidelines by William Cobbett. Reprints of Foxe's *Book of Martyrs*, Burnet and Strype upheld the hero-narrative, aided by counter-attacks on Cranmer's Catholic detractors from H. J. Todd and other contemporaries. The rival tradition of detraction from High Church Anglicans deplored Cranmer's support for King Edward's destructive policies, frequently attributed his actions to undue and unEnglish influence from foreign divines, and often decried the 1552 Book in comparison with that of 1549; if they stood in the Non-Juror tradition, they were also likely to see him as an Erastian contemptibly subservient to the State. When the Oxford Movement came to criticize Cranmer in turn, it picked up all these critical themes.

We need not spend much time listening to nineteenth-century High Churchmen, except to note a new obfuscation. The pre-Tractarian High Churchman Walter Hook, Vicar of Leeds and latterly Dean of Chichester, had a lot of good to say about Cranmer in his two-volume biography published in 1868. He did criticize his subservience to Henry VIII, to whom Hook felt that Cranmer displayed 'a culpable weakness both of character and of principle'; Hook's chief charge was that 'he bequeathed to us an ecclesiastical atmosphere so charged with Erastianism, as to render it difficult, at certain times, to extricate the religious from the political element'. Yet Hook began a new line of defence among High Churchmen; rather than deplore Cranmer, he rewrote him in a way which would have horrified the archbishop, making him into a proto-High Churchman. 'As the primate of an ancient church, while he laboured to remove the abuses by which, in the lapse of ages, it had been encrusted, he was careful to preserve its continuity, and he resisted successfully the attempts incessantly made to supplant, by the introduction of a modern sect, the church of Augustine.'[51]

Hook's remarkable reinterpretation of Cranmer's agenda paralleled a general rewriting of the English Reformation which became a speciality of the Oxford Movement, minimizing the disruption which the English Reformation had caused or had been intended to cause.[52] Even if not all rewriting on Cranmer was so unblushing as Hook's, still the twentieth century saw nuanced accounts of Cranmer which were damage-limitation exercises. The one serious twentieth-century effort at a study of Cranmer's theology from within the Anglican tradition was clearly unhappy with his lack of a doctrine of objective Eucharistic presence, and managed entirely to omit a salient fact of his theology: he was a thoroughgoing predestinarian.[53] One popularizing High Church biography from 1927 concentrated in its final judgements on the lack of harm caused by Cranmer to the Church because of his weakness of character: a stronger man might have been removed and replaced by someone really obnoxious like John Hooper or John Knox.[54]

A similar tone was set as late as 1951 in the influential 'Teach Yourself History' series: Cranmer's life was here presented by a High Church scholar-clergyman, F. E. Hutchinson. The Thirty-Nine Articles could have been worse, Canon Hutchinson felt, because they could have contained more Reformation doctrine, and 'if in the Prayer Book of 1552, more was sacrificed of ancient and approved liturgical use than need have been, each revision . . . has recovered things that have improved the service book'. This last thought led Hutchinson to reflect (with obvious relief) that 'the religious life of the English people has been far more influenced by their familiarity with the Prayer Book than by the Articles'.[55] By now, with literary criticism as established an academic industry as historical research, a favourite topos of all treatments of Cranmer was that whatever one thought of his conduct or his theology, his stately formal prose in the Prayer Book made up for a multitude of sins. An extreme example can be found in the Anglo-Catholic periodical the *Church Quarterly Review* for 1891, where the anonymous reviewer, probably the distinguished liturgical scholar F. E. Brightman, bluntly says 'the only deed for which we feel that we owe any gratitude to Cranmer is for his unrivalled liturgical translation'; he goes on to say that with popes like the Borgia Alexander VI around in the period, it is hardly any wonder that sixteenth-century Europe was flooded with immorality and unbelief, or that 'we have a Cranmer, a Becon, a Hooper, or a Ridley controlling events in England'.[56] This is damning with faint praise indeed.

Unexpectedly, Hilaire Belloc made Cranmer's literary talents the exonerating factor in the archbishop's career, and almost extinguished the Catholic Harpsfield legacy. His generous thoughts on Cranmer's prose are one of the best summary meditations on Cranmer's particular genius. Belloc (not unfairly) found most of Cranmer's private or polemical prose 'as dull, turgid and confused as all his generation were', but

> When he says to himself 'Now I have something special to do; here I am on my mettle, I must produce some fine thing' – *then* he constructs with a success only paralleled by the sonnets of Shakespeare . . . most of the Collects, which with the isolated phrases of the Litany are his chief triumph, consist in single sentences – but they are sentences which most men who know the trade would give their eyes to have written. And since that endures which is carved in hard material, they have endured, and given endurance to the fabric – novel and revolutionary in his time, the institution at the root of which he stands – the Church of England.[57]

The late nineteenth century brought the first studies by professional historians, who inevitably had their own prejudices but were less likely to subordinate their findings to a religious agenda. James Gairdner, an editor of that monument to disinterested scholarship, *Letters and Papers, Foreign and Domestic, Henry VIII*, produced an accomplished little essay in 1888 for the *Dictionary of National Biography*, managing to avoid any major value-judgements. In 1905 A. F. Pollard produced an outstanding biography among his studies of the great names of Tudor England. Despite Belloc's characterization of it as hero-worship, it is noticeably fair-minded, particularly in a masterly chapter on 'Cranmer's character and private life'. Cranmer was again well served by Jasper Ridley in 1962. It was therefore with a somewhat heavy heart that I embarked on a commission to add to the total of Cranmerian lives. Was there anything more to say?

Ultimately I was reassured. I did have a number of lucky new archival finds, but more interesting was the way in which the whole body of material on Cranmer began pulling me towards a picture which I had not found in existing biographies. The evidence had been there, but it had not been treated with the perspective that I found thrust upon me, and which was still taking shape as I brought my text to a close. Cranmer had usually been treated as an English churchman with a few foreign friends, rather than as a major player in a European-wide revolution with a cosmopolitan outlook exceptional among his English contemporaries. A brilliant young scholar of the 1920s, Charles Smyth, had given the clues here in a remarkable little book, *Cranmer and the Reformation under Edward VI*, but there was much more.[58] This alerted me to how unAnglican Cranmer was. His Reformation was part of a larger event, and its nearest relative was the Strassburg of Martin Bucer. Cranmer had no affection for much of what gives Anglicanism its particular character; he showed no affection for cathedrals and their music, and would have been unenthusiastic about choral evensong, one of the chief glories of the modern Anglican tradition. He had no time for ideas of apostolic succession of the episcopate. His theology was structured by predestination, a theological concept which Anglicanism has on the whole decided to treat with caution. He would have been shocked by the idea of a *via media* between Rome and Protestantism. It had been in no one's interest to point out these obvious facts since the seventeenth century, and every reason as Anglicanism constructed its tribal identity to enrol the chief actor in the English Reformation as an honorary Anglican. It was with the foreignness of Cranmer in mind that I chose to enter the battle of the beard. For the dust-jacket of my book, I took the Lambeth bearded portrait of the archbishop, not the famous Flicke image, which was still the dominant note of the quincentenary exhibition on Cranmer at the British Museum in 1989.[59]

When the book appeared, it was instructive to find how live an issue the Reformation still was, and how a biography whose author did not espouse any active religious viewpoint was enrolled in contemporary religious battles. In that, its nearest parallel was another large book from Yale University Press, Eamon Duffy's *Stripping of the Altars*, said to be on the coffee tables of all well-informed Roman Catholic clergy, and a prolonged, elegant and creative scholarly lament that the Reformation had ever happened. I was both gratified and intimidated to find my work on the bedside table of Dr Ian Paisley, alongside the Bible and a biography of 'King William III, Prince of Orange: the first European'.[60] Reviewers, as always, used the book for their own purposes. William J. Tighe, a conservative academic writing in the American *New Oxford Review*, celebrated the biography's undermining of Anglo-Catholic views of Anglicanism, adding in a curious non sequitur that the 'Gadarene rush' of Anglicanism 'into theological, moral, and practical libertinism . . . reveals Anglicanism to be leaving behind the modicum of common Christian orthodoxy that it has retained'.[61] The ultra-conservative American Roman Catholic commentator Richard Neuhaus (who misread me as 'a relentless Protestant') turned the biography towards current developments in the Roman Catholic Church, seeing the story as vindicating papal authority against contemporary calls for conciliarism, which would 'plunge the Church back into the perpetual commotion of national and ideological factionalism'.[62]

Perhaps the most surprising intervention of *Thomas Cranmer: a Life* was in the internal politics of the Anglican diocese of Sydney in Australia. Here, the last decades have seen a steady move to consolidate power in the already formidable conservative evangelical group dominating this wealthy and influential diocese. A major ecclesiastical row was generated during 1999 by one stage in this campaign: a strongly supported proposal to introduce lay presidency at the Eucharist. An ordinance to that effect was passed by two-to-one majorities of both clergy and laity in the Synod of Sydney Archdiocese, and only vetoed by the Archbishop of Sydney despite his personal sympathy for the ordinance because of the effect of unilateral action on the Anglican Communion. During the discussions, one of the chief proponents of the move, Dr Robert Doyle, put forward arguments that Cranmer had believed that a layman may ordain a bishop, appealing to my biography as a principal source for this claim. It took an opponent of the measure, Dr Ivan Head, to go back to the book and point out that the relevant material quoted by Doyle indicated that Cranmer believed that the only layperson who could thus ordain a bishop was a monarch like King Henry VIII: hardly the most apposite parallel in modern Australia.[63]

To speak of Thomas Cranmer is still to enter culture wars. There are ears to hear, far more so than if one writes about Henry VIII or Elizabeth I. It may be that Anglicans will have to realize that it is one of the glories of their tradition that it is a tradition without logic or consistency, which depends on the strong clash of opposites, and which in the end provides heroes who are examples of human frailty rather than role-models for uncomplicated courage – which forces the individual to undertake a good deal of hard thinking in order to make sense of the world around, rather than reaching for some simple model in a book. Such a heritage is a healthy corrective to the common relish of the religiously minded for telling other people what to do – and that corrective may be the diaconal task of Anglicanism within the Christian faith.

20

Richard Hooker's Reputation

From my undergraduate days in Cambridge, I remember a lecture by the late Sir Geoffrey Elton in which he pronounced not altogether kindly on the achievement of another giant of early modern historical writing, Professor Lawrence Stone. Elton said of Stone's magnum opus, *The Crisis of the Aristocracy*, 'Lawrence Stone has written a great book. [*Pause*] A huge book. An ENORMOUS book.' In a similar fashion, Richard Hooker's many admirers, detractors and manipulators can agree on one thing: Hooker wrote a very big book. Everyone remembers that. Take, for instance, the early seventeenth-century clerk of Canterbury Archdeaconry Court who compiled the index to the probate register volume which deals with Richard Hooker: when the clerk came to Hooker's name in his index, he showed an uncharacteristic spark of interest, and he commented in the margin 'he wrote an Ecclesiastical Polity'.[1]

Now we know that it was not just *an* Ecclesiastical Polity, but *the* Ecclesiastical Polity, a majestic and hallowed testimony to the character of Anglicanism and the *via media* of the Church of England. But it may give us pause to find, if we take up the formidable task of reading Hooker's works – all seven volumes of them in the standard edition, including commentary and notes – that nowhere in any of his writings does Hooker use either the word Anglicanism or the phrase *via media*.[2] That may suggest that the legacy of Hooker is not as straightforward as it has sometimes been portrayed; indeed, it may mean that Anglicanism and the *via media* are more interesting and fluid concepts than the complacent version of Anglican historiography has sometimes made them.[3] Did Hooker defend Anglicanism in his book, or did he, as Professor Peter Lake once famously suggested, actually invent Anglicanism?[4] Did he write a great book, or just a huge and enormous one? To find out who he was and what he has been understood to have intended requires an exploration of the extraordinarily varied ways in which he and his big book have been encountered over four centuries.

Hooker started his public career as a rather predictable Reformed Protestant, one among the swelling number of young clergymen whose formation in early Elizabethan Oxford fitted them to lead a Church very conscious of its place in the wider family of European Reformed Churches. Hooker's family back in Devon was precociously Protestant. His uncle, John Vowell alias Hooker, was a passionately committed historian of the Hookers' home city, Exeter, but also a cosmopolitan scholar whose higher education had included time in Cologne and Strassburg.[5] More important still was the young Richard's debt to his patron, Bishop John Jewel, first defender of the Elizabethan Protestant Settlement and veteran both of Edwardian Oxford and the Zürich of Heinrich Bullinger. In the 1590s, Richard Hooker remembered Jewel with affection and awe as 'the worthiest Divine that Christendome hath bred for the space of some hundreds of yeres'.[6] Both the elder Hooker and Jewel had sat at the feet of the great exile theologian Peter Martyr Vermigli, who above all others symbolized the international links of the English Reformation – the Italian whose fate took him as mediator of Reformed religion to Strassburg, Oxford and Zürich. Their Reformation was caught up in a war against the forces of popery, in the person of whose bishop in Rome was to be found a prime representative of Antichrist. When Hooker can first be glimpsed on the public stage, preaching some time in 1582 or 1583 as a young Oxford don on the Book of Jude, he was still recognizably part of that world. Like his mentors, he referred repeatedly to the Roman Pontiff as 'the man of sinne'.[7] Such orthodox Reformed sentiments were natural in a man who was not only the spiritual heir of John Hooker and John Jewel, but who in his Oxford career was the close associate of the great Dr John Rainolds, President of Corpus Christi College and doyen of moderate Puritans in the university.[8]

Yet something more odd and individual began emerging later in the 1580s. It is possible that Rainolds's was not the only influence to work on the young man. In its foundation, after all, Corpus had been a flagship of Catholic humanism in Oxford, and when Hooker came up as an undergraduate in 1568 it maintained its distinctive emphasis on learning Greek: he would have been given more exposure to the writings of the Greek Fathers than most of his contemporaries.[9] Although, in the very year that he arrived there was a major clear-out of the strongly Catholic Fellows who had continued to dominate the College after Elizabeth's accession, even then the victory of properly Reformed Protestants in Corpus was by no means complete.[10]

We cannot know whether or how these patristic and sacramentalist elements in his environment affected Hooker. What is clear, however, is that the issue on which he first publicly struck out in his own direction was that which would preoccupy him throughout his mature literary and theological career: the nature of a Church, of ecclesiastical polity. Already in his *Learned Discourse of Justification*, in many ways a mainstream piece of Reformed soteriological discussion in the tradition of Archbishop Cranmer's official *Homilies*, there emerges the assertion that the Church of Rome, although in error, is a true Church and that therefore members of it might well be saved.[11] It was not the first time that Reformed Protestants had recognized some shadow of the Church in popery – Hooker was careful to quote impeccably Reformed foreign divines saying just that – but normally there was a more grudging tone to the admission. Moreover, the concession tended to be treated by Reformed commentators as a logical corollary of the fact that the pope was Antichrist: after all, Antichrist needed a true Church in which to squat and do his foul deeds. Now Hooker had bidden Antichrist goodnight, and he showed a disturbing tendency to take more interest in the visible Church than in the true Church.[12]

The same theme emerged in the first public row in which Hooker was involved: a confrontation in 1586 with his colleague at the Temple, Walter Travers, a leading representative of those clergy who would have liked to push the Church of England on its logical Reformed road towards a presbyterian polity. Travers did not choose to oppose Hooker publicly on episcopacy versus presbyterianism, but instead on the issue of the status of the Church of Rome. The differences between them on this matter were narrow, but the difference was more important than its dimensions: Travers accused Hooker of going beyond the norm in saying in a sermon at the Temple that it was possible for Romanists who had lived *and died* in the superstitions of Rome to be saved (normally the convention was that generations of papist forefathers predestined to salvation had died not positively believing in Romish error, but in simple ignorance of the truth).

It is possible that Hooker did not in fact take this fatal step outside the bounds of Elizabethan orthodoxy, but that is certainly what Travers heard him as saying. Travers was entitled to feel suspicious, because he heard Hooker expressing unorthodox views on an allied matter: the stricter versions of predestinarian theology, as expounded by the great masters like Calvin or Peter Martyr. It is noticeable that although Hooker's patron, the Archbishop of Canterbury, John Whitgift, intervened against Travers on Hooker's behalf, he did not give decisive backing to Hooker's arguments. He might heartily dislike Puritans like Travers who did not give bishops the respect which they deserved, but he was not going to be led out of the doctrinal consensus which he shared with moderate Puritanism.[13] The historian Thomas Fuller's celebrated dictum seventy years later, that at the Temple Hooker preached 'pure Canterbury' in the morning and Travers 'pure Geneva' in the afternoon, could thus hardly be further from the truth. Yet since being canonized by quotation in Izaak Walton's biography of Hooker, this phrase of Fuller's has become an essential cliché in the construction of the Anglican version of him.[14]

After the confrontation with Travers, we can begin to see Hooker as having a public reputation, and a slightly strange one. He was a champion of the establishment who championed it in distinctly unestablishment terms; an oddity who puzzled and irritated his opponents by his stance of disinterested aloofness. He was beginning to distance himself from the community of international Reformist Protestantism represented by Rainolds, which had nurtured him in his early Oxford years. In a fine piece of detective work in 1974, James Cargill Thompson detected a tiny but significant instance of Hooker's rebellion against Rainolds which has not been sufficiently marked by subsequent commentators: the marginalia which accompany Hooker's well-known admission in Book VII of his *Ecclesiastical Polity* that he had changed his mind about the origins of episcopacy.

The marginal references on this passage consist of a list of authors who provided evidence for the commonplace Elizabethan stance that episcopacy was a human institution, a standpoint which Hooker commented that he 'did sometimes judge a great deal more probable than now I do'. The list is not original to Hooker, but is borrowed from a widely circulated manuscript treatise by Rainolds which had attacked Richard Bancroft's claim (made in a famous Paul's Cross sermon of 1589) that episcopacy was of apostolic institution. In the course of that work, Rainolds gives a marginal list of authorities who bear witness against Bancroft's view. Thus only a year or two later, at the beginning of the 1590s, Hooker silently plagiarized and condensed Rainolds's list in order to signal his dissent from his former patron; the gesture is almost a private joke in the discretion of its reference.[15]

Such a miniature literary fossil in Hooker's text is an indication of how problematically he might have been perceived by his contemporaries. In the feverishly polarized atmosphere of the early 1590s, when the bishops were waging war on churchmen who promoted presbyterianism, Hooker's clash with Travers was in any case a much more salient reason for Puritans to regard him as a marked man. As early as 1590, we find a passing sneer at Hooker as an episcopal lapdog in a polemical work by Job Throckmorton, flamboyant Puritan gentleman and probable mastermind of the scurrilously funny Puritan Martin Marprelate tracts. In the course of a discussion of the question which had divided Travers and Hooker – the fate of papists in the afterlife – Throckmorton snapped that 'in this point if either M. Hooker, M. Some, or all the reverend B[ishops] of the land do stand against us, it shall little dismaie us' (by us, he meant the godly).[16] Once the presbyterians were officially humiliated and routed by government action in 1591, some of the conformists who had written against them in defence of the establishment returned to another form of defence – writing against Rome. Hooker, however, did not.[17] He decided to press on with the work against presbyterianism which he had probably been preparing since his troubles at the Temple had confronted him with Travers, a presbyterian sympathizer red in tooth and claw. Job Throckmorton's anonymously published *Petition to her Majestie* of 1592 is indeed quoted sarcastically in the text of the *Ecclesiastical*

Polity, although we cannot be certain as to whether Hooker could have identified the author.[18]

Hooker's book, the first half of which appeared in 1593, was not to be merely another work of anti-presbyterian polemic: just as well, because after 1591, the struggle with presbyterianism was yesterday's news. Polemic there did remain, and despite Hooker's reputation for 'judiciousness', polemic is plain to see in his text, which sometimes drips with sarcasm. The reader can hardly fail to notice that large sections of the whole work consist of an irritable dialogue with a book published in the mid-1570s by the leading presbyterian theologian Thomas Cartwright, itself a riposte to a work by Hooker's patron Whitgift, and now answered rather belatedly.[19] The occasion of Hooker's publication was also highly partisan: the parliamentary campaign against sectary Protestants which resulted in the first Elizabethan legislation specifically directed towards Protestant rather than Roman Catholic nonconformity.[20] But the scale of Hooker's work was grander than its occasion. Its arguments combated the whole mindset which had created presbyterianism and those arguments were placed in the framework of a philosophy of human action, motivation and discipline, analysed as an expression of God's law for his creation. Specifically, Hooker said in his 1593 advertisement to the reader that these first four published books were about 'generalities', and that the 'particulars' which arose from them were to follow in the next four books.[21]

The eight-volume version of Hooker's *Ecclesiastical Polity*, which we will find emerging in the late seventeenth century from a convoluted and conflicted history of publication, has in the course of several centuries come to be seen as the cornerstone of Anglican theological method: a faithful transcription of what the early divines of the Church of England regarded as the way in which theology ought to be done, and a classic exposition of the way in which Anglicans have always thought. It is necessary now to rescue it from this cocoon of hindsight, to tease out Hooker's intentions and how he achieved them.[22] Brooding behind its intricate structure and byways of intellectual exploration is a preoccupation with how authority operates in constructing religious truths or untruths. Central to the argument was a careful sifting of the ways in which scripture should be used as an authority for Christian life and practice, and the ways in which it should not. The purpose was to widen the areas which could be regarded as matters indifferent, *adiaphora*, which might therefore be considered using a variety of norms and so were open to the authorities of Church and Commonwealth to regulate in the wider public interest. By meticulous definition and argument, Hooker extended these areas way beyond those which scripturally minded Protestants would consider appropriate, notably in the field of Church government. In such matters which did not affect salvation, the criteria for making decisions were as much the weight of collective past experience and the exercise of God-given reason as the commands of scripture itself. That is not the same, of course, as the common Anglican notion that Hooker created a Trinitarian authority of scripture, tradition and reason as the basis of deciding doctrinal questions. Scripture for Hooker remained paramount, even if its competence was given stricter bounds.[23]

The second four books dealt, as Hooker had promised, with the practical outworkings of his principles: first, in a massive Book V, the defence of aspects of English church practice attacked by Puritans, then an analysis, now partly lost, of church penitential discipline (Book VI), followed by a discussion of how to view episcopal authority (Book VII), and finally an analysis of the relationship between ecclesiastical and secular political power (Book VIII). Of these other four books, only Book V was published in Hooker's lifetime and the consequences of that delayed publication we will see unravelling over three centuries. Book V is a remarkable performance in its relentless defence of the exact shape of the 1559 Settlement of Religion – a settlement created by political accidents, consisting of an arbitrary snapshot of the Edwardian Church as it had happened to exist in autumn 1552.[24] If some ecclesiastical practice or phenomenon survived beyond the 1559 Settlement, then Hooker defended it, neither more nor less. After reading Book V, one feels that if the parliamentary legislation of 1559 had prescribed that English clergy were to preach standing on their heads, then Hooker would have found a theological reason for justifying it.

It is possible to see Hooker as still standing in the Reformed Protestant camp.[25] Certainly, when setting out to say unconventional things on predestination, Hooker was extremely careful (at least in his works intended for publication) not to challenge Reformed orthodoxy too directly. His sacramental views were not in themselves particularly exceptional for a Reformed commentator: nearer to Calvin than to Zwingli in his sacramental outlook, he was typical of English theologians of his time in briskly dismissing Lutheran real presence views of the Eucharist as much as the Romish doctrine of transubstantiation.[26] A celebrated section of Book V is a sensuous expression of Eucharistic participation, yet it has an impeccably Reformed climax: a rhapsodic quotation which Hooker had borrowed from a twelfth-century text edited by a French Reformed pastor.[27] What was individual, however, was what Hooker did with this generally unexceptional discussion. He deliberately and at some length re-emphasized the role of the sacraments and liturgical prayer at the expense of preaching; he felt that the sermon had been over-emphasized in the English Church. The unworthy thought may occur that his reassessment of preaching may have had something to do with the fact that, notoriously, he was not very good at it. Nevertheless, Hooker valued preaching enough to leave money in his will for a new pulpit in his parish church at Bishopsbourne, and one might more charitably place the origins of his attitude in the wider context of his educational formation and teaching priorities at Oxford.[28] In the later testimony of Daniel Featley in his memorial biography of John Rainolds, Hooker was considered to have made his name as a lecturer in logic, at a time when the nature of the university curriculum encouraged students to make a choice between considering logic or rhetoric a priority. Hooker's Oxford patron, Rainolds, was, by contrast, the exponent of rhetorical studies as set out in Aristotle's *Rhetoric*, as Featley also pointed out. It might not therefore be surprising that the master of logic should look down on the claims of pulpit rhetoric.[29]

Whatever his motivation, Hooker's attitude to preaching was not a popular stance to take at the time. One of the major and admirable features of his work is that he was not out to please anyone. He was an unusually wealthy clergyman who had apparently turned away from the clerical career ladder to serve in unimportant country parishes, and he seems to have written to satisfy himself. Most strikingly of all in this respect, despite his discreet questioning of Rainolds's views on episcopacy, he refused to follow fellow conformist polemicists who increasingly emphasized divine right claims for episcopacy in order to outface divine right claims for presbyterian polity. Indeed, astonishingly, in Book III of his work, he says that it is 'altogether too late' to reintroduce episcopacy into the established Church of Scotland, hardly the sentiment of someone who believes in the universal necessity of bishops in the Church. It is not surprising that when that classic Oxford Movement enthusiast for episcopal apostolicity John Keble quoted (in his 1836 editorial preface to Hooker's works) the passage in which this remark occurs, Hooker's opinion was too much for him to take, and he silently censored it out of the quotation.[30] In a similar independent fashion, when it came to secular government, Hooker did not let his anti-Puritanism take him down the road of producing arguments for divine right secular monarchy, unlike many contemporary ecclesiastical lawyers who might otherwise be congenial to him. For him, government or 'dominion' might arise out of direct provision by God, but equally it might arise out of conquest, or – in a statement with major implications for future political theory – an original act of consent by the 'multitude'.[31]

It was this sheer individuality, the variety of hares started by Hooker's indefatigable quest, which was to make him such a protean source for commentators in the future. Yet one person would have been pleased if she had read the *Ecclesiastical Polity* – Queen Elizabeth I. Hooker had few recorded encounters with the queen. His one known invitation to preach at court, immediately after the publication of his Book V in 1598, was in mid-Lent, at the prompting of Archbishop Whitgift, and in view of what we know of Hooker's other ventures into the pulpit, it may have been a particularly penitential Lenten exercise for the ageing monarch.[32] Nevertheless, the accumulated vision of Hooker's work is uncannily close to what we can glean of the idiosyncratic private religious opinions of this very private woman. She too defied contemporary wisdom in her reluctance to characterize Rome as Antichrist; she too was sceptical about excessive claims for episcopacy; she too had an ambiguous attitude to preaching and valued prayer more than sermons; and she too loved dignified church ceremonial. Even her views on the Eucharist had veered towards Reformed formulations because of her growing irritation with German Lutheran dogmatism, and so she would have sympathized with Hooker's Calvin-like talk of mystical participation.[33]

For the time being, however, Hooker's work was a damp squib. The reading public was perhaps baffled by a book which grounded its assault on its opponents on axioms from Aristotle, Plato and the medieval scholastics, rather than getting straight down to satisfyingly direct insults. Puritanism was in any case more fun than conformist argument: one witness's later memory of Hooker's dismal sales was that 'bookes of that Argument and on that parte were not saleable'.[34] In the end Hooker was forced to reduce the price of his book to try to move it along. A few friends and enemies took some notice of him. Thomas Rogers, another conformist client of the bishops, writing in the mid-1590s, listed Hooker among the literary enemies of the Cambridge Puritans who were his own enemies in the parishes of West Suffolk, and Rogers went on to cite Hooker elsewhere in his own writings.[35] In 1594 or 1595, Hooker's previous tormentor Job Throckmorton (in the one work published under his own name during his lifetime) borrowed a phrase from the *Polity* about laying aside the gall of bitterness in controversy, and had some polemical fun at Hooker's expense – evidently he disliked Hooker and was irritated by his affectation of sweet reasonableness.[36] But no wave of criticism appeared to indicate that Hooker's work was considered of great importance: in fact, only one answer to the *Ecclesiastical Polity* was published before his death in 1600, a work entitled *A Christian Letter* (1599).[37] Yet this attack was to prove the beginning of the long contest for the identity of Richard Hooker.

A Christian Letter was anonymous, but we can be reasonably certain that it was either exclusively or mainly the work of Andrew Willet. Willet was a prominent Cambridge moderate Puritan, much respected for his attacks on the Church of Rome, which, unlike the works of Hooker, were major bestsellers. Willet went on to attack Hooker posthumously in works published in 1603 and 1605.[38] It seems the world of militant Reformation from which Hooker had emerged was now decisively and openly rejecting him. The *Christian Letter* emphasized in its title and text that its anonymous supposed multiple authors were not Nonconformists but 'unfained favourers of the present state of religion': the theme of their work was that Hooker was disloyal to the Church of England. Willet pointed to specific doctrinal features of the *Ecclesiastical Polity* which 'seeme to overthrow the foundation of Christian Religion, and of the church among us', among them a mishandling of the authority of scripture and its relationship to the use of human reason, a weakening of the doctrine of predestination, an underestimation of preaching and a disrespect for Calvin.[39] Cruelly but effectively, the book climaxed in an attack on Hooker's peculiar method of presenting his arguments, 'so long and tedious, in a stile not usuall'; it elaborated on this in a 252-word-long sentence which was a hilarious and deliberate parody of the Hookerian period.[40]

Relentlessly, Willet claimed that the views that he was championing against Hooker were central to the Church of England. Hooker's already celebrated stylistic moderation signalled his determination to claim the middle ground in the English Church; while Willet was determined to seize the same territory for himself and repeatedly put himself on the side of Cranmer and the Oxford martyrs and even of Archbishop Whitgift (to whom he had dedicated other works). Hooker was the outsider, the deviant from the Church of England's norm. To many Elizabethan readers, it would have seemed a plausible case. Willet was seeking for Hooker something like the fate which had befallen a Cambridge scholar, William Barrett, only four years before: for attacking predestinarian doctrine, Barrett had been expelled from the university and, not long after, he converted to Roman Catholicism. Presiding over Barrett's humiliation had been Hooker's patron Archbishop Whitgift.[41] *A Christian Letter* was thus a serious attack which could have had dire consequences. Hooker's fury is evident from his surviving manuscript notes on his copy of the *Christian Letter*, which illustrate neither moderation nor judiciousness. But he had little chance to prepare a public answer: he died at his Kentish benefice of Bishopsbourne on 2 November 1600, at the age of forty-six. His friend and admirer Lancelot Andrewes, writing to another close friend only a few days later, lamented their loss, but he was also sadly conscious that most of the Church of England had no idea what it had lost.[42]

At the moment of his death, let us take stock of the man before he passes into myth. Izaak Walton would later want to picture him as a simple country parson, akin to Walton's literary portrait of George Herbert, but with an extra dimension: Hooker's humble country garb as described by Walton gave him touches of John the Baptist in the wilderness – the implication being that he made straight the way for the glories of the Anglican Church of Charles II's Restoration.[43] However, even Walton was forced to complicate this picture by a slightly awkward admission that Hooker was a wealthy man when he died. He left around £1,100 to his daughters, and his probate inventory reveals the parsonage at Bishopsbourne stuffed with furniture and belongings worth more than £600, including the staggering sum of £300 for his library, which must have been one of the best private book collections of his day.[44] Far from Hooker being a sequestered rural clergyman, the consistent pattern of evidence finds him in London, long after he had left his post at the Temple in 1591.

He spent a great deal of time at the home of his father-in-law, a prominent London merchant; his children were baptized and buried not at his country benefices but in London or Middlesex.[45] His angry annotations to his copy of the *Christian Letter,* evidence of his preoccupations in the last year of his life, show a man still intimately involved in London life; his inside knowledge of the publishing world meant that he knew of books which were still in the press, and in the year that Shakespeare's *Julius Caesar* may have been first performed in London, the death of Julius Caesar sprang into his mind as he reflected on Willet's false protestations of friendship.[46] More alarmingly, it had been while walking in the suburbs of London in the early 1590s that he had had an unfortunate, though probably innocent, encounter with a prostitute which had led to blackmail: it may have been the scandal arising from this murky incident which caused his abrupt resignation of the Temple Church and presentation to an obscure Wiltshire benefice, curtailing any further movement up the ecclesiastical *cursus honorum* during his short life. Finally, it was while travelling back from London to his final parish in Kent that he caught the cold which led to his death.[47]

This rather metropolitan – not to say cosmopolitan – Hooker was lost to sight after his death by the confusion and ill-will into which his family fell. Bitter quarrels between his executors, his wife and daughters and his wife's second husband led to a proliferation of lawsuits over his wealth, all rediscovered seventy years ago by the scholar-poet C. H. Sisson. The epic struggle was notorious: that most metropolitan of dramatists Ben Jonson even took the gossip about it as far as Edinburgh when he visited the poet William Drummond of Hawthornden, eighteen years after Hooker's death.[48] The result was gradually to remove the real Hooker from the scene. He received no monument until 1635 and then it was not put up by his family but by William Cowper, who managed to get the date of his death wrong by three years. His daughter's gravestone of 1649 confusedly boasted that he had been Dean of Salisbury.[49] By the later 1650s, those trying to produce memoirs of him even thought that he had died unmarried, and once more got his death-date wrong. Meanwhile, the obscure and slightly controversial figure of Hooker was being transformed into an iconic and much-contested authority.

The process began in 1603 with an attempt to answer Willet's *Christian Letter*, published in London as *A just and temperate defence*. It proclaimed itself as 'published by authority', which was nothing less than the truth, because it was written by William Covell, a chaplain of the man who was about to succeed John Whitgift as Archbishop of Canterbury, Richard Bancroft. Moreover, it had been licensed for publication by a chaplain of Whitgift's, one John Buckeridge, and the combination of author and licenser is a significant one. Buckeridge was a prime representative of a new element in the establishment of the English Church. He was a colleague and friend of William Laud at St John's College, Oxford, though since he was an older and more senior man than Laud, it makes little sense to call him and those like him Laudians. The term 'High Church' is likewise too blunt an instrument for Buckeridge's new mood of sacramentalism, clericalism and distaste for the style of the earlier English Reformation: the most accurate recent term coined by modern historians is 'avant-garde conformist'. That distinguishes Buckeridge and his fellows from two generations of conformists like Whitgift and Bancroft, who had not so decisively parted with the Reformed mainstream of the rest of Europe.[50]

Already, therefore, one party in the Church was reaching out to embrace Hooker, a party with a very definite agenda to move the

Church on and refashion in its own mould England's worship, theology and general ecclesiastical style. That was not, of course, how Covell presented his task. He repeatedly stressed Hooker's 'temperate' or 'grave' moderation: this was essential if he was to counter Willet's effort to push Hooker to the margins of the Church. In reality, however, Covell sharpened every one of the positions which Willet had attacked in Hooker, at the same time quoting extensively and generally without acknowledgement directly from the *Ecclesiastical Polity.* For Covell, attack was the best form of defence. On the inflammatory question of the Church of Rome, for instance, he was much more explicit than Hooker had been in saying that members of the Church of Rome could live and die in that Church and be saved. He even implied that all who denied Rome to be a true Church were Puritans. This was heady stuff at the time; it was an early instance of the rhetorical strategy whereby those who criticized Hooker might be labelled Puritans, and could thus be written off as having nothing to do with the Church of England. Covell indeed wrote with more sympathy about moderate Roman Catholic authors than he did about Puritans.[51] The only point where Covell beat a strategic retreat in the face of an assault by Willet on Hooker's message was on predestination. Here Covell rather unhappily asserted a fairly orthodox Reformed position, said that the whole matter was a mystery, and for once, did not assert the essential clarity of Hooker's position. The Barrett affair was too recent for comfort; it was not yet time for avant-garde conformists to show their hand on predestination.[52]

So now the avant-garde conformists were choosing those aspects of Hooker's work which eloquently and at length defended their case, and they were using his 'moderation' to manoeuvre themselves into the rhetorical centre-ground of the Church. It was a strategy with a major long-term future. One of the earliest quotations of Hooker by a conformist writer after Covell is a passing piece of anti-Puritan abuse from Hooker's Preface to *Of the Lawes of Ecclesiastical Polity* and comes from Thomas Rogers, like Covell a client of Bancroft, in 1607.[53] Only eighteen years after Hooker's death, Ben Jonson, a good hater of Puritans, could tell William Drummond in Scotland that Hooker's book was authoritative in England 'for church matters'.[54] Hooker could be quarried for two themes which appealed to avant-garde conformists: his polemical role against Puritans and his conciliatory attitude to the Church of Rome. But Hooker's stance on Rome had a wider use. It became unexpectedly fashionable with the accession of James VI to the English throne. Despite the unfortunate hiccup caused by Guy Fawkes's spirited attempt to remove James and his Parliament from the scene, a major element of James's policy was a national and international ecumenicism. At home, he wanted to reconcile his Roman Catholic subjects to his rule, as he had done so successfully in Scotland; thus when the new English order of baronets was instituted in 1611, prominent Roman Catholics were among the leading beneficiaries (albeit at a price).[55] Internationally, James made overtures to Rome for the general reunion of Christendom, and he was even prepared to suggest that the pope could be the patriarch of a reunited Church.[56] An author who provided a sustained rhetoric of moderation on this subject was liable to find his stock suddenly rising.

Particularly unexpected was a client base which Hooker's work now developed on top of this – English Roman Catholic propagandists. Catholics could make use of a Church of England writer who denigrated Puritans, and who might be taken as readjusting the role of scripture in discussing questions of doctrinal authority. Hooker could be read as stressing the importance of tradition as an arbiter of doctrine. If such an author says such things, the argument ran, then the Catholic case is made by the Church's opponents. This was a particularly effective line in the atmosphere created by James I's ecumenical busyness. However, if this strategy was to work, it was essential for Roman Catholics to stress the authority of Hooker's works. A precocious example of this was provided in the Parliament of 1604, when a crypto-papist MP, John Good, got up and attacked Puritans as being no better than Protestant sectaries. This was a standard innuendo promoted in the *Ecclesiastical Polity*, and it was grist to Good's mill to quote the book which he styled the 'absolute and unanswerable works of reverend Mr. Hooker'.[57] The move is soon after exemplified in print, first in the work of an adroit pseudonymous Catholic writing under the name John Brereley. Brereley's 1608 *Protestants Apology for the Roman Church* is entirely based on the technique of quoting Protestants to make Roman Catholic arguments. In using Hooker and Covell, Brereley takes them as representative of the Church of England, punctiliously pointing out that Covell had published his work with Bancroft's authority.[58]

Brereley's writings provoked response and counter-response for half a century, and his strategy on Hooker became common in Roman Catholic polemic throughout the seventeenth century.[59] It also achieved results. For instance, Elizabeth, Lady Falkland (writer, translator and mother of the patron of the Great Tew circle) said of her conversion to Catholicism around 1604 that the *Polity* 'had left her hanging in the air; for having brought her so far (which she thought he did very reasonably) she saw not how, nor at what, she could stop, till she returned to the Church from whence they were come'. Equally, James II attributed his conversion primarily to reading Hooker. This is the most backhanded of tributes to Hooker's authority.[60] Such Roman Catholic use of Hooker may have been the origin of the almost certainly spurious anecdote in Izaak Walton that Pope Clement VIII expressed his admiration for Hooker's writings when two leading English Catholic clergy read out extracts to him, translating into Latin as they went along.[61] In fact Hooker was never put into print in Latin and thus never gained an international audience, despite an early hint in the 1620s from William Camden that such a translation would be a good idea, and despite a complete effort from Bishop John Earle which remained in manuscript and was then lost.[62] Hooker's impact remained entirely confined within the English-speaking world.

The mischievous Roman Catholic praise of Hooker would have to be answered. One possibility would be to ignore him, and thus deny him authority, and for many Puritan-minded heirs of Andrew Willet, this was the answer. The great Puritan lecturer Samuel Ward of Ipswich (1577–1640) conspicuously failed to include Hooker's works in the town library whose contents he masterminded for the benefit of his successors as borough lecturers.[63] The Calvinist Bishop William Bedell, the beginning of whose career was spent in Ward's world of East Anglian Puritanism, said briskly in 1630, and without a hint of apology about his personal library, 'Mr Hooker I have not.'[64] This was hardly surprising, since Bedell recalled on another occasion that his friend James Wadsworth, another Suffolk parson and eventual convert to Rome, had picked up anti-Calvinist notions in his youth by misreading the works of Hooker, Bancroft and Hooker's friend Hadrian Saravia, misunderstanding them as opposing Calvin's doctrine as well as Calvinist discipline.[65]

A more constructive line would be to reclaim Hooker for the mainstream and stress his Protestant arguments against Rome: to find in him an acceptable champion of the Reformed Church and range him alongside other great names of the cause. This seems to have been the agenda behind a burst of publication of Hooker's lesser works in 1612–14 by Henry Jackson, assistant to Hooker's literary executor, Dr John Spenser, Rainolds's successor as President of Corpus Christi College. Jackson provided prefaces for two of these works, printed in Oxford by the university printer. The first, prefacing Hooker's *Discourse of Justification*, spoke of the necessity of publication because 'it will free the Author from the suspition of some errours, which he hath been thought to have favoured'; Jackson darkly added the Latin proverb, 'he who lacks an enemy will be crushed by his friends'.[66] The most obvious candidate for this thrust by Jackson was Hooker's defender Covell. Notably, this work merited a second edition in 1613 – interest in Hooker was evidently picking up. Jackson's second preface, to the 1614 publication of Hooker's early and notably Reformed sermons on Jude, was even more remarkable in that it managed to omit any mention of Hooker by name, and concentrated on a passionate defence of that flower of Reformation martyrs, Bishop Hugh Latimer, against attacks by papists.[67] That was product placement with a vengeance.

A useful literary trope used by other forward Protestants was to take the happy coincidence of three recent members of Corpus Christi College who were all Devon men – John Jewel, John Rainolds and Richard Hooker – and treat them as a trio: that necessarily associated Hooker with two safely Protestant names. This is what was done in the memorial biography for Dr Rainolds written by his relative Daniel Featley, later to be chaplain to George Abbot, the eminent Reformed divine who became Archbishop of Canterbury: the three Corpus men were 'Devonienses triumviros literatos'.[68] The establishment Calvinist and Oxford divine Dr George Hakewill used the same conceit in 1627 when he dedicated his bestselling book on providence to the University of Oxford; in the main text of the same work,

Hakewill was careful to further associate Hooker with the great names of the European Reformation, Zwingli and Bullinger.[69]

With Hooker thus safely reclaimed, the old guard mainstream of the Jacobean Church could give him due praise and put him to use.[70] They tended to cite what he said on fairly minor matters, but not always. Samuel Ward of Sidney Sussex College, Cambridge, a different man from the Puritan lecturer of Ipswich, but also a hero of the godly and a devout disciple of the arch-Puritan William Perkins, approved strongly of Hooker's views on the Eucharist. In good Calvinist fashion, he disapproved of the general run of English Protestant sacramental discussion because it minimized the efficacy of the sacraments; he termed this view 'obsignation', something closer to Zürich than to Geneva. Taking a healthier viewpoint, he recommended more than once what Hooker had to say about the sacraments.[71] When the moderate Puritan and future bishop Joseph Hall preached the keynote sermon to the clergy of the Convocation of Canterbury in 1624, he placed Hooker in a succession of twenty-one leading scholarly lights of the Church since the Reformation; together they made the learning of the English clergy '*stupor mundi*', the wonder of the world. The list began with Jewel, and thereafter it was weighted towards Reformed heroes, so that Hooker was to be found cheek by jowl with the great Puritan bestseller William Perkins as well as with anti-Calvinist John Overall, but, even more remarkably, with his erstwhile tormentor Andrew Willet![72]

Yet Hooker the respectable Protestant divine could be challenged by Hooker the Protestant ceremonialist and theologian of the middle way in order to aid and comfort the growing power of Laudianism in the English Church in the last years of James I and in the reign of Charles I. On ceremonies, Hooker did not entirely chime in with Laudian preoccupations: he couched his defence of them too much for Laudian sensibilities in terms of legal validity and 'things indifferent', rather than affirming their directly divine institution.[73] However, his exhaustive discussion of the subject in Book V could hardly be other than a resource for the ceremonially minded, and there was much else in Hooker for Laudians to savour. All those avant-garde aspects of his work which Covell had emphasized against Willet were there for the heirs of Covell and Buckeridge to seize on and develop, much to the shock and fury of the conformist mainstream in the Church hierarchy.[74] The Laudians increasingly emphasized their own centrality at the expense of the Church's old guard – and not simply in the English Church, but a wider centrality in the riven state of Latin Christianity. Laudians developed the ecumenicism promoted by King James by repositioning the Church of England as the representative of true Catholicism, standing aloof from most Protestants as well as from the Church of Rome. Thus in July 1624 one of the most uninhibited spokesmen of the movement, Richard Montague, said that he sought a Church of England that would 'stand in the gapp against Puritanisme and Popery, the Scilla and Charybdis of antient piety'.[75] This was the true beginning of *via media* discussion, which would have a major future in the Anglican tradition. Hooker's precocious irenicism towards Rome and his constant stress on the Aristotelian mean were of great use here.

Besides Hooker's irenicism, his moderation was important. That had been part of his literary self-image, and undoubtedly it formed an authentic part of his personal outlook. The earliest effort at quasi-biographical description of him, John Spenser's preface to the 1604 edition of the *Polity*, had stressed his 'soft and mild disposition'.[76] Given the Laudian claim to represent the centre ground of English religion in the face of opposition from much of the rest of the Church, it was particularly useful for the Laudians to celebrate the moderate style and measured learning of Hooker. So it seems to have been the Laudians who first made much of the adjective which would come to characterize the man: 'judicious Hooker'. An early instance came in 1631, in a book by the Laudian William Page aimed against William Prynne and defending bowing at the name of Jesus.[77] Not long afterwards, the sacramentally minded Kentish gentleman William Cowper, who with the encouragement of his Laudian incumbent finally provided a monument for Hooker at Bishopsbourne in 1635, added the description 'judicious' to Hooker's name when he made an English translation of a Latin epitaph for him. By 1675, after much emphasis on the 'judicious Hooker' in Izaak Walton's biography, it was enough of a cliché to need no explanation in the title of a Hooker selection entitled *Judicious Hooker's illustrations of Holy Scripture*.[78]

Laudian celebration of Hooker brought him his most socially

exalted admirer yet: King Charles I. Sir Philip Warwick, servant to the king during the 1640s, reminisced that 'Bishop Andrewes, Laud and Hooker were this Prince's three great authors'.[79] This is not surprising, given the crucial role of Lancelot Andrewes at the beginning of the 1620s in turning Charles away from the international Reformed tradition in which his father and elder brother had stood.[80] Andrewes, one of the literary executors and consistent champion of Hooker, would naturally point the king to his work; after that, in the 1630s Andrewes and Hooker were destined habitually to be paired by Laudians as reliable precursors of their own activity.[81] Laud himself naturally reinforced Andrewes's message about Hooker. In 1636, as Chancellor of Oxford, he masterminded Charles's visit to the University with his brother-in-law the Elector Palatine. The University authorities made a point of presenting a copy of Hooker's works to the exiled Elector while Charles looked on – a delicate instance of their habitual sensitivity to the enthusiasms of the great and the good.[82] Charles's devotion to Hooker was displayed as much in the worst as in the best of times. In an appendix to his supposed meditations before his death, the mammoth bestseller *Eikon Basilike*, his daughter Princess Elizabeth recalled that in their last interview, 'Hee bid mee read Bishop Andrew's Sermons, Hooker's Ecclesiastical Politie, and Bishop Laud's Book against Fisher'.[83] So Hooker was thereafter canonized by association in the martyrology of a Laudian saint. The association would moreover suggest that Hooker's undoubted defence of reverent ceremonial was paired with the sort of divine right principles advocated by the martyred king, an assumption which, as we have already begun to note, was not justified.

At the same time, Hooker took on a different valence. He became a hero of the loose grouping of intellectuals who gathered around the second Viscount Falkland at his Oxfordshire mansion at Great Tew, notably the polymath scholar William Chillingworth. The group equally deplored Reformation dogmatism and the new clericalist ceremonialism of the Laudians, even though Chillingworth was a personal friend of Laud. Chillingworth, a convert to Rome who had then thought better of it, was well aware of the misuse of Hooker by Brereley and similar Catholic writers, and the chief themes which they had explored were also what attracted him in Hooker: the discussion of reason, to which Hooker appeals so frequently throughout his work, and of moderation, a quality which meant much to the Great Tew circle. Reason and moderation were concepts equally important to Laud and his associates, but they heard very different things when they read of these concepts in Hooker. The contrast was at its most stark on the subject of reason. For Chillingworth, reason was principally a faculty of the individual mind, brought to bear on problems of scriptural authority as a final court of appeal; it became virtually his primary authority in matters of belief. For Laud, tussling with concepts of the Church's authority promoted by Roman Catholics in his 'conference' with 'Fisher the Jesuit', reason was a communal wisdom, to be associated closely with the tradition of the Church. Church tradition was not something which was divinely instituted, but controlled by God's gift of reason. In this three-cornered contest for the meaning of reason and authority between Chillingworth, Laud and the Jesuit Fisher, Hooker was an ambiguous force, whose pronouncements were sufficiently capacious for all sides to be able to quote him.[84]

The crowning testimony to Hooker's early Stuart reputation, finally nailing into place his authority in relation to the Church of England, came paradoxically from fierce critics in Scotland. Their venom had been aroused by the political crisis provoked by Charles I's mishandling of his northern kingdom and imposition of a new Prayer Book in 1637. In the national revolution which followed, the Scots' aim was to reject what they saw as English arrogance and ecclesiastical imperialism. Charles I's theological hero made a good figurehead to attack. When in 1637 the uncompromising Scots divine George Gillespie published his *Dispute against the English-Popish ceremonies, obtruded upon the Church of Scotland*, Hooker was the first English theologian whom Gillespie named as part of the assault on Scottish purity. With Gillespie, we have returned to the Hooker of Willet's assault. Significantly, Gillespie's vitriol was republished in 1660; it became part of the Presbyterian effort to resist a partisan Anglican settlement of the Church question in the three kingdoms.[85]

Other Scots were perhaps more discriminating than Gillespie in their hostility to Hooker, but only because they hated Archbishop Laud more. In his vicious literary attack on Laud in 1640, Robert Baillie contrasted the work of Laud and his associates in virtually restoring the mass with the earlier and slightly less offensive Eucharistic discussion of 'Andrews, Hooker, Mountague, or the grossest of the English Divines'.[86] The intellectual historian Conal Condren has expressed it neatly: Hooker's reputation as an authoritative representative of the Church of England was 'assured by an uneasy alliance of his church's enemies' – Jesuits on the one hand, and angry Scots Presbyterians on the other.[87] It was an astonishing turnaround in the fortunes of the man who, at his death, had seemed to be the author of a large and unsuccessful work of conformist propaganda. In the forty years from 1600, Hooker's big book had been transformed into a great book. Protean Hooker had become a standard-bearer for a bizarre spectrum of moderate Protestants, high-flying Laudians, gentle rationalists at Great Tew and converts to Roman Catholicism. But there was more to come.

With the outbreak of Civil War in 1642, England dissolved into more than political and social confusion: the new and uncontrollable situation produced ideological confusion and bewilderment. Any writer like Hooker who represented stability and continuity was therefore at a premium. His varied old admirers predictably clung to him throughout the next two decades. So apologists for the old Prayer Book like Anthony Sparrow, Henry Hammond or Peter Heylyn found him their mainstay.[88] Admirers of the shattered episcopal Church of England began taking a belated interest in finding out who Hooker actually was. Thomas Fuller, in his *Church-History of Britain* of 1655, began to scrape together what he could find out about the man's life. Even the defenders of what little stability had been re-established in the 1650s tried to use Hooker's name: nervous Presbyterians worried about Independents and the excesses of the radical sects, and apologists for Interregnum governments who were trying to persuade recalcitrant Anglicans to offer de facto allegiance and ecclesiastical conformity to the new order in church and state.[89] The one significant silence comes from the man who most passionately sought stability after the national catastrophe, but did so in his own distinctively bleak fashion: Thomas Hobbes. It is not surprising that the sacramental mysticism of Hooker's theology, his moderation and his defence of the Church's distinctive identity should hold little appeal for the expounder of an ultra-Erastian absolutism.

Nevertheless Hooker was beginning to take on wider political significance because the full scope of his writings was now being put into print. It will be remembered that at his death, three of the eight books of the *Polity* were still in manuscript. Despite several proclamations of intent to get these properly published, nothing had been done, for reasons which are still not entirely clear, but which to begin with had a great deal to do with the vicious in-fighting and lawsuits among Hooker's heirs and literary executors.[90] The monument put up to him in 1635 made a point of stating that the three last books '*desiderantur*' (were lost), but that was not true. There may indeed have been a deliberate ambiguity in the inscription, for a second resonance of the verb '*desiderantur*', if the epitaph had added a qualifying '*adhuc*' ('still' or 'hitherto'), would be that the books were looked for and their absence should be ended. Part of Book VI was indeed lost for ever during the early seventeenth century, and what remained of it included a long section on the practice of confession which now seems curiously incongruous with the general thrust of the *Polity*, since it is directed against Roman Catholics rather than presbyterian Puritans.[91] However, Book VII on episcopacy and Book VIII on Church and State remained intact, although to varying degrees not in a final polished state. They were always well known to some through manuscript circulation: Lancelot Andrewes, for instance, was able to quote from Book VIII in a sermon preached before James I in 1606, although he did not acknowledge the citation in print.[92]

What is interesting is that, after the dust of the Hooker family lawsuits had begun to settle in the 1630s, and the manuscript books were safe in the hands of reliable leading churchmen like Archbishop Laud, they were still not finally put into print. This may well not have been because they were unknown, but because their content was too well known. In Book VII, Hooker would have been unacceptably minimalist in Laudian eyes on the apostolic origins of the episcopate, in line with the fact that in Book III he had already written off episcopacy in James VI's Church of Scotland. Equally, in Book VIII, he did not uphold the universal divine right of monarchs, and he enlarged on the theme of an original contract between governed and governors. His stance should not surprise us. The man who had financially underwritten Hooker's original publications, his friend Edwin Sandys, was an enthusiastic conformist in the religious terms of the late Elizabethan Church, but Sandys had gone on after Hooker's death to become a major thorn in the side of Jacobean government: suspected by some of republicanism, and capable in 1614 of asserting that a king was elected 'with reciprocal conditions betweene King and People'.[93]

With such associations, an extended version of Hooker was not what the ruling clique in Church and State wanted to read in the 1630s. Laud's Victorian admirer John Keble did his best delicately to extenuate what he clearly suspected was deliberate suppression on Laud's part: 'a false notion might prevail, of undue countenance likely to be afforded to the innovators by certain portions'.[94] There were indeed many who gave the missing text an eager audience; manuscripts of Book VIII were in particular demand.[95] It is possible that when the Westminster Parliament confiscated Laud's copies of Hooker's manuscripts in 1641 and put them in the hands of the leading radical preacher Hugh Peter, the intention was to publish them in order to damage Laud and the king's party. In the end, publication of Books VI and VIII had to wait until 1648, and it became the responsibility of Archbishop James Ussher, former discreet opponent of Laud and now the focus for many of hopes for a moderate Protestant settlement.[96]

With this 1648 publication began a new and paradoxical phenomenon: the efforts of some High Churchmen and exponents of royal divine right to combat or discredit the newly revealed message of Hooker; this was matched by an interest in him from some who supported the new order in Church and State. The leading contribution on divine right was the work of Sir Robert Filmer, *Patriarcha*, which during the 1650s gradually emerged into the general political consciousness in the same manner as the later parts of the *Ecclesiastical Polity* – through the circulation of manuscript copies before its belated appearance in print. Filmer, probably writing originally in the early 1630s, had argued that absolute monarchical power derived from the original power enjoyed by fathers over their households, an idea which Hooker had explicitly rejected. Encountering the manuscript versions of Hooker's Book VIII, with their objectionable message of an original contract, Filmer could hardly belittle the great man, given the reputation which the published portion of Hooker's work enjoyed among Laudians. His reaction was to express rhetorical respect for

Hooker's authority, ranking him along with Aristotle as a giant, while describing himself as a dwarf in their company: this was a springboard for selective and minimal quotation from Hooker's work.

Already in 1658, Edward Gee, Presbyterian propagandist for the Interregnum government, could in response use Hooker in his attack on Filmer's still-manuscript work in order to propound a theory of government based on original consent by the people – even to justify the deposition of usurpers.[97] This was prophetic of how the political Hooker would be positioned in the future. Equally prophetic was Jeremy Taylor's silence in January 1660 about Hooker's last three books. With the exciting prospect of a new religious dispensation in the three kingdoms, he recommended to Irish friends a list of books to form the basis of a reliable Anglican library. He must have known of Archbishop Ussher's 1648 publication of Books VI and VIII, but he only mentioned Hooker's first five, highlighting Book V on liturgy.[98]

Then in 1660 came the collapse of the Interregnum government and the restoration of Charles II. The immediate problem to be solved was the future shape of English religion. Could the English Church be rebuilt on the basis of episcopacy, yet heal the wounds of the previous twenty years and recreate the Protestant comprehensiveness which it had enjoyed in the reign of James I? There were many who wished this to happen, both episcopalians and moderate Presbyterians. Others among the returning royalist exiles and the royalist gentry of the English provinces were determined to take revenge on those who had helped to destroy not just the king but the old Church and commonwealth, and as part of that revenge they intended to draw the boundaries of conformity as narrowly as any pre-war Laudian would have wished. Among this latter group was a determined set of clergy led by a politician of genius, Gilbert Sheldon, who soon became Archbishop of Canterbury: we may safely apply to them that term so often now misleadingly backdated into the sixteenth century – Anglicans. Soon the most extreme and politically active among them would acquire the label of High Churchmen. The question now was which party could most effectively shape the identity of the new Church. It will be no surprise to discover that the identity of Richard Hooker was part of the answer to that question.

The moderates did their best to claim back Hooker for themselves, just as their predecessors had tried to do in the 1620s. They included no less a figure than Edward Hyde, Earl of Clarendon, a veteran of the pre-war Great Tew circle and, despite the many bitternesses which he had accumulated over two decades, now doing his best as Chief Minister of the Crown to stem the tide of Cavalier extremism and the hard line of the clerical grouping around Gilbert Sheldon.[99] It is well known that the opening sentence of Clarendon's *History of the Rebellion and Civil Wars in England* is an imitation of the opening sentence of Hooker's Preface in the *Ecclesiastical Polity*; Hugh Trevor-Roper has gone so far as to say that Clarendon intended his work 'to be the secular counterpart' of the *Polity*.[100] However, as Jessica Martin has more recently discovered, there are two other significant examples of the same phenomenon: the first sentences in biographies of two moderate Protestant figures of the pre-1640 era, Bishop Thomas Morton and Robert Sanderson.[101] Biography was now to prove the chief battleground for Hooker.

The cue in this had been given by the biographical fragments published from 1655 onwards by Thomas Fuller in his monumental and delightfully miscellaneous history of the English Church. Despite the compliments which Fuller heaped on Hooker, the result was by no means hagiography. Not once but twice Fuller alludes to the story of Hooker's blackmail by a London prostitute, part of the hidden reputation of the great divine which had not previously surfaced in print. Notably, in Fuller's extended account in the *Church-History* of the row between Travers and Hooker, there is more praise of Travers than of Hooker, including the fact that Travers was a much better preacher, and there is a definite suggestion that Hooker came off worst in the whole affair. Fuller was also careful to minimize the hostility between the presbyterian and the conformist, a strategy with obvious resonances in the 1650s.[102] Significantly, in the changed conditions of 1662, in the revised account provided in his *History of the Worthies of England*, Fuller felt more inclined to stress the conflict between the two men, so it was then that he added his famous phrase contrasting the sermons of pure Geneva and pure Canterbury.[103] But already his earlier work had been subsumed into a pioneering attempt to write a full life of Hooker by Bishop John Gauden: the introduction to the first complete assemblage of the surviving text of the *Ecclesiastical Polity*.

Gauden had been the ghost-writer of Charles I's bestselling *Eikon Basilike* and he was rewarded at the Restoration with the bishopric of Exeter for keeping reasonably quiet about this operation. He was nevertheless a moderate episcopalian who had managed to conform throughout the Interregnum, and as plans for the king's Restoration were gathering momentum, he published an extended study of how the new Church might move forward in a comprehensive way; Hooker played an important supporting role in his case.[104] He was an ambitious man who was no doubt eager to seize the chance of promoting his abilities in such an important literary venture as the Hooker edition, but he was to be disappointed in his hopes of further advancement through his efforts: his introductory biography appalled Sheldon and resolute High Churchmen when it appeared in January 1662. It is indeed a strange production. In its forty quarto pages of rambling moralizing and shameless padding, it adds virtually nothing to the scraps which had already appeared in print, apart from a guess at Hooker's exact birthplace in Exeter (culled from one of Gauden's recently acquired flock in that city), and, alarmingly, more than a page fleshing out in detail Fuller's hints about the blackmail attempt, exploiting gossip from Gauden's undergraduate days in Oxford.[105] Gauden also takes his cue from Fuller in being less than hagiographical, particularly on the subject of Hooker's dull preaching. He gives a broad hint that he finds Book V of the *Polity* fairly tedious, and his encomium of Hooker is less than overwhelming: 'in whom some things were admirable, many things imitable, and all things commendable'.[106]

Perhaps more offensive and dangerous in the eyes of observers like Archbishop Sheldon was Gauden's aggressive moderation. He was openly and repeatedly rude about pre-war Laudianism, giving it its share of blame for the catastrophe of the 1640s:

> the strength of the Church of England was much decayed and undermined, before it was openly battered; partly by some superfluous, illegal and unauthorized innovations in point of Ceremony, which some men affected to use in publique, and impose upon others, which provoked people to jealousie and fury . . .

Such remarks were paired with irenic remarks about moderate nonconformists of the 1590s, who were carefully distinguished from doctrinaire presbyterians.[107] Hooker was repeatedly presented as a counterweight to excess, and Gauden's own view of episcopacy remained resolutely pragmatic: 'Episcopacy rightly managed, is manifested to be the great Interest of Gods glory, and our Saviours honor, as they have by precepts and examples constituted a visible Church, regular Flock, and orderly Family in this world.' His parting exhortation to his readers (whom he envisaged as 'us ... Bishops and Presbyters') was that they should be inspired by Hooker, 'Neither losing friends by negligences in the main concerns of holiness and peace, nor multiplying enemies by causeless exasperations and extravagancies'.[108] Amidst the triumphalist Anglican crackdown of 1662, this was subversive talk. Something would have to be done, and when in the same year Fuller's *Worthies* appeared, correcting his own errors on Hooker, which Gauden had copied, the perfect excuse was provided.

The result was famously that Gilbert Sheldon commissioned Izaak Walton to write a replacement life. It was a labour of love which Walton had in any case previously contemplated undertaking; it proved a delightful and masterly shaping of what was known about Hooker into an image which back-projected Walton's own gentle sacramentalist Anglicanism onto the gentle divine of the previous century.[109] The life was first published separately in 1665, but from 1666 it permanently shouldered aside Gauden's biography from the collected edition of Hooker's works: a rather feline introductory epistle from Walton regretted Gauden's 'many material mistakes, and more omissions'.[110] Even Walton's title-page for the whole work was subtly remodelled in appropriate fashion from the title-page of Gauden's edition, while being broadly identical to it. Gauden's Hooker had been described as 'learned, godly, judicious and eloquent'; Walton's Hooker was just 'learned and judicious'. Gauden's Church of England had been 'duly Reformed'; Walton deleted that whole phrase. 'Godly' and 'Reformed' had the wrong sound in the Anglican world of Sheldon.

One of the most remarkable features of Walton's work was its deliberate effort to undermine the authenticity of the three last books of the *Polity*, which contained such unpalatable material on divine right and episcopacy; indeed, Walton devoted a substantial appendix to arguing the case against the three books. Using circumstantial anecdotes and statements derived from partisans in the family feuds of Hooker's heirs, Walton did his best to show that Books VI to VIII had been tampered with by ideologically motivated subversives, and so they did not now represent Hooker's true intentions. It was a remarkable exercise in having one's cake and eating it: Hooker the defender of Anglican ceremony and of the established polity of the Church of England could continue to provide authoritative aid and comfort to high-flying Anglicanism, while his problematic political statements could be quarantined. Some royalists who had embraced ideas about political contract in their earlier days and who now wanted to affirm their fervent belief in divine right, found it very convenient to discover the problematic status of Book VIII: they could now claim that they had been misled by a spurious work.[111]

Few editors can have striven as hard as Walton to shake their readers' confidence in the work which they have edited, and few can have achieved such success in their aim. Commentators of radical or Whig sympathies, such as the young Samuel Taylor Coleridge or the constitutional historian Henry Hallam, were always able to point out the self-serving nature of High Church doubts about the last three books.[112] Yet thanks to the affection in which Walton's work was held, the authenticity of these sections of Hooker's works was still in question right down to the twentieth century – quite unnecessarily.[113] The story of Hooker's reputation and influence after the Walton biography now becomes two stories, distinct although repeatedly overlapping: one, his reputation as ecclesiastical authority; the other, his usefulness as a political theorist of consent and contract. Those who commented on the ecclesiastical strand tended to reject or ignore the last three books; those who commented on the political strand would affirm their authenticity. Both camps were nevertheless anxious to apply Hooker's now axiomatic authority to the repeated crises which they faced.

The result was to pitch a gentle, clerical High Church Hooker against a Whig, contractarian Hooker. Those old-fashioned enough to continue to uphold Calvinism in the Church occasionally appealed to Hooker's statements on predestination in order to recall their former dominance in English theology, or to embarrass his High Church and Arminian admirers, but theirs were very much the minority voices.[114]

Nonconformists, many of them heirs of the moderate Reformed tradition which had once embraced his writings, generally lost interest in the ecclesiastical Hooker following the events of 1662.[115] This was understandable, particularly after a new wave of Anglican anti-Nonconformist publications, sparked by the political crisis of 1679–81, which sought to exclude James, Duke of York, from the throne: Hooker figured largely in this High Church publication drive, with much selective quotation and a new edition of his works in 1682.[116]

By contrast, politicians standing up against the claims of divine right theory were stimulated to embrace Hooker by the fact that their chief ideological enemy, Sir Robert Filmer, had both attacked and distorted him. During the Exclusion Crisis, Filmer's *Patriarcha* was put into print as a central polemical statement for the Tory grouping supporting James. The republican-minded Algernon Sidney, in his opposition to Filmer, gratefully drew on Hooker as a respectable authority for his own views, although in the process of advocating the rule of aristocracy against arbitrary monarchy, he pushed Hooker's political thought out of its political context almost as radically as Filmer had done.[117] Of greater long-term significance was John Locke's contest with Filmer, part of the same Exclusion Crisis literature. As in Sidney's work, Locke used Hooker as a respectable traditional authority opposing the sort of absolutism championed by Filmer as a testimony to the existence of an original contract behind government, and then as a smokescreen for his own more radical conclusions. Where Hooker had spoken of the paramountcy of consensus and custom in political activity, Locke in his *Two Treatises of Government* emphasized individual rather than corporate possession of political wisdom. He stripped natural law of its intimate association with the active divine will, and he stressed the natural rights of an individual, neither of which premises were part of Hooker's mental furniture.[118]

The Glorious Revolution of 1688 succeeded in ousting James where Exclusionists had failed. As an anxious political nation considered how to explain to itself what it had done in ejecting King James, it was not at first the radical contractarianism of Locke's *Two Treatises* which provided the answer. The new Whig establishment did not want to endanger its fragile alliance with Anglican Tories who in desperation had backed James's removal, nor did it wish to suggest that it had done anything as radical or populist as had emerged in the Civil War. It therefore looked away from Locke to seek a more conservative model of government that emphasized the role of the elite: a lawfully constituted Parliament and not a popular uprising had brought the change of regime, and so had saved England from extremes both of radicalism and Roman Catholicism. The Revolution's defenders had no inhibitions in using providential religious rhetoric: William III was God's agent in defending the English Church. Given these preoccupations, Hooker was a reassuringly conservative figure to quote, particularly if one emphasized that James and not his opponents had brought unwelcome innovation into English politics.[119] As the nation painfully regained its composure in 1689, at least two provincial quarter-sessions' grand juries were treated to doses of Hooker in their charges from the presiding justice: at Cambridge, Sir Matthew Dudley praised Hooker as having refuted those 'dangerous spirits', the Marprelates, lauded his 'charity and meekness' and quoted the first sentence of his preface. The Earl of Stamford in Leicestershire garnished the published version of his grand jury charge with a citation from the 'incomparable Hooker' and his (of course unquestionably authentic) Book VIII: 'There is the best Established Dominion, where the Law doth most rule the King.'[120]

The aftermath of the Glorious Revolution had also finally destroyed the reality of the polity which Hooker had described. Hooker had known a Church which had embraced virtually all the Protestants of the nation, and despite his polemical rhetoric which implied that Puritans were separatists, he had in reality been addressing opponents who were part of the same broad national Church as himself. Indeed, his text implied that everyone in England, Catholic recusants included, was part of that same ecclesial body.[121] In the wake of the Revolution, with the failure of a Comprehension Bill intended to make a space in the Church of England for at least some of those who objected to bishops and the Prayer Book, this was no longer the case even for Protestants; a comprehensive Protestant Church was not rebuilt. Protestant Dissenters there had been, ever since the completion of the Anglican Settlement in 1662; now they were to form a permanent feature of the national religious landscape. The Toleration Act, passed in 1689, turned out over the next decades to concern not a small minority of separatists, as had been intended, but a substantial proportion of the Protestant population. The eighteenth-century evangelical revival and the gradual separation of Methodism from the Church of England only exacerbated the situation. Judith Maltby puts it neatly: 'in 1689 a *national* church was finally replaced by the more pragmatic idea of an *established* church'.[122]

Far from rendering Hooker obsolete, this new situation added yet further dimensions to his usefulness. If Whigs used him to discuss original contracts, then Tories nostalgic for a truly national church would look to him as part of their ongoing attempts to restore the Church of England to its old position of virtual monopoly. Other Tories, however, had been unable to cope at all with the new political order. They had taken the radical step of leaving the Established Church to remain faithful to their oath of loyalty to the Stuarts, and had formed the Church grouping known as the Non-Jurors. As time went on, some of them even began to profit from their separation, to glory in the unsullied purity of their Church, and to assert that there was no necessary link between Church and State. Now Hooker could be used against the Non-Jurors by those Tories who had accepted the post-1689 regime and remained within the establishment, because Hooker had insisted on an undivided Church and State in a Christian society. That did not stop some Non-Jurors reading his defence of episcopal government as a basis for their insistence on the sacred commission of bishops to preserve the integrity of the Church.[123]

Thus Hooker entered the eighteenth century as a moderate Whig, a Lockean Whig, a moderate Tory, a ceremonialist parson and a Non-Juring defender of the Church's apostolic government. By now, anyone in English politics who needed a name to command instant respect or who wanted to score a debating point for their cause was ready to quote Hooker; even those beyond the orthodox Christian pale like Socinians and Deists tried it on.[124] Virtually any commentator could have said what was in fact said by a Whig, Sir John Willes, when defending England's constitution on the basis of Hooker, just after Queen Anne's death: 'Mr Hooker is an Author of unquestionable Credit, and has been always esteemed a Man of great Learning as well as a truly Orthodox Divine: And therefore his Authority will be of much greater Weight than any thing that I can say.'[125] Neverthe-less, it is not surprising that the noisiest claimants for Hooker were whoever happened to be in power. During the brief Tory renaissance under Queen Anne, it was his Tory aspect, the organic union of Church and State, which was most stridently proclaimed. Once the Hanoverians were on the throne and the Tories routed, then varia-tions on Hooker the Whig re-emerged as paramount. As Locke gradually became more widely esteemed by the establishment, many read Hooker through his eyes.[126] The arch-Whig churchman Benja-min Hoadly had little time for Locke, but he devoted a whole book in 1710 to *A Defense of Mr. Hooker's Judgment*, which was a defence of a Latitudinarian Church given its shape by a single act of consent safely back in 1689, and of an Erastian Church securely under the control of the Crown in Parliament.[127]

However, Bishop Hoadly provoked Church controversies which frightened many of his fellow Whigs looking for a quiet life in Church and State, and his extreme Erastianism offended Whig clergymen who may have been Whigs but who were still also clergymen. A creative answer to this problem, and an acceptable reformulation of Hoadle-ian themes, was provided from 1736 by Bishop William Warburton, quintessential establishment or court Whig cleric of Hanoverian Eng-land. His *Alliance between Church and State: Or, the Necessity and Equity of an Established Religion and a Test-Law Demonstrated* first appeared in 1736, and was thereafter expanded to become a best-seller.[128] Warburton was not an especially original thinker, but there is an engaging realism in his analysis of the Hanoverian constitution which gave his work a lasting popularity. In the third edition of his work, he boasted about this pragmatism to his dedicatee, the Earl of Chesterfield: 'I have still kept our own happy Constitution in my eye: And, under the direction of so safe a guide, I was secure from the danger of those visions, by which the best Writers who have treated these subjects only in the abstract, have been misled.'[129] His pedes-trian representativeness merits extended consideration.

Warburton's realism included the startlingly simple insight which has eluded most English commentators on the British constitution over the last three centuries: the existence of an established Presby-terian Church in Scotland as an essential part of a united kingdom. It was a body with a very different ethos from the Church of England, and Warburton felt little warmth towards it, talking sourly in the *Alliance* of the Kirk's reluctance to cooperate with the State.[130] However, the Kirk was unavoidably there after the constitutional deals of 1689 and 1707, and it represented the majority of the Scottish population, just as the Church of England did in England. It thus provided a justification for the English Church's continuing privileged position, as well as providing a bulwark against the Jacobitism of the Scottish Non-Juring episcopal clergy. As the index in the 1741 version of the *Alliance* succinctly put it, the alliance of Church and State 'must always be with the largest Religious Society, if more than one in the same state; in England with the Episcopal, in Scotland with the Presbyterian'. This, then, was a primary basis of what has been termed Warburtonianism: the alliance of Church and State was an association (Warburton preferred to talk of a 'convention' rather than a contract) which had been freely entered into by two separate societies – one secular, one religious. The state should have the greater voice in the association, but the association was not irrevocable. Nor did association imply an exclusive Church which included all worshipping Christians: an Established Church had a leading and privileged role, guaranteed by the seventeenth-century Test Acts which disadvantaged other Christians in public life, but also guaranteed their other rights. A Church was established only as long as it commanded majority support.[131]

Such clear-sighted observations of eighteenth-century Britain were fundamentally opposed to Hooker's vision of Elizabethan England. Warburton's state had no divine character; like Locke before him, he had attenuated the connection between natural law and its divine origin. Consequently, when Warburton wrote about Hooker, he neatly exemplified all the tensions which the post-1689 Settlement embodied in relation to the judicious divine. In early versions of the *Alliance*, he ignored the problem. He used Hooker a great deal in standard moderate Whig ways, praising his attacks on fanaticism, ridiculing High Church distortions of his views on episcopacy, and making admiring citations which are largely decorative. He also defended Hooker against what he saw as unjust criticisms by the dissenting historian Daniel Neal.[132] However, during the 1740s, Warburton's tangled relationship with the Tory political writer Henry, Lord Bolingbroke, erupted into a bitter feud and eventually provoked Warburton into further expansions of the *Alliance*. Bolingbroke had cited Hooker extensively in his campaigns against the great Whig Robert Walpole, and naturally Bolingbroke's Hooker was a Tory exponent of the organic union of Church and State.[133]

In the 1766 edition of the *Alliance*, Warburton confronted Bolingbroke in various respects, partly asserting that he had misread Hooker. However, he also decided that on the basic principle of the organic union of Church and State, Bolingbroke was all too accurate in his perception of Hooker: both writers must now be refuted.[134] Warburton in other respects reaffirmed his admiration for Hooker: he now called him 'the BEST GOOD MAN of our order', noted his incompatibility with Filmer and emphasized the authenticity of Book VIII. Nevertheless, unlike Warburton himself, Hooker had failed to discover 'that capital idea of an ALLIANCE', and he 'was wrong in thinking, church and state was only one society under different names'. In a remarkable rhetorical sleight of hand, Warburton managed to link Hooker, Elizabethan Puritans, Thomas Hobbes and Bolingbroke in a common Erastianism, a catch-all list which also had the advantage of silently reproving the missing name, the obstreperous Bishop Hoadly, for being excessively Erastian. Warburton also pointed out (perfectly correctly) that any conception of organic union between Church and State such as Hooker's led inevitably to the principle of persecution for religious opinions.[135]

Warburton's work never achieved universal admiration, for all its usefulness to the mid-eighteenth-century Whig establishment. It disturbed the illusion of Anglican country clergy that they still served a national and not an Established Church; in any case, many of them distrusted members of the hierarchy like Warburton who were more realistic than they were, and they also loathed Warburton's clear intellectual debt to Locke.[136] Warburton's attack on Hooker therefore focused High Church and Tory devotion to Hookerian principles of Church and State, and this devotion in turn was given a far more dramatic and urgent stimulus by the catastrophe of the French Revolution. When a king was executed and a national Church overthrown, Warburtonianism was at a discount. When Edmund Burke described the

Church as 'an oblation of the state itself', one hears a very different note from Warburton's exposition of a secular State in free alliance with a majority Church.[137] Pre-Tractarian High Churchmen like Bishop Samuel Horsley, Hutchinsonian divines and the Hackney Phalanx were contemptuous of Warburton, whom ironically they viewed as an extreme Erastian: they praised Hooker, but also toyed a little uncomfortably with the high-flown sacramentalism and clericalism embodied in Non-Juror theologies of the Church.[138]

The debacle for such Hookerian High Church hankerings came with the transformation of the basis of British national government in 1828–32: a series of legislative measures extending a raft of civil and political rights to Protestant Dissenters and even Roman Catholics dealt the death-blow to the long-wounded idea of a confessional English state. Not merely Tories were affected: the Whig interest disintegrated, and Hooker's long association with Whig political preoccupations became relegated to intellectual history. Among Tories, one reaction to the developing new situation was that of Samuel Taylor Coleridge in his *On the Constitution of Church and State* (1830). Here Coleridge, a great admirer of Hooker, may be said to have creatively misunderstood him. Coleridge envisaged a national Church which had a cultural as well as a religious function, a Church which could be distinguished from the Church of Christ: if the two had any relationship, it was 'a blessed accident'. Coleridge then identified his two faces of the Church in Hooker's discussion of the visible and invisible Church. But Coleridge's visible Church, whose primary role is as bearer of a nation's civilization, is hardly the same as Hooker's visible Church, the embodiment of divine truth and divine action in the world.[139]

Coleridge was in any case idiosyncratic in his relationship to the older High Church grouping to which he had in some sense returned after his Unitarian years. More representative, and also an epitaph on the Hookerian ideal of Church and State, was W. E. Gladstone's monumental and ill-fated work, *The State in Its Relations with the Church* (1838). Gladstone, a realistic politician as well as devout churchman, was aware that Hooker could not be fitted directly onto the situation of post-1832 England: 'church and commonwealth' could no longer be 'personally *one society*'. Nevertheless he drew the conclusion from

Hooker, 'the great doctrine that the state is a person, having a conscience, cognisant of matter of religion, and bound by all constitutional and natural means to advance it', and he scorned Bishop Warburton for his contrary secular vision of the state.[140] Yet in defending British Church establishments in this way, Gladstone was the last advocate of a world which had already disappeared: the England in which to be fully English was to be a member of the Church of England, not a Dissenter or a Roman Catholic. Characteristically, when he found that virtually no one else in the country agreed with him, he rewrote his book at twice the length, just to make sure that he had not been misunderstood. Still no one agreed. By the late 1860s, Gladstone himself had abandoned his theoretical justification of Church Establishment, and he outraged his constituents in Oxford University when he spearheaded the disestablishment of the Protestant Church of Ireland.

If Hooker's political legacy was effectively dead from the 1830s, his ecclesiastical and liturgical arguments continued to be useful to the Church of England as it rethought its role in the nation. The Oxford Movement was one distinctive and innovative response to the new situation, an attempt to rescue the Catholic character of the English Church from liberal and rationalist distortions, while showing a flexibility towards the notion of an intimate union between Catholic Church and confessional state which had sustained High Church theology since the days of William Laud. Much inspiration for the Oxford Movement's new departures came from its explorations of Non-Juror spirituality and theology, coupled with a re-examination of the Church of England's past in order to find inspiration for the present. Who better to explore than Hooker?

Central to the Oxford project in the 1830s, therefore, was a new edition of Hooker which would have a contemporary relevance: it was undertaken by John Keble, an old High Churchman who was prepared to move beyond the world which he knew, and who was openly determined to rescue Hooker from the multifarious uses to which he had been put over the previous century. The particular trigger for Keble's project was a three-volume edition of Hooker's works published in 1830 by Benjamin Hanbury, an accomplished Congregationalist historian. Hanbury naturally felt that the sixteenth-century

English Reformation had been incomplete and that the Church Establishment was its least desirable feature. He admired much about Hooker, with the very considerable exception of his views on Church and State and on episcopacy; his annotations to Book VII of the *Polity* are notably different from the rest of his editorial work and amount to a considerable critique of the text. No doubt with that particular part of Hanbury's labours in mind, Keble described the edition in his own preface as 'executed . . . with considerable spirit and industry, but in some parts with a degree of haste, and in many with an expression of party feeling, tending to lessen its usefulness greatly'.[141] He would also have been annoyed by Hanbury's clear-headed summing-up of two centuries of Hooker's reputation: 'in Politics what we understand by the term a Whig, but in Church affairs a Tory'. In reaction to this, Keble denounced 'the rationalists . . . and the liberals of the school of Locke and Hoadly', as the chief kidnappers of Hooker: Hanbury had indeed specifically asserted that Hooker was 'ably supported by Locke and Hoadly'. Keble was slightly disingenuous in wanting Hooker 'to become more generally read and known': his edition was intended to supplant Hanbury's and to make Hooker's works known in a particular way. '[S]urely the better they are known, the more entirely will they be rescued from the unpleasant association, and discreditable praise, just mentioned.'[142]

Keble's edition, a monument of meticulous scholarship for its day, was the most important event in Hooker scholarship since Izaak Walton's biography, yet its one notably traditionalist feature was that Keble (unlike Hanbury) strongly upheld Walton's reliability and thus prolonged the old High Church case against the last three books of the *Polity*. Keble adopted wholesale the attitudes of Laudians who had annexed Hooker from the Reformed mainstream in the early seventeenth century. He saw Hooker as training up successors in the Church from Laud onwards, to whom 'we owe it, that the Anglican Church continues at such a distance from that of Geneva, and so near truth and apostolical order'.[143] Keble said with little equivocation that the English Reformation was a deplorable event, inspired largely by foreigners, and that Hooker had been raised up by God to undo its unfortunate consequences: repeatedly, Keble contrasted Hooker with Archbishop Cranmer, to Cranmer's disadvantage.[144] Altogether, Keble's editorial preface, despite its genuine insight and probing of previously unused manuscript sources, is a formidable exercise in special pleading designed to turn Hooker's ecclesiological, sacramental and liturgical outlook towards the best possible approximation to a Tractarian of the 1830s. Keble does not ignore the problems in doing this: he deals at length with Hooker's attitude to divine right episcopacy, his receptionist Eucharistic views and his generally Reformed discussion of predestination, but the reader is left with the impression that such unfortunate features of the Elizabethan divine can more or less be nuanced out of sight.[145] Any regrettable aspects of Hooker's theology were in Keble's eyes more than compensated for by the mystical beauty of his sacramental outlook.[146]

Keble was at his least happy with Hooker's views on Church and State, which smacked to him of an obsolete Erastianism – a word fast becoming one of the most tainted in the Tractarian vocabulary. In this he was encouraged by the forthrightness of the Oxford Movement's most turbulent child, Hurrell Froude. Applying brutal logic to the post-1832 situation of the Church of England, Froude picked up the most radical stance of some eighteenth-century Non-Jurors in their rejection of the state link, and took it further. He produced assertions not merely of the Church's autonomy but of its supremacy; when his *Remains* were posthumously and perhaps unwisely published by his grieving friends, these sounded as startling as the pronouncements of any Roman Catholic ultramontane. Froude's contempt for Hooker's ecclesiology bred a more general irreverence towards him. Froude was prepared to take on the great man on a wider front: in 1835, exalting the rule of bishops in the Church against any possibility of lay participation in synods, he said, 'I don't know enough to have an opinion; but as far as I see I disagree with Hooker . . . Neither the laity nor the presbyters seem to me to have any part or lot in the government of the church.'[147] Such open selectivity also typified his friend John Henry Newman's attitude to Hooker: rather than seek to explain Hooker's views on justification in a sense compatible with his own interpretation of what was Catholic, Newman simply said, flatly, 'since we are not allowed to call any man our master on earth, Hooker, venerable as is his name, has no weight with any Christian, except as delivering what is agreeable to Catholic doctrine'.[148] Soon, in any case, Newman was to leave behind Hooker's Church for the Church of Rome.

There continued to be some attempts to rescue Hooker from the Tractarian grip. Professor R. D. Hampden, so much harassed by intolerant Tractarians in Oxford, must have enjoyed the moment when in 1844 he was able to fail a BD presented by the Tractarian R. G. Macmullen on the specific grounds that Macmullen had not disowned a presence in the elements apart from their reception, as Hampden maintained Hooker had done.[149] Evangelicals also took up the cudgels. Some Evangelicals objected strongly to the wholesale appropriation by the Tractarians and their successors of the mainstream divinity of the Stuart Church of England. Henry Fish, in his diatribe *Jesuitism traced in the movements of the Oxford Tractarians*, criticized E. B. Pusey, the doyen of the Oxford Movement, for citing Hooker and Andrewes 'in confirmation of Mr Newman's views of Justification: whereas the views of both those men were the very reverse of Mr. Newman's'. Less confrontationally, Anne Tyndale, an Evangelical correspondent of Pusey, told him that the eighteenth-century Evangelical revival had represented a revival of the theology not merely of the sixteenth-century Reformers, but also of 'Hooker, Ussher, Hall, and other great divines of the early seventeenth century' – an interesting succession which is a surprisingly accurate evocation of those moderate Protestant churchmen who had sought to appropriate Hooker in their day. There was indeed a Reformed Hooker to be rediscovered, as we have seen.[150]

Yet on the whole, the effect of Keble's magisterial edition was to cement Hooker firmly into the Victorian High Church tradition. In late Victorian England, Anglo-Catholics rather than Evangelicals wrote Anglican Church history. Different wings of a diverse Catholic movement chose different features of Hooker's works to exploit. Moderate Tractarians excavated him for discussion of the *via media*, a concept by then given canonical status in the Anglican writings of John Henry Newman. More extreme Anglo-Catholics selectively savoured what Hooker had to say about the Eucharist and episcopacy. Others revelled in a theologian of the Reformation who was not afraid to cite medieval scholasticism and canon law, no doubt not realizing how common this had been in the later years of the sixteenth century. The Church of England as a whole, no longer merely a national Church, but enjoying a newly central status in a worldwide Anglican communion, was happy to find an Anglican saint viewed through the agreeable filters provided by Izaak Walton and John Keble. As statues of saints came back into architectural and theological fashion, and proliferated amid the newly restored or rebuilt Gothic of Anglicanism's churches, Hooker's statue was often to be found, usually clutching his great book.[151]

Perhaps one can see this finally Anglican and specifically Tractarian victory in the contest for Hooker's identity as Pyrrhic. No one else wanted to exploit him any more. The central assumption around which his theology evolved, a unitary Church and State in which the national Parliament is the expression of the will of a Christian commonwealth, was gone for ever. It is notable that the main commentator from outside the Anglican tradition who chose to revisit Hooker's theories of government, that courageous anti-Fascist pioneer of Italian political philosophy, Alessandro Passerin d'Entrèves, did so because he wanted to explore alternatives to liberal political thought.[152] An added paradox in the story of Hooker's reputation is that no one has ever wanted to adopt everything which he propounded; everyone has made choices to suit themselves. There is no Hookerian Movement.

Yet it would be a mistake for theologians entirely to leave Hooker to the historians. Hooker's intricate discussion of what constitutes authority in religious matters gives him a contemporary usefulness. The disputes which currently wrack Western Christianity are superficially about sexuality, social conduct or leadership style: at root, they are about what constitutes authority for Christians. The contest for the soul of the Church in the West rages around the question of how a scripture claiming divine revelation relates to those other perennial sources of human revelation, personal and collective consciousness and memory; whether, indeed, there can be any relationship between the two. Hooker provides a major discussion of these problems in one historical context, and it would be foolish for modern Christians to ignore such a resource. But finally, if one feels any gratitude for the shape of modern Anglicanism – its exhilarating variety, its engaging inability to present a single identity, its admirable unwillingness to tell people what to do – much of this is to do with the protean nature of Richard Hooker: for no one since his death in 1600 has been able permanently to pin him down or to say what exactly constitutes the message of his huge, his enormous – his great book.

21

Forging Reformation History: a cautionary tale

In 1547 Archbishop Thomas Cranmer preached a pithy and dramatic sermon at the Coronation of King Edward VI, urging the royal youth to renew the scriptural role of young King Josiah of Judah in his own kingdom. In the early 1560s, Queen Elizabeth I berated Dean Alexander Nowell, in his own cathedral church of St Paul's, for subversion of her Protestant religious settlement through his ill-judged gift to her of a presentation copy of the Book of Common Prayer, enriched with devotional pictures. Both events are still repeatedly to be met with in accounts of the English Reformation, and the first has recently become something of a fixture in references to King Edward, but there is one problem: neither of them happened. They are fictions created by Robert Ware of Dublin (1639–97).[1] This Irish gentleman, second son of the distinguished Irish antiquarian and historian Sir James Ware (1594–1666), had an acute historical imagination, but he was also a liar and a forger, whose criminal deceptions had a malign effect on the politics and historiography of his day and have shown remarkable staying power since. Although Ware was unmasked by three late Victorian scholars, and by others since in passing, his forgeries still pollute the historical pool of sources about English and Irish history. Hence Ware needs to be exposed afresh, in an effort finally to exorcize him from our understanding of the sixteenth century. Turning our gaze on Ware may also reveal something about the preoccupations and temptations to which historians are prone, even in modern historiographical practice.

Robert Ware's background was in the Irish Protestant governing group that maintained a fierce loyalty to the episcopally ordered

Established Protestant Church of Ireland through all the vicissitudes of the seventeenth century: they were what in the eighteenth century would be termed 'the Ascendancy'. Ware was born at the heart of this embattled elite and lived in the parish of St Werburgh, in the shadow of Dublin Castle and a street away from Christ Church Cathedral. His father, Sir James Ware, was a graduate of Trinity College Dublin and a protégé of the great James Ussher, sometime Vice-Provost of Trinity and Vice-Chancellor of Dublin University, and later Archbishop of Armagh. Ussher was an exceptional scholar, now unjustly remembered in the public mind solely for his over-precise historical dating of the Creation.[2] Proudly conscious of his 'Old English' descent, giving him a centuries-long Irish inheritance, the archbishop was nevertheless aware that many of his relatives and most of his fellow Old English had made a different choice, preserving their religious loyalty to Rome.

Ussher devoted his career to defending the episcopally governed Church of Ireland, and spent much energy supplying as scholarly a demonstration as possible of the historical truth of Protestantism, patiently sifting primary source historical evidence to persuade the world out of error. Regularly in contact with politicians, churchmen and historians in London, he was a well-known and welcome collaborator, amid a European-wide range of correspondents, with such towering figures of early Stuart English historical scholarship and major collectors of manuscripts as Henry Spelman and Robert Cotton. In his English retirement during the Interregnum, Ussher came to be regarded as a Reformed Protestant statesman of international stature. His genius for original research set the highest standards of assessment of ancient documents, albeit combined with an emphatically polemical purpose, and established the tone of Protestant Irish scholarship into the modern age.

Ussher therefore exemplified, and really created, the outlook of the closely related knot of Dublin elite families of whom Robert Ware represented a third generation in scholarship and education: proudly Protestant, with a consciousness of its international Reformed character.[3] Most of its membership was, unlike the Usshers, drawn from recent Protestant English migration; so the Wares had their roots in Yorkshire, with marriage connections to Suffolk. Robert Ware's father James had, however, been born beside Dublin Castle, to a senior civil servant also called James, who provided the Wares with the office of Irish Auditor-General, which became well nigh hereditary in the family for nearly a century. Both Jameses received knighthoods, and at one stage the two knights, father and son, shared the family home. Like Ussher, such people were convinced of the importance of episcopacy, but were also deeply suspicious of Laudian sacramentalism (Archbishop William Laud of Canterbury had repeatedly been a thorn in Ussher's side), and they therefore looked back with affectionate awe to the first two generations of properly Protestant English bishops in the reigns of Edward VI and Elizabeth. Looking further back to remote antiquity, they also discerned a Celtic or 'British Church' that owed nothing to the Roman mission of Augustine of Canterbury except corruption, and which could now provide an identity to embrace the Protestant Churches of England, Ireland and Scotland, and endorse their model of Reformed episcopacy.[4]

The traumas of the mid-century civil wars meant that Sir James the younger was mostly exiled in England or France from the late 1640s until Robert was nineteen, returning permanently to Ireland at Charles II's Restoration.[5] This experience of family disruption not only strengthened the Ware circle's detestation of popery, but also added a deep loathing of Protestant Dissent, a contrast to Ussher's determined irenicism towards Protestants who opposed episcopacy. After Ussher died in 1656, his moderating influence disappeared, and Sir James Ware's sufferings were largely at the hands of Dissenters: as he judiciously reminded James Butler, Duke of Ormond, on the Restoration in 1660, his lucrative office of Auditor-General had been taken from him only to be regranted to a duo, one of whom had been an 'Anabaptist'.[6] Now, royalist Protestant episcopalians were spurred on to a conviction that there was a hidden connection between the two adversaries: Dissent was infiltrated by a fifth column of disguised papists, among whom the Jesuits were most prominent. All these motives can be discerned in the literary creations of Robert Ware.

Archbishop Ussher directed Robert's father towards antiquarian scholarship, and Sir James's achievements were outstanding. His publication of *De Hibernia et antiquitatibus eius, disquisitiones* in 1654 remains one of the most important pioneering surveys of Irish history, law and physical antiquities.[7] Behind the publications lay Sir James's manuscript collections: original manuscripts, some medieval or Celtic, together with a rich and meticulous set of transcriptions which earned him the title 'the Camden of Ireland' from contemporaries, and which were rendered all the more important by the destruction of so much manuscript material in Ireland as late as the twentieth century. Sir James published a catalogue of his collections in a small edition in Dublin in July 1648, apparently the only book published in the city in that unpropitious year for scholarship: Primate Ussher and John Selden were among the recipients of specimens of the short print run.[8]

This catalogue is precious for subsequent historians, as will become clear from the troubled fate of Ware's manuscript collections: the story turns from the highest reaches of seventeenth-century scholarship to abject deceit. For by Sir James Ware's will, his manuscripts ended up in the hands of his second son Robert, thereby becoming entangled in a troubled family history. As a boy, Robert suffered severe epileptic fits, and was not expected to live or remain sane if he did. Accordingly, Sir James resolved to create a strong entail on his estates in favour of his elder boy (yet another James), only to be confounded by seeing his second son grow out of the epileptic fits into health and exceptional academic ability. According to Robert's descendants, whose reminiscences provide echoes of his frustration at his lost opportunities, Sir James subsequently refused both a baronetcy and a viscountcy, regarding them as pointless, since the entail descended to the eldest son's daughter and her descendants in default of a male heir to continue the name. In his last years, Sir James tried to compensate Robert, building up a fund amounting to the astonishing sum of £1,000 each year for the remaining half a dozen years of his life. In his will of 1666, he left the young man all his non-entailed estates available around Dublin, but equally significantly, all goods, debts, books, money and plate of which he might die possessed.[9]

This act of generosity was to have consequences over three centuries and more, since Robert was to make very particular use of his literary inheritance. Over the next few years, he augmented his father's collections on the blank pages of the old books in his own distinctive hand, and also created new notebooks of his own. But in contrast to his father's careful accumulation, the new material was precisely that:

new, elaborate, extensive forgeries of documents, ostensibly dating from a century and a half before his own time, interspersed with what material he chose to gather from printed historical sources available to him, Archbishop Ussher's works included, to provide a spurious air of authenticity for his creations. He never attempted to disguise his hand with any archaisms, always presenting his interpolations as a transcript from some older document. Robert had a genuine feel for the past, and an eclectic knowledge of it worthy of his father. No evidence has been found that he attended a university, which, given Britain's troubled decade of the 1650s, is perhaps unsurprising; his father probably educated him, and introduced him to the fascination of history, with fatal results. His father had also secured him an appropriately archival position, *Custos Brevium* and chirographer in the Irish Court of Common Pleas in 1660, affording Robert yet more access to documents of antiquity.[10]

Thanks to his father's belated generosity, Robert was not poor, and in the years immediately after his father's death he was frequently a creditor for large sums in the Irish Statute Staple books, never a debtor: either these were transactions resulting from his father's financial settlement, or he was using resultant capital for money-lending.[11] His house in Dublin was sufficiently grand to attract the attention of no less a person than Richard Butler, Earl of Arran, son of the long-term Lord Lieutenant of Ireland, James, Duke of Ormond. As military governor of Dublin, in 1678 Arran sought to lease the property, very conveniently placed next to his father's official residence in the Castle; his subsequent lease would prove somewhat awkward when Robert Ware became ranged politically against the Castle establishment, as we will discover.[12] What evidence Ware has bequeathed gives the impression of a powerful and driven personality, acutely conscious of the disadvantaged place which accident of birth had awarded him in his family. Tellingly, in one of the title-pages which he constructed for a volume of his father's doctored papers, he strikes out 'second' in his first draft 'put together out of Sr. James Wares Manuscripts by his second son Robert Ware Esqr'.[13] It would have been understandable if he brooded on the contrast between his own specialist historical knowledge and the fact that his elder brother, Sir James's heir, could trade on their father's reputation, with much less talent than Robert to justify his advantage. When in 1667, Lord Lieutenant Ormond was discussing with the Archbishop of Canterbury what should happen to the office of Auditor-General of Ireland, vacant by the death of Sir James, the duke spoke with indulgent contempt of the heir, James Ware, who held its reversion: he 'has little other merit then that of his father to plead for him, and that was so emminent in his way that his sonns defects ought to bee borne with in consideration of him'.[14]

Certainly, Robert adored his native city, and took enormous pride in Dublin's beauty and historic buildings, though with Puritan preciseness he criticized the hedonism and materialism of its present inhabitants. It has been said by the compiler of a comprehensive finding-list of his father's extant collections that Robert's unpublished manuscript – 'History and antiquities of Dublin' – is his most 'respectable' work, but in view of what follows, everything from the hand of Robert Ware must be under suspicion.[15] In particular, his prefatory remarks in his Dublin history might provoke hollow laughter:

> My scope is only to comply with those inducements which have been often vehemently urged unto me for the publishing in the best method I can such observations of my deceased father Sir James Ware kt, and other particulars of moment relating to the city of Dublin since the conquest of Ireland as I find in the several volumes of these manuscripts which he was pleased to bequeath unto me as a legacy of great price and for the regulation and conduct of myself in this undertaking I shall look up no other pole, nor have any other scope than the impartial representation of truth out of authentic memorials compiled with the secure warranty of faithful dealing.[16]

Despite this ringing protestation, the reality of Robert's history of Dublin is already characteristic of his other work. It ignores most of his father's genuine medieval collections in favour of material on the sixteenth and seventeenth centuries, including some beguilingly specific and detailed but also hair-raisingly inaccurate or unverifiable material from all dates. Some of the history sounds as if it is meant to tease the reader with absurdity, the sort of cheerfully wild exaggeration which was to become so characteristic of Dublin's literary tradition. One cannot imagine that Robert Ware was being entirely serious when he affected not to know that the dedication 'Christ

Church' in the nomenclature of the cathedral so close to his home is equivalent to the Holy Trinity; instead, he solemnly stated that it was actually a corruption of 'Chrite Church', in allusion to a rich merchant called Crite who had helped in the building's restoration.[17] There is a playful, celebratory character to such Joycean stuff, but the playfulness was soon to turn ugly.

The character of Ware's forgeries is extraordinary. I well remember my first real acquaintance with it in 1997, in the form of two transcripts among the Tanner papers in the Bodleian Library: two fragments apparently from the history of the Irish Church under Edward VI. They provoked contrasting emotions in me: astonishment and excitement at these sudden shafts of light on a very obscure aspect of the Reformation, with vivid dialogue between Archbishop Dowdall and Lord Deputy Croft, plus equally highly coloured letters between the two – but also unease, a feeling that it was all too good to be true, and some puzzlement at the seventeenth-century cast of the literary style. Luckily, I decided to leave the texts alone and not to make use of them.[18] With hindsight, I see that I had already encountered and been deceived by two much more influential forgeries. But what strikes anyone reading the originals of any of the forgeries in London, Oxford or elsewhere, is their sheer leaden relentlessness and repetitiveness – drafts, redrafts, extra copies, plus the constant obsessive authentication of the supposed transcripts: 'Ex Bib. Cottonens. I got thes memories on the 6th of October 1657', or 'Ex Bib. Cottonens. July 7th 1658' – suggesting the work of a conscientious copyist, copying (crucially) during Sir James Ware's lifetime.[19] So both the supposed original and supposed copy vie for the reader's credulous attention, in an audacious parody of the seventeenth century's new enthusiasm for primary source manuscript verification.

Ware's productivity on the basis of his father's papers seems to have begun to take its finished or published form in 1678, when he was aged thirty-nine. It is to that year that he ascribes his unpublished Dublin history, but by now there was more than local history, even on the scale which Ireland's capital demanded, to excite Ware. His opportunity to use (and indeed no doubt greatly expand) his literary creations for a specific political and religious cause derived from the atmosphere of hysteria which arose in the late 1670s, when members of the Established episcopal Churches suddenly felt their hard-won gains threatened by a monarchy which seemed ready to betray them to Roman Catholics and to use Protestant Dissent as a means to that end. So the agitation to exclude James, Duke of York, from succession to the throne reached fever-pitch. It was fuelled by a bizarre character whose ability to lie on a heroic scale must have aroused Robert Ware's admiration and envy: Titus Oates, inventor of the Popish Plot which so transfixed the Atlantic Isles between 1678 and 1681. There is no positive evidence that Oates and Ware ever met, but the atmosphere created by Oates's fictions gave Ware his chance to poison English and Irish historiography.

At the beginning of the Popish Plot crisis, there appeared a small work of eight pages entitled *Strange and remarkable prophesies and predictions of . . . James Ussher*, a tribute to the continuing domin-ance of the late archbishop's personality in the Ware circle.[20] The pamphlet's material was presented anonymously, but in its mode of distancing itself slightly from its supposed original material, while presenting a detailed and circumstantial narrative, it has all the hall-marks of a Robert Ware production. Its point of departure was a passage from Nicholas Bernard's biography of Ussher which described a sermon preached by the future archbishop in his twenty-second year in 1602, predicting the coming of civil war in 1641 on the basis of a passage in Ezekiel (the redactor for better effect in his pamphlet, tidied the sermon back to 1601).[21] Ussher's more recent – and more trust-worthy – biographer, Alan Ford, gives credence to the original story, but the redactor's version of the sermon with the archbishop's rather vague predictions of Britain's mid-century calamities nevertheless occupies only a couple of pages before the remaining five. The com-piler of the 1678 pamphlet had his own new material to present.[22]

Introduced afresh by the editor, this new story told of the encounter between Ussher and a main narrator (not the editor) a year before the archbishop's death, in 1655. It is a detailed and circumstantial narra-tive by someone who claimed to have heard much of the material directly from Ussher himself, a mixture of written word and conversa-tion. There is additional citation of named corroborative witnesses, one of them Ussher's daughter, the other the wife of Sir James Ware's colleague in the Irish Exchequer, Chief Baron John Bysse. Hence, already Robert Ware was exploiting the names of the great and the good in the previous two generations of his family and acquaintance, while posing (albeit anonymously) as a mere editor and compiler, a tactic that would become characteristic of his forgeries. In this account, Ussher did what any respectable Reformed Protestant theologian ought to do, first expounding with awe and humility the relationship between justification and sanctification, before solemnly warning of the likelihood of further persecution and massacres by papists, as part of their continued worldwide conspiracy against godliness. So it was the latter prophecy which really mattered in the pamphlet's seven pages: Ussher had been predicting the Popish Plot twenty years before it had supposedly taken shape. When various subsequent pirated and doctored versions of the Ussher prophecies were issued, it was usually this material, rather than that supplied by Bernard, which interested redactors.

The slim production which was the source of all subsequent versions was published at a crucial moment, its licence dated 16 November 1678. Only a month earlier, Titus Oates had delivered his sensational testimony to the English House of Commons. Ware's pamphlet proved a bestseller: Oxford libraries hold no fewer than eight copies of the 1678 edition alone; there was an immediate translation into Dutch apparently produced by the same publisher in London; a further edition was published in Cork in 1679; and the sequence of subsequent reprints did not end with the Exclusion Crisis, but proliferated up to the mid-nineteenth century, each addressing the latest manifestation of Romish malevolence.[23] Already in 1681 came the first tidied-up and shortened plagiarism of the text concentrating on the matter relevant to the moment.[24] The enthusiastic reception for the first of Ware's fictions evidently inspired him to subsequent forgeries which should have been much more straightforward to discredit, but which have proved remarkably enduring.

In 1679, Ware issued another slim eight-page quarto pamphlet: the first forgery of supposed older manuscripts which would later become his special genre, *The examinations of Faithful Commin Dominican Fryar, as Sir James Ware had them from the late Lord Primate Usher.* This edition was furnished with Elizabethan literary pedigrees which would become familiar in his forgeries, from papers of 'Lord Cecil' (i.e. Sir William Cecil, later Lord Burghley), conveyed to the manuscript collections of Archbishop Ussher and then 'my dear Father' Sir James Ware. This account from 1567 described the activities of one 'Faithful Commin', a Dominican who had pretended to be 'a Strict Protestant' to sow discord in the Protestant Church of England. The material was wonderfully circumstantial, including verbatim cross-examinations of Commin by Matthew Parker and Queen Elizabeth herself. The fraudulent Dominican had gathered England's first independent Protestant congregation. It would all confirm to readers a great conspiracy between Romanists and Protestant Dissenters of more than a century's duration, and Ware ended the sensational material by promising that there were 'many other Memorandums in the same Book worth the Printing'. Evidently he was setting up the beginning of a rich stream of revelations for a horrified Protestant public.[25]

Robert's forgeries, presenting the Popish Plot as part of a long design against Protestant Britain, with the Irish Rebellion of 1641 as prime exhibit, were only one aspect of his activity in promoting this fiction. What conspiracy existed was in reality the work of people like himself, with his own role not insignificant. At the height of the Exclusion hysteria in summer 1680, Ware was in London, as an agent of Henry Jones, sometime Vice-Chancellor of Trinity College Dublin and now Bishop of Meath (the most senior bishopric in the Church of Ireland after the archbishoprics, Meath carried with it a seat on the Irish Privy Council). A veteran Irish politician whose resourcefulness and adaptability served a ruthless commitment to advancing traditional Reformed Protestantism, Jones was central to the Irish dimension of the Popish Plot. Up to his death on 5 January 1682, the bishop was a close associate of Anthony Ashley Cooper, Earl of Shaftesbury and Arthur Capel, Earl of Essex, in stoking the alarms of 1679–81. Jones was also one of the most active in maintaining momentum in the execution for treason of the hapless Catholic Primate of Armagh, Oliver Plunket, against the Duke of Ormond's dogged attempts as viceroy to lower the temperature of public excitement.[26] Ormond's strategy during the Popish Plot was of a piece with his consistent attempts to draw the fangs of the memory of 1641, in the interests of creating national harmony across the religious divide. The publication of Archbishop Ussher's supposed predictions about 1641 must thus have annoyed him sorely.[27]

By contrast, Jones was only too conscious of the atrocities in the 1641 rising, having early in his career edited the considerably exaggerated account of the crisis, as 'beyond all parallel of former ages, a most bloody and anti-Christian combination and plot'. Presented to the English Parliament in 1642, the depositions in his account were frequently reprinted to keep bitter memories alive, and the original manuscripts were punctiliously preserved after Jones's death, acquiring something of the same canonical status afforded to Sir James Ware's manuscripts. One of Jones's most celebrated sermons, preached in Christ Church Dublin in 1676, invoked the memory of 1641 in a fashion anticipating the Ussher prophecy pamphlet of 1678, and his sermon was duly reprinted in London in 1679, with a dedication to Essex, the Whig promoter of Popish Plot hysteria.[28] Moreover, Jones was yet another member of the Ussher/Ware circle. As well as being Archbishop Ussher's nephew, Jones married Sir James Ware's niece as his second wife, and was thus cousin by marriage to Robert Ware; for his part, Robert Ware married Elizabeth Piers, another cousin, and one of Jones's nieces.

It is therefore unsurprising to find Ware working for Jones in London in summer 1680, at the time when Archbishop Plunket's trial was beginning in Dundalk. Ware was in the company of another Irish conspirator active with Shaftesbury and Essex, Colonel Roderick Mansell; the conspirators sought to implicate Ormond himself in allegations that Catholics were plotting to secure a French invasion of Ireland.[29] The fragments of Ware's letters to Jones are racy and gossipy, and Ormond's agent, who was trying to head off this plotting and who had intercepted these letters, referred to him familiarly as 'Robin Ware'.[30] Here is a further echo of a conspirator given to high-spirited mischief. This incident is not the only evidence suggesting Henry Jones as the *éminence grise* behind the utilization of Ware's talents in both conspiracy and forgery; nor was it the end of Ware's dabblings in the Exclusion Crisis.

Through his crowded years of political activity, Ware greatly expanded the range of his historical fictions, first in partnership with an English clergyman, incumbent of Doddington in Cambridgeshire, John Nalson. Nalson's connection to Ware remains a puzzle, but amid the excitements of 1678–81, with Ware travelling regularly between

Dublin and England, it hardly needs explanation. R. C. Richardson comments that '[w]ithout doubt Nalson was fixedly anchored in the tempestuous years around 1680', which was equally true of Ware: a double case of cometh the hour, cometh the man.[31] Nalson was an ultra-royalist pamphleteer whose talents had been exploited by the Danby administration through the 1670s, yet in the early stages of the Exclusion Crisis, this was to prove no obstacle to collaboration with an Irishman who was linked to English Whigs. There were plenty of loyal subjects of King Charles who quickly came to hate Shaftesbury and his collaborators, yet who had no doubt through most of the Exclusion Crisis that the Popish Plot was a reality.[32] It was by no means impossible for a classic Anglican royalist and admirer of Archbishop Laud like Nalson to see an exotic Irish ally in a royalist episcopalian like Ware. Ware's idol was the very different Archbishop Ussher, but even Ussher was an object of suspicion to radical Whigs as a propagandist for *jure divino* monarchy.[33] Nalson would also know that the Ware family had been unbending in its royalist allegiance throughout Ireland's civil wars and had suffered accordingly. Both men were obsessed with the historical lessons of the 1640s, and both saw the rebels against Charles I as the enemies of liberty in his kingdoms. Now there was a new threat to liberty, and as the Exclusion Crisis took shape, it was not easy for royalists obsessed with 1641–2 to see exactly where the chief threat came from: Puritans or Papists.[34]

Like so many Anglican royalists, the two propagandists were equally firm in their hatred of Roman Catholics and Protestant Dissenters, including Presbyterians, and that shared animus was a firm basis for their unholy temporary collaboration. The year before the Popish Plot was announced, Nalson had published a hyper-royalist diatribe detecting 'no great difference between those of the foundation of Loyola and Geneva', something of a Cavalier commonplace at the time.[35] Now, in the summer of 1680, while Ware was busy plotting in London, this view was consolidated into the claim of an actual conspiracy of popery and Dissent, as revealed in a hugely successful thirty-three-page collection largely consisting of Ware forgeries, published in London by Nalson and resonantly entitled *Foxes and firebrands, or, A specimen of the danger and harmony of popery and separation.*[36]

The title was a clever conceit, which was already a commonplace in

Restoration royalist circles, much encouraged by conspiracy theories around the popish origins of the Great Fire of London.[37] The alliteration and resonant echo of Foxe's *Book of Martyrs* was only the most superficial appeal. Its main point was its biblical allusion to the story of Samson sowing confusion among the Philistines by sending pairs of foxes with burning torches tied to their tails into Philistine farmlands (Judges 15: 4–5), and it also satisfyingly lined up papists as cunning foxes and Dissenters as headstrong firebrands. The work was sarcastically dedicated to the leading Presbyterians Richard Baxter and William Jenkins, and while not actually accusing them of being hidden papists, it certainly directed that accusation against Quakers and Fifth Monarchy Men, with the aid of material which Nalson was not too squeamishly Tory to derive from Titus Oates's accusations. Besides the newly produced material in the pamphlet, there was the story of Faithful Commin taken directly from Ware's previous publication, as Nalson pointed out, providing its pedigree from William Cecil to Ussher to Sir James Ware, whose 'son Robert Ware Esq. has obliged the Publick by the communication of them'.[38]

In effect, this was a relaunch of Ware's 1679 pamphlet, which to judge by its minimal present-day survival, had not made a great impact, perhaps because it had only been published in Ireland. Now Ware's forgeries were being rebranded for the London market, with exciting extras, fulfilling the promise he made in his Commin pamphlet. To the treachery and duplicity of Faithful Commin was added the very similar and supposedly contemporary story of Thomas Heath, brother of Nicholas Heath (slightly curiously described as Bishop of Rochester rather than taking notice of the culmination of his career as Archbishop of York). Heath had, in a similar fashion to Commin, inveighed from the pulpit against set prayer, but examination by Bishop Edmund Guest of Rochester exposed him as a Jesuit. This made a fine prelude to material from the combined pens of Titus Oates and Robert Ware dated to the early seventeenth century, further demonstrating how the Jesuits planned this subversion of Protestants.

The collaboration between Nalson and Ware in 1680 proved fleeting; the differing nature of their passion for the Established Church must have driven a wedge between them. Thereafter, Nalson enthusiastically supported the royal ascendancy of Charles II's last years, no doubt encouraged by the revelation of what Whig radicalism might lead to in the Rye House Plot in 1683; the parson of Doddington shared in the crystallization of a 'Tory' group which was happy to embrace the label, and now knew more clearly whom it hated.[39] Notable was Nalson's publication in 1684 of an edition of the record of Charles I's trial ostentatiously dedicated to James, Duke of York, including a diatribe against those who 'should so violently endeavour to Exclude the Son from the Right of Succession, who so inhumanely and barbarously Excluded his Father from the Possession both of his Crown and his Life'. Nalson's introduction to the text further attempted to gratify his dedicatee by ridiculing those former supporters of the Commonwealth who attempted to excuse their own guilt by asserting 'that the late King was murdered by the Papishes, as they call them' – precisely the charge which Robert Ware had made in the Preface to the Reader in his first outing of Faithful Commin in 1679.[40] For Nalson there was to be no more talk of collusion between Romanists and Dissenters; he exemplifies Jonathan Scott's aphoristic remark that '[f]rom 1678 to 1683 people remained convinced of an imminent threat to the church and government: in 1681 they changed their minds about where the greatest threat was coming from'.[41]

Accordingly, Ware was obliged to maintain momentum without Nalson's help. The year 1681 proved to be his literary *annus mirabilis,* with three separate new works published in London or Dublin. The slimmest was a previously unknown Celtic prophetic text, 'of late casually found, and drawn out of the Archives of Sir James Ware's rich and careful preserved Antiquities'. This rebuke by Gnatus, a hermit of true British religion, to popish Augustine of Canterbury soon after his landing in Kent was another supposed trophy from the Rochester archives, transmitted to the Wares in an Elizabethan transcription by a chaplain of Bishop Guest. As Ware poetically described it, the fragment 'now breaks forth like a Star newly created in the firmament of Heaven, which draws all the World to look upon it with admiration', with prophecies of events still to come, 'depending on the behaviour of Nobles, and people practising and maintaining the true Religion against Idolatry'. The prophet had taken the trouble to inform Augustine of the coming Reformations of Edward VI and Elizabeth, while Ware authenticated his text with learned references to Bede and Lambarde's *Perambulation of Kent,* John Stow and Thomas Fuller among the supporting cast.[42]

A further Dublin pamphlet of 1681 told the story of an Irish Franciscan friar and nephew of Archbishop Hugh Corwen of Dublin who supposedly converted to Protestantism in 1589. This was allegedly drawn from the papers of John Garvey, one of Ussher's predecessors as Primate of Armagh, which was (as Ware put it on the title-page with delicious ambiguity, perhaps savouring the joke) 'now entered amongst Sir James Ware's manuscripts', a phrase he used on more than one occasion. Naturally, the pamphlet climaxed with reports of murderous plots among Elizabethan Irish Catholics.[43] Most ambitious was a publication in 1681 in Dublin and London editions (with a new London title-page specifically aimed at a general English market), which took Ware back to the reigns of Henry VIII, Edward VI and Mary Tudor, consisting of a biography of George Browne, Reformation Archbishop of Dublin, accompanied by a long sermon of Browne's against idolatry. Idolatry had quickly emerged as a favourite theme for Ware, underlining the gulf between his variety of Anglican Royalism and that of English High Churchmen, but to echo the Corwen material, his present work also contained the account of yet another murderous plot against Irish Protestants in Mary's reign which had been foiled. Transmission of some of the material was credited to Sir James Ware's mentor, the Trinity scholar Anthony Martin, Ussher's immediate successor and Jones's predecessor as Bishop of Meath.[44]

The background to Ware's publications in 1681 was his continued political activity, amid the efforts of Jones and his associates to keep alive the non-existent Irish side of the Popish Plot and contribute to Exclusion agitation. In September and October 1681, Ware took a pivotal role in gathering Irish material which might assist Shaftesbury's defence in his trial on capital charges of high treason, much to the fury of Ormond and Michael Boyle, Protestant Archbishop of Armagh, who were still desperately trying to avoid an explosion of sectarian violence in Ireland. Monitoring Ware's visits in the Dublin Marshalsea prison to an English informer called William Smith, Ormond and Boyle found themselves trying to sort out a bewildering set of accusations and counter-accusations, particularly involving one Dr Theophilus Harrison, titular Protestant Dean of Clonmacnoise Cathedral.

What Ormond and Boyle discovered was that it was Ware who was transmitting such material to Sir Robert Clayton, one of Shaftesbury's leading Whig associates in London. Its effect would be to show that Roman Catholics were trying to invent accusations against mainstream members of the Church of Ireland, like Harrison, that these royalist Protestants were in turn inventing a Popish Plot. The depositions would incidentally supply evidence implying that the Dublin administration was dangerously soft on Catholics, in order to vindicate Shaftesbury's three years of agitation.[45] Little more than a month after Clayton received and exploited the material which Ware had gathered in the Marshalsea, a sympathetic jury returned an *ignoramus* verdict in Shaftesbury's case. Archbishop Plunket had not been so lucky, having been executed on 11 July 1681.

It is this background of conspiracy against the Ormond administration which effectively rules out a tempting attribution of yet a fourth pamphlet to Ware, also published in 1681 in Dublin. Raymond Gillespie has suggested that Ware was the author of the anonymous *The mischiefs and unreasonableness of endeavouring to deprive his majesty of the affections of his subjects* ... Certainly, this effusion shared its printer Joseph Ray and publisher Samuel Helsham with *The prophecy of Gnatus* and its printer with *The conversion of Philip Corwine*.[46] There was, however, not much choice of printers in Dublin, and Ware's authorship of this piece is unlikely. The prose style is much more formal, there is none of the usual Ware accumulation of picturesque incidents or forged documents and no mention of Sir James Ware's collections, Roman conspiracy or idolatry. Instead, there is a reasoned appeal to passive loyalism, not merely with no hint of papist conspiracy, but also with no allegations of conspiracy between papists and Dissenters. Crucially, the resonant year 1641 is only mentioned in connection with the deplorable breakdown of English order at that time; the Irish rebellion is not mentioned at all. The writer goes out of his way to ridicule those who claim 'that we are galloping to Mass as fast as we can' or that 'care has been taken by the Papists (who say they have Govern'd these three kingdoms these twenty years) that none should be preferr'd to any thing considerable but those who were for their purpose'.[47]

Reading *The mischiefs and unreasonableness*, one conjectures that, far from being its author, Robert Ware was actually in the sights of a writer who speaks with sorrow of 'the people, who are led and managed by these Discoverers' and whose 'Zeal for the Protestant Religion will make them hate all who they suspect design its subversion. . . . rash and forward men who were for too violent counsels, and too close a prosecution of things as circumstances then were'. A pamphlet which spends a page praising the government and character of Ormond, including his 'firmness to the Protestant religion, . . . most notorious to all who have heard of him', and the assertion that the pope had called the duke 'one of the most considerable and dangerous Enemies they had in Christendom', does not sound as if it emanates from one of the Jones circle.[48] Moreover, it was being sold just by the main gate of Dublin Castle, by a man who was official printer to the Irish executive and the corporation of Dublin.[49] And all this in a work dated 24 May 1681, only three weeks after Plunket's arraignment in Westminster Hall, as the agitation for his destruction was gathering momentum with the aid of Jones and Ware. In this moment of crisis, to make Robert Ware its author seems too illogical a double-game even for that master of lies; after all, what would have been the advantage for Ware in an anonymous encomium of the Lord Lieutenant? There was indeed to be a reconciliation between Ormond and Ware, but not yet.

The 'authentic' works of Ware continue consistent in the incendiary themes of earlier works. In the following year, 1682, he returned to Nalson's *Foxes and firebrands*, reprinting it from a Dublin press, but now enriched by his own second part of further material without any collaboration from Nalson. Both collections were separately prefaced by Ware, while he punctiliously acknowledged an author whom he referred to as 'the learned Dr Henry Nalson'. Maybe the mistaken Christian name was just inadvertence, but the paranoid alert for in-jokes in Ware's *oeuvre* might consider it a distancing device, or even a conflation of John Nalson with Ware's own patron, Henry Jones.[50] Ware also gloried in having

> disobliged the two extreme factions in Religion, (the Papist and the Puritan) by exposing their Combinations for the ruine of the Protestant Faith which is by Law happily established and setled among us . . . I

hope the Reader will look upon it as an argument of my candor and sincerity, that I do not studie to gratifie any party in Religion, but have rather invited their prejudices upon my self, by saying these things that are disobliging to them both.[51]

It was at the beginning of the new second part that there appeared, as the very first primary source item, the forgery which has enjoyed the longest life among all Ware's creations, curiously separate in its supposed time frame from, and earlier than, everything else in the collection: the supposed speech by Archbishop Thomas Cranmer at King Edward VI's Coronation in 1547. As in the sermon of Archbishop George Browne, its major theme was the fight against idolatry, which Cranmer urged upon his young King Josiah. Otherwise, the materials ranged from the Elizabethan period to the era of the 1641 rising, taking in en route the Duke of Buckingham's assassination of 1628 as a Jesuit plot, and including a letter from a Jesuit which made it clear that 'that sovereign drug Arminianism' was all part of the Society's grand design.[52]

In 1683 came a new variant on the fox theme: *The hunting of the Romish fox*, which added another layer of allusion to *Foxes and firebrands*, derived from Ware's antiquarian knowledge. Its title was a version of titles of a celebrated sequence of literary attacks from the 1540s by the evangelical William Turner on the arch defender of traditional religion, Bishop Stephen Gardiner. The title theme had already been reused in a new work of the 1590s, and like that production, Ware's work had nothing to do with the original Tudor text; its entirely new content, original in every sense, cited a mixture of his usual fictional sources, ranging from Archbishop Cranmer to Archbishops Laud and Ussher.[53] But there was something new: the work is notable for its ostentatious (and I would argue in Ware's works, unprecedented) courting of Ormond, who, by this stage in his lieutenancy, had become an absentee in England. Ormond's name was emblazoned on the title-page via the work's publisher, who carried the title of the ducal bookbinder in Dublin, yet Ware's fulsome dedication to Ormond notably does not repeat any of the phraseology or sentiments of *The mischiefs and unreasonableness*.

This looks like a politic reconciliation of the former plotter against the Castle administration, now that Exclusion was a lost cause and his patron Henry Jones was dead. Admittedly, Ware was still causing trouble in March 1683 for Ormond's son and substitute in Dublin, Richard Butler, Earl of Arran, but now in civic rather than national politics and with a Dissenter also in his sights. Ware was leading the opposition to a major building project in his beloved city whose projector was using the Ormond name to further the scheme, 'Ormond Market' north of the Liffey, and it can only have exacerbated Ware's opposition that the chief promoter, amid many other improvement schemes, was a notorious Presbyterian, the Lord Mayor Sir Humphrey Jervis.[54] Arran reported to Ormond that the row over the market's construction was finally quelled only after a noisy meeting of the city Corporation on 19 March 1683. In view of Ware's frequent sneering deployment of the word 'fanatic' for Protestant Dissenters, not least in the dedication of *The hunting of the Romish fox* to Ormond, he would have been mortified by Arran's irritated private characterization of the market scheme's opponents as 'fanatics', with 'Robin Ware the busiest among the mutineers'.[55]

The hunting of the Romish fox represents a peak in Ware's publications, and it is key to his self-perception and political outlook. It reveals him as the proponent of a 'British Empire', a phrase which he used without inhibition for the polity created by the Tudor and early Stuart Reformations, 'after our pious Kings, with their learned Bishops and Clergy, had canonically purg'd and reform'd the Brittish Church from the Innovations and Superstitions of Rome'. In this, Ware was echoing a genuinely sixteenth-century anti-popish theme: the rhetoric of an 'Empire of Great Britain' dated to the last years of Henry VIII and the reign of Edward VI, when the prospect of a common Protestant state for the Atlantic archipelago had first seemed a real possibility. Yet the exact phrase Ware used, apparently a sixteenth-century coinage, came more naturally from an Irish than an English Protestant, and it would not enter into common use until the decades after the Act of Union of 1707.[56] Ware's concept of a 'British Empire' was for him, as the notion of a British Church had been for Archbishop Ussher, a defence of his beloved episcopally ordered Church of Ireland, binding it into an archipelago-wide Protestant polity which looked beyond Roman usurpation to an earlier purity.

Once more, Ware made an elaborate show of irenicism to excuse his sectarian bile, addressing himself not only to Protestants but also to Roman Catholics, so that 'my dear Countryman the Papist, who is zealous in the simplicity of his heart, may begin to suspect and examine the constitution of that Religion that supports itself by such disingenuous arts and unchristian methods'. And again there was that unblushing claim to authenticity, enriched by its purity from any taint of idolatry:

> These Papers are not the product of a fictitious Romantick Brain, they contain no Legends, nor empty Fables, to entertain and amuse the credulous part of mankind; they are extracted out of faithful Records, and the Memoirs of the ablest Statesmen of the last Age, and Sir James Ware's Manuscripts; or they have fallen within our own Ken and Observation, or have been handed down to us by conveyed sense, and can be proved as clearly as matters of Fact and things of that nature can. The Collector of these Remarks hath no private Interest to serve, he cries not up any Diana, because he lives by forging her Shrines; he only desires to undeceive his deluded Countrymen, to cement their Schisms, and unite 'em in God-like Love and Obedience, that they may live in the holy Communion of their National Church, which is most agreeable to the Catholick and Apostolick Doctrines and Constitutions.[57]

The hunting of the Romish fox confidently anticipated more Ware publications, for at the end of the text it advertised the imminent publication of his history of Dublin 'in large Folio, with a good Character, containing above an Hundred Sheets and near Forty Copper Plates', offered the prospect of specimen pages and sought subscriptions.[58] But this was not to be; that work remained in manuscript, and there was a five-year hiatus in Ware's literary productivity, during which only reprints and adaptations appeared. This possibly resulted from the catastrophes of James II's reign which can only have confirmed Robert in his Manichean world-view. We have Ware's account of what happened, which, given all his other falsehoods, should be treated with caution, but evidently he became involved in the dramatic escalation of confrontation between Protestants and Catholics at James II's accession.[59] If we take at face-value Ware's account (mediated through his grandson-by-marriage Walter Harris), the author of such bitter publications in the Exclusion Crisis was a marked man when James II sent Richard Talbot, Earl of Tyrconnell, to govern Ireland in

1687. Ware fled to England on the day of Tyrconnell's arrival, his estates were ravaged as were those of many absentees, and he was not to return until after William of Orange's victory at the Boyne in 1690.

One reason to withhold complete credence from Ware's story of catastrophe is that he had actually parted company with his father's manuscripts apparently peaceably and by sale to James II's previous viceroy, the royal brother-in-law Henry Hyde, second Earl of Clarendon. Having arrived in Ireland in 1685, Clarendon was also, according to Harris, responsible for advising Ware to flee in 1687. Clarendon took Ware's papers back to London and deposited them in an impeccably Anglican and Latitudinarian setting, the new public library of St Martin-in-the-Fields which had been founded in 1684 by the rector and future Archbishop of Canterbury, Thomas Tenison. So, most of Sir James's papers with their augmentations by Robert were out of harm's way – not least from any further harm which could be done to them by Robert Ware. There was a rough catalogue of them at that stage, but a much more careful inventory was undertaken by another scholar and future English bishop, Edmund Gibson. Their repose was to be short-lived: at some stage in the 1690s, amid the tumultuous politics of the Williamite Revolution, a resentful Clarendon, now a pariah from William and Mary's court, repossessed most of them from the objectionably Williamite Tenison and made his own plans for cataloguing. However, Clarendon sold his entire great manuscript collection, just before his death, in 1709. Later, the Ware papers were sold again to James Brydges, Duke of Chandos, and in the dispersal of Chandos's vast possessions they were once more sold by auction in 1746. Some papers were bought by the Non-Juring bibliophile bishop Richard Rawlinson and are now in the Bodleian Library. Others were bought by the leading antiquary Jeremiah Milles, Dean of Exeter; they have ended up in the British Library.[60]

Following this complicated history of transmission, it took William O'Sullivan's heroic efforts in the 1990s to provide a proper concordance of what Sir James had collected, and how it descended from Clarendon's purchase.[61] With the exception of some manuscripts now in Armagh Public Library which were piecemeal purchases by Irish worthies from the Chandos sale, the Ware originals were fated to remain permanently in English exile. This fact may have helped obscure what Robert Ware had done to them – but there was another signifi-cant factor. Those manuscripts that had remained with Ware throughout his life were copies of his originals, made by Anthony Dopping, Bishop of Meath, and another antiquary, John Madden, before Clarendon had removed the Ware manuscripts from Ireland. These duplicates ended up in Trinity College Dublin, and were the basis for the eighteenth-century Irish publications of Sir James Ware's work, principally by Walter Harris, who married Robert Ware's grand-daughter. That is significant, for once the manuscripts had been copied it became well-nigh impossible to distinguish between an interpolation by Robert Ware and genuine material compiled by his father.[62]

Whatever Ware's sufferings in James II's reign, his productivity resumed after James's flight from England, but the royal succession still remained unresolved for the archipelago as a whole because of the continuing war in Ireland between the Jacobite and Williamite armies. Ware clearly felt that there was an urgent need for more falsehood. Two works appeared in London, the first in 1689, yet another instal-ment of *Foxes and firebrands*, which was explicitly presented as Ware's swansong – *the Third and last part*.[63] It is longer than the other two parts combined. After beginning in the reigns of Edward, Mary and Elizabeth with an intricate mixture of historical fact and imagined documents, most of the volume is concerned with seventeenth-century history, duly forged. Besides cross references to the two earlier parts, the new Elizabethan material documents a supposed clash between Queen Elizabeth and Dean Alexander Nowell in St Paul's Cathedral, credited to two of Ware's favourite authorities, Sir Robert Cotton and Sir Henry Sidney.[64] Like the earlier Cranmer speech, this dialogue between queen and dean is particularly concerned with the perils of idolatry, which naturally good Queen Bess is portrayed as against.

Finally, at the beginning of 1690, came a short tract on the congen-ial and appropriately fictional subject of Pope Joan, pointing out in its dedication that it was a deliberate riposte to a Catholic refutation of the story of that apocryphal lady, published anonymously in Dublin in 1686. Ware's dedicatee was that now-triumphant Protestant cham-pion Henry Compton, Bishop of London, a fitting successor in Ware's esteem to Bishop Jones in ecclesiastical and political ruthlessness.[65] Appropriately after the valedictory tone of the last instalment of

Foxes and firebrands, Ware now laid aside his own creativity and relied on the venerable fictions of others, including those of his equal in heroically extensive historical forgery from a previous century, Abbot Johannes Trithemius of Sponheim. This tract, uniquely among Robert's acknowledged works, contains no reference to Sir James's collections, and in contrast to Ware's deployment of the theme of 'British Empire' in 1683, his interest in Pope Joan was the last gasp of a Reformation theme in British anti-Catholicism, as the national hatred of popery moved on to new topoi.[66] Thus ended, apparently, the publishing career of Robert Ware, seven years before his death in his fifty-eighth year.

What was passing through Ware's mind when he created his huge mass of historical fiction? It was far greater in volume than any immediate polemical necessity demanded. His early years would have been spent hearing the names of Ussher and Sir Robert Cotton in family conversation, and with much talk doubtless of the heroic days of the early English Reformation, together with mealtime gossip from the slightly less heroic days of the early Irish Reformation, which frustratingly bequeathed no testimony in manuscript form. Moreover, Ware would have grown up with Sir James's manuscripts, pored over them and thereby acquired an impressive (but by no means impeccable) degree of familiarity with a world of a century earlier. Perhaps Ware wished to outdo, or equal, his formidably learned father, and behind him the even more formidable Ussher, or maybe he just wanted to impress the scholarly society in which he lived, including such Trinity men as Henry Jones. One is reminded of another weaver of new ancient texts from a century later with a far more wretched fate than Ware's: Wordsworth's 'marvellous boy' of Bristol, Thomas Chatterton, brooding on the medieval archive of St Mary Redcliffe and thus inspired to express himself through the voice of an imaginary poet long dead. Chatterton loved Bristol as Ware had loved Dublin, and their love may have been one of the factors in turning them from honesty or even sanity. Ware's activity seems as much pathological as criminal.[67]

Ware's own publications perpetuated his forgeries in Ireland, but as the flames of sectarian hatred burned lower in England, they would no doubt have disappeared from view had they not been taken up by one of the most influential historians to project the Anglican narrative of English history into the future. The Revd John Strype's voluminous publications became the conduit whereby certain of Ware's stories became fixed in the record. Since Strype's works were long regarded as authoritative (we have met him more than once before in these essays), and they were indeed more reliable in transmitting primary sources than many contemporary historians, these Ware forgeries gained a respectability which they might otherwise have quickly shed; some still remain with us. Hence Strype emerges as a key player in the Ware saga, because in this case he suffered a rare lapse from his generally high evidential standards.[68]

James II was safely exiled overseas when Strype's first biography, his *Memorials of Thomas Cranmer*, appeared in 1694, during Robert Ware's lifetime. Here Strype included Ware's Cranmer Coronation speech from the second part of *Foxes and firebrands* of 1681, 'found among the inestimable Collections of Archbishop Usher; and though published of late years, yet I cannot but insert it here, tending so much to illustrate the memory of this great and good Archbishop'.[69] Interestingly, Strype placed the speech in the main body of his text rather than summarizing it and including the whole text in the appended collection of primary sources, as was his normal practice with important documents. That was a precocious indicator that Ware's material would never be treated in quite the same way as Strype's primary source evidence from manuscripts; but the speech was too useful for his purposes to be ignored. The selections which Strype was subsequently to use from Ware revealed how closely Strype's outlook chimed with that of the Dublin Protestant elite: discreetly hostile to the successors and partisans of William Laud within the Church of England, but violently opposed to both Roman Catholicism and those Protestants who attacked episcopacy. It was a fatal correlation of sympathies which undermined Strype's ability to assess properly what he found in *Foxes and firebrands*. His use of this material was the one great exception to his proud claim in his Preface to the Reader in *Cranmer*, the first statement of the principle on which all his voluminous publications would be based:

> And I do here protest once for all, that I have not inserted into this
> Book any one single Historical Passage out of mine own head, but such

as I have either found in some credible published History, or in some old Book printed in those times, or the Prefaces and Epistles to them; or lastly, in some good MS. or other.[70]

This avowal, ironically reminiscent of Ware's Preface to his Dublin collections two decades earlier, was all too true of the rather mindless scissors-and-paste structure which characterizes Strype's works, but it is also mocked by the use Strype was now making of Ware, whose material had indeed been inserted in his publications out of his own head.

Strype evidently remained uneasy about including the Ware material in his volumes; he could see that it was outside the normal range of his primary sources and not up to the standards set by the remarkable quantity of original manuscript material which he had built up by fair means or foul in his own home.[71] Although he does not say so, he must have known of a pioneering and substantial demolition of Ware's fictions, made in 1700, six years after the publication of *Cranmer*, as part of a debut treatise by that unusually independent-minded and clear-sighted young gentleman-philosopher Anthony Collins (1676–1729), Strype's fellow resident in Essex.[72] Collins was not attacking Strype or his *Cranmer*, but the High Church Tory controversialist Dr John Scott (1639–95), who had used John Nalson's first part of *Foxes and firebrands* only four years after its publication, and had made the stories of Faithful Commin and Thomas Heath the culminating swipe in his two-part assault on Protestant dissent.[73] Collins enjoyed some extended fun at the expense of Scott's use of the pseudo-Elizabethan material, using both logic and his very considerable historical knowledge to dissect its improbabilities with well-informed relish. He was coldly sarcastic about the pedigrees of such a 'Romance', rounding it off with a crushing dismissal of Nalson:

> a pretended Abstract, and that of a Relation of Matter of Fact more than a hundred Years Old (it were worth something to see it) and this communicated to the World, after I know not how many Descents. My Lord Burleighs, the Primates, Sir James Ware, and at last at the Second Hand, not by him that had this Relick, but by one who hath not given the World much Cause to be confident of the Truth of what he hath wrote.[74]

It was an analysis that could not have been bettered. In the same passage, Collins triumphantly pointed out that Scott had only been borrowing from a yet more immediate adaptation of *Foxes and firebrands*. This was by no less a scholar than Edward Stillingfleet, then Dean of St Paul's and so a senior colleague of Scott in London. In the Preface to his celebrated appeal to moderate nonconformists against the threat of popery, *The unreasonableness of separation* (1681), Stillingfleet had cited the Commin and Heath stories from the Nalson/ Ware collaboration within a year of its publication. Collins elaborately extended his sarcasm from Scott to Stillingfleet, though he failed to point out Stillingfleet's most unfortunate faux pas. With misplaced erudition, the Dean had criticized Ware's inadequate understanding of his sources, by cross-referencing the stories to references Stillingfleet had discovered for himself in Thomas Fuller's *Church History*, Peter Heylyn's *Aerius redivivus* and William Camden's *Annals*. These provided further information and a fresh perspective on three individuals whom Ware had inserted in his material as disguised papists – Hallingham, Coleman and Benson. When Stillingfleet commented that the editor of *Foxes and firebrands* had misunderstood their role, and proceeded to clarify it from his trio of authors, it was he who was being duped: clearly Ware had borrowed the surnames of these popish conspirators from one of the three historians (and following their unanimous lead, he had not provided his characters with Christian names). So Stillingfleet's condescending critique only boosted the basic authenticity of Ware's account at the outset of his productivity.[75]

In the wake of Collins's assault on *Foxes and firebrands*, but also in the face of many other criticisms, Strype felt it necessary in his Preface to his biography of Archbishop Parker (1711) to set out at length a general 'Declaration of my Impartiality and truth . . . against the Censure of some Parties, who, by reason of Prepossession, may not like some things they read here, not so agreable to their espoused Principles and Inclinations'.[76] He felt vindicated by the impressive list of manuscript sources which he had personally consulted, and the list (whose brevity was equally impressive) of manuscripts consulted only through the manuscript transcripts of others among his acquaintances. At the end of this list, however, uniquely, stood his use of material derived from a printed book: 'the MSS in Ireland, sometimes belonging to the Learned Sir James Ware, Knight. Printed in two Books, called *The Hunting of the Romish Fox*, and, *Foxes and Firebands* [*sic*]'.[77]

Equally without any parallel among Strype's confident citations of his sources was the fact that, in the case of these works from Ware, he felt compelled to appeal to others to vouch for 'the credit of the transcripts therein inserted'. It is this appeal which gives the first clue as to what had happened. Strype based his confidence not on any reference to Stillingfleet or Scott, but on extracts from a letter to him from 'a very reverend and worthy Dean in Ireland', Dr Theophilus Harrison, Dean of Clonmacnoise Cathedral. Whilst this formulation might suggest the disinterested testimony of some august prelate of the Irish Church, the truth was rather different. Strype did not reveal to the reader that he and Harrison had known each other and regularly corresponded over more than two decades; Harrison was in the habit of calling Strype his 'Brother', kept him in touch with Irish affairs and moreover acted as his agent in collecting subscriptions for Strype's historical publications in Ireland.[78] It was in that context that, in spring 1709, Strype asked Harrison, in the course of a routine business letter about the Irish sales of Strype's *Annals of the Reformation*, for reassurance about the now deceased Robert Ware and Sir James Ware's papers. On 9 May, he was gratified to read Harrison's testimony:

> I did not forget to speake to Mr Ware [i.e. Robert Ware's son], and he assures me that his grandfather had his collections from the persons you mention and from Sir Robert Cotton. I had the same account many years since from Dr Jones Bp of Meath deceased a man of great learning and a nephew of Primate Ushers, and indeed the s'd manuscripts are generally of good esteem among us.[79]

Strype duly reproduced this paragraph, in his usual fashion in close paraphrase, in his *Life of Parker* published two years later; and his magisterial reputation seems thereafter to have eclipsed Collins's whistle-blowing on *Foxes and firebrands*, no doubt aided by the earlier support from Stillingfleet. The next effort to expose Ware would have to wait for more than a century and a half.

It is interesting that Dr Harrison called to witness that wily, but by then long-deceased, patron of Robert Ware, Bishop Henry Jones. This is not the only reason to recall the Irish end of the Popish Plot, because we have met the Dean of Clonmacnoise before. In 1681, he had apparently been the victim of a Roman Catholic accusation that he had effectively helped to invent the Popish Plot: that same accusation which Robert Ware had transmitted across the Irish Sea to Sir Robert Clayton at the time of Shaftesbury's trial. It is impossible to say from the evidence whether or not Harrison colluded with Ware in that affair, but he had certainly known him at that time. Harrison, a Trinity College Dublin graduate and Doctor of Divinity, who in 1681 had been resident in Dublin during that affair in some sort of pastoral capacity, was predictably an absentee from his supposed cathedral. Knowing the Church of Ireland, Strype would not have worried too much that for more than a century Clonmacnoise Cathedral had been a roofless ruin without even the shadow of its own diocese, and that its ghostly Chapter consisted solely of Dean Harrison; the evanescence of Clonmacnoise seems appropriate to someone vouching for Robert Ware's respectability.[80] From 1696, Harrison was Rector of St John's, Dublin, the next parish to Robert Ware's home in St Werburgh's.[81] Like Ware, Harrison had suffered exile in England during the turbulent years of James II's reign (probably then spending time in Strype's own Essex parish of Low Leyton), and he had returned to find devastation in his parishes wrought by triumphant Roman Catholics.[82] He would have known of Ware's troubles in James II's time; Ware as Confessor for the Protestant faith would seem all the more convincing an historical source, and that consideration would still any doubts that the conscientious dean might have harboured.

For Strype, there was another equally important Irish voucher for Ware: his own much-loved cousin and Cambridge undergraduate contemporary, James Bonnell, an English-born civil servant who made his career in Ireland in the financial departments of Irish government, which had also long been an almost hereditary home for the Wares. Bonnell was a deeply pious Anglican who never quite made it to the priesthood, yet whose biography by an eighteenth-century archdeacon of Armagh has been described as 'more a Book of Devotion, than Biography'.[83] Bonnell was also a good friend of Harrison, using him as a courier for correspondence with Strype at least as early as 1691, and he may indeed have been responsible for introducing them.[84] Four years before the dean gained the benefice of St John's Dublin, Bonnell told Strype of having come across him 'in Town t'other day very plump and jolly'.[85] Bonnell was buried in St John's church during Harrison's incumbency. He had been dead for more than a decade when Strype invoked Harrison to sponsor Ware's respectability; in any case Bonnell would not have cut such an impressive figure of testimony with Strype's public as a dean, even an Irish dean.

In reality, Bonnell was as much an agent for the transmission of Ware to Strype as Harrison. Among Bonnell's many letters in Strype's correspondence are a number of references, beginning in 1691, to his sending Strype publications or documents of Ware's (among much perfectly genuine Irish historical material), confirming that he knew the man himself.[86] In one of his letters, Bonnell spoke of Ware's material on George Browne as 'ramblingly put together by Robbin Ware, the son of the great Sir James Ware'; thus he knew Ware, but not especially well or with any great respect, just the right degree of acquaintance or lack of personal interest not to suspect any problem. Indeed, if there was a problem, it was simply Ware's scholarly mediocrity, not dishonesty, exactly as Stillingfleet had observed as early as 1681.[87] In none of Bonnell's references was there any hint of doubt about the content of Ware's publications, particularly because the agent who had obtained this material for Strype was Anthony Dopping, the scholarly and respected successor of Henry Jones as Bishop of Meath. It will be remembered that Dopping was one of the antiquaries who had copied the Ware manuscripts before they had left Ireland.[88] Given this tangle of associations among Strype, Bonnell and Harrison, it was not surprising that Strype was prepared to take the Ware material on trust.

Gilbert Burnet, an Anglican historian with a great deal more native wit and historical acuity than Strype, did not make the same mistake by allowing Ware wholesale into his historical publications. In the first instance, this was more by luck than judgement, because the first volume of Burnet's instantly successful *History of the Reformation* appeared in 1679, before Ware had publicly launched any forgeries of English history. But in the margin of one of Ware's concoctions in the British Library Ware manuscripts, stories from the days of Henry VIII through to Elizabeth, is a note in a hand which may or may not be

Ware's: 'Anno 1679 April the 6th lett Henry Bishop of Meath take coppyes hereof to send to Dr Burnett' (see Plate 14).[89] This early attempt to draw Burnet into the circle of deceit during the Popish Plot (supplying further proof of Jones's centrality to the Ware forgery enterprise) did not succeed, either because Jones failed to follow it up, or because Burnet refused to become interested. The second volume of Burnet's *History*, published in 1681 with parliamentary acclaim proudly positioned opposite the title-page, could easily have drawn on the exciting documentation of the two Elizabethan supposed causes célèbres of Faithful Commin and Thomas Heath, newly made available in *Foxes and firebrands*; but Burnet held back. This was in line with the fact that, despite some wavering, Burnet had never been impressed by Titus Oates or the Popish Plot's existence, and had reassured King Charles II about his scepticism more than once.[90]

Later, in the different crisis of the Glorious Revolution, when Roman Catholic political action seemed more real than in 1679–81, Burnet appears to have weakened in his resolve to ignore Ware's abundant anti-Catholic material. In a sermon preached before the Commons on the exciting day of 31 January 1689, when Parliament was giving thanks for the happy outcome of the convulsions in England, Burnet discussed the detail of the Elizabethan Settlement, saying 'I my self have seen the Letters of the chief Bishops of the time, from which it appears that the queen's Stiffness in maintaining some Ceremonies flowed not from their Councils, but from the Practices of some disguised Papists.' This was in fact a reference to Ware's forgeries.[91] Furthermore, there is one small later instance of Ware influencing Burnet, and that at second-hand through Strype, in revisions and additions to Burnet's *History* published as a new volume in 1714. By now, Strype had published his *Annals of the Reformation* (first edition, 1709), and when Burnet first published the newly discovered letters from English Reformers preserved in Zürich, he added a little material drawn from Ware via Strype's *Annals* in his English translation of one of them from John Jewel. With his characteristic attention to sources, Burnet nevertheless allowed diligent readers to notice this by also publishing a faithful transcript of the Latin original of the letter from Bishop John Jewel to Peter Martyr Vermigli which lay behind the reference in the main text, and which naturally did not contain the

Ware material. It was the indefatigable Victorian investigator T. E. Bridgett who noticed this single pollution of Burnet's historical text by Ware's forgeries.[92]

Although Robert Ware died in 1697, there was evidently interest in extending his fictions further into print, using his father's good name as a cover. In 1704–5 there appeared simultaneously in Dublin and London a work purporting to publish Sir James's collections, but containing a significant number of characteristic forgeries from Robert. Dublin Corporation subsidized the Dublin edition after its publication, at the request of the publisher, Matthew Gunne, which indicates that Robert Ware's stridency on behalf of his beloved city was not forgotten.[93] It is not certain who finally edited this material, though in his petition to the Corporation, Gunne implied that it was himself. Gunne nevertheless presents the text as if edited by the late Robert Ware, including a reference in the first person to Ware's publication of material on George Browne in 1681 'about two years since', while the London publisher was Awnsham Churchill, who had helped to bring out Ware's final work in his life, the last version of *Foxes and firebrands*, in 1689.[94] Gunne's publication is also notable in beginning a false tradition that Robert Ware's grandmother, Mary Briden, was the daughter of a Kentish knight rather than the daughter of Ambrose Briden, admittedly a leading burgess in the Suffolk town of Bury St Edmunds, but no more than a wealthy haberdasher with a keen interest in books. One detects a specimen of Robert Ware's efforts to reinforce his status as an esquire; a pointless endeavour in a man who was the son and grandson of a knight.[95]

The responsible agent in 1704 was certainly not the next editor of the Ware manuscripts, Walter Harris, who was then only an eighteen-year-old undergraduate at Trinity College Dublin, and whose own initiative seems to have arisen from his dissatisfaction with the 1704–5 publication. Harris's much enlarged edition in 1739 of *The whole works of Sir James Ware concerning Ireland*, with some important new illustrations of Ireland's medieval cathedrals, was one of the first fruits of a prolific, if mediocre, publishing career in Irish history. His ambitious project was connected with his second marriage to Robert Ware's granddaughter, whose father supplied a portrait of Sir James for his frontispiece. Nevertheless, it may be that the marriage arose from a previous interest: Harris tells the reader in his Preface that his project began in his own attempts to correct the errors of the previous English edition. There was a further edition of Harris's work in 1764, still polluted by Robert Ware forgeries, as well as Harris's own more straightforward additions.[96]

Although Harris lacked his predecessor's criminal flair, the history and status of his numerous additions to Sir James Ware's original text remain to be investigated, while he fully shared Robert Ware's hatred of the papacy and its current protégé, the Stuart pretender, who had been 'nurtured at Rome in all the bigotry and cruelty of that Church'.[97] One of Harris's polemical attacks on Irish Catholic contemporaries and their alleged distortion of the past was entitled *Fiction unmasked*.[98] This was an unwise claim, since in his historical magnum opus, Harris was, like Ware, prepared to distort the past by silence, in this case on account of disputes which still raged in the Ware family over that fatal entail made by Sir James in the mid-seventeenth century. In his biographical accounts of Sir James and Robert Ware, Harris omitted all mention either of the historian's second marriage or of the second marriage of Robert Ware's elder brother, which had produced issue affecting the entail.[99]

In the sectarian tensions periodically renewed in Ireland into the nineteenth century, the preoccupations of *Foxes and firebrands* and Ware's other works, from the prophecies of Ussher onwards, continued to enjoy a broad appeal. One finds a lurid public example in the Irish parliamentary proposal of 1719–23 for the compulsory castration of Roman Catholic priests, eventually rejected only at the English Privy Council's insistence, in one of the more benevolent operations of Poynings' Law. The idea originated in just such a proposal to geld Jesuits, attributed to George Villiers, Duke of Buckingham, but confined to the second part of *Foxes and firebrands*.[100] Still, in the nineteenth-century Church of Ireland, beleaguered by Catholic revival and for the first half of the century fighting to maintain its established status, Ware's obsessions with perfidious papists and deluded dissenters struck a chord, and his budget of stories was repeatedly quarried.[101]

By contrast, English historians encountered Robert Ware's forgeries mainly through the pages of Strype. Victorian editors, properly concerned to improve on Stuart and Georgian citation of primary sources to produce a greater standard of scholarly rigour, repeatedly came up against the buffers in trying to authenticate Strype's Ware fragments. Hence the Parker Society editor of Cranmer's whole works said in perplexity of the Coronation speech: 'Dr Jenkyns was unable to meet with the original, search having been made in vain for it in Dublin . . . A farther search for it has also been made for the present edition, but equally without success.'[102] The editor of a new freestanding edition of Strype's *Cranmer*, who meticulously re-edited all Strype's primary sources from the originals, equally had to admit defeat, informing his readers, 'The original copy of this speech has never been met with. The text is corrected from the book, from which Strype quoted' – in other words, *Foxes and firebrands*, in all its mendacious glory.[103] Ware would have been delighted at thus receiving the attentions of his only ever truly scholarly editor.

It was noticeable, however, that even among Strype's borrowings from Ware, English historians passed over much in silence. Interest began to fade in the stories of cunningly disguised Catholic fifth columnists like 'Faithful Commin', although polemical works like *Rome's tactics* by William Goode, a stridently Evangelical Dean of Ripon, would occasionally trot out the full panoply of *Foxes and firebrands* forgeries, with the aim of denouncing High Church Anglicans as much as Rome.[104] The main twins to survive to the end of the century were Cranmer's Coronation speech and the confrontation between Queen Elizabeth and Dean Nowell over his illustrated presentation Prayer Book. This latter encounter, which had been given a new airing in a biography of the dean in 1809,[105] was of interest in the perpetual skirmishes between Ritualists and Low Churchmen about the role of images in Church and the nature of the Prayer Book, while the former was a small contribution to filling a conspicuous gap in the English Reformation record: an entire absence of examples of any preaching from the archbishop who was the most prominent English Protestant of the century, and who was accordingly known to have preached important and prominent sermons at various stages of his public career. It was so tempting to reproduce the Coronation sermon text, and therefore many did.

Ware's Victorian nemesis was a Roman Catholic priest, Fr Thomas E. Bridgett, a Derby man who had travelled to Rome from Unitarianism via High Church Anglicanism, and who became a Redemptorist priest, working in Limerick and in England.[106] Bridgett was a thorough and conscientious historian. His life of Sir Thomas More has been deemed by Richard Marius as 'the first and best of the modern biographies', and Bridgett was devoted to the cause of correcting prejudiced Protestant accounts of Roman Catholic history.[107] What Bridgett lacked in flair, he made up in tenacity, and although he shows no signs of knowing that Anthony Collins had anticipated his work in 1700, his eighty-plus-page exposure of Ware, first published in the *Tablet* and then republished separately, is a fascinating piece of ruthless detective work which would greatly have satisfied his predecessor.[108] Bridgett investigated the publication history of Ware's pamphlets, and rightly identified Strype as the chief source of their material's infiltration into the mainstream historical record. He also noted a characteristic tic of Ware's forgeries which is a useful first clue in picking them up: invariably, when Ware placed one of his creations in the pen of a Catholic, he would use the phrase 'the mother Church'.[109]

It did not suit most mainstream English historians in Bridgett's time to take notice of something published in an apparently polemical Roman Catholic context, first in the *Tablet* and then from a press with a recently converted Catholic proprietor, Kegan Paul (of the firm Kegan Paul, Trench and Trübner). Nevertheless, only a year after the republication, one obviously scholarly commentator outside the fairly marginal world of English Roman Catholicism took up the cudgels from Bridgett and published further material in the house journal of England's new scientific history, the *English Historical Review*.[110] He was George Frederick Warner (1845–1936), Assistant Keeper of Manuscripts in the British Museum, who realized that one of the Grenville MSS in his care (Additional 33746) was an entire manuscript by Robert Ware, an intricate combination of Morgan Godwin's *Annals of England* (published 1630 and 1675) and Ware's own material. The forgery which had drawn his attention was a highly coloured account of the destruction of St Thomas Becket's shrine at Canterbury in 1538 in the presence of Henry VIII and his Privy Council: a circumstance which was simply impossible and not corroborated elsewhere. Spurred by this fresh specimen of Ware's work, Warner encouraged Fr Bridgett to return to the hunt of 'his special game', but Bridgett apparently did nothing further.

Warner was a private man whose stammer deterred him from public speaking; he was not likely to do much further to advertise Ware's perfidy, beyond those initial three pages among the *EHR*'s *Notes and Documents*. Warner's detective work is nevertheless clearly apparent in the British Museum's catalogue entries for the Ware material in the Additional Manuscripts, which meticulously point out the spurious material, but outside the BM catalogues, the Irish forger once more sidled his way out of terminal exposure.[111]

In the twentieth century, Irish and English historical interests increasingly diverged, yet Robert Ware continued to haunt and mislead historians on both sides of the Channel. The predominantly Catholic historiography of Ireland took more notice of Fr Bridgett than did the English; so an Irish historian and bibliographer, Philip Wilson, was spurred to a further demolition of Ware, after having been deceived by one of his forgeries. Ware still seemed capable of tainting even his adversaries with malpractice, since Wilson evidently used Bridgett's pioneering work in his exposé of the forger, but made no acknowledgement of the fact.[112] In any case, Wilson's restatement of the case against Ware failed to make an impact on English historians, perhaps because they were inattentive to bibliographical studies, or because Wilson's paper appeared amid Ireland's Home Rule crisis and in the last year of the First World War.

Soon after, one can observe the great Irish historian Robert Dudley Edwards coming to a horrified realization of how he had been deceived by Ware on the Irish Reformation, in a series of careful corrections to the *Dictionary of National Biography* which Dudley Edwards submitted to the British *Bulletin of the Institute of Historical Research* in 1933. Yet it was easy to ignore this new condemnation of Ware in the small print at the back of the *Bulletin* and in an article whose title did not refer to its main subject; in any case, Dudley Edwards had only detected the Irish part of the Ware forgeries.[113] Ware fictions continued to beguile Irish historians in single fragments, because of their sheer diversity. One of Ware's forgeries concerning a controversy in 1587 about which grammar textbook to use in Dublin emerged into the daylight of Irish educational history in 1976 from one of the British Library Ware manuscripts.[114] Equally, Robert's tantalizing references to a manuscript about the death of the Celtic hero Cormac in the library of Sir Robert Cotton have unsurprisingly been among the Ware inventions which have excited anthologists of Irish literature in the last two decades.[115]

England was secondary to Ireland in Ware's original work, but it has remained a last refuge for the active use of his material, even as the Irish mostly came to see through their compatriot. One pitfall for historians of the English Reformation, apart from their general neglect well into the twentieth century of sources without an Anglican provenance, was the fact that Fr Bridgett had not drawn attention to, or even mentioned, the two most spectacular and long-lasting forgeries from Ware to be found in Strype: Archbishop Cranmer's speech at Edward VI's Coronation and Elizabeth I's encounter with Dean Alexander Nowell. The Nowell story is perhaps the more puzzling survival of the two, since it was self-evidently anomalous, precisely reversing the known religious stances of the two protagonists. The real Dean Nowell was an advanced Reformed Protestant who drew generously on John Calvin in his much-circulated catechism; in fact, in a genuine clash with Elizabeth, Nowell had landed himself in trouble in 1565 by preaching before the queen against images and idolatry. He would have been the last person to present her with an illustrated Prayer Book, while in her furious reaction to Nowell's sermon of 1565 Elizabeth had revealed herself, as on many other occasions, as a stubborn defender of visual images of the sacred: an awkward position in the iconophobic Church of which she was Supreme Governor. What was she doing attacking images in a Prayer Book on the other occasion, and what was Dean Nowell doing putting them there? The incident seemed merely a proof of Elizabeth's feminine inconsistency, a cliché against which male historians would do well to guard themselves.

Another reason for the survival of both the Nowell and Cranmer forgeries was that in both, unusually in his creations, Ware had minimized the possibility of triangulation: he had not left any hostages to fortune in the form of extra characters whose movements might be traced elsewhere to disprove the fiction, and both dialogues were comparatively short. In the one, the conversation is entirely between the queen and the dean; and in the other, Cranmer is the only speaker before a silent king and congregation. Throughout the twentieth century and right up to the present, the Cranmer sermon has remained a firm favourite among historians, among whom, until very recently, I numbered myself, though with increasing unhappiness.[116] It chimed all too well with our rediscovery of the importance of iconophobia in the Tudor Reformation, and it seemed to provide the perfect example of the contemporary characterization of Edward VI as King Josiah which was indeed a common topos in authentic sources of the time.[117] The Nowell anecdote has received less attention, but has been adduced in evidence at least four times in the last four decades, and has found its way into Stanford Lehmberg's account of the dean in the current *Oxford Dictionary of National Biography*.[118] It is time to say goodbye to both these fictions, or rather to reassign them to their rightful place and importance as an influential product of the late seventeenth-century crisis of the Three Kingdoms.

Bridgett's tools for analysing Ware were set out in respect to his stories about the Marian bishops removed from their sees in the Church of England under Elizabeth, but they furnish a useful forensic armoury for judging all Ware's work and isolating the pollution that he has caused. Bridgett is worth quoting at length:

> I reject as apocryphal certain histories of the deposed bishops. 1. Because they are in themselves improbable and out of harmony with the known character of the actors. 2. Because they are filled with impossibilities when compared with ascertained facts and dates. 3. Because, being of a public nature, they should have been chronicled by contemporaries, whereas they were unheard of until a century and a quarter after their supposed occurrence. 4. Because there is no record of them in any existing State Papers. 5. Because the 'Memorials' from which it is pretended that they have been derived do not exist and are not known to have existed. 6. Because the book which first records them is full of palpable forgeries, whereby these things also are rendered suspected; and 7, lastly, Because the purpose of their invention is clear, which is to throw odium on the Church and her bishops, as unscrupulous agents of Rome, ready to bully or to lie according to circumstances, but crushed by Protestant simplicity and truth, of which these books are a curious specimen.[119]

There is a wider maxim to be observed in dealing with the Ware *oeuvre*. None of the posthumously published works of Sir James

Ware are fully trustworthy. No statement in them should be taken as a valid piece of historical evidence without checking the manuscript collections on which they are based – works printed in Sir James's lifetime – and also taking guidance from the manuscripts' existence in Sir James's original published catalogue of 1648. If Robert Ware intended this as revenge on his father, then the revenge has been the sweeter for being drawn out over three centuries.

22

And Finally: the nature
of Anglicanism

'Anglican' is one of many religious labels which started as a term of contempt, like 'Methodist', or probably indeed, 'Christian'. In the 1590s, King James VI of Scotland assured his suspicious Scottish clergy that he was not thinking of foisting 'Papistical or Anglican bishops' on them (the wily king changed his mind when he became James I of England). But thereafter the word was hardly used at all until the 1830s, when English High Churchmen rediscovered it, using it to emphasize how different their Church was from any other – neither Roman nor Protestant. Then 'Anglican' quickly lost its 'party' connotations, because everyone realized how useful it was for describing a new reality: two national Established Churches, the Churches of England and Ireland, had transmuted into something else, spawning a worldwide ecclesiastical family which spread in tandem with the British Empire. What to call it? Anglican. And so the 'Anglican Communion' was born, in the happy unplanned fashion which has characterized the history of this now global form of the Christian faith, ever since its birth in the Reformation.

Make no mistake: Anglicanism is a product of the Reformation, though a peculiar one. If around 1570 you had scrutinized all three Churches officially established in these islands, you would of course have called them Protestant – but which sort? Two European groupings of Protestant Churches were developing. One was the Lutheran bloc; the other, those not signed up to the Lutheran party line, looked more to Churches in Zürich or John Calvin's Geneva. These non-Lutherans were coming to be called 'Reformed' Protestants. Emphatically, the Churches of England, Scotland and Ireland were all Reformed, not

Lutheran. They all had bishops (the Established Scottish Church only definitively got rid of bishops in 1690), but so did other Reformed Churches, like the Hungarians, Poles or Transylvanians.

Still, one thing made the Church of England different, and gradually alienated it from its Reformed neighbour in Scotland. For reasons locked deep in the mind of Queen Elizabeth I, it kept its cathedrals: an accident which has been a major theme in this book. Other Protestant Churches also kept the buildings (with uncharacteristic lack of logic, the Church of Scotland still calls its former cathedrals cathedrals, despite ejecting their bishops three centuries ago) – but what made England unique was the survival of the whole medieval shebang: deans, chapters, prebends, organs, choirs, closes, the lot. Above all, what survived was the cathedral ethos: dedication to a regular round of beautifully performed ceremony and sacred music. Cathedrals annexed the Tudor prose of Thomas Cranmer's Book of Common Prayer for this ancient (and very unProtestant) liturgical duty, and still do. What is more Anglican than Sung Evensong? Yet Cranmer would have been underwhelmed by it, not having much time for cathedrals.

That's the glory of the Anglican tradition. It is a double helix, intertwining two mutually antagonistic strands of Christianity which elsewhere bitterly clashed in the Reformation: Catholic and Reformed. At first, the balance was extremely unstable, and that was a major element in seventeenth-century civil wars which cost King Charles I his head – but most of the English were thoroughly frightened by what they had done, and in 1660 they brought back Charles II, and with him, bishops, cathedrals and the Prayer Book of the Church of England. It is one of the astonishments of English history that the nobility and gentry of England meekly surrendered all the church lands that they'd cheerfully acquired from Oliver Cromwell, just to recreate those majestic institutions, which have been there ever since. It is really only with Charles's Restoration in 1660 that we can speak about Anglicanism existing, even though it was yet to be named.

Another characteristic of that Restoration Anglicanism is that ever afterwards, it has lived not only with internal contradictions, but with a vigorous external Protestant critique: no other Protestant Church in Europe apart from the Reformed Church of the Netherlands (for very different reasons) has had this experience. Many Protestants who, before the Civil Wars, would just about have stayed within the Established Church of England, could not stomach its renewed ceremonial flummery. These gritty souls were christened 'Dissenters', then 'Nonconformists' or 'Free Churchmen'. A hundred years later, John Wesley released such spiritual energies in the C of E that they burst its bounds and reluctantly regrouped outside the Church, as Methodism. Part of the richness of English Protestantism is that it is a babble of cussed voices, exuberant Free Church percussion enlivening the majestic orchestra that is Anglican spirituality. From the eighteenth century, the English and their American relatives have shared hymns across the divides: as a result, much of the world's hymnody comes from the divided and argumentative strands of anglophone religion.

The next contribution to the Eton Mess of Anglicanism was the nineteenth-century Oxford Movement, emphasizing the Catholic ethos which had clung on in Good Queen Bess's cathedrals and sometimes pretending that it was the only thing of any value in the Church of England. More nuanced followers of this 'Anglo-Catholic' movement have always realized that it's not that simple. They have brought a combination of seriousness, artistic sensitivity and deft humour to the Anglican worship of God, and in the process, have widely transformed Anglican worship. They have valued reflection on the complex past (inevitable if you're an Anglican). Very often, they have realized that to be Catholic is not to be wedded to the past, but to listen to what the present is telling us, for instance about ordaining women to the priesthood or treating gay people properly. Others, at the moment no more than a handful, have given up the struggle and decided that Rome knows best. That's a shame, because the whole basis of the Church of England's Reformation, and the reason for Anglicanism's separate existence, has always been that Rome does not know best, though it would be nice if it currently did.

Journalists love to write about the crisis of Anglicanism over women and gays, for it makes a great headline. 'NOT ALL THAT MANY GO OVER TO ROME' or 'EVANGELICALS END UP NOT MAKING QUITE SUCH A FUSS AS THEY HAD PLANNED' don't pack a punch in big type. Headline-writers don't seem to realize that the Anglican crisis began in 1533, and has not stopped since. That is why it is so satisfying to be an Anglican. Anglicanism is a trial-and-error form of Christianity; it has made mistakes in the past (losing the Dissenters and the Methodists being two of the worst, not to mention killing Roman Catholics), and it can feel honestly rueful about them. Anglicanism is an approach to God which acknowledges that He is often good at remaining silent and provoking more questions than answers. Anglicans are not afraid to argue in public.

Thanks to Archbishop Cranmer and a fleet of committees who thoughtfully revised his Prayer Book, Anglicanism has a liturgy whose dignity and solemnity can act as a sure support through choppy waters. Seek out Cranmer's Evensong, hearken beyond its beautiful choral performance to some ghostly tut-tutting from a dead archbishop, and enjoy the way in which the past mocks our dogmatism and asks us to think again.

Acknowledgements

The original versions of these articles were published as follows:

Christianity: the bigger picture: 'Reassessing Christian History', in *Religion: the 2014 Engelsberg Seminar* (2015)

Angels and the Reformation: 'Recent studies of angels in the Reformation', *Reformation* 14 (2009), pp. 179–86

The Virgin Mary and Protestant Reformers: 'Mary and 16th-century Protestants', in R. N. Swanson (ed.), *The Church and Mary*, Studies in Church History 39 (Woodbridge: Boydell and Brewer for the Ecclesiastical History Society, 2004), pp. 191–217

John Calvin: 'Calvin: fifth Latin doctor of the Church?', in I. Backus and P. Benedict (eds), *Calvin and his influence, 1509–2009* (Oxford University Press, 2011), pp. 33–45

The Council of Trent: 'One enormous room', *London Review of Books*, 9 May 2013

The Italian Inquisition: 'Evil just is', *London Review of Books*, 13 May 2010, pp. 23–4

Tudor Royal Image-Making: 'Paraphernalia', *London Review of Books*, 19 November 2009, pp. 24–5

Henry VIII: pious king: 'Henry VIII and the reform of the Church', in Diarmaid MacCulloch (ed.), *The Reign of Henry VIII: Politics, Policy and Piety* (Basingstoke: Macmillan, 1995), pp. 159–80

Tolerant Cranmer?: 'Archbishop Cranmer: Tolerance and Concord in a changing Church', in O. Grell and R. W. Scribner (eds), *Tolerance and Intolerance in the European Reformation* (Cambridge University Press, 1996), pp. 119–215

The Making of the Prayer Book: 'Mumpsimus, Sumpsimus', *London*

Review of Books, 24 May 2012, pp. 13–15

Tudor Queens: Mary and Elizabeth: 'Something about Mary', *London Review of Books*, 18 October 2007, pp. 15–16

William Byrd: 'Young Man's Nostalgia', *London Review of Books*, 31 July 2014, pp. 19–20

The Bible before King James: extract from E. Solopova and D. MacCulloch, 'Before the King James Bible', in H. Moore and J. Reid (eds), *Manifold Greatness: The Making of the King James Bible* (Oxford: Bodleian Library Publications, 2011), pp. 13–40

The King James Bible: 'How Good is it?', *London Review of Books*, 3 February 2011, pp. 20–22

The Bay Psalm Book: Introduction to *The Bay Psalm Book: imprinted 1640* (Oxford: Bodleian Library Publications, 2014)

Putting the English Reformation on the Map: 'Putting the English Reformation on the Map', *Transactions of the Royal Historical Society*, 6th series 15 (2005), pp. 75–96

The Latitude of the Church of England: 'The Latitude of the Church of England', in K. Fincham and P. Lake (eds), *Religious Politics in Post-Reformation England: essays in honour of Nicholas Tyacke* (Woodbridge: Boydell Press, 2006), pp. 41–59

Modern Historians on the English Reformation: 'Changing perspectives on the Reformation: the last fifty years', in P. Clarke and C. Methuen (eds), *The Church on its Past*, Studies in Church History (Woodbridge: Boydell and Brewer for the Ecclesiastical History Society, 2013), pp. 282–302

Thomas Cranmer's Biographers: 'La Reforma Inglesa a judicio: percepciones biográficas del Arzobispo Thomas Cranmer', in J. C. Davis and Isabel Burdiel (eds), *El Otro, el Mismo: biografía y autobiografía en Europe (siglos XVII–XX)* (Valèncìa: Universitat de Valèncìa, 2005), pp. 89–114

Richard Hooker's Reputation: 'Richard Hooker's Reputation', *English Historical Review* 117 (2002), pp. 773–812

Forging Reformation History: a cautionary tale: 'Foxes, Firebrands and Forgery: Robert Ware's pollution of Reformation history', *Historical Journal* 54 (2011), pp. 307–46

And Finally: the nature of Anglicanism: 'Unplanned product of a very English Reformation', *Times* series for Holy Week, 18 April 2011

Notes

1. Christianity: the bigger picture

1. Diarmaid MacCulloch, *A History of Christianity: the First Three Thousand Years* (London, 2009), p. 1.
2. For a fuller explanation, see my essay 'John Calvin', below.

2. Angels and the Reformation

Originally published as a review of *Angels in the Early Modern World*, edited by Peter Marshall and Alexandra Walsham, Cambridge University Press, 2006, 340pp; *In the Anteroom of Divinity: The Reformation of the Angels from Colet to Milton* by Feisal G. Mohamed, University of Toronto Press, 2008, 248pp.

1. See my essay 'John Calvin', below.
2. *Angels in the Early Modern World*, ed. P. Marshall and A. Walsham (Cambridge, 2006), p. 204.
3. J. Arnold, *Dean John Colet of St Paul's: humanism and reform in early Tudor England* (London, 2007).

3. The Virgin Mary and Protestant Reformers

1. G. C. G. Thomas, 'The Stradling Library at St. Donat's, Glamorgan', *National Library of Wales Journal* 24 (1986), pp. 402–19, at 408. There are several notices of this incident: [?N. Harpsfield], *Bishop Cranmer's Recantacyons*, ed. Lord Houghton with introduction by J. Gairdner (Philobiblon Society Miscellanies 15, London, 1877–84), p. 15; *A Chronicle of England . . . by Charles Wriothesley, Windsor Herald*, ed. W. D. Hamilton (2 vols, Camden Society, 2nd series 11, 20, 1875, 1877),

vol. 2, p. 10; *Chronicle of the Grey Friars of London*, ed. J. Gough Nichols (Camden Society, 1st series 53, 1852), p. 58. For the surviving account of the trial of the antinomian radical John Champneis, see Lambeth Palace Library, Cranmer's Register, fo.71v; other accounts in the register, notably that of the later martyr Joan Bocher, have been lost.

2. L.-E. Halkin, *Erasmus: a critical biography* (Oxford, 1993), pp. 224-5, 229. The *Ciceronian* is translated in *Collected Works of Erasmus, XXVIII*, ed. A. H. T. Levi (Toronto, 1986), see pp. 381-2. Erasmus's main Marian works are to be found in *Collected Works of Erasmus, LXIX: Spiritualia and Pastoralia*, ed. J. W. O'Malley (Toronto, 1999): cf. pp. 25, 44-5, and for his embarrassment, ibid., p. 40.

3. *Collected Works of Erasmus, LXVI: Spiritualia: Enchiridion; de contemptu Mundi; De vidua Christiana*, ed. J. W. O'Malley (Toronto, 1988), p. 71.

4. Halkin, *Erasmus*, p. 230.

5. Halkin, *Erasmus*, p. 229. Halkin points out that Erasmus's close friend John Fisher continued in his preaching to make use of the Song of Songs in relation to Mary.

6. Halkin, *Erasmus*, p. 225: cf. *Modus Orandi Deum: Opera Omnia Desiderii Erasmi Roterodami* (Amsterdam, 1969–), vol. 5, part i, pp. 146-7.

7. Halkin, *Erasmus*, p. 209. Cf. *Opus Epistolarum Des. Erasmi Roterodami . . .*, eds P. S. Allen, H. M. Allen and H.W. Garrod (12 vols, Oxford, 1906-58), vol. 8, p. 421, for a preacher's attack on Erasmus for this change.

8. *Opera Erasmi*, 6.5, pp. 490-92.

9. On the Colloquies, see M. Aston, *England's Iconoclasts I: Laws against Images* (Oxford, 1988), pp. 197-9.

10. Cf. interesting remarks on this in J. Pelikan, *Mary through the centuries: her place in the history of culture* (New Haven and London, 1996), pp. 210-11.

11. *Collected Works of Erasmus, XXXIX-XL: Colloquies*, ed. C. R. Thompson (Toronto, 1997), vol. 2, pp. 630-33, 636; *An admonition showing the advantages which Christendom might derive from an Inventory of Relics*, printed in *Tracts relating to the Reformation by J. Calvin*, ed. H. Beveridge (3 vols, Edinburgh, 1844-51), vol. 1, pp. 287-341, esp. pp. 316-18.

12. *Collected Works of Erasmus: Colloquies*, vol. 1, p. 355; *Opera Erasmi* 5.1 (*Modus Orandi Deum*), pp. 155-6, 172; cf. Halkin, *Erasmus*, p. 222.

13. *Certain Sermons or Homilies appointed to be read in Churches in the Time of the Late Queen Elizabeth . . .* (London, 1852), pp. 206-8. For discussion, see Aston, *England's Iconoclasts*, pp. 320-25, esp. n. 96.

14. *Precationes aliquot novae* (Basel, 1535): *Collected Works of Erasmus, LXIX*, pp. 117–52, at pp. 126–7, cited by Halkin, *Erasmus*, pp. 261, 334. Cf. Erasmus's attempts to balance his material in the *Colloquies* and elsewhere in his writings of the 1530s: Aston, *England's Iconoclasts*, p. 199; Halkin, *Erasmus*, p. 225.

15. Halkin, *Erasmus*, pp. 226–8: *Collected Works of Erasmus, LXIX*, pp. 79–108, esp. at pp. 98–9.

16. Halkin, *Erasmus*, p. 331.

17. For the texts of their correspondence, see B. Collett, *A long and troubled pilgrimage: the correspondence of Marguerite D'Angoulême and Vittoria Colonna 1540–1545 (Studies in Reformed Theology and History* new series 6, 2001), pp. 125–43, and for Colonna, the Virgin and Michelangelo, Collett., pp. 87, 89–92.

18. B. Cottret, *Calvin: A Biography* (Grand Rapids and Edinburgh, 2000), p. 62.

19. H. A. Oberman, *The impact of the Reformation* (Edinburgh, 1994), p. 213, quoting *Die Chronik des Bernhard Wyss*, ed. G. Finsler, p. 16.

20. *To the Christian Nobility of the German Nation*, in *Luther: Three Treatises* (Philadelphia, 1970), p. 75: *D. Martin Luthers Werke* (Weimar, 1883–) [hereafter *WA*], vol. 6, pp. 447, 18 and n. For an illustration of a copy of Michael Ostendorfer's 1520 print of the Regensburg pilgrimage, with an added hostile MS comment of 1523 by Albrecht Dürer, S. Michalski, *The Reformation and the visual arts: the Protestant image question in western and eastern Europe* (London, 1993), pl. 3. For the noticeable late medieval association between Marian devotion and anti-Semitism, see M. Rubin, 'Europe remade: purity and danger in late medieval Europe', *Transactions of the Royal Historical Society*, 6th series 11 (2001), pp. 101–24, at pp. 118–19.

21. Aston, *England's Iconoclasts*, pp. 35–6.

22. R. Bireley, *The refashioning of Catholicism, 1450–1700* (London, 1999), p. 111.

23. H.-J. Goertz, *Thomas Müntzer: apocalyptic mystic and revolutionary* (Edinburgh, 1993), pp. 114–16.

24. Michalski, *Reformation and visual arts*, p. 92.

25. On Paris, 1528, and Geneva, 1532, see Cottret, *Calvin*, p. 49. On the image from Cadiz at St Alban's College Valladolid, see A. Shell, *Catholicism, controversy and the English literary imagination, 1558–1660* (Cambridge, 1999), pp. 200–207.

26. Aston, *England's Iconoclasts*, pp. 39–43. Lutherans nevertheless got no credit from Orthodox Christians for their positive attitude to the visual: the memories of 1520s northern atrocities like Riga remained

strong. Michalski, *Reformation and visual arts*, pp. 102, 114, 134–5, 148, 154.

27. Useful treatments in English are P. Newman Brooks, 'A lily ungilded? Martin Luther, the Virgin Mary and the saints', *Journal of Religious History* 13/2 (1984), pp. 136–49, and G. Müller, 'Protestant veneration of Mary: Luther's interpretation of the *Magnificat*', in *Humanism and Reform: the Church in Europe, England and Scotland, 1400–1643. Essays in Honour of James K. Cameron*, ed. J. Kirk, *Studies in Church History, Subsidia* 8 (1991), pp. 99–112. The work is to be found in WA, vol. 7, pp. 538–604.

28. WA, vol. 7, p. 568, ll. 11 and 15–16; vol. 7, p. 573, ll. 32–3.

29. WA, vol. 7, p. 569, ll. 33; p. 570, ll.3.

30. Cf. Halkin, *Erasmus*, p. 105.

31. WA, vol. 7, p. 569, ll. 14–15.

32. WA, vol. 7, p. 601, ll. 8–11.

33. W. Tappolet with A. Ebneter, *Das Marienlob der Reformatoren: Martin Luther, Johannes Calvin, Huldrych Zwingli, Heinrich Bullinger* (Tübingen, 1962), pp. 357–65. For further discussion of Luther and Mary, see H. Düfel, *Luthers Stellung zur Marienverehrung* (Göttingen, 1968).

34. On Luther's hymnology, Tappolet, *Marienlob*, pp. 127–44, and on this poem, pp. 141–4. See also Brooks, 'A lily ungilded', p. 147, and Pelikan, *Mary*, p. 13.

35. Tappolet, *Marienlob*, p. 156. The editors of the Rheims Testament underlined Luther's rationale when they complained that English Protestants only retained Marian feasts which were really Christocentric, 'so that she by this meanes shal have no festivitie at al': *The New Testament of Jesus Christ* (Rheims, 1582), p. 191. For Luther's remarks on the feast of the Immaculate Conception in 1516–17, see Rubin, 'Europe remade', p. 121.

36. *Martin Bucer and the Book of Common Prayer*, ed. E. C. Whitaker, Alcuin Club Collections 55 (1974), pp. 140–41. It is a token of Cranmer's characteristic self-effacement that the Feast of the Visitation was his birthday.

37. For a modernized and abridged text, Tappolet, *Marienlob*, pp. 221–39. For a similar Marian sermon from Bullinger, preached and published in 1558 because 'contumeliose nos loqui de beate virgine', see Tappolet, *Marienlob*, pp. 275–302.

38. G. W. Locher, *Zwingli's Thought: New Perspectives* (Leiden, 1981), p. 60; on the Marian festivals, ibid. pp. 89, 91, and K. Biegger, *'De invocatione beatae Mariae Virginis': Paracelsus und die Marienverehrung*

(*Kosmosophie* 6, 1990), p. 86. For Zwingli's defence of using the scriptural 'Hail Mary', see Oberman, *Impact*, p. 243. Note cautious comments on the liturgical use of the angelic salutation by the prominent Zürich pastor Ludwig Lavater, *De ritibus et institutis ecclesiae Tigurinae* (1559), qu. *Private Prayers put forth by authority during the reign of Queen Elizabeth*, ed. W. Keatinge Clay (Parker Society, Cambridge, 1851), p. viii.

39. 'Hac caussa credimus et Deiparae virginis Marie purissimum thalamum et spiritus sancti templum, hoc est, sacrosanctum corpus eius deportatum esse ab angelis in coelum': H. Bullinger, *De origine erroris libri duo* (Zürich, 1539), fo. 69v, and subsequent editions; the sentence does not occur in the much shorter first version, Zürich, 1529. On Zwingli and the Assumption, see Locher, *Zwingli's Thought*, pp. 89–90.

40. Tappolet, *Marienlob*, p. 327.

41. *Calvin's Theological Treatises*, vol. 1, pp. 118–20; this is Calvin's riposte to twenty-five Articles put out on 10 March 1542 by the doctors of theology in the University of Paris. On Luther, see Tappolet, *Marienlob*, p. 126.

42. J. Cadier, 'La Vierge Marie dans la dogmatique réformée au XVIe et au XVIIe siècle', *La revue réformée* 9/no. 36 (1958/4), pp. 46–58, at p. 46 makes the point that there is no reference to Mary in Marlorat's index to the *Institutes*.

43. W. J. Bouwsma, *Calvin: a sixteenth-century portrait* (New York and Oxford, 1988), pp. 123, 267.

44. Taking their cue from Calvin, the notes to the Geneva Bible are remarkably taciturn on Mary, even in passages where it would be obvious to comment on her, with the notable exception of condemnations of papist misattribution to her of honorific titles at Ezekiel 7:18 and 44:17: *The Bible: that is the Holy Scriptures conteined in the Old and New Testament* (London, 1606), sigs HH8v and KK6r.

45. *Sermons and Remains of Hugh Latimer . . .*, ed. G. E. Corrie (Parker Society, Cambridge, 1845), p. 393. On Mary and the Lollards, see Aston, *England's Iconoclasts*, pp. 130–39; C. Marsh, *Popular Religion in sixteenth century England: holding their peace* (Houndmills, 1998), p. 165.

46. *Sermons of Hugh Latimer*, ed. G. E. Corrie (Parker Society, Cambridge, 1844), pp. 383, 515; *Sermons and Remains of Latimer*, ed. Corrie, pp. 91, 117, 157–8; *An Answer to Sir Thomas More's Dialogue, the Supper of the Lord . . . and William Tracy's Testament expounded. By William Tyndale . . .*, ed. H. Walter (Parker Society, Cambridge, 1850), p. 207.

Latimer was nevertheless equally prepared to use Mary's silence (Luke 2:51) as an example to other women to keep silent: *Sermons and Remains of Latimer*, ed. Corrie, p. 91.

47. C. W. Foster, *The state of the church ... as illustrated by documents relating to the Diocese of Lincoln*, vol. 1 (Lincolnshire Record Society 23, 1926), p. 370.

48. *The Sources of Swiss Anabaptism: the Grebel Letters and related documents*, ed. L. Harder (Scottdale, PA, 1985), p. 362 and n. 1, p. 719: the number seven derives from Mark 6:3, where the mention of four brothers and plural sisters of Jesus indicates a minimum of seven children in the Holy Family.

49. Quoted in E. Mâle, *Religious Art* (London, 1949), p. 167. On the medieval background to celestial flesh doctrine, see G. H. Williams, *The Radical Reformation* (London, 1962), pp. 325–35.

50. A. Duke, 'The face of popular religious dissent in the Low Countries, 1520–1530', *Journal of Ecclesiastical History* 26 (1975), pp. 41–67, at p. 52, quoting Gemeentearchief Gouda, Oud-rechterlijk archief 147, fo. 45v. and *Corpus documentorum inquisitionis haereticae pravitatis Neerlandicae*, ed. P. Fredericq (5 vols, Ghent/The Hague, 1889–1902), vol. 4, p. 372.

51. *Sermons of Latimer*, ed. Corrie, p. 60.

52. Williams, *Radical Reformation*, p. 245.

53. Williams, *Radical Reformation*, pp. 329, 330–32. Hofmann may have been aware that one of Bernard of Clairvaux's best-known sermons on Mary employed the metaphor of an aqueduct to describe her role in mediating grace. See D. Spivey Ellington, *From sacred body to angelic soul. Understanding Mary in late medieval and early modern Europe* (Washington DC, 2001), p. 128.

54. On Bocher's beliefs, and those of her contemporary English radicals, see I. B. Horst, *The Radical Brethren: Anabaptism and the English Reformation* (Nieuwkoop, 1962), pp. 109–15. See Williams, *Radical Reformation*, pp. 394–5, 490–92.

55. Williams, *Radical Reformation*, pp. 176–8.

56. Williams, *Radical Reformation*, pp. 490–93, 562, 610, 666–8, 745. For a late sixteenth-century echo of Italian unitarianism in Menocchio the Friulian miller, see A. del Col, trans. J. and A. Tedeschi, *Domenico Scandella known as Menocchio: his trials before the Inquisition (1583–1599)* (Binghamton, NY, 1996), esp. pp. liii–liv, 4, 6–8, 54.

57. One notices, for instance, that when a group of Swiss radicals in Appenzell fell under the spell of a local woman, she proclaimed herself to be a new and female Messiah, but not the new Mary: A. Jelsma, 'A "Messiah for women": religious commotion in the north-east of Switzerland,

1525–1526', in *Women in the Church*, ed. W. J. Sheils and D. Wood (Studies in Church History 27, Oxford, 1989), pp. 295–306.

58. K. Biegger, *'De invocatione beatae Mariae Virginis': Paracelsus und die Marienverehrung* (Kosmosophie 6, 1990) provides an edition of the main Marian tract and invaluable general discussion; see also U. Gause, *Paracelsus (1493–1541): Genese und Entfaltung seiner frühen Theologie* (Tübingen, 1993). Biegger, *Marienverehrung*, pp. 60–68, seeks to date *De Invocatione* at c.1527, but much is uncertain in Paracelsus chronology. The text of *De Trinitate* can be found in *Paracelsus: sammtliche Werke II: theologische und religionsphilosophische Schriften III: dogmatische und polemische einzelschriften*, ed. K. Goldammer (Stuttgart, 1986), pp. 233–66, and see discussion, ibid., pp. xlii–xliv. I am much indebted to Charles Webster for pointing me to material on Paracelsus.

59. Biegger, *Marienverehrung*, pp. 26–38, 201.

60. Biegger, *Marienverehrung*, pp. 51, 163, 197, 254–5.

61. Biegger, *Marienverehrung*, pp. 238, 248, 262.

62. Williams, *Radical Reformation*, pp. 286–8, 292.

63. J. Boehme, *The way to Christ* (New York, 1978), esp. pp. 9, 44, 150. The English conformist polemicist Thomas Rogers claimed in the 1580s that the women of the radical sect the Family of Love believed that they were all Marys, 'and say, that Christ is come forth in their fleshe': P. Crawford, *Women and Religion in England, 1500–1720* (London, 1993), p. 122, quoting T. Rogers, *The Family of Love*, sigs. kv, kii. The beliefs expressed by the Familists themselves contain no trace of this canard: cf. e.g. C. Marsh, *The Family of Love in English Society* (Cambridge, 1993), Ch. 2.

64. Cf. e.g. *Zwingli and Bullinger*, ed. G.W. Bromiley (London, 1953), p. 256, and Locher, *Zwingli's Thought*, p. 87; *A Disputation on Holy Scripture ... by William Whitaker*, ed. W. Fitzgerald (Parker Society, Cambridge, 1849), pp. 538, 603.

65. Cf. e.g. *Doctrinal Treatises and Introductions to Different Portions of the Holy Scriptures. By William Tyndale ...* , ed. H. Walter (Parker Society, Cambridge, 1848), p. 315; *An Answer to Sir Thomas More's Dialogue ... by Tyndale*, ed. Walter, p. 28; Tappolet, *Marienlob*, p. 55 (Luther); H. Hackett, *Virgin Mother, Maiden Queen: Elizabeth I and the cult of the Virgin Mary* (Basingstoke, 1995), p. 204 (William Perkins). It may be that some early Reformers saw the Assumption as a possible argument against the doctrine of psychopannichia (soul-sleep) held by some radicals.

66. For some English examples, *Treatises by Tyndale*, ed. Walter, p. 159; *An Answer to Sir Thomas More's Dialogue ... by Tyndale*, ed. Walter, p.

131; H. Joliffe and R. Johnson, *Responsio venerabilium sacerdotum, Henrici Joliffi et Roberti Jonson* (Antwerp, 1564), fo. 165v (John Hooper); *The Works of John Jewel, Bishop of Salisbury*, ed. J. Ayre (2 vols. in 4, Parker Society, Cambridge, 1845–50), vol. 3, p. 611, vol. 4, pp. 1045–6, 1053; *A defence of the sincere and true translations of the Holy Scriptures . . . by W. Fulke*, ed. C. H. Hartshorne (Parker Society, Cambridge, 1843), p. 35; *A disputation on Holy Scripture by William Whitaker*, ed. W. Fitzgerald (Parker Society, Cambridge, 1849), pp. 504–5.

67. D. Steinmetz, *Calvin in context* (New York and Oxford, 1995), p. 86, citing *WA*, vol. 44, p. 324: Luther's lectures on Genesis, 1545.

68. *The Works of Roger Hutchinson*, ed. J. Bruce (Parker Society, Cambridge, 1842), p. 148.

69. On More, see *An Answer to Sir Thomas More's Dialogue . . . by Tyndale*, ed. Walter, p. 96; cf. *Remains of Myles Coverdale . . .*, ed. G. Pearson (Parker Society, Cambridge, 1846), p. 414.

70. [T. Swynnerton], J. Roberts [pseud.], *A mustre of scismatyke bysshoppes of Rome* (London, 1534), sigs. Eviiir–Fir. For the importance of the argument over 'unwritten verities', see P. Marshall, 'The debate over "unwritten verities" in early Reformation England', in B. Gordon, ed., *Protestant history and identity in 16th century Europe* (Aldershot, 1996), pp. 60–77.

71. *Documents on the Continental Reformation*, ed. W. R. Naphy (Basingstoke, 1996), p. 97 (Zwingli); Tappolet, *Marienlob*, pp. 227, 246 (Zwingli and Osiander); *The Decades of Henry Bullinger*, ed. T. Harding (4 vols, Parker Society, Cambridge, 1849–52), vol. 4, p. 437; Cadier, 'Vierge Marie', p. 47 (Calvin); *Works of Archbishop Cranmer*, ed. J. E. Cox (2 vols, Parker Society, Cambridge, 1846), vol. 2, p. 60; *The Examinations and Writings of John Philpot . . .*, ed. R. Eden (Parker Society, Cambridge, 1842), pp. 426–7 (Caelius Curio and Philpot); *Sermons and Remains of Latimer*, ed. Corrie, pp. 104–6; *Early Writings of Bishop Hooper . . .*, ed. S. Carr (Parker Society, Cambridge, 1843), p. 161; *Works of Jewel*, ed. Ayre, vol. 3, p. 440.

72. Tappolet, *Marienlob*, pp. 245, 280. More cautiously, Archbishop Cranmer's theological commonplace books noted that the allegorical argument from Ezek. 44 was a possible direction to take: *Works of Cranmer*, vol. 2, p. 60.

73. *An Answer to Sir Thomas More's Dialogue . . . by Tyndale*, ed. Walter, p. 33; Bouwsma, *Calvin*, p. 267; *Fulke's Answers to Stapleton, Martiall and Sanders*, ed. R. Gibbings (Parker Society, Cambridge, 1848), p. 272; *Disputation by Whitaker*, p. 538.

74. *Ecclesiastical Polity* I.7.5 (*Folger Library Edition of the Works of Richard Hooker*, ed. W. R. Speed Hill et al. (7 vols, Cambridge and Binghamton, 1977–94), vol. 1, p. 179, line 27. On Catholic awareness of the Protestant problem in relation to the perpetual virginity, see [P. de la Place], *Commentaires de l'estat de la religion et Republique soubs les Rois Henry et Francois seconds et Charles neufieme* ([Paris], 1565), pp. 291–4, and S. M. Manetsch, *Theodore Beza and the quest for peace in France 1572–1598* (Brill, 2000), pp. 274–5. I am grateful to Philip Benedict for pointing me to these references.

75. *Documents*, ed. Naphy, p. 97.

76. *Documents*, ed. Naphy, p. 101.

77. Tappolet, *Marienlob*, p. 246.

78. A. Walsham, *Providence in early modern England* (Oxford, 1999), pp. 80, 91–3.

79. T. Watt, *Cheap Print and popular piety* (Cambridge, 1991), pp. 120–21, and on Protestant attitudes to Joseph, cf. *A Defence of the sincere and true translations of the Holy Scriptures into the English tongue by William Fulke*, ed. C. H. Hartshorne (Parker Society, Cambridge, 1843), pp. 535–6.

80. Cf. *Calvin, Theological Treatises*, ed. J. K. S. Reid (Library of Christian Classics 22, London, 1954), p. 97, the Latin catechism of Geneva, 27 November 1545, almost certainly composed by Calvin; *A catechism in Latin by Alexander Nowell . . . together with the same catechism translated into English by Thomas Norton . . .*, ed. G. E. Corrie (Parker Society, Cambridge, 1853), p. 150; I. Green, *The Christian's ABC: Catechisms and catechizing in England c. 1530–1740* (Oxford, 1996), p. 336.

81. *Certain Sermons or Homilies (1547) and A Homily against Disobedience and Wilful Rebellion (1570)*, ed. R. B. Bond (Toronto, 1987), p. 200, a 1547 reference where an allusion to Luke 1:52 in the Magnificat was made more explicit in 1563 (cf. *Certain Sermons or Homilies appointed . . . in the Time of the Late Queen Elizabeth*, p. 139); *Homilies*, ed. Bond, p. 169; *Certain Sermons or Homilies appointed . . . in the Time of the Late Queen Elizabeth*, p. 150.

82. E. A. McKee, *Katharina Schütz Zell. 1. The life and thought of a 16th century Reformer. 2. The writings: a critical edition* (2 vols, Leiden, 1999). For similar comment, see P. Russell, *Lay Theology in the Reformation: Popular Pamphleteers in Southwest Germany 1521–1525* (Cambridge, 1985), pp. 201, 222. On Counter-Reformation discussion of the humility of Mary, see particularly Ellington, *From sacred body to angelic soul*, pp. 182–4.

83. C. B. and J. B. Atkinson, 'The identity and life of Thomas Bentley, compiler of *The Monument of Matrones'*, *Sixteenth Century Journal* 31 (2000), pp. 323–47, at p. 328.

84. Perhaps most telling is Hackett's balanced discussion of the much-exploited sermon of Dr John King preached immediately after Elizabeth's death: Hackett, *Virgin Mother*, p. 225.

85. For the importance of the private chapel of the statesman Robert Cecil at Hatfield, begun in 1607, see P. Croft, 'The religion of Robert Cecil', *Historical Journal* 34 (1991), pp. 773–96, at pp. 787–9.

86. Cadier, 'Vierge Marie', pp. 49–53: C. Drelincourt, *De l'honneur qui doit estre rendu a la saincte et bienheureuse Vierge Marie: Auec la response à Monsieur l'euesque de Belley sur la qualité de cét honneur* (Paris, 1642).

87. *Works of Jewel*, ed. Ayre, vol. 3, p. 578.

4. John Calvin

1. A. N. S. Lane, *Calvin and Bernard of Clairvaux* (Studies in Reformation Theology and History new series, 1, Princeton, 1996).

2. J. Calvin, *Institutes of the Christian religion*, ed. J. T. McNeill and F. L. Battles (2 vols, Philadelphia, 1960), vol. 1, pp. 164–5 [*Institutes* I.xiv.4].

3. I. Backus, *Historical method and confessional identity in the era of the Reformation (1378–1615)* (Leiden, 2003), pp. 71, 79, 86, 99–100.

4. See a judicious treatment of this in A. N. S. Lane, *John Calvin: student of the Church Fathers* (Grand Rapids, 1999), pp. 226–9.

5. The discussion of leadership for rebellion which became *Institutes* IV.xx.31 (Calvin, *Institutes*, ed. McNeill and Battles, vol. 2, pp. 1518–19) is most usefully studied for its variants in Latin and French and over the various editions of the *Institutes* in *Luther and Calvin on Secular Authority*, ed. H. Höpfl (Cambridge, 1991), pp. 82–3.

6. J. Calvin, *Institutes of the Christian religion, 1536 Edition*, ed. F. L. Battles (London, 1975), p. 12: cf. Preface in Calvin, *Institutes*, ed. McNeill and Battles, vol. 1, pp. 28–9.

7. *Institutes* IV.xx.8 (Calvin, *Institutes*, ed. McNeill and Battles, vol. 2, pp. 1493–5), helpfully laid out with its variants in Latin and French and over the various editions of the *Institutes* in *Luther and Calvin on Secular Authority*, ed. Höpfl, pp. 56–7, 84–6.

8. J. Calvin, *Sermons on the Acts of the Apostles*, ed. W. Balke and W. H. T. Moehn (Neukirchen, 1994), pp. 160–61.

9. J. Calvin, *Confessio Genevensium praedicatorum de Trinitate*, ed. M. Vial [second part of *Instruction et Confession de Foy dont on use en l'Eglise de Geneve*, ed. A. Zillenbiller, *Ioannis Calvini Opera omnia denuo recognita et adnotatione critica instructa notisque illustrata*, III/2 (Geneva, 2002)], pp. 123–52, gives the text with a fine Introduction. The dispute and the literature which sprang out of it are described in detail in E. Bähler, 'Petrus Caroli und Johannes Calvin. Ein Beitrag zur Geschichte und Kultur der Reformationszeit', *Jahrbuch für Schweizerische Geschichte* 29 (1904), pp. 39–168, esp. at pp. 62–96, and are briefly dealt with in W. de Greef, *The Writings of John Calvin: an introductory guide* (2nd edn, Louisville and London, 2008), pp. 158–60.

10. On this, see J. I. Israel, *Radical Enlightenment: philosophy and the making of modernity 1650–1750* (Oxford, 2001).

11. Calvin, *Confessio Genevensium praedicatorum de Trinitate*, ed. M. Vial, p. 129 and n.

12. Calvin, *Confessio Genevensium praedicatorum de Trinitate*, ed. M. Vial, pp. 151–2.

13. On Calvin's traumas over Caroli in 1545, J.-F. Gilmont, *John Calvin and the Printed Book*, trans. K. Maag (Sixteenth Century Essays and Studies 72, Kirksville, MO, 2005), pp. 1–3.

14. Calvin, *Institutes*, ed. McNeill and Battles, vol. 2, p. 1052 [*Institutes* IV.ii.11].

15. See a similar assertion about God's continual care to preserve 'a hidden seed, that the Church should not be utterly extinguished' in Calvin's last and posthumously published work: J. King (ed.), *Commentary on Ezekiel ii* (Calvin's Commentaries 23, Edinburgh, 1847–50), vol. 2, p. 165, on Ezek. 16:53; 'greatest sacrilege': Calvin, *Institutes*, ed. McNeill and Battles, vol. 2, p. 1050 [*Institutes* IV.ii.9].

16. There is excellent discussion of this and allied shifts in Calvin's perspective in R. C. Zachman, 'Revising the reform: what Calvin learned from dialogue with Roman Catholics', in *John Calvin and Roman Catholicism: critique and engagement, then and now*, ed. R. C. Zachman (Grand Rapids, 2008), pp. 165–91, esp. p. 186.

17. Pastors' memorandum on Castellio, February 1544, *Corpus Reformatum*, vol. xxxix, cols. 673–75, quoted in translation in *John Calvin: Documents of Modern History*, ed. G. R. Potter and M. Greengrass (London, 1983), p. 101. For Theodore Beza's echo of this championing of Church tradition in his later attacks on Castellio, see Backus, *Historical method and confessional identity*, pp. 118–21.

18. For further discussion of Calvin, Luther and Mary, see my essay 'The Virgin Mary and Protestant Reformers', above.

19. For discussion of the incarnation and the nature of humanity, see Calvin, *Institutes of the Christian religion, 1536 Edition*, ed. Battles, p. 52, and compare its development in Calvin, *Institutes*, ed. McNeill and Battles, vol. 1, p. 482 [*Institutes* II.xiv.1]. For explicit references to Chalcedon added in 1543, see *Institutes* II.xiv.4; IV.v.4; IV.vii.2; IV.vii.4; IV.vii.15; IV.ix.11.

20. Backus, *Historical method and confessional identity*, Ch. 4.

21. Calvin, *Institutes*, ed. McNeill and Battles, vol. 2, p. 1367 [*Institutes* IV.xvii.7]. For his comments on Luther and Zwingli in the 1550s, B. Cottret, *Calvin: A Biography* (Grand Rapids and Edinburgh, 2000), p. 66.

22. *Short treatise on the Lord's Supper* (1541), quoted in P. Rorem, 'Calvin and Bullinger on the Lord's Supper', *Lutheran Quarterly* 2 (1988), pp. 155–84 and 357–89, at p. 156. The English text may conveniently be found in a contemporary translation (but misattributed to Miles Coverdale) in *Writings and translations of Myles Coverdale*, ed. George Pearson (Parker Society, Cambridge, 1844), pp. 434–66.

23. Calvin, *Institutes*, ed. McNeill and Battles, vol. 2, pp. 1379–1403 [*Institutes* IV.xvii.16–31].

24. *Commentary on Isaiah* (published 1551), p. 211, quoted in *Calvin*, ed. Potter and Greengrass, p. 36.

25. Calvin, *Institutes*, ed. McNeill and Battles, vol. 1, pp. 486–7 [*Institutes* II.xiv.4]. A fine treatment of the question is H. A. Oberman, 'The "Extra" dimension in the theology of Calvin', *Journal of Ecclesiastical History* 21 (1970), pp. 43–64, esp. pp. 56–7.

26. Calvin, *Institutes*, ed. McNeill and Battles, vol. 2, p. 1277 [*Institutes* IV.xiv.4].

27. B. A. Gerrish, 'Sign and reality: the Lord's Supper in the Reformed Confessions', in Gerrish, *The Old Protestantism and the New* (Edinburgh, 1982), pp. 118–30.

28. The key discussion here is that developed for the 1559 version of the *Institutes*, IV.xvii.16–34 (Calvin, *Institutes*, ed. McNeill and Battles, pp. 1379–1411).

29. Calvin, *Institutes*, ed. McNeill and Battles, p. 1412 [*Institutes* IV.xvii.36], and cf. other instances from Calvin cited by Zachman, 'Revising the reform', pp. 177–9. See also C. B. Kaiser, 'Climbing Jacob's ladder: John Calvin and the early church on our Eucharistic ascent to heaven', *Scottish Journal of Theology* 56 (2003), pp. 247–67.

30. Cf. T. Harding (ed.), *The Decades of Henry Bullinger* (4 vols, Parker Society, Cambridge, 1849–52), p. 4 [The Fifth Decade], p. 309. With a not uncharacteristic contrariness, Martin Bucer disapproved of the ana-

logy to *sursum corda*: see D. F. Wright (ed.), *Common Places of Martin Bucer* (Appleford, Oxon, 1972), p. 79.

31. A fine treatment of the genesis of the *Consensus* is Rorem, 'Calvin and Bullinger on the Lord's Supper'.
32. L. W. Levy, *Treason against God: a history of the offense of blasphemy* (New York, 1981), esp. pp. 135–47.
33. On Calvin as David, see H. Selderhuis, *Calvin's theology of the Psalms* (Grand Rapids, 2007). On the impact of Genevan psalmody on northern Europe quite apart from francophone and anglophone societies, see *Der Genfer Psalter und seine Rezeption in Deutschland, der Schweiz und den Niederlanden 16.–18. Jahrhundert*, ed. E. Grunewald, H. Jürgens and J. R. Luth (Tübingen, 2004).

5. The Council of Trent

Originally published as a *review of Trent: What Happened at the Council* by John O'Malley, Harvard University Press, 2013, 326pp.
1. In this reconstruction of the Chisholm careers, I have drawn on K. Lualdi, 'Persevering in the faith: Catholic worship and communal identity in the wake of the Edict of Nantes', *Sixteenth Century Journal* 35 (2004), pp. 717–33.
2. J. W. O'Malley, *Four Cultures of the West* (Cambridge, MA, 2004), p. 197.
3. O'Malley, *Four Cultures of the West*, p. 175.

6. The Italian Inquisition

Originally published as a review of *The Italian Inquisition* by Christopher F. Black, Yale University Press, 2009, 352pp.

7. Tudor Royal Image-Making

Originally published as a review of Selling the Tudor Monarchy: Authority and Image in Sixteenth-Century England by Kevin Sharpe, Yale University Press, 2009, 512pp.
1. See my essay 'William Byrd', below.
2. C. S. L. Davies, 'The Tudor Delusion', *Times Literary Supplement*, 13 June 2008.
3. See my essay 'Forging Reformation History', below.
4. E. Ives, *Lady Jane Grey: a Tudor mystery* (Chichester, 2009).

8. Henry VIII: pious king

1. J. C. Dickinson, *An Ecclesiastical History of England: the Later Middle Ages from the Norman Conquest to the eve of the Reformation* (London, 1979), pp. 66–8.

2. B. Bradshaw, *The Dissolution of the Religious Orders in Ireland under Henry VIII* (Cambridge, 1974), Ch. 1; I. B. Cowan, *The Scottish Reformation: Church and Society in 16th century Scotland* (London, 1982), Chs 1–3.

3. R. L. Storey, *Diocesan Administration in Fifteenth Century England* (Borthwick Papers 16, 1972), pp. 29–30.

4. [Anon., possibly F. E. Brightman], 'Cranmer's Liturgical Projects', *Church Quarterly Review* 31 (1891), pp. 446–62, at p. 459. Cf. R. O'Day, *The Debate on the English Reformation* (London and New York, 1986), Ch. 4.

5. The 'Walsingham Hymn' was written by Sir William Milner (8th baronet, 1893–1960).

6. On Grynaeus and his mission, see D. MacCulloch, *Thomas Cranmer: a life* (New Haven and London, 1996), Ch. 3. The second major Reformer to meet the king was Friedrich Myconius, Superintendent of Gotha, a member of the Lutheran delegation to England in 1538.

7. For Henry's friendly response in August/September 1538 to a gift from Zwingli's successor at Zürich, Heinrich Bullinger, see *Original Letters relative to the English Reformation . . .*, ed. H. Robinson (2 vols, Parker Society, Cambridge, 1846–7), pp. 610, 617, but for his negative response to the book's contents, see J. J. Scarisbrick, *Henry VIII* (London, 1968), p. 418.

8. On Cuddington Church and Rewley Abbey, see *The History of the King's Works*, ed. H. M. Colvin et al. (6 vols, plus plans, 1963–82), vol. 4, pp. 179, 132.

9. Act from *Rotuli Parliamentorum* VI, 270, conveniently presented in G. R. Elton, *The Tudor Constitution* (2nd edn, London, 1982), p. 4.

10. On this royal activity, see V. Murphy, 'The literature and propaganda of Henry's divorce', in *The Reign of Henry VIII: Politics, Policy and Piety*, ed. D. MacCulloch (Basingstoke, 1995), Ch. 6.

11. W. Ullmann, '"This realm of England is an Empire"', *Journal of Ecclesiastical History* 30 (1979), pp. 182–4. I agree with Pamela Tudor-Craig against Ullmann that it is most unlikely that Henry drafted this oath in 1509 or then used it; nor was it subsequently used. P. Tudor-Craig, 'Henry VIII and King David', in *Early Tudor England*, ed. D. Williams (Woodbridge, 1989), pp. 187–9, 199.

12. *Works of Archbishop Cranmer*, ed. J. E. Cox (2 vols, Parker Society, Cambridge, 1844, 1846), vol. 2, pp. 100, 106.

13. Cf. discussion of the manuscripts in Tudor-Craig, 'Henry VIII and King David', pp. 193–7. For a late draft of a revision for the *King's Book* by Henry, see PRO, SP 1/178 fos 107–9 (*Letters and papers, foreign and domestic, of the Reign of Henry VIII*, ed. J. Gairdner, J. S. Brewer, and R. H. Brodie, 21 vols in 33 parts, 1862–1910 and revision of vol. 1, and 2-part addenda, by Brodie, 1920–32, vol. 18, Pt I, no. 609.2).

14. M. K. Jones and M. G. Underwood, *The King's Mother: Lady Margaret Beaufort, Countess of Richmond and Derby* (Cambridge, 1992), especially pp. 208–10.

15. Colvin et al., *History of the King's Works*, vol. 3, pp. 195–6, vol. 4, pp. 105, 227–8.

16. J. K. McConica, *English Humanists and Reformation Politics under Henry VIII and Edward VI* (Oxford, 1965), p. 63. *A Chronicle of England ... by Charles Wriothesley, Windsor Herald*, ed. W. D. Hamilton (2 vols, Camden Society, 2nd series 11, 20, 1875, 1877), p. 109.

17. *Expositions and Notes on sundry portions of the Holy Scriptures together with the Practice of Prelates. By William Tyndale ...*, ed. H. Walter (Parker Society, Cambridge, 1849), p. 81. 'Friars' in this instance is a loose usage for 'brothers'.

18. Scarisbrick, *Henry VIII*, p. 29.

19. A. Fox and J. Guy, *Reassessing the Henrician Age: Humanism, Politics and Reform 1500–1550* (Oxford, 1986), p. 167.

20. T. F. Mayer, 'Tournai and tyranny: imperial kingship and critical humanism', *Historical Journal* 34 (1991), esp. pp. 263–8.

21. Scarisbrick, *Henry VIII*, pp. 110–17, 270–71.

22. On Suffolk's religious outlook, see S. G. Gunn, *Charles Brandon Duke of Suffolk c.1484–1545* (Oxford, 1988), esp. pp. 103–7, 159–64, 199–201.

23. J. Guy, 'Thomas More and Christopher St. German', in Fox and Guy, *Reassessing the Henrician Age*, Ch. 5.

24. *Calendar of State Papers, Spanish*, ed. P. de Gayangos, G. Mattingly, M. A. S. Hume and R. Tyler (15 vols in 20 parts, HMSO, 1862–1954), vol. 4, Pt I, no. 224, pp. 349–50. On the aristocratic programme, see J. Guy, *The public career of Sir Thomas More* (New Haven and London, 1980), pp. 106–7 and Appendix 2 (cf. *Letters and papers*, ed. Gairdner, Brewer and Brodie, vol. 4, Pt III, no. 5749).

25. For the debate around Anne Boleyn, see G. W. Bernard, 'Anne Boleyn's religion', *Historical Journal* 36 (1993), pp. 1–20, answered by the various writings of E. W. Ives, lastly and concisely in E. W. Ives, 'Anne

Boleyn on trial again', *Journal of Ecclesiastical History* 62 (2011), pp. 763–77.

26. For pioneering uses of the word 'Protestant' by Edward Underhill in 1553, see *Narratives of the Reformation*, ed. J. G. Nichols (Camden Society, 1st series, 77, 1859), pp. 141, 148, 163, and for gingerly use of it by Marian martyrs, *The Works of Thomas Becon*, ed. J. Ayre (3 vols, Parker Society, Cambridge, 1843–4), vol. 3, p. 211; *The Writings of John Bradford . . .*, ed. A. Townsend (2 vols, Parker Society, Cambridge, 1848, 1853), vol. 1, p. 452; *The Works of Nicholas Ridley . . .*, ed. H. Christmas (Parker Society, Cambridge, 1843), p. 14.

27. D. MacCulloch, 'England', in *The Early Reformation in Europe*, ed. A. Pettegree (Cambridge, 1992), esp. pp. 169–74. Cf. also C. Trueman, *Luther's Legacy* (Oxford, 1994), *passim*.

28. On Stokesley, see *Narratives of the Reformation*, ed. Nichols, pp. 277–8. On Gardiner: G. Redworth, *In Defence of the Church Catholic: the life of Stephen Gardiner* (Oxford, 1990), pp. 159–64. On Fisher, R. Rex, *The Theology of John Fisher* (Cambridge, 1991), pp. 149, 158–9.

29. On Wilkinson's Boleyn connection, see 'William Latymer's Chronickille of Anne Bulleyne', ed. M. Dowling, *Camden Miscellany* 30 (Camden Society, 4th series, 39, 1990), p. 28. Astonishingly, Christina Garrett did not think that Wilkinson or indeed any other woman merited a separate entry in Garrett's *Marian Exiles: a study in the origins of Elizabethan Puritanism* (Cambridge, 1938): cf. p. 334. Wilkinson's will of 1556 (National Archives, Kew, PROB 11/42B fos 233–234v) is ample proof of her importance.

30. This letter-book is now in London: British Library MS Harley 6148. It contains letters to other key political figures, such as the king himself.

31. The best treatments of this episode and its relation to the Vicegerency are in F. D. Logan, 'Thomas Cromwell and the Vicegerency in Spirituals: a revisitation', *English Historical Review* 103 (1988), pp. 658–67, and P. Ayris in *Thomas Cranmer: Churchman and Scholar*, ed. P. Ayris and D. Selwyn (Woodbridge, 1993), pp. 122–9.

32. Bod. Lib. MS Jesus 74, fo. 299v.

33. For Cranmer's involvement in 1535, see *Letters and papers*, ed. Gairdner, Brewer and Brodie, vol. 8, no. 846; he also seems obliquely to be describing his interrogation of Anabaptists in a letter of 25 May 1535, *Works of Archbishop Cranmer*, ed. Cox, vol. 2, p. 306.

34. R. Rex, 'The New Learning', *Journal of Ecclesiastical History* 44 (1993), pp. 26–44.

35. For Robert Wakefield as an example of this breach, see Rex, *Theology of John Fisher*, p. 168; another case was Richard Croke, although his quarrel with Fisher predated the annulment controversy: ibid., p. 56.

36. D. MacCulloch, *Suffolk and the Tudors: Politics and Religion in an English County* (1986), pp. 151-3.

37. R. W. Hoyle, 'The origins of the dissolution of the monasteries', *Historical Journal* 38 (1995), pp. 275-305.

38. For suggestions about approachable discussions of the doctrinal statements, see bibliographical note. Six Articles text: Elton, *Tudor Constitution*, pp. 399-401; cf. P. Avis, *The Church in the Theology of the Reformers* (Cambridge, 1981), esp. p. 25. I am indebted to Sir Geoffrey Elton for reminding me of the presence of 'congregation' in the Articles.

39. E. Hall, *The Triumphant Reigne of Kyng Henry the VIII*, ed. C. Whibley (2 vols, London, 1904), vol. 2, p. 356; S. E. Lehmberg, *The Later Parliaments of Henry VIII 1536-1547* (Cambridge, 1977), pp. 229-31.

40. Cf. Hall, *Triumphant Reigne of Kyng Henry the VIII*, ed. Whibley, vol. 2, p. 357 and *Works of Archbishop Cranmer*, ed. Cox, vol. 2, pp. 118-25, esp. p. 122.

41. *Letters and papers*, ed. Gairdner, Brewer and Brodie, vol. 18, Pt II, p. 353, quoting Corpus Christi Colleges, Cambridge MS 128, f. 245.

42. *Sermons and Remains of Hugh Latimer ...*, ed. G. E. Corrie (Parker Society, Cambridge, 1845), pp. 379-80.

43. London, Lambeth Palace MS 1107, fos 125-32. Discussion of these documents has been unnecessarily complicated by their modern editor who, for no strong reason, printed them as if they were associated with a later document of 1540, and also failed to notice that they comprised two different drafts: *The Rationale of Ceremonial 1540-1543 with Notes and Appendices and an essay on the Regulation of Ceremonial during the Reign of Henry VIII*, ed. C. S. Cobb (Alcuin Club Collections 18, 1910), pp. 44-52. For the text of the Ten Articles, see *English Historical Documents 1485-1558*, ed. C. H. Williams (London, 1967), pp. 795-805.

44. *Sermons and Remains of Latimer*, ed. Corrie, p. 247.

45. A. Kreider, *English Chantries: the road to Dissolution* (Cambridge, MA, 1979), p. 152, and cf. ibid., pp. 127, 134-8.

46. Scarisbrick, *Henry VIII*, pp. 412-18.

47. Redworth, *In Defence of the Church Catholic*, pp. 98-9. Cf. *Miscellaneous writings of Henry the Eighth ...*, ed. F. Macnamara (London, 1924), pp. 97-9.

48. The annotations are printed in Tudor-Craig, 'Henry VIII and King David', pp. 200-202: NB Henry's comments on Psalms 53(54), 96(97), 105(106).

49. See the debate between Henry and Cranmer, *Works of Archbishop Cranmer*, ed. Cox, vol. 2, pp. 83-114.

50. G. Rupp, *Studies in the Making of the English Protestant Tradition* (Cambridge, 1947), pp. 140–41.

51. Scarisbrick, *Henry VIII*, p. 419.

52. M. St. Clare Byrne, *The Letters of King Henry VIII* . . . (London, 1936), p. 86.

53. January: *Works of Archbishop Cranmer*, ed. Cox, vol. 2, pp. 414–17. August: *The Acts and Monuments of John Foxe*, ed. G. Townshend and S. R. Cattley (8 vols, 1837–41), vol. 5, pp. 561–4. For a good introduction to Henry's last year, see D. Starkey, *Henry VIII: Personalities and Politics* (London, 1985), pp. 140–67.

54. C. Haigh, *English Reformations* (Oxford, 1993), p. 162 and R. Rex, *Henry VIII and the Reformation* (1993), pp. 169–70, are both sceptical that Henry VIII consciously chose evangelicals as tutors. McConica, *English Humanists*, pp. 213–18, presents a still convincing case to the contrary, except that he probably overstresses the role of Catherine Parr.

55. *The Gratulation of the most famous Clerk M. Martin Bucer* . . ., trans. and with Preface by T. Hoby (London, 1548), sigs. Biv–Bv.

56. See the excellent discussion in P. Tudor-Craig, 'Henry VIII and King David', *passim*.

9. Tolerant Cranmer?

1. M. Turchetti, 'Religious concord and political tolerance in 16th and 17th century France', *Sixteenth Century Journal* 22 (1991), pp. 15–26; M. C. Smith, 'Early French advocates of religious freedom', *Sixteenth Century Journal* 25 (1994), pp. 29–51.

2. Here I am moving on from the point made by Smith, 'Early French advocates', p. 35 n. 13, to accept Turchetti's assumption that both these forms represent varieties of concord.

3. Smith, 'Early French advocates', p. 29; B[R. W.]. Scribner, 'Preconditions of tolerance and intolerance in sixteenth-century Germany' in *Tolerance and intolerance in the European Reformation*, ed. O. Grell and B. Scribner (Cambridge, 1996), pp. 32–47, at p. 34, has a slightly weaker formulation as 'indifference to certain kinds of difference', but I vividly remember the more snappy version from his original version of this paper, given at Corpus Christi College, Cambridge, in 1994.

4. On this aspect of More's thought, see G. R. Elton, 'Persecution and Toleration in the English Reformation', in *Persecution and Toleration*, ed. W. J. Sheils (Studies in Church History 21, Oxford, 1984), pp. 164–71.

5. F. E. Brightman, *The English Rite* (2 vols, London, 1915), vol. 1, p. 372.

6. On the dating of Cranmer's adoption of belief in the Royal Supremacy, see D. MacCulloch, *Thomas Cranmer: a life* (New Haven and London, 1996), Chs 2–3. On his battles with Henry VIII over justification by faith alone, ibid., Chs 6, 8.

7. The questions and answers are to be found in London, Lambeth Palace MS 1108, fos 69–141; National Archives, SP 1/1605 fos 2–5, SP 6/6/9, fos 77–81; London, British Library, MS Cotton Cleopatra E V, fos 38, 53, 113 (*Letters and papers, foreign and domestic, of the Reign of Henry VIII*, ed. J. Gairdner, J. S. Brewer and R. H. Brodie, vol. 15, no. 826). Cranmer's replies are conveniently presented in *Works of Archbishop Cranmer*, ed. J. E. Cox (2 vols, Parker Society, Cambridge, 1844, 1846), vol. 2, pp. 115–17.

8. Quoted in M. Brock, *The Great Reform Act* (London, 1973), p. 40.

9. MacCulloch, *Thomas Cranmer*, *passim*.

10. *A Chronicle of England . . . by Charles Wriothesley, Windsor Herald*, ed. W. D. Hamilton (2 vols, Camden Society, 2nd series 11, 20, 1875, 1877), pp. 33–4, and *Sermons of Hugh Latimer*, ed. G. E. Corrie (Parker Society, Cambridge, 1844), p. 49. Cf. *An Answer to Sir Thomas More's Dialogue, the Supper of the Lord . . . and William Tracy's Testament expounded. By William Tyndale . . .*, ed. H. Walter (Parker Society, Cambridge, 1850), and *Expositions and Notes on sundry portions of the Holy Scriptures together with the Practice of Prelates. By William Tyndale . . .*, ed. H. Walter (Parker Society, Cambridge, 1849), p. 183 (1532). For further comment on this sermon, MacCulloch, *Thomas Cranmer*, Ch. 5.

11. *Letters and papers*, ed. Gairdner, Brewer and Brodie, 8, no. 846; this refers to a 'Dr. Chramuel', but I think it more likely that the Archbishop rather than Cromwell is intended, particularly since the Vice-gerency was not fully developed at this stage. Cf. I. B. Horst, *The Radical Brethren: Anabaptism and the English Reformation to 1558* (Nieuwkoop, 1972), p. 59; *Tudor Royal Proclamations*, ed. P. L. Hughes and J. F. Larkin (vols 1, 2, New Haven and Yale, 1964, 1969), vol. 1, no. 155; MacCulloch, *Thomas Cranmer*, Ch. 5.

12. *The Works of Thomas Becon*, ed. J. Ayre (3 vols, Parker Society, Cambridge, 1843–4), vol. 3, p. 41.

13. *Works of Thomas Becon*, ed. Ayre, vol. 3, pp. 40–41. For another list of Becon's, including simply 'papists' alongside varieties of radicalism, see ibid., p. 401.

14. *Sermons and Remains of Hugh Latimer . . .*, ed. G. E. Corrie (Parker Society, Cambridge, 1845), p. 197. Cranmer himself in the Homilies,

possibly assisted by Becon, referred to the religious orders as 'sects', without making the comparison with radicals: *Certain Sermons or Homilies (1547) and A Homily against Disobedience and Wilful Rebellion (1570)*, ed. R. B. Bond (Toronto, 1987), pp. 110–12.

15. For discussion of Henry's views and his rhetoric of the middle way, see 'Henry VIII: pious king', above.

16. MacCulloch, *Thomas Cranmer*, pp. 274–5.

17. I consider these incidents in MacCulloch, *Thomas Cranmer*, Chs 5, 7.

18. *Works of Archbishop Cranmer*, ed. Cox, vol. 2, p. 218.

19. London, British Library MS Harley 6148, fo. 25r; *Works of Archbishop Cranmer*, ed. Cox, vol. 2, p. 246 (17 June 1533).

20. L. W. Levy, *Treason against God: a history of the offense of Blasphemy* (New York, 1981), pp. 124–30.

21. On the Latimer affair at Bristol, see M. C. Skeeters, *Community and Clergy: Bristol and the Reformation c.1530–c.1570* (Oxford, 1993), pp. 38–46, and discussion in MacCulloch, *Thomas Cranmer*, Ch. 4. On Stokesley's prohibition, *Acts and Monuments of John Foxe*, ed. Townshend and Cattley, vol. 7, p. 459; Appendix VII.

22. *The Acts and Monuments of John Foxe*, ed. G. Townshend and S. R. Cattley (8 vols, 1837–41), vol. 5, p. 11; vol. 8, pp. 697–9; vol. 5, p. 9.

23. See Foxe's account of these events, *Acts and Monuments of John Foxe*, ed. Townshend and Cattley, vol. 5, pp. 227–36; all details are taken from there unless otherwise stated.

24. John Husee said that Lambert denied the 'corporal substance' of the presence at his trial; that is not the same as addressing the question of transubstantiation. *The Lisle Letters*, ed. M. St. C. Byrne (6 vols, Chicago, 1980), vol. 5, p. 1273 (*Letters and papers*, ed. Gairdner, Brewer and Brodie, vol. 13, Pt II, no. 854).

25. National Archives, SP 1/135 fos 86–7 (*Letters and papers*, ed. Gairdner, Brewer and Brodie, vol. 13, Pt II, no. 97).

26. See MacCulloch, *Thomas Cranmer*, Ch. 9.

27. M. Parker, *De Antiquitate Britannicae Ecclesiae ...* (London, 1572), p. 396; this was after the so-called Prebendaries' Plot, on which see MacCulloch, *Thomas Cranmer*, Ch. 8.

28. National Archives, SP 1/92, fo. 120, *Works of Archbishop Cranmer*, ed. Cox, vol. 2, p. 303 (*Letters and papers*, ed. Gairdner, Brewer and Brodie, vol. 8, no. 616).

29. National Archives, SP 1/143 fos 30–31, *Works of Archbishop Cranmer*, ed. Cox, vol. 2, p. 361 (redated to 1539 by *Letters and papers*, ed. Gairdner, Brewer and Brodie, vol. 14, Pt II, no. 244). On Forest and

Payne, see MacCulloch, *Thomas Cranmer*, respectively Chs 6 and 5, and for comment on other Observants, ibid., Ch. 4.

30. *Works of Archbishop Cranmer*, ed. Cox, vol. 1, p. 6.

31. The text is from *Narratives of the Reformation*, ed. J. G. Nichols (Camden Society, 1st series, 77, 1859), pp. 246–7.

32. On this, see A. Null, *Thomas Cranmer's Doctrine of Repentance: renewing the Power to Love* (Oxford, 2001), *passim*.

33. For details of Anabaptist trials under Edward VI, see P. Ayris in *Thomas Cranmer: Churchman and Scholar*, ed. P. Ayris and D. Selwyn (Woodbridge, 1993), pp. 148–52. Corpus Christi College, Cambridge MS 105, pp. 233–4 is an interesting paper which appears to be a dialogue between Cranmer and an Anabaptist, probably as part of an examination for heresy. A third burning of a heretic at Maldon, Essex, in 1549, is revealed in W. J. Petchey, *A Prospect of Maldon 1500–1689* (Essex Record Office Publications 113, 1991), p. 171.

34. For a useful discussion of the relationship between the two documents, see L. R. Sachs, 'Thomas Cranmer's "Reformatio Legum Ecclesiasticarum" of 1553 in the context of English Church Law from the Later Middle Ages to the Canons of 1603' (Catholic University of America J.C.D., Washington DC, 1982), pp. 111–16.

35. On Bocher, see J. Davis, 'Joan of Kent, Lollardy and the English Reformation', *Journal of Ecclesiastical History* 33 (1982), pp. 225–33.

36. The omitted passage was printed by the nineteenth-century editors as an appendix, *Acts and Monuments of John Foxe*, ed. Townshend and Cattley, vol. 5, p. 860. For discussion of Cranmer, Edward VI and Bocher, see J. G. Ridley, *Thomas Cranmer* (Oxford, 1962), pp. 291–3, and of Foxe on toleration, see Elton, 'Persecution and Toleration', pp. 171–80.

37. A. Pettegree, *Foreign Protestant Communities in Sixteenth-Century London* (Oxford, 1986), p. 31, and for the general outline of what follows, ibid., Ch. 2.

38. *Joannis a Lasco opera tam edita quam inedita*, ed. A. Kuyper (2 vols, Amsterdam, 1866), vol. 2, pp. 655–62, where Laski's letter is dated to 1551, but it is more likely to be of autumn 1550.

39. MacCulloch, 'Two Dons in Politics', pp. 12–13, and MacCulloch, *Thomas Cranmer*, Ch. 2.

40. For this initiative, see *Works of Cranmer*, ed. Cox, vol. 2, pp. 431–3; *Epistolae Tigurinae de rebus potissimum ad ecclesiae Anglicanae Reformationem pertinentibus* ... (Parker Society, Cambridge, 1848), pp. 462–3, or *Original Letters relative to the English Reformation* ..., ed. H. Robinson (2 vols, Parker Society, Cambridge, 1846–7), p. 711;

Gleanings of a few scattered ears, during the period of the Reformation in England . . ., ed. G. C. Gorham (London, 1857), p. 277; C. G. Bretschneider (ed.), *Corpus Reformatorum* 42 (Calvini Opera 14), col. 370.

41. *The Chronicle and Political Papers of Edward VI*, ed. W. K. Jordan (Ithaca, NY, 1966), p. 37.

42. D. W. Rodgers, *John à Lasco in England* (New York and Frankfurt, 1994), pp. 67, 93 n. 139.

43. Pettegree, *Foreign Protestant Communities*, pp. 65–6.

44. Cf. especially his letter to the Queen, September 1555, *Works of Cranmer*, ed. Cox, vol. 2, pp. 447–54.

45. Elton, 'Persecution and Toleration', pp. 183–4.

10. The Making of the Prayer Book

Originally published as a review of *The Book of Common Prayer: The Texts of 1549, 1559, and 1662*, edited by Brian Cummings, Oxford University Press, 2011, 830pp.

1. *The bibliography of the Book of Common Prayer, 1549–1999*, ed. D. N. Griffiths (London/New Castle, DE, 2002).

2. D. MacCulloch, Introduction to *The Book of Common Prayer 1662 Version* (London, 1999), pp. ix–xxxiv.

3. Margaret Houlbrooke, *Rite out of Time: a study of the churching of women and its survival in the twentieth century* (Donington, Lincs, 2011).

4. George Herbert, 'Love (III)', from *The Temple* (1633).

11. Tudor Queens: Mary and Elizabeth

Originally published as a review of Mary Tudor: *The Tragical History of the First Queen of England* by David Loades, The National Archives, Kew, 2006, 240pp.

1. E. Ives, *The Life and death of Anne Boleyn* (Oxford, 2004).

2. A. Weikel, 'The Marian Council revisited', in *The Mid-Tudor Polity c.1540–1560*, ed. J. Loach and R. Tittler (Basingstoke, 1980), Ch. 3.

3. E. Duffy, *The Stripping of the Altars: traditional religion in England 1400–1580*, especially the Preface to the second edition (London and New Haven, 2005); C. Haigh, *English Reformations: Religion, Politics and Society under the Tudors* (Oxford, 1993); *Reforming Catholicism in the England of Mary Tudor: the achievement of Friar Bartolomé*

Carranza, ed. J. Edwards and R. Truman (Aldershot, 2005); D. M. Loades, 'The piety of the Catholic Restoration in England, 1553–1558', in *Humanism and Reform: the Church in Europe, England and Scotland, 1400–1643. Essays in Honour of James K. Cameron*, ed. J. Kirk (Studies in Church History, Subsidia 8, Oxford, 1991), pp. 289–304, repr. in D. Loades, *Politics, Censorship and the English Reformation* (London, 1991), pp. 200–212.

4. A. G. Dickens, *The English Reformation* (London, 1967), p. 384.
5. G. Cavendish, ed. S. W. Singer, *Life of Cardinal Wolsey* (2 vols, London, 1825), vol. 2, pp. 136, 164.

12. William Byrd

Originally published as a review of *Byrd* by Kerry McCarthy, Oxford University Press, 2013, 282pp.
1. K. McCarthy, *Byrd* (Oxford, 2013), p. 71.
2. See the essay above, 'The Making of the Prayer Book'.
3. McCarthy, *Byrd*, p. 62.
4. McCarthy, *Byrd*, p. 237.

13. The Bible before King James

1. J. Kloczowski, *A History of Polish Christianity* (Cambridge, 2000), p. 84.
2. D. Daniell, 'William Tyndale, the English Bible, and the English language', in *The Bible as book: the Reformation*, ed. O. O'Sullivan (New Castle, DE, and London, 2000), pp. 39–50, at pp. 3, 65f.
3. A. J. Brown, *William Tyndale on priests and preachers with new light on his early career* (London, 1996). Chs 1 and 2 provide to my mind a persuasive relocation of his boyhood.
4. D. Daniell, *William Tyndale: a biography* (New Haven and London, 1994), p. 1.
5. *The Bible as book*, ed. O'Sullivan, p. 47.
6. R. Rex, *The Theology of John Fisher* (Cambridge, 1991), pp. 149, 158–60.
7. *Tudor Royal Proclamations*, ed. P. L. Hughes and J. F. Larkin (vols 1, 2, New Haven and Yale, 1964, 1969), vol. 1, pp. 193–7 (no. 129); cf. G. R. Elton, *Policy and Police: the enforcement of the Reformation in the age of Thomas Cromwell* (Cambridge, 1972), pp. 218–20, and A. Fox, *Thomas More: history and providence* (Oxford, 1982), pp. 169–70.

8. *Letters and papers, foreign and domestic, of the Reign of Henry VIII*, ed. J. Gairdner, J. S. Brewer, and R. H. Brodie (21 vols in 33 parts, 1862–1910), vol. 7, no. 1555.

9. Parker's reminiscence is in M. Parker, *De Antiquitate Britannicae Ecclesiae* ... (London, 1572), p. 385: Gardiner's letter is printed in *State Papers published under the authority of His Majesty's Commission, King Henry VIII* (11 vols, 1830–52), vol. 1, pp. 430–31 (*Letters and papers*, ed. Gairdner, Brewer and Brodie, vol. 8, no. 850). James Gairdner the historian of Lollardy charitably suggested that Gardiner's translations were destroyed in the sack of his library in 1554 by Sir Thomas Wyatt's rebels: J. A. Muller, *Stephen Gardiner and the Tudor Reaction* (New York, 1926), p. 350 n. 23.

10. *Chronicle of the Grey Friars of London*, ed. J. G. Nichols (Camden Society, 1st series 53, London, 1852), p. 38.

11. A. Freeman, 'To Guard his words', *Times Literary Supplement*, 14 December 2007, pp. 13–14.

12. *Works of Archbishop Cranmer*, ed. J. E. Cox (2 vols, Parker Society, Cambridge, 1844, 1846), vol. 2, p. 344.

13. On its printing in Antwerp, see G. Latré, 'The 1535 Coverdale Bible and its Antwerp origins', in *The Bible as book*, ed. O'Sullivan, pp. 89–102, at pp. 92–8.

14. On the first launch of Cromwell's injunction about Bible provision and its slow take-up, see MacCulloch, *Thomas Cranmer*, p. 166n.

15. N. Tyacke, 'Introduction', in *England's Long Reformation*, ed. N. Tyacke (London, 1998), pp. 1–32, at pp. 7–8, 28.

16. M. Dickman Orth, 'The English Great Bible of 1539 and the French Connection', in *Tributes to Jonathan J. G. Alexander: the Making and Meaning of Illuminated Medieval & Renaissance Manuscripts, Art and Architecture*, ed. S. L'Engle and Gerald B. Guest (London, 2006), pp. 171–84.

17. I owe this point to my former student Dr Ellie Gebarowski-Shafer.

18. *Tudor Royal Proclamations*, ed. Hughes and Larkin, vol. 1, pp. 296–8 (no. 200).

14. The King James Bible

Originally published as a review of *The Holy Bible: King James Version, 1611 Text*, edited with an anniversary essay by Gordon Campbell, Oxford University Press, 2010, 1552pp; *Bible: The Story of the King James Version 1611–2011* by Gordon Campbell, Oxford University

Press, 2010, 354pp; *The King James Bible: A Short History from Tyndale to Today* by David Norton, Cambridge University Press, 2011, 218pp; *The King James Bible after 400 Years: Literary, Linguistic and Cultural Influences*, edited by Hannibal Hamlin and Norman W. Jones, Cambridge University Press, 2010, 364pp; *Begat: The King James Bible and the English Language* by David Crystal, Oxford University Press, 2010, 327pp.

1. A. Nicolson, *Power and Glory: Jacobean England and the making of the King James Bible* (London, 2003).
2. *Ecce the New Testament of our Lords and Saviours, the House of Commons at Westminster . . .* (London, 1648/9), p. 2.

15. *The Bay Psalm Book*

1. *The Bay Psalm Book: imprinted 1640* (Oxford, 2014).
2. S. Ahlstrom, *A religious history of the American people* (New Haven and London, 1972), p. 136.
3. On Cotton and the origins of 'Congregationalism', *John Cotton on the Churches of New England*, ed. L. Ziff (Cambridge, MA, 1962), p. 2.
4. B. Wendell, *Cotton Mather: the Puritan priest* (Cambridge, MA, 1926), p. 12.
5. See, for instance, T. D. Bozeman, *To Live Ancient Lives: The Primitivist Dimension in Puritanism* (Chapel Hill, 1988), p. 149.
6. K. J. Höltgen, 'New verse by Francis Quarles: the Portland manuscripts, metrical psalms, and *The Bay psalm book* (with text)', *English Literary Renaissance* 28 (1998), pp. 118-41.

16. Putting the English Reformation on the Map

1. One can sample mature Anglo-Catholic distortions and obfuscations throughout the entries relating to the English Reformation in the first edition of an otherwise excellent reference work, *The Oxford Dictionary of the Christian Church*, ed. F. L. Cross (Oxford, 1957). This is emphatically not the case in the *Dictionary*'s present incarnation, edited by E. A. Livingstone (3rd edition, Oxford, 1997, and subsequent revisions). An up-to-date compendium of 'in-house' Anglican historiographical attitudes in scholarly form is embodied in Paul Avis, *Anglicanism and the Christian Church: theological resources in historical perspective* (rev. edn, Edinburgh and New York, 2002).
2. P. Nockles, 'Survivals or new arrivals? The Oxford Movement and the nineteenth-century historical construction of Anglicanism', in *Anglican-*

ism and the Western Christian tradition, ed. S. Platten (Norwich, 2003), pp. 144–91. I also discuss this further in my essay 'Thomas Cranmer's Biographers' below.

3. For discussion of the fugitive use of the term 'Anglicanism' before the nineteenth century, and its possible origins in the mouth of King James VI of Scotland, see *The Short Oxford History of the British Isles: the sixteenth century*, ed. Patrick Collinson (Oxford, 2002), pp. 110–11.

4. On Hooker's later impact in England, see my essay 'Richard Hooker's reputation', below.

5. For further discussion, see my essay 'Henry VIII', above.

6. This is a formulation invented by Peter Marshall: cf. A. Ryrie, 'The strange death of Lutheran England', *Journal of Ecclesiastical History* 53 (2002), pp. 64–92, at p. 67.

7. J. Estes, 'Melanchthon's confrontation with the "Erasmian" *via media* in politics: the *De officio principum* of 1539', in *Dona Melanchthoniana*, ed. J. Loehr (2001), pp. 83–101, at pp. 93–5.

8. Estes, 'Melanchthon's confrontation', at pp. 96–7.

9. T. String, 'A neglected Henrician decorative ceiling', *Antiquaries Journal* 76 (1996), pp. 139–52, at pp. 144–5. For an illustration of the Great Bible and discussion, see D. MacCulloch, *Thomas Cranmer: a life* (New Haven and London, 1996), pp. 238–40.

10. Gordon Donaldson, *The Scottish Reformation* (Cambridge, 1969), p. 30.

11. For useful discussion, see George Bernard, 'The making of religious policy, 1533–1546: Henry VIII and the search for the middle way', *Historical Journal* 41 (1998), pp. 321–51.

12. See a very different argument throughout Richard Rex, *The Lollards* (Basingstoke, 2002), esp. Ch. 5 and Conclusion.

13. Amid the great mass of literature on Lollardy, see especially Margaret Aston, *Lollards and Reformers: images and literacy in late medieval religion* (London, 1984), A. Hudson, *Lollards and their books* (London, 1985), A. Hope, 'Lollardy: the stone the builders rejected?', in *Protestantism and the national Church in 16th century England*, eds. P. Lake and M. Dowling (London, 1987), pp. 1–35. There is still much to discover about the theology of post-Wyclifite Lollard groups, but see P. Hornbeck, *What is a Lollard? Dissent and Belief in Late Medieval England* (Oxford, 2010).

14. I develop these ideas at greater length in D. MacCulloch, *The Later Reformation in England, 1547–1603* (Basingstoke, 1990), pp. 55–65.

15. See e.g. D. MacCulloch, *Tudor Church Militant: Edward VI and the Protestant Reformation* (London, 1999), pp. 2, 4.

16. MacCulloch, *Thomas Cranmer*, p. 192.

17. For a masterly treatment of the 1540s, see A. Ryrie, *The Gospel and Henry VIII: evangelicals in the early English Reformation* (Cambridge, 2003).

18. MacCulloch, *Thomas Cranmer*, pp. 393–4 and other index refs. s.v. von Wied, Hermann. See also J. K. Cameron, 'The Cologne Reformation and the Church of Scotland', *Journal of Ecclesiastical History* 30 (1979), pp. 39–64, and R. W. Scribner, 'Why was there no Reformation at Cologne?', *Bulletin of the Institute of Historical Research* 49 (1976), pp. 217–41.

19. H. E. Jannsen, *Gräfin Anna von Ostfriesland: eine hochadelige Frau der späten Reformationszeit (1540/42–1575)* (Munich, 1988).

20. Andrew Pettegree, *Marian Protestantism: six studies* (Aldershot, 1996), pp. 80–84. The best overall treatment of Łaski is to be found in *Johannes à Lasco: Polnischer Baron, Humanist und europäischer Reformator*, ed. Christoph Strohm (Tübingen, 2000), particularly, on his Eucharistic views, C. Zwierlein, 'Der reformierte Erasmianer a Lasco und die Herausbildung seiner Abendmahlslehre 1544–1552', ibid., pp. 35–100.

21. Andrew Pettegree, *Foreign Protestant Communities in sixteenth century London* (Oxford, 1986), Chs 2–4.

22. MacCulloch, *Thomas Cranmer*, pp. 538–40.

23. MacCulloch, *Thomas Cranmer*, pp. 461–2, 504–8.

24. See especially the *Reformatio*'s section on heresy in *Tudor Church Reform: the Henrician Canons of 1535 and the Reformatio Legum Ecclesiasticarum*, ed. Gerald Bray (Church of England Record Society 8, Rochester, NY, 2000), pp. 186–213.

25. On this, see MacCulloch, *Thomas Cranmer*, pp. 531–5, and on the precise circumstances and nature of the defeat, J. F. Jackson, 'The *Reformatio Legum Ecclesiasticarum*: politics, society and belief in mid-Tudor England' (D.Phil. thesis, Oxford University, 2003), pp. 222–4.

26. Two of the most important recent contributions to opening up this field have been E. Duffy, *The Stripping of the Altars: traditional religion in England 1400–1580* (London and New Haven, 2005), pp. 524–63, and T. F. Mayer, *Cardinal Pole: priest and prophet* (Cambridge, 2000), pp. 203–301.

27. The construction of the Settlement is described in detail (including a thoroughgoing and effective demolition of Sir John Neale's reconstruction of events in 1558–9) in N. L. Jones, *Faith by Statute: Parliament and the Settlement of Religion, 1559* (London, 1982).

28. MacCulloch, *Thomas Cranmer*, pp. 620–21.

29. *Pace* arguments to the contrary in Roger Bowers, 'The Chapel Royal, the First Edwardian Prayer Book, and Elizabeth's settlement of religion,

1559', *Historical Journal* 43 (2000), pp. 317–44. The centre of his case is the assertion that some particularly sumptuous musical settings of the 1549 liturgy could not possibly have been written in 1549–52, and must postdate musical innovations in the Catholic restoration of Queen Mary. This *a priori* assumption is undermined by the fact that one of Bowers's examples, a 'Second Service' by John Sheppard, is most unlikely to have been written for Elizabeth, since Sheppard made his will a fortnight after Elizabeth's accession and died a fortnight later (Bowers has mistaken his date of death). Sheppard probably had other concerns in his dying weeks than providing music for the Chapel Royal. If Sheppard's elaborate music can thus be reassigned to the period 1549–52, there is no reason why any of the other supposed 1559 settings of the 1549 texts should not be likewise, and no reason to assign any of them to 1559.

30. The atmosphere is well captured in the letters of the period 1559–61 between Zürich reformers and leading English returned exiles, *The Zürich Letters . . .*, ed. H. Robinson (2 vols, Parker Society, Cambridge, 1842, 1845), *passim*. See also D. MacCulloch, 'Peter Martyr Vermigli and Thomas Cranmer', in *Peter Martyr Vermigli: Humanism, Republicanism, Reformation*, ed. E. Campi et al. (Geneva, 2002), pp. 173–201, at pp. 199–200. For an interesting argument from an unexpected quarter that the Eucharistic adjustments may perfectly plausibly be seen as an effort to update the liturgy to developments in Reformed Protestant thinking, see C. S. Carter, 'The Anglican "Via Media": a study in the Elizabethan Religious Settlement', *Church Quarterly Review* 97 (1924), pp. 233–54.

31. The full extent of the queen's fury has been revealed in Pettegree, *Marian Protestantism*, pp. 144–8, 197–9.

32. See MacCulloch, *Thomas Cranmer*, pp. 278–9, 460–61.

33. For an interesting late seventeenth-century discussion of the consecration, innocent of later High Church preoccupations, but clearly setting out the pre-Oxford Movement issues in controversy with Roman Catholics about Parker's consecration, see J. Strype, *The Life and Acts of Matthew Parker . . .* (3 vols, Oxford, 1821), vol. 1, pp. 112–22. On the Barlow controversy, see A. S. Barnes, *Bishop Barlow and Anglican Orders: a study of the original documents* (New York and London, 1922).

34. On Westminster Abbey, see particularly J. F. Merritt, 'The cradle of Laudianism? Westminster Abbey, 1558–1630', *Journal of Ecclesiastical History* 53 (2001), pp. 623–46 and various essays in *Westminster Abbey Reformed 1540–1640*, eds C. S. Knighton and R. Mortimer (Aldershot, 2003), pp. 38–74.

35. The foundational work on the divergence between cathedral and parish church music is N. Temperley, *The Music of the English Parish Church* (Cambridge and New York, 1979), and very important also is R. A. Leaver, 'Goostly psalmes and spirituall songes': English and Dutch Metrical Psalms from Coverdale to Utenhove, 1536–1566 (Cambridge, 1991). On the wider European phenomenon of psalmody, see D. MacCulloch, *Reformation: Europe's House Divided 1490–1700* (London, 2003), pp. 146, 307–8, 326, 352, 460, 511, 536, 588, 590–91.

36. On Łaski's troubles in Scandinavia in 1553, see O. P. Grell, 'Exile and tolerance', in *Tolerance and intolerance in the European Reformation*, eds O. Grell and B. Scribner (Cambridge, 1996), pp. 164–81. On Wesel and Aarau, *Original Letters relative to the English Reformation . . .*, ed. H. Robinson (2 vols, Parker Society, Cambridge, 1846–7), vol. 1, pp. 160–68.

37. P. Lake, 'Calvinism and the English Church 1570–1635', *Past and Present* 94 (February 1987), pp. 32–76: another useful perspective on that debate is provided by Nicholas Tyacke, 'The ambiguities of early-modern English Protestantism', *Historical Journal* 34 (1991), pp. 743–54. For a contrasting perspective, see Peter White, *Predestination, policy and polemic: conflict and consensus in the English Church from the Reformation to the Civil War* (Cambridge, 1992), usefully reviewed by P. Lake, 'Predestinarian propositions', *Journal of Ecclesiastical History* 46 (1995), pp. 110–23. For a statesmanlike afterview, see S. F. Hughes, '"The Problem of Calvinism": English theologies of predestination c. 1580–1630', in *Belief and practice in Reformation England*, eds S. Wabuda and C. Litzenberger (Aldershot, 1998), pp. 229–49.

38. MacCulloch, *Tudor Church Militant*, pp. 173–4, 176.

39. For Samuel Ward of Sidney Sussex's opinion to this effect, see B. D. Spinks, *Two Faces of Elizabethan Anglican Theology: Sacraments and salvation in the thought of William Perkins and Richard Hooker* (Lanham, MD, 1999), p. 164.

40. On this, see N. Tyacke, *Anti-Calvinists: The rise of English Arminianism, c. 1590–1640* (Oxford, 1987), especially pp. 20, 39, 59.

41. I am very grateful to Peter McCullough for drawing my attention to Lancelot Andrewes's use of Martin Chemnitz's *Examinis Concilii Tridentini* (Frankfurt, 1574), which McCullough notes in particular in relation to Andrewes's sermon on Isaiah 6:6–7, preached on 1 October 1598 and published in L. Andrewes, *Αποσπασμάτια Sacra* (London, 1657), pp. 515–22. Andrewes is clearly also silently drawing on Luther's analogy of Eucharistic presence as like heat in red-hot iron in this sermon. We await McCullough's biography of Andrewes. For Luther's uneasy place in English Reformation polemic and self-

defence, see R. H. Fritze, 'Root or link? Luther's position in the historical debate over the legitimacy of the Church of England, 1558–1625', *Journal of Ecclesiastical History* 37 (1986), pp. 288–302.

42. For more extended discussion, see MacCulloch, *Later Reformation in England*, Ch. 6.

43. On Andrewes's successful operation to gain control of the Chapel Royal of Charles as Prince of Wales and hence of the theological future of the court, see Peter McCullough, *Sermons at Court: politics and religion in Elizabethan and Jacobean preaching* (Cambridge, 1997), pp. 194–209.

44. MacCulloch, *Tudor Church Militant*, p. 173.

45. Anne Oakley, 'Archbishop Laud and the Walloons in Canterbury', in *Crown and Mitre: religion and society in Northern Europe*, ed. W. M. Jacob and N. Yates (Woodbridge, 1993), pp. 33–44.

46. See F. J. Bremer, *John Winthrop: America's forgotten founding father* (Oxford, 2003).

47. For a subtle and sensitive overview of English religion in the American colonies, see P. Bonomi, *Under the cope of heaven: religion, society and politics in Colonial America* (Oxford, 1986). On the continuing links between Old and New England, F. J. Bremer, *Congregational communion: clerical friendship in the Anglo-American puritan community, 1610–1692* (Boston, MA, 1994).

17. The Latitude of the Church of England

This paper was originally given at All Souls in the series 'Doubt and Belief in early modern Europe', and I am grateful to those who commented on it on that occasion. I am also grateful to Nicholas Tyacke for inspiring so much of the new direction in discussion of Reformation Church history which has helped to shape this paper. My debt will be apparent from the following endnotes.

1. See essay above, 'Putting the English Reformation on the Map'.

2. For a fine overview of the revised historiography of the English Reformation, see N. Tyacke, 'Re-thinking the "English Reformation"', in *England's Long Reformation 1500–1800*, ed. N. Tyacke (London, 1998), pp. 1–32, reprinted in N. Tyacke, *Aspects of English Protestantism c.1530–1700* (Manchester, 2001), pp. 37–60.

3. James I's apparent invention of the word 'Anglican' is to be found in D. Calderwood, *History of the Church of Scotland*, ed. T. Thomson (8 vols, Wodrow Society, Edinburgh, 1842–9), vol. 5, p. 694.

4. See my essay 'Putting the English Reformation on the Map', above.

5. A. Ryrie, 'The strange death of Lutheran England', *Journal of Ecclesiastical History* 53 (2002), pp. 64–92. See also K. Maas, *The Reformation and Robert Barnes: history, theology and polemic in early modern England* (Woodbridge, 2010).

6. D. MacCulloch, *Thomas Cranmer: a life* (New Haven and London, 1996), pp. 232–4, and see essay above, 'Tolerant Cranmer?'.

7. On this and what follows on relations with Zürich, see more detailed discussion in D. MacCulloch, 'Heinrich Bullinger and the English-speaking world', in P. Opitz and E. Campi (eds), *Heinrich Bullinger (1504?–1575): Leben, Denken, Wirkung* (Zürcher Beiträge zur Reformationsgeschichte, 24, 2006), pp. 891–934.

8. I intend to deal with this theme at much greater length in my envisaged biography of Thomas Cromwell.

9. See my essay 'Putting the English Reformation on the Map', above.

10. For an account of these events, see MacCulloch, *Thomas Cranmer*, pp. 352–5.

11. MacCulloch, 'Bullinger'.

12. C. Euler, 'Heinrich Bullinger, marriage, and the English Reformation: *The Christen state of Matrimonye in England, 1540–53*', *Sixteenth Century Journal* 34 (2003), pp. 367–94.

13. D. MacCulloch, *Tudor Church Militant: Edward VI and the Protestant Reformation* (London, 1999), pp.173–4.

14. N. L. Jones, *Faith by Statute: Parliament and the Settlement of Religion, 1559* (London, 1982).

15. I say more about this in 'Putting the English Reformation on the Map'.

16. Anglo-Catholics did not always relate the clause to the parliamentary authorization of the 1549 Prayer Book, and seized on the wording's reference to the second year of King Edward VI as referring to the whole of 1548, when in theory there had been much more liturgical leeway possible than survived the first English Prayer Book. In context, however, it is quite clear that the reference is to the 1549 Prayer Book authorized by a session of Parliament beginning in the second year of Edward VI (in fact November 1548): it was not therefore authorizing the pre-1549 situation. See the text in *Documents of the English Reformation*, ed. G. Bray (Cambridge, 1994), p. 334, and compare the similar reference in the 1559 Act of Uniformity to the 1552 Book of Common Prayer, in terms of its authorization by Act of Parliament in the fifth and sixth years of Edward VI: ibid., p. 329. The rubric preceding Mattins in the 1559 Prayer Book specifically refers to this ornaments clause in the 1559 Act of Parliament: *The First Prayer Book*

of Edward VI compared with the successive revisions of the Book of Common Prayer, ed. J. Parker (Oxford and London, 1877), p. 64. The main effect would be to authorize the alternatives of a 'vestment or cope' over plain white alb for use at Holy Communion. Cf. The two Liturgies ... of King Edward VI, ed. J. Kettley (Parker Society, Cambridge, 1844), p. 76: the 'vestment' was the chasuble, traditionally appropriate to the Eucharist, while the cope was not a Eucharistic garment. This represents a wide latitude indeed.

17. For an example of a Suffolk clergyman, Thomas Shackleton of Kenton, finding himself in the 1570s embattled and isolated for wearing a cope in worship, see D. MacCulloch, 'Catholic and Puritan in Elizabethan Suffolk: a county community polarises', Archiv für Reformationsgeschichte 72 (1981), pp. 232-89, at p. 254.

18. Washington DC, Folger Shakespeare Library, MS V.b.303, pp. 183-6, quoted in P. Collinson, 'Puritans, Men of Business and Elizabethan Parliaments', Parliamentary History 7 (1988), pp. 187-211, at p. 192.

19. The Works of John Jewel, Bishop of Salisbury, ed. J. Ayre (2 vols in 4, Parker Society, Cambridge, 1845-50), vol. 3, p. 109.

20. For John Williams's reminder to Laud in 1637 that there were different canonical provisions for cathedrals and parish churches, see The Work of Archbishop John Williams, ed. B. Williams (Sutton Courtenay, 1988), p. 182. As late as 1680 there was an attempt to institutionalize in legislation the different liturgical styles, when in parliamentary negotiations over comprehension for nonconformists, there was a proposal that surplices should be worn only in cathedrals and the Chapel Royal: J. T. Cliffe, The Puritan Gentry besieged, 1650-1700 (London and New York, 1993), p. 183. On parochial music, N. Temperley, The Music of the English Parish Church (Cambridge and New York, 1979), and J. Ottenhoff, 'Recent Studies in Metrical Psalms', English Literary Renaissance 33 (2003), pp. 252-75.

21. MacCulloch, Tudor Church Militant, pp. 204-8, 210-15; J. F. Merritt, 'The cradle of Laudianism? Westminster Abbey, 1558-1630', Journal of Ecclesiastical History 53 (2001).

22. Curiously, Archbishop Laud contributed to the subsequent neglect of the surviving texts of these sermons when he did not embody them in his carefully presented selection of Andrewes's works. We await Peter McCullough's biography of Andrews: cf. the foretaste in P. McCullough, 'Making dead men speak: Laudianism, print and the works of Lancelot Andrewes, 1626-1642', Historical Journal 41 (1998), pp. 401-25. Of the few Cripplegate period sermons which Laud did allow into the ninety-six sermons, the most striking and audacious is that on Imagin-

ations 15, preached and written in January 1593 at the height of the campaign against separatist nonconformity which also saw the publication of the first part of Hooker's *Ecclesiastical Polity*. This sermon takes the trope of idolatry, so familiar in a Reformed Protestant context, and turns it against Puritan and separatist positions on Church polity and liturgy, with a few token swipes at Roman Catholics. I am grateful to Prof. McCullough for our discussions on this remarkable sermon.

23. See N. Tyacke, 'Lancelot Andrewes and the myth of Anglicanism', in *Conformity and Orthodoxy in the English Church, c.1560–1660*, ed. P. Lake and M. Questier (Woodbridge, 2000), pp. 5–33, at pp. 19–24.

24. On the Articles, see E. Gilliam and W. J. Tighe, 'To "Run with the Time": Archbishop Whitgift, the Lambeth Articles and the politics of theological ambiguity in late Elizabethan England', *Sixteenth Century Journal* 23 (1992), pp. 325–40. The best overview of the Arminian movement and its antecedents remains N. Tyacke, *Anti-Calvinists: The rise of English Arminianism, c.1590–1640* (Oxford, 1987); see especially the introduction to the paperback edition, 1990.

25. E. Evenden, 'The Michael Wood mystery: William Cecil and the Lincolnshire printing of John Day', *Sixteenth Century Journal* 35 (2004), pp. 383–94.

26. This remark so often misquoted and so often attributed to Elizabeth herself is to be found in *The Works of Francis Bacon*, ed. James Spedding, Robert Leslie Ellis and Douglas Denon Heath (14 vols, London, 1857–74): *Lord Bacon's Letters and Life*, vol. 1, p. 178. It occurs in Bacon's 'Observations on a Libel' of 1592, but is also to be found word for word with its surrounding material in a letter of Francis Walsingham to M. de Critoy, written between 1589 and Walsingham's death in 1590: ibid., p. 98. Spedding is almost certainly correct in postulating that Bacon had ghost-written this letter of Walsingham's.

27. On these and the 'third way', see D. MacCulloch, *Reformation: Europe's House Divided 1490–1700* (London, 2003), pp. 253–5, 290, 310, 317–19, 354, 570, and above, 'Putting the English Reformation on the Map'.

28. C. W. Marsh, *The Family of Love in English Society, 1550–1630* (Cambridge, 1993), pp. 131–3.

29. Marsh, *Family of Love*, pp. 282–3. Marsh's seminal book remains the definitive account of the Familists in England.

30. D. Wootton, 'Deities, devils, and dams: Elizabeth I, Dover Harbour and the Family of Love', *Proceedings of the British Academy* 162 (2009), pp. 45–67. Noel Malcolm has suggested (in discussion and private correspondence) that the poem is not an original composition, but perhaps

the queen's translation from a Spanish original. For the text, see S. W. May and A. L. Prescott, 'The French Verses of Elizabeth I', *English Literary Renaissance* 24 (1994), pp. 9–43.

31. On Perne and Whitgift, see P. Collinson, 'Andrew Perne and his times', in P. Collinson et al., *Andrew Perne: Quatercentenary studies,* Cambridge Bibliographical Society 11 (1991), pp. 1–34, at pp. 2, 20, 24, 34.

32. On Perne and Baro, see H. C. Porter, *Reformation and Reaction in Tudor Cambridge* (Cambridge, 1958), p. 376.

33. W. McFadden, 'The life and works of Antonio del Corro, 1527–91' (unpublished Ph.D. thesis, Queen's University Belfast, 1953; I am indebted to Dr Ronald Trueman for access to this work). For a treatment in print of Corro, I am much indebted to McFadden's work, but for additional material, see C. M. Dent, *Protestant Reformers in Elizabethan Oxford* (Oxford, 1983), pp. 119–22.

34. McFadden, 'Corro', pp. 350–52; on Corro's anti-predestinarian views and unitarianism, ibid., pp. 362–6, 373–84, 512, 624–32, 648–9, 737–8. The French national Protestant synod meeting at La Rochelle in 1571 explicitly made the connection between eastern European unitarianism and Corro: ibid., p. 398.

35. McFadden, 'Corro', p. 498.

36. McFadden, 'Corro', p. 508 (quoting the view of the Spanish Ambassador Mendoza), and on Leicester's patronage to Corro generally, ibid., pp. 365–8, 405–7, 434–5, 445–65, 484, 494–6, 508, 511–13, 527–8.

37. On patronage from Cecil, see McFadden, 'Corro', pp. 337–8, on Hatton, ibid., pp. 482, 539–42.

38. McFadden, 'Corro', pp. 379–80. On Lady Dorothy Stafford, *History of Parliament: The House of Commons 1509–1558,* ed. S. T. Bindoff (3 vols, London, 1982), vol. 3, p. 365, and C. H. Garrett, *Marian Exiles: a study in the origins of Elizabethan Puritanism* (Cambridge, 1938), p. 296.

39. *The Zürich Letters . . .,* ed. H. Robinson (2 vols, Parker Society, Cambridge, 1842, 1845), vol. 2, p. 259. To extend further the interesting tangle of these orthodox and unorthodox clergy, Corro's principal adversary at Oxford in his troubles from 1576 to 1582 was Richard Hooker's patron (from whom Hooker was later to distance himself), John Raignoldes of Corpus Christi College: see Dent, *Protestant Reformers in Elizabethan Oxford,* pp. 119–25.

40. On these nuances, see MacCulloch, *Thomas Cranmer,* pp. 620–21.

41. *Zürich Letters,* ed. Robinson, vol. 2, p. 127.

42. Cf. especially *Works of Jewel,* ed. Ayre, vol. 3, p. 69.

43. Cf. Bishop Parkhurst's gleeful reaction to the destruction of the silver crucifix in Elizabeth's Chapel Royal: *Zürich Letters,* ed. Robinson, vol.

1, pp. 121, 128; *The Letter Book of John Parkhurst, Bishop of Norwich, compiled during the years 1571–5*, ed. R. A. Houlbrooke (Norfolk Records Society, Norwich, 43, 1975), p. 62.

44. For general accounts, see especially J. H. Primus, *The Vestments Controversy* (Kampen, 1960), and H. Horie, 'The influence of Continental Divines on the making of the English Religious Settlement ca. 1547–1590: a reassessment of Heinrich Bullinger's contribution' (unpublished Cambridge University Ph.D. thesis, 1991), pp. 243–68.

45. *Zürich Letters*, ed. Robinson, vol. 1, p. 357: cf. Gwalther's comments to Bishop Cox in 1572, ibid., vol. 1, p. 362.

46. A. Mühling, *Heinrich Bullingers europäische Kirchenpolitik* (Bern and Frankfurt am Main: Zürcher Beiträge zur Reformationsgeschichte 19, 2001), pp. 116–17.

47. On this large theme, see J. W. Baker, 'Erastianism in England: the Zürich connection', in *Die Zürcher Reformation: Ausstrahlungen und Rückwirkungen*, ed. A. Schindler and H. Stickelberger (Zürich, 2001), pp. 327–49. K. Rüetschi, 'Rudolf Gwalthers Kontakte zu Engländern und Schotten', in ibid., p. 368, sounds a useful note of caution, pointing out the differences in the polities of England and Zürich, as does Horie in 'Heinrich Bullinger's contribution', p. 297.

48. D. J. Keep, 'Bullinger's Defence of Queen Elizabeth', in *Heinrich Bullinger 1504–1575: Gesammelte Aufsätze zum 400 Todestag, Bd. 2: Beziehungen und Wirkungen*, ed. U. Gäbler and E. Herkenrath (Zürich, 1975, Zürcher Beiträge zur Reformationsgeschichte 8), pp. 231–41.

49. M. Taplin, *The Italian Reformers and the Zürich Church, c.1540–1620* (Aldershot, 2003), *passim* and p. 191.

50. *Zürich Letters*, ed. Robinson, vol. 2, p. 254.

51. *Zürich Letters*, ed. Robinson, vol. 1, p. 276; *The Works of John Whitgift ...*, ed. J. Ayre (3 vols, Parker Society, Cambridge, 1851–3), vol. 3, pp. 496–7.

52. *Works of John Whitgift ...*, ed. Ayre, vol. 1, p. 184. Cf. Whitgift's very similar quotation from Gwalther, ibid., vol. 1, p. 186.

53. The story is well told in Horie, 'Heinrich Bullinger's contribution', pp. 302–66, from where citations are taken unless otherwise stated.

54. A. B. Emden, *A Biographical Register of the University of Oxford A.D. 1501 to 1540* (Oxford, 1974), p. 135.

55. *The Decades of Henry Bullinger*, ed. T. Harding (4 vols, Parker Society, Cambridge, 1849–52), vol. 1, pp. 8, 9.

56. On Grindal and the prophesyings, see P. Collinson, *Archbishop Grindal 1519–1583: the Struggle for a Reformed Church* (London, 1979), Part 4. On the other uses, Horie, 'Heinrich Bullinger's contribution', p. 318.

57. The best account of this period is P. Collinson, *The Elizabethan Puritan Movement* (London, 1967), Parts 5 and 6.

58. For a superb study of these tensions, see G. Murdock, *Calvinism on the frontier 1600–1660: international Calvinism and the Reformed Church in Hungary and Transylvania* (Oxford, 2000).

59. See a later essay in this book, 'Richard Hooker's Reputation'.

60. M. E. C. Perrott, 'Richard Hooker and the problem of authority in the Elizabethan Church', *Journal of Ecclesiastical History* 49 (1998), pp. 29–60, esp. pp. 32, 37, 39, 49.

61. Perrott, 'Richard Hooker and the problem of authority', pp. 50, 51, quoting R. Hooker, *Folger Library Edition of the Works of Richard Hooker*, ed. W. R. Speed Hill et al. (7 vols, Cambridge and Binghamton, 1977–94), vol. 1, pp. 179–80, 185.

62. P. Collinson, *The Religion of Protestants* (London, 1983), p. 90.

63. *The Autobiography of Richard Baxter*, ed. N. H. Keeble, abridged by J. M. Lloyd Thomas (London, 1974), pp. 84, xvii.

64. *Autobiography of Richard Baxter*, ed. Keeble, p. 9.

65. *Autobiography of Richard Baxter*, ed. Keeble, p. 11.

66. *Autobiography of Richard Baxter*, ed. Keeble, p. 111.

67. R. Askew, *Muskets and Altars: Jeremy Taylor and the last of the Anglicans* (London, 1997).

18. Modern Historians on the English Reformation

I gave an earlier version of this paper at a Colloquium on 30 April 2011 to honour Dr Felicity Heal on her retirement. In view of her central place in Reformation studies in the last half-century, I have not found it necessary to remove very many of the original references to Felicity, and I am happy to celebrate her ongoing career with this present augmented version.

1. I will not repeat my sarcasm on this usage of 'Continent': see D. MacCulloch, M. Laven, and E. Duffy, 'Recent Trends in the Study of Christianity in Sixteenth-Century Europe', *Renaissance Quarterly* 59 (2006), pp. 697–731, at pp. 697–8.

2. E. G. Rupp, *The Righteousness of God: Luther Studies* (London, 1953); E. G. Rupp, *Religion in England 1688–1791* (Oxford, 1985).

3. For one fatal lapse on Strype's part, see my essay 'Forging Reformation History', below. On Williams, whose scholarship has been in my view underrated, see *The Work of Archbishop John Williams*, ed. B. Williams (Sutton Courtenay, 1988), and for another healthy revision of

Williams's reputation, see S. Hampton, 'The Manuscript Sermons of Archbishop John Williams', *Journal of Ecclesiastical History* 62 (2011), pp. 707–25.

4. On Victorian Evangelicals, see D. Rosman, *Evangelicals and Culture* (London, 1984).

5. A. Milton, *Laudian and Royalist Polemic in 17th-century England: the Career and Writings of Peter Heylyn* (Manchester, 2007). A fine overview is provided by P. Nockles, 'A disputed legacy: Anglican historiographies of the Reformation from the era of the Caroline divines to that of the Oxford Movement', *Bulletin of the John Rylands Library* 83 (2001), pp. 121–67.

6. For examples (in which I must confess having had a hand), compare successive entries across editions of the *Oxford Dictionary of the Christian Church*, s.v. Browne, Robert (no longer 'clearly mentally unstable'); Real Presence (now without a mendacious attribution of the doctrine to Hugh Latimer); Stubbs, John (no longer a 'fanatic').

7. H. Butterfield, *The Whig Interpretation of History* (London, 1931). An enlightening portrait of Butterfield is M. Bentley, *The Life and Thought of Herbert Butterfield: History, Science and God* (Cambridge, 2011).

8. C. Dugmore, *The Mass and the English Reformers* (London, 1958). To be fair to Dugmore, in the journal which he himself edited, he published a polite but distinctly sceptical review of his work by that acute ecclesiastical historian, Norman Sykes: *Journal of Ecclesiastical History* 10 (1959), pp. 246–8.

9. H. Davies, *Worship and Theology in England. I. From Cranmer to Hooker, 1534–1603* (Princeton, 1970), p. 54.

10. Davies, *From Cranmer to Hooker*, pp. 236, 440.

11. Davies, *From Cranmer to Hooker*, p. 34.

12. H. Davies, *Worship and Theology in England. II. From Andrewes to Baxter and Fox, 1603–1690* (Princeton, NJ, 1975), p. 159.

13. There are of course honourable exceptions in Germany, and one particular witness of this, arguably pioneering in its concern to reach over divides, is a volume of essays (to which I contributed), D. Wendebourg (ed.), *Sister Reformations /Schwesterreformationen: the Reformation in Germany and in England – Die Reformation in Deutschland und in England* (Tübingen, 2010).

14. P. Hughes, *The Reformation in England* (3 vols, London, 1950–54).

15. E. Duffy, *The Stripping of the Altars: traditional religion in England 1400–1580* (London and New Haven, CT, 2005); E. Duffy, *Fires of Faith: Catholic England under Mary Tudor* (London and New Haven, 2009).

16. D. Knowles, *The Religious Orders in England* (3 vols, Cambridge, 1948, 1955, 1959).

17. D. Knowles, *The Religious Orders in England*, III: *the Tudor Age* (Cambridge, 1959), p. 464, and cf. ibid., p. 460: 'With the exception of the Carthusians, the Bridgettines and the Observant Franciscans, the religious life in England was humanly speaking easier and less spiritually stimulating in 1530 than it had been a century earlier.'

18. J. G. Clark, 'The Culture of English Monasticism', in *The Culture of English Monasticism*, ed. Clark (Woodbridge, 2007), pp. 1-18.

19. See C. Brooke's delicate and engaged meditation on Knowles's career, 'Dom David Knowles and his vocation as a monastic historian', *Downside Review* 110 (1992), pp. 209-25.

20. For an incisive analysis of one example of this tendency in the Anglican-Roman Catholic International Commission (ARCIC) documents, see J. Maltby, 'Anglicanism, the Reformation and the Anglican-Roman Catholic International Commission's Agreed Statement, *Mary: Grace and Hope in Christ*', *Theology* 110 (2007), pp. 171-9.

21. A. L. Rowse, *Tudor Cornwall* (London, 1941). Trevelyan's remark in his *Sunday Times* review of Rowse's *England under Elizabeth: the Structure of Society* (London, 1950) is quoted in H. P. R. Finberg, *The Local Historian and his Theme* (Leicester University Department of English Local History Occasional Papers 1, 1952), p. 8.

22. That was certainly Sir John Neale's attitude to such subjects as prosopography on which so much of his work on Parliament was based: that was left to women, who could not progress beyond MAs. On this, see P. Collinson, *The History of a History Man: or, the Twentieth Century viewed from a Safe Distance* (Woodbridge, 2011), p. 78. At least Neale put Collinson on the road to his study of Puritanism: ibid., pp. 77-8.

23. A. G. Dickens, *The English Reformation* (1st edn, London, 1964).

24. Collinson, *History of a History Man*, pp. 5-37.

25. C. Haigh, *Reformation and Resistance in Tudor Lancashire* (Cambridge, 1975).

26. *The English Reformation Revised*, ed. C. Haigh (Cambridge, 1987).

27. I am grateful to Felicity Heal for this reminiscence: the year appears to be 1974 in anticipation of the 1976 Colloquium.

28. J. J. Scarisbrick, *The Reformation and the English People* (Oxford, 1983).

29. C. Haigh, 'The English Reformation: a Premature Birth, a Difficult Labour and a Sickly Child', *Historical Journal* 33 (1990), pp. 449-59: an extended review article of key texts over the previous few years. Haigh's latest work might be said to celebrate the effectiveness of the

Reformation: C. Haigh, *The Plain Man's Pathways to Heaven: Kinds of Christianity in Post-Reformation England* (Oxford, 2007).

30. P. N. Brooks, *Thomas Cranmer's Doctrine of the Eucharist* (London, 1965; revised edn, Basingstoke, 1992). For my critical remarks about the terminology which Brooks used to characterize the change, see D. MacCulloch, *Thomas Cranmer: a life* (New Haven, CT, and London, 1996), pp. 182-3, 392.

31. P. Lake, *Moderate Puritans and the Elizabethan Church* (Cambridge, 1983).

32. D. MacCulloch, 'The importance of Jan Laski in the English Reformation', in C. Strohm (ed.), *Johannes à Lasco: Polnischer Baron, Humanist und europäischer Reformator* (Spätmittelalter und Reformation, New series, 14, 2000), pp. 325-46; D. MacCulloch, 'Peter Martyr Vermigli and Thomas Cranmer', in *Peter Martyr Vermigli: Humanism, Republicanism, Reformation*, ed. E. Campi et al. (Geneva, 2002); D. MacCulloch, 'Heinrich Bullinger and the English-speaking world', in P. Opitz and E. Campi (eds), *Heinrich Bullinger (1504?-1575): Leben, Denken, Wirkung* (Zürcher Beiträge zur Reformationsgeschichte, 24, 2006).

33. To appreciate one fine example of the usefulness of juxtaposing a deep understanding of the English Reformation with literature, see D. Womersley, *Divinity and State* (Oxford, 2010).

34. A. Ryrie, 'The strange death of Lutheran England', *Journal of Ecclesiastical History* 53 (2002), pp. 64-92; A. Ryrie, *The Gospel and Henry VIII: evangelicals in the early English Reformation* (Cambridge, 2003).

35. G. Murdock, *Calvinism on the frontier 1600-1660: international Calvinism and the Reformed Church in Hungary and Transylvania* (Oxford, 2000), p. 65. The title of the book might be said to be its least happy feature, since Murdock is describing something much wider than 'Calvinism'.

36. B. D. Spinks, *Two Faces of Elizabethan Anglican Theology: Sacraments and salvation in the thought of William Perkins and Richard Hooker* (Lanham, MD, 1999); and see also W. B. Patterson, 'William Perkins as apologist for the Church of England', *Journal of Ecclesiastical History* 57 (2006), pp. 252-69. On Walton, see also J. Martin, *Walton's Lives: Conformist Commemorations and the Rise of Biography* (Oxford, 2001).

37. See J. Maltby, *Prayer Book and People in Elizabethan and Early Stuart England* (Cambridge, 1998); K. Fincham and S. Taylor, 'Vital Statistics: Episcopal Ordination and Ordinands in England, 1646-60', *English Historical Review* 126 (2011), pp. 319-44.

38. F. Heal, *Reformation in Britain and Ireland* (Oxford, 2003). I can testify that my attendance in 2000 at Felicity Heal's preliminary seminar

paper laying out how she was proposing to structure this book impelled me to give up a similar writing project, which I felt would simply be duplicating the excellent prospectus which she presented.

39. See a very suggestive little discussion, R. Biebrach, 'Conspicuous by their absence: rethinking explanations for the lack of brasses in medieval Wales', *Transactions of the Monumental Brass Society* 18 (2009), pp. 36–42.

40. M. Aston, 'Public Worship and Iconoclasm', in *The Archaeology of Reformation 1480–1580*, ed. D. Gaimster and R. Gilchrist (Leeds, 2003), pp. 9–28, at pp. 16–17.

41. P. Everson and D. Stocker, 'The Archaeology of Vice-regality: Charles Brandon's Brief Rule in Lincolnshire', in Gaimster and Gilchrist (eds), *The Archaeology of Reformation*, pp. 145–58.

42. N. Oakey, 'Fixtures or Fittings? Can Surviving Pre-Reformation Ecclesiastical Material Culture be used as a Barometer of Contemporary Attitudes to the Reformation in England?', in Gaimster and Gilchrist (eds), *The Archaeology of Reformation*, pp. 58–72. This ideological destruction with a 'Catholic' agenda is of course widely paralleled in the Counter-Reformation rearrangement of churches across Europe: see E. C. Tingle, 'The Catholic Reformation and the Parish: the Church of Saint Thégonnec (Finistère, France) 1550–1700', in Gaimster and Gilchrist (eds), *The Archaeology of Reformation*, pp. 44–57.

43. Heal, *Reformation in Britain and Ireland*, p. 478.

44. For some of the ways in which they achieved that, see I. Green, *The Christian's ABC: Catechisms and Catechizing in England c.1530–1740* (Oxford, 1996), T. Watt, *Cheap Print and Popular Piety* (Cambridge, 1991) and R. A. Leaver, *'Goostly psalmes and spirituall songes': English and Dutch Metrical Psalms from Coverdale to Utenhove, 1536–1566* (Cambridge, 1991); L. Dixon, 'Richard Greenham and the Calvinist Construction of God', *Journal of Ecclesiastical History* 61 (2010), pp. 729–45.

19. Thomas Cranmer's Biographers

1. D. MacCulloch, *Thomas Cranmer: a life* (New Haven and London, 1996), pp. 584–5. On Harpsfield, see A. B. Emden, *A Biographical Register of the University of Oxford A.D. 1501 to 1540* (Oxford, 1974), p. 269.

2. T. S. Freeman, 'Did Cranmer equal six hundred Beckets? John Foxe, Nicholas Harpsfield and the martyrs of the English Reformation', in

Sanctity and Martyrdom in Early Modern England, ed. T. S. Freeman and T. Mayer (Woodbridge, forthcoming).

3. 'tanquam institor, merces in operto exportabat, ut ad singula divortia presto adesset capsa cum impedimento': [?N. Harpsfield], *Bishop Cranmer's Recantacyons,* ed. Lord Houghton with introduction by J. Gairdner (Philobiblon Society Miscellanies 15, London, 1877–84), p. 8.

4. MacCulloch, *Thomas Cranmer,* p. 250.

5. *A treatise on the pretended divorce between Henry VIII and Catherine of Aragon, by Nicholas Harpsfield* . . ., ed. N. Pocock (C.S. 2nd series 21, London, 1878), p. 292, and on the box, ibid. p. 275. On Cranmer and the monasteries, MacCulloch, *Thomas Cranmer,* pp. 166–9, 263–4.

6. J. A. Champion, *The Pillars of Priestcraft Shaken: the Church of England and its Enemies, 1660–1730* (Cambridge, 1992), p. 87, quoting J. Bossuet, *History of the variations of the Protestant Churches* (2 vols, Antwerp, 1742), vol. 1, p. 303.

7. A. Woodhead, *A compendious discourse on the Eucharist with two appendixes* (Oxford, 1689), p. 155.

8. Champion, *Pillars of Priestcraft Shaken,* p. 84, quoting P. Manby, *A Reformed Catechism, in two dialogues concerning the English Reformation* (London, 1687), epistle to the reader.

9. R. O'Day, *The Debate on the English Reformation* (London, 1986), pp. 60–80.

10. H. Belloc, *Cranmer* (London, 1931): see prefatory note.

11. H. Belloc, *Characters of the Reformation* (London, 1955 edn), pp. 80–89. On Cranmer's prose, Belloc, *Cranmer,* pp. 30–31, 244–6.

12. MacCulloch, *Thomas Cranmer,* pp. 633–6. On Nevinson, see my entry on him, s.v. Nevinson, Stephen, in *The Oxford Dictionary of National Biography.*

13. London, British Library MS Harley 417, fos 90–93. J. Foxe, *Rerum in ecclesia gestarum commentarii* (2 vols, Basel, 1559–63).

14. J. Foxe, *Acts and Monuments of these latter and perilous days* . . . (1583), pp. 1859–93.

15. Foxe, *Acts and Monuments* (1583), pp. 1121, 1870.

16. Foxe, *Acts and Monuments* (1583), p. 1862. Foxe may have derived the idea from an English tract of 1536 which was then ascribed to Luther's authorship, *A descrypcyon of the images of a verye Chrysten bysschop and of a counterfayte bysshop*: J. Martin, *Walton's Lives: conformist commemorations and the rise of biography* (Oxford, 2001), pp. 72–4.

17. Foxe, *Acts and Monuments* (1583), pp. 1862–3.

18. Martin, *Walton's Lives,* pp. 78–81.

19. P. J. Olsen, 'Was John Foxe a millenarian?', *Journal of Ecclesiastical History* 45 (1994), pp. 600–624, at p. 601.

20. Augustinus Jonas, *Historia von Thoma Cranmero dem Ertzbischoff zu Cantuaria in Engellend . . . durch J.F . . . bescrieben, und itzt aus dem Latein verdeutscht* (Weissenfels, 1561): the British Library copy is shelf-mark 1126.h.11. I am indebted to Dr Thomas Freeman for pointing me to this reference.

21. M. Sztárai, *Historia Cranmerus T. Erseknek az igaz hitben valo alhatatosagarol . . . Sz M. által énekben szeresztetet* (Debrecen, 1582): the copy held in the British Library (C.38.e.14) is thought to be the only surviving example. See discussion in K. Erdös, 'Sztárai Mihály Cranmerus Thamásrol szólór historiás énekének forrása', *Irodalomtörténeti Közlemények* 24 (1914), pp. 215–19. I am most grateful to Graeme Murdock for our discussions on this work and for providing me with translations of part of the poem.

22. M. Parker, *De Antiquitate Britannicae Ecclesiae . . .* (London, 1572), pp. 381–405.

23. [Anon., ?J. Stubbs], *The life off the 70. Archbishopp off Canterbury presentlye sitting Englished . . .* (n.p., 1574), sigs. E1v, E6r.

24. *Tudor Church Reform: the Henrician canons of 1535 and the Reformatio legum ecclesiasticarum*, ed. G. Bray (Church of England Record Society, 8, London, 2000), pp. 164–65; cf. M. Graves, *Thomas Norton: the Parliament Man* (Oxford, 1994), pp. 299–301.

25. Parker, *De Antiquitate*, pp. 398–9.

26. From innumerable examples of this collective treatment of the Prayer Book, I instance an unjustly neglected Roman Catholic who was a perceptive (though vitriolic) analyst of the Reformation – Abraham Woodhead – an Oxford don who converted to Roman Catholicism: cf. Woodhead, *Church-Government Part V. A relation of the English Reformation, and The lawfulness thereof examined by the Theses deliver'd in the Four former Parts* (Oxford, 1687), pp. 129, 143–51.

27. On these, see D. MacCulloch, *Tudor Church Militant: Edward VI and the Protestant Reformation* (London, 1999), pp. 176–9.

28. MacCulloch, *Thomas Cranmer*, pp. 624–5. For similar use of Cranmer by both Puritans and anti-Arminian churchmen to annoy or criticize Archbishop Laud, see ibid., pp. 626–7.

29. *A brief discourse of the troubles at Frankfort 1554–1558 A.D.*, ed. E. Arber (London, 1908), p. 75 (the report of a 'Master H.' who cannot be more definitely identified among the exiles; it may have been Christopher Hales, see C. H. Garrett, *Marian Exiles: a study in the origins of*

Elizabethan Puritanism (Cambridge, 1938), pp. 171–2. See also *Brief discourse*, ed. Arber, pp. 37, 45.

30. MacCulloch, *Tudor Church Militant*, pp. 218–20.

31. MacCulloch, *Thomas Cranmer*, pp. 626–7. The precedent for this was the twitting of that ultimate champion of the Elizabethan Settlement, Richard Hooker, by the Puritan consortium who attacked him in 1599 in *A Christian Letter*: cf. the edition of their work with Hooker's annotations, *Folger Library Edition of the Works of Richard Hooker*, ed. W. R. Speed Hill et al. (7 vols, Cambridge and Binghamton, 1977–94), vol. 4, pp. 47, 64, 71, 228–9.

32. D. Nussbaum, 'Laudian Foxe-hunting? William Laud and the status of John Foxe in the 1630s', in *The Church Retrospective*, ed. R. N. Swanson (*Studies in Church History* 33, Oxford, 1997), pp. 329–42.

33. P. Heylyn, *Cyprianus Anglicus, or the history of the life and death of . . . William by divine providence Lord Archbishop of Canterbury* (London, 1668), p. 532. In a revealing little slip, Laud in his speech promoted Cyprian from bishop to archbishop.

34. G. Burnet, *History of the Reformation of the Church of England* (2 vols, London, 1679–81).

35. Champion, *Pillars of Priestcraft shaken*, p. 87.

36. On Burnet and Strype, see O'Day, *Debate on the English Reformation*, pp. 38–53.

37. Cf. e.g. Foxe, *Acts and Monuments* (1583), p. 1294 with the original in Cranmer's 'Osiander' catechism of 1548, illus. in e.g. MacCulloch, *Thomas Cranmer*, p. 388.

38. On the portraits and pictures, MacCulloch, *Thomas Cranmer*, pp. 338–47, 602, 621: beards: ibid., pp. 361–2, 472.

39. MacCulloch, *Tudor Church Militant*, p. 78.

40. C. Lever, *The history of the Defendors of the Catholique Faith. Wheareunto are added Observations Divine, Politique, Morrall . . .* (London, 1627): illus. in MacCulloch, *Tudor Church Militant*, p. 16.

41. Burnet, *History of the Reformation*, p. i, facing p. 179. Strype and Burnet shared the same publisher, Richard Chiswell, who reused various portraits between the two volumes.

42. For this discussion, I have used two copies of Strype's *Memorials* in the Bodleian Library which retain their frontispieces: Douce S.542 and C.19.Theol. That both these frontispieces are original and integral is shown by the fact that both of them have rather crudely but identically printed on their reverse 'THE LIFE OF ARCH-BISHOP CRANMER'.

43. *Fox's original and complete book of martyrs*, ed. P. Wright (issued in parts, London, 1811–17), illustrations of Cranmer's last sermon and his burning,

facing pp. 486, 487. For similar rhetorical treatment of Richard Hooker by Izaak Walton, see my essay 'Richard Hooker's reputation', below.

44. Champion, *Pillars of priestcraft shaken*, p. 84.

45. The copy is now Oxford Bodleian Library K.5.13.Art.

46. MacCulloch, *Thomas Cranmer*, pp. 475–6. On Foxe's attitudes generally, see Elton, 'Persecution and Toleration', pp. 171–80.

47. On the radicals, MacCulloch, *Thomas Cranmer*, pp. 474–7, *The Catholic doctrine of the Church of England . . . by Thomas Rogers . . .*, ed. J. J. S. Perowne (Parker Society, Cambridge, 1854), p. 350; G. H. Williams, *The Radical Reformation* (London, 1962), pp. 789–90, and cf. J. R. Knott, *Discourses of martyrdom in English literature, 1563–1694* (Cambridge, 1993), p. 116.

48. J. Hayward, *The Life and raigne of King Edward the Sixt* (London, 1630), pp. 7–8. On his Tacitean borrowings, see L. Richardson, 'Sir John Hayward and early Stuart Historiography' (Cambridge Ph.D., 1999).

49. W. Cobbett, *A History of the Protestant Reformation in England and Ireland* (London, 1925), para. 64. Cobbett presented a copy of this work to Pope Pius VIII in 1829: see a description of that presentation copy in St Philip's Books (Oxford) sale catalogue no. 33, item 1551. Cf. O'Day, *Debate on the English Reformation*, pp. 73–7, and A. G. Dickens and J. M. Tonkin, *The Reformation in Historical Thought* (Oxford, 1985), pp. 193, 195, 265, 344.

50. Cobbett, *Protestant Reformation*, para. 64. On Gibbon, see Dickens and Tonkin, *Reformation in Historical Thought*, p. 136.

51. W. F. Hook, *Lives of the Archbishops of Canterbury* (12 vols, London, 1860–76), new series, vol. 2, p. 418.

52. See above on H. Davies, *Worship and Theology in England. II. From Andrewes to Baxter and Fox, 1603–1690* (Princeton, 1975), in my essay 'Modern Historians on the English Reformation', above. A fine account is P. Nockles, 'A disputed legacy: Anglican historiographies of the Reformation from the era of the Caroline divines to that of the Oxford Movement', *Bulletin of the John Rylands Library of Manchester* 82 (2002), pp. 121–67.

53. G. W. Bromiley, *Thomas Cranmer, Theologian* (London, 1956), esp. pp. 67, 75; and cf. MacCulloch, *Thomas Cranmer*, pp. 209–12.

54. A. C. Deane, *The Life of Thomas Cranmer Archbishop of Canterbury* (London, 1927), pp. 240–41.

55. F. E. Hutchinson, *Cranmer and the English Reformation* (London, 1951), pp. 182–3. Hutchinson was a former Fellow of All Souls (his All Souls colleague A. L. Rowse was the General Editor of the Teach Yourself series).

56. [Anon., possibly F. E. Brightman], 'Cranmer's Liturgical Projects', *Church Quarterly Review* 31 (1891), pp. 446–62, at pp. 457, 462.

57. Belloc, *Cranmer*, pp. 30–31. Coming on Belloc's observations after publishing my own biography, I found them both gratifyingly and embarrassingly similar to my own observations.

58. C. H. Smyth, *Cranmer and the Reformation under Edward VI* (London, 1926). There are faults of interpretation and occasionally of fact in this essay which do not detract from its significance.

59. See the catalogue, P. N. Brooks (ed.), *Cranmer in Context: Documents from the English Reformation* (London, 1989).

60. *The Guardian*, section 2, 6 July 1998, p. 4.

61. *New Oxford Review* (December 1998), pp. 41–3, at p. 43.

62. *First Things* (November 1996), pp. 66–74, at p. 72.

63. I am grateful to Dr David Hilliard for passing me the relevant papers in this case, including a circular letter of 9 November 1999 from Archbishop Goodhew and a circulated essay by Dr Head of 5 June 2000.

20. Richard Hooker's Reputation

A version of this paper formed the first in a series of lectures sponsored by Corpus Christi College, Oxford, in autumn 2000, commemorating the quatercentenary of Hooker's death. I am extremely grateful for the generosity of the following in allowing me access to their unpublished work: the late Patrick Collinson, Susan Doran, Jessica Martin and Peter Nockles. I must also thank Steven McGrade for his invaluable detailed comments on a draft of the paper, Peter Groves for assistance in Pusey House Library, Séan Hughes for some provocative conversations in seminars, and Conal Condren for supplying various secondary sources. My particular debt to Michael Brydon is apparent from these endnotes, in which I have endeavoured to specify precisely where I have used him: M. Brydon, *The Evolving Reputation of Richard Hooker: an examination of responses* (Oxford, 2006).

1. R. Keen, 'Inventory of Richard Hooker, 1601', *Archaeologia Cantiana* 70 (1957), pp. 231–6, at p. 231. I am grateful to Dr Kenneth Fincham for alerting me to this reference.

2. *The Folger Library Edition of the Works of Richard Hooker* [FLE], ed. W. R. Speed Hill et al. (7 vols, Cambridge and Binghamton, 1977–94).

3. For useful citations of conventional discussion of Hooker's role, see *Richard Hooker and the Construction of Community*, ed. A. S. McGrade (Tempe, 1997), pp. 221, 261; for further discussion, Brydon, *Evolving Reputation of Hooker*, Introduction.

4. P. Lake, *Anglicans and Puritans? Presbyterianism and English Conformist Thought from Whitgift to Hooker* (London, 1988), p. 230.

5. On John Hooker alias Vowell, see *The History of Parliament: The House of Commons 1558–1603*, ed. P. W. Hasler (3 vols, London, 1982), vol. 2, pp. 334–5, and W. T. MacCaffrey, *Exeter, 1540–1640: The Growth of an English County Town* (Cambridge, MA, 1958), pp. 3, 7–8, 50, 120, 139, 144, 225, 272–4.

6. *FLE*, vol. 1, p. 171, ll. 2–4 (II.6.4).

7. *FLE*, vol. 5, p. 33, ll. 6–7; v.49, ll. 9–10; cf. also vol. 5, p. 112, l. 6; cf. R. Bauckham, 'Hooker, Travers and the Church of Rome in the 1580s', *Journal of Ecclesiastical History* 29 (1978), pp. 37–50, at pp. 37–40; A. Milton, *Catholic and Reformed: the Roman and Protestant Churches in English Protestant Thought, 1600–1640* (Cambridge, 1995), pp. 211–12. It was not surprising that John Keble's Anglo-Catholic sensibilities were offended by the Jude sermons, and that he included them in his 1836 edition of Hooker's works with a health warning about their authenticity: *The Works of that learned and judicious divine Mr. Richard Hooker*, ed. J. Keble (3 vols in 4, Oxford, 1836), vol. 1, pp. xlvi–xlviii.

8. On Rainolds, see C. M. Dent, *Protestant Reformers in Elizabethan Oxford* (Oxford, 1983), index, *sub nomine*.

9. *The History of the University of Oxford*, vol. III, *The Collegiate University*, ed. J. McConica (Oxford, 1986), pp. 21–2, 24–8, 658, 693.

10. Dent, *Protestant Reformers*, pp. 25–8, 43; *Collegiate University*, ed. McConica, pp. 381, 408.

11. *FLE*, vol. 5, pp. 146–8.

12. Cf. Milton, *Catholic and Reformed*, pp. 106, 146–7, 286; A. Milton, in *The Early Stuart Church, 1603–1642*, ed. K. Fincham (Basingstoke, 1993), pp. 206–7.

13. Bauckham, 'Hooker, Travers and the Church of Rome', pp. 41–50.

14. T. Fuller, *The Worthies of England*, ed. J. Freeman (London, 1952), p. 133; I. Walton, *The Lives of John Donne, Sir Henry Wotton, Richard Hooker, George Herbert and Robert Sanderson*, ed. G. Saintsbury (Oxford, 1927) [reproduction of 1675 edn of Hooker's life], p. 200.

15. W. D. J. Cargill Thompson, 'The source of Hooker's knowledge of Marsilius of Padua', *Journal of Ecclesiastical History* 25 (1974), pp. 75–81.

16. [J. Throckmorton], *M. Some laid open in his colors* ([La Rochelle], 1590), p. 29. C. Condren, 'The creation of Richard Hooker's public authority: rhetoric, reputation and reassessment', *Journal of Religious History* 21 (1997), pp. 35–59, at p. 38, discusses this reference but accepts the older mistaken attribution to John Greenwood: for identification, see P. Milward, *Religious Controversies of the Elizabethan Age:*

A survey of printed sources (Lincoln, NE, and London, 1977), p. 85, no. 311. For Patrick Collinson's renewed doubts about the authorship of the Marprelate Tracts, see *The Reign of Elizabeth I: Court and culture in the last decade*, ed. J. Guy (Cambridge, 1995), pp. 157–8.

17. Milton, *Catholic and Reformed*, p. 48. The one partial exception is the discussion of confession which now forms part of Book VI of the *Ecclesiastical Polity*.

18. L. H. Carlson, *Martin Marprelate, gentleman: Master Job Throckmorton Laid Open in his Colors* (San Marino, CA, 1981), pp. 117–18, 377.

19. T. Cartwright, *The second replie . . . agaynst Maister Doctor Whitgiftes second answer* (1575) and *The rest of the second replie . . . agaynst Master Doctor Whitgifts second answer* (1577).

20. On this context, see P. Collinson, 'Richard Hooker and the construction of Christian community', in *Richard Hooker*, ed. McGrade, pp. 149–80, at pp. 161–70.

21. *FLE*, vol. 3, p. xxiv.

22. The literature on the reception of the work is vast, but one of the best short guides is provided by Brydon, *Evolving Reputation of Hooker*, Introduction. See also Lake, *Anglicans and Puritans?*, pp. 145–252, and M. Perrott, 'Richard Hooker and the problem of authority in the Elizabethan Church', *Journal of Ecclesiastical History* 49 (1998), pp. 29–60.

23. For incisive discussion of this point, see W. D. Neelands in *Richard Hooker*, ed. McGrade, pp. 75–94, esp. p. 89.

24. I present the case for this in my *Tudor Church Militant: Edward VI and the Protestant Reformation* (London, 1999), pp. 191–2.

25. N. Atkinson, *Richard Hooker and the Authority of Scripture, Tradition and Reason: Reformed Theologian of the Church of England?* (St Ives, 1997) rather overdid this aspect of Hooker, by taking too monolithic a view of what Reformation Protestantism consisted. For instance, he took no notice of Hooker's hostility towards Lutheran Eucharistic doctrine. More nuanced treatments are T. Kirby, 'Richard Hooker's theory of natural law in the context of Reformation theology', *Sixteenth Century Journal* 30 (1999), pp. 681–703, and Kirby in *Richard Hooker*, ed. McGrade, pp. 219–36.

26. B. D. Spinks, *Two Faces of Elizabethan Anglican Theology: Sacraments and salvation in the thought of William Perkins and Richard Hooker* (Lanham, 1999), is a careful and useful analysis of the subject.

27. *FLE*, vol. 2, pp. 340–43 (V.67.12). See *Richard Hooker*, ed. McGrade, p. 145, and see *FLE*, n. to vol. 2, p. 343.6–26.

28. Hooker's will of 26 October 1600 is printed in *Works of Hooker*, ed. Keble, vol. 1, pp. 12–113n.

29. Featley's biography of Rainolds is translated in T. Fuller, *Abel Redevivus, or the Dead yet speaking. The lives and deaths of the modern divines,* ed. W. Nichols (2 vols, London, 1867): cf. vol. 2, p. 219. I am indebted to Brian Vickers for our conversation on Hooker and logic.

30. *FLE,* vol. 1, p. 264, ll. 3–15 (III.11.16). Cf. quotation at *Works of Hooker,* ed. Keble, vol. 1, p. lxxiv.

31. *FLE,* vol. 3, pp. 333–5. On the growing commitment of civil lawyers to absolutist theories in Church and State, see J. Guy, in *The Reign of Elizabeth I,* ed. Guy, pp. 126–49.

32. P. E. McCullough, *Sermons at Court: Politics and religion in Elizabethan and Jacobean preaching* (Cambridge, 1998), p. 97. Hooker's absence from court preaching is in striking contrast to the constant presence of his close friend Lancelot Andrewes, and is remarkable considering that we know that he had preached at Paul's Cross as long ago as 1581.

33. S. Doran, 'Elizabeth I's religion: the evidence of her letters', *Journal of Ecclesiastical History* 50 (2000), pp. 699–720; see also MacCulloch, *Tudor Church Militant,* pp. 185–95.

34. C. H. Sisson, *The Judicious Marriage of Mr. Hooker and the birth of The Laws of Ecclesiastical Polity* (Cambridge, 1940), p. 134; cf. also pp. 132, 145, 149, 151, 156.

35. Chicago University Joseph Regenstein Library, MS 109, fo. 21r. The MS of this short satire clearly post-dates the publication of the *Lawes,* and so is later than the accompanying longer MS tract by Rogers of 1590, dealt with by J. Craig, 'The "Cambridge Boies": Thomas Rogers and the "Brethren" in Bury St. Edmunds', in *Belief and Practice in Reformation England: A Tribute to Patrick Collinson,* ed. S. Wabuda and C. Litzenberger (Aldershot, 1998), pp. 153–76. For Rogers's citations of Hooker, see ibid., p. 174n, and T. Rogers, *The Catholic Doctrine of the Church of England, an exposition of the Thirty-Nine Articles,* ed. J. J. S. Perowne (Parker Society, Cambridge, 1854), p. 359.

36. J. Throckmorton, *The defence of Iob Throkmorton, against the slaunders of Maister Sutcliffe* ([London], 1594), sigs. Ciiiv–Civ; cf. Carlson, *Martin Marprelate,* p. 124.

37. [?A. Willet], *A Christian Letter, of certaine English Protestants, unfained favourers of the present state of English Religion, authorised and professed in England: unto that Reverend and learned man, Mr. R. Hoo.,* . . . (Middelburg, 1599); the text with Hooker's marginalia is printed in *FLE,* vol. 4, pp. 1–80.

38. The case for Willet's authorship is presented in *FLE,* vol. 4, pp. xix–xxv. For Willet's later attacks, see Milton, *Catholic and Reformed,* pp. 17,

20, 128. *A Short Title Catalogue of Books printed in England, Scotland, and Ireland and of English Books Printed Abroad before the year 1640* (3 vols, London, 1976–91) lists forty-eight separate pre-1640 editions of Willet's works (pp. 25672–707), to Hooker's twenty (*Short Title Catalogue of Books ... before the year 1640*, pp. 13706–23).

39. [Willet], *A Christian Letter*, title-page.

40. [Willet], *A Christian Letter*, p. 45.

41. I am indebted to Peter Lake for this point: P. Lake, 'Business as usual? The immediate reception of Hooker's *Ecclesiastical Polity*', *Journal of Ecclesiastical History* 52 (2001), pp. 456–86. On Barrett, see H. C. Porter, *Reformation and Reaction in Tudor Cambridge* (Cambridge, 1958), Chs 15–17; on his conversion, pp. 362–3.

42. Andrewes to Henry Parry, 7 November 1600, pr. *Works of Hooker*, ed. Keble, vol. 1, pp. 115n–116n.

43. For relevant passages, see Walton, *Lives*, ed. Saintsbury, pp. 166, 216. Walton's original formulations of the Baptist motif were more indirect: Brydon, *Evolving Reputation of Hooker*, p. 115.

44. Keen, 'Inventory'; cf. Walton, *Lives*, ed. Saintsbury, p. 229, Sisson, *Judicious Marriage*, pp. 133, 136, and Hooker's will, pr. *Works of Hooker*, ed. Keble, vol. 1, pp. 112n–113n.

45. Sisson, *Judicious Marriage*, pp. 124–6.

46. *FLE*, vol. 4, p. 70, ll. 15–17 and nn.; p. 78, ll. 4–7; see also the extended evidence of his dealings with publishers in Sisson, *Judicious Marriage*, pp. 132–56. Cf. *Works of Hooker*, ed. Keble, vol. 1, pp. xiv, cxiii. Keble, evidently wishing to protect Hooker's rural seclusion, accounted for his knowledge of current publication plans by saying that Whitgift must have told him. G. M. Young made a similar suggestion about the Julius Caesar reference: *FLE*, vol. 4, pp. 233–4. I am grateful to Brian Vickers for pointing out the possible significance of Hooker's reference to Cassius and Brutus.

47. Walton, *Lives*, ed. Saintsbury, p. 223. For the story of the prostitute, see *The Works of Mr. Richard Hooker (that learned, godly, judicious and eloquent Divine) ... with an account of his holy life and happy death ...*, ed. J. Gauden (London, 1662), pp. 32–3.

48. *Conversations of Ben Jonson with William Drummond of Hawthornden* (London, 1906), ed. P. Sidney, p. 20.

49. Sisson, *Judicious Marriage*, p. 126.

50. For an excellent introduction to the idea of 'avant-garde conformity', see P. Lake, 'Lancelot Andrewes, John Buckeridge, and Avant-Garde Conformity at the Court of James I', in *The Mental World of the Jacobean Court*, ed. L. L. Peck (Cambridge, 1991), pp. 113–33.

51. Milton, *Catholic and Reformed*, p. 240.

52. Lake, 'Business as usual?', pp. 475–81.

53. Rogers, *Catholic Doctrine of the Church of England*, ed. Perowne, p. 359.

54. *Conversations of Ben Jonson with William Drummond*, ed. Sidney, p. 20.

55. P. Croft, 'The Catholic gentry, the Earl of Salisbury and the Baronets of 1611', in *Conformity and Orthodoxy in the English Church, c. 1560–1660*, ed. P. Lake and M. Questier (Woodbridge, 2000), pp. 262–81.

56. W. B. Patterson, *King James I and the Reunion of Christendom* (Cambridge, 1997).

57. Lake, 'Business as usual?', p. 483.

58. Condren, 'Hooker's public authority', discusses Brereley at pp. 40–41: however, at p. 40 and nn. 25–27, Condren mistakes Robert Parsons's references to Richard Hooker's uncle, the chronicler John Hooker alias Vowell, as referring to Richard Hooker himself. This is impossible in the context: cf. N. D. [R. Parsons], *A Treatise of Three Conversions of England from Paganisme to Christian Religion* . . . ([St Omer, F. Bellet] 1604), pp. 92, 162, 169, 623. [J. Anderton], J. Brereley, *pseud.*, *The Protestants Apologie for the Roman Church* (St Omer, 1608), p. 169.

59. For excellent demonstrations of this, see Condren, 'Hooker's public authority', pp. 41–2; Brydon, *Evolving Reputation of Hooker*, pp. 150–57. For an illustration of the long-term resonances of the Brereley debate through the writings of William Laud and beyond, see [T. Thorold], T. Carwell , *pseud.*, *Labyrinthus Cantuariensis: or Doctor Lawd's labyrinth* (?London, 1658), pp. 93–6.

60. On Lady Falkland, Brydon, *Evolving Reputation of Hooker*, pp. 35, 151; on James II, *Works of Hooker*, ed. Keble, vol. 1, pp. civ–cv, and J. Miller, *James II: A study in kingship* (London, 1978), pp. 57–8. Michael Brydon observes how little Hooker was used by Anglicans in the polemical battle with Roman Catholics in James II's reign, and attributes that to the success of earlier Catholic exploitation of Hooker's writings: Brydon, *Evolving Reputation of Hooker*, pp. 156–7.

61. Walton, *Lives*, ed. Saintsbury, pp. 211–12.

62. For efforts and proposals to translate Hooker, see Walton, *Lives*, ed. Saintsbury, pp. 213–14; *Works of Hooker*, ed. Keble, vol. 1, pp. 92n–3n; R. Eccleshall, 'Richard Hooker and the peculiarities of the English: the reception of the *Ecclesiastical Polity* in the 17th and 18th centuries', *History of Political Thought* 2 (I) (Spring 1981), pp. 63–117, at p. 68; H. R. Trevor-Roper, *Catholics, Anglicans and Puritans* (London, 1987), p. 191; *Oxford Dictionary of National Biography*, s.v. Earle, John; C. H. Miller, 'Seventeenth-Century Latin Translations of Two English

Masterpieces: Hooker's Polity and Browne's Religio Medici', *Acta Conventus Neo-Latini Abulensis: Proceedings of the Tenth International Congress of Neo-Latin Studies*, Avila, 4–9 August 1997 (Medieval and Renaissance Texts and Studies, 207, 2000), pp. 55–72.

63. J. Blatchly, *The Town Library of Ipswich ... a history and catalogue* (Woodbridge, 1989), p. 79. Whitgift, Bridges and Saravia were also absent.

64. Spinks, *Two Faces of Elizabethan Anglican Theology*, p. 168.

65. Milton, *Catholic and Reformed*, p. 427.

66. 'Cui deerat inimicus, per amicos oppressus': R. Hooker, *A learned discourse of justification, workes, and how the foundation of faith is overthrowne* (Oxford, 1612); [*FLE*, vol. 5, pp. 83–170], Preface, sig. A2. John Keble commented sourly on Jackson that he was 'evidently of the Reynolds school in theology': *Works of Hooker*, ed. Keble, vol. 1, p. xlviii.

67. R. Hooker, *Two sermons upon part of S. Judes epistle* (Oxford, 1614 [*FLE* vol. 1, pp. 1–57]), Preface, *passim*.

68. Collinson, 'Hooker and the construction of Christian community', p. 158.

69. G. Hakewill, *An apologie of the power and providence of God in the government of the world* (3rd edn, London, 1635), sig. A2v; Condren, 'Hooker's public authority', p. 41. It is interesting to find Gauden, the deliberately moderate biographer of Hooker, reviving the 'triumvirate' trope in 1662: *Works of Hooker*, ed. Gauden, *Life*, p. 10.

70. See Milton, *Catholic and Reformed*, p. 533, and Brydon, *Evolving Reputation of Hooker*, pp. 37–9, for a number of examples.

71. Spinks, *Two Faces of Elizabethan Anglican Theology*, pp. 164–5. For Hooker's later influence on sacramental discussion by the Calvinist Edward Reynolds, see B. Spinks, *Sacraments, ceremonies and the Stuart Divines: sacramental theology and liturgy in England and Scotland 1603–1662* (Aldershot, 2001).

72. Text cited in P. Collinson, *The Religion of Protestants: the Church in English Society, 1559–1625* (Oxford, 1982), p. 92n.

73. Cf. Milton, *Catholic and Reformed*, pp. 496–7. Prynne and Burton were quick to seize on this contrast between Hooker and the Laudians: Brydon, *Evolving Reputation of Hooker*, pp. 50–51.

74. For examples of such reaction, see Milton, *Catholic and Reformed*, p. 533; Brydon, *Evolving Reputation of Hooker*, p. 38 (on Robert Sanderson).

75. *Correspondence of Cosin*, Surtees Soc. 1869, p. xxi.

76. *FLE*, vol. 1, p. 347.

77. W. Page, *A treatise or justification of bowing at the name of Jesus* (Oxford, 1631), dedicatory, p. *3.

78. London, 1675: no editor is named. Cf. Brydon, *Evolving Reputation of Hooker*, p. 76, for another instance from the 1650s, by the Laudian gentleman Sir Robert Shirley. On John Warner, incumbent of Bishopsbourne in the 1630s, ibid., p. 50.

79. *Early Stuart Church, 1603–1642*, ed. Fincham, p. 42.

80. McCullough, *Sermons at Court*, pp. 200–209.

81. E.g. in the charge by Bishop Skinner of Bristol to his Dorset clergy in 1637: *Early Stuart Church*, ed. Fincham, p. 81. For Laudian adaptation of Andrewes to their purposes in a similar fashion to Hooker, see N. Tyacke, 'Lancelot Andrewes and the myth of Anglicanism', in *Conformity and Orthodoxy*, ed. Lake and Questier, pp. 5–33, especially pp. 7 and 12.

82. P. Heylyn, *Cyprianus Anglicus, or the history of the Life and Death of . . . William by divine providence, Lord Archbishop of Canterbury . . .* (London, 1668), p. 318. For an early instance of Laud quoting Hooker in a sermon before James I, see his court sermon of 24 March 1622: McCullough, *Sermons at Court*, microfiche listing of sermons, s.v. 24 March 1622.

83. [J. Gauden], *Eikon Basilike . . .* (London, 1649), appended material, p. 9 (copy in my possession; pagination is irregular).

84. Condren, 'Hooker's public authority', pp. 45–6; Eccleshall, 'Hooker', pp. 71–4.

85. G. Gillespie, *A dispute against the English-Popish ceremonies obtruded upon the Church of Scotland, Wherein not only our own arguments against the same are strongly confuted, but likewise the answers and defences of our opposites, such as Hooker, Mortoune, Burges, Spring, Paybody, Andrewes, Saravia, Tilen, Spotiswood, Lindsey, Forbesse &c., Particularly confuted* (Edinburgh, 1637). For excellent comment, see Condren, 'Hooker's public authority', pp. 42–3; Brydon, *Evolving Reputation of Hooker*, pp. 55–6, 83–4.

86. R. Baillie, *Ladensium autokatakrisis, the Canterburians self-conviction . . .* (Amsterdam, 1640), p. 109.

87. Condren, 'Hooker's public authority', p. 43.

88. Eccleshall, 'Hooker', pp. 66–7; Brydon, *Evolving Reputation of Hooker*, pp. 71–4.

89. Eccleshall, 'Hooker', p. 88; Brydon, *Evolving Reputation of Hooker*, pp. 74–5.

90. There has been much recent sensible discussion of this complicated problem: for the most definitive analysis, see *FLE*, vol. 3, pp. xiii–lxxv, but see also Sisson, *Judicious Marriage, passim*.

91. For a useful analysis of the problem, see A. S. McGrade, 'Repentance and spiritual power: Book VI of Richard Hooker's *Of the Laws of*

Ecclesiastical Polity', *Journal of Ecclesiastical History* 29 (1978), pp. 163–76.

92. Steven McGrade lists various examples of stylistic incongruity in Book VII in *FLE*, vol. 6, p. 309n; see also his discussion, in *FLE*, vol. 6, pp. 243–6.

93. *Hooker*, ed. McGrade, pp. 308n, 340.

94. *Works of Hooker*, ed. Keble, vol. 1, p. xxiv.

95. On the popularity of Book VIII, *FLE*, vol. 3, p. xxix. Keble also noticed this phenomenon: *Works of Hooker*, ed. Keble, vol. 1, pp. xxiv–xxvi.

96. On Hugh Peter, see Brydon, *Evolving Reputation of Hooker*, pp. 58, 61, 108. On Usher's earlier publication of a minor Hooker text in 1641, see R. P. Almasy, 'They are and are not Elymas: the 1641 "causes" notes as postscript to Richard Hooker's "Of The Lawes of Ecclesiasticall Politie"' in *Hooker*, ed. McGrade, pp. 183–201.

97. Eccleshall, 'Hooker', pp. 89–90; Condren, 'Hooker's public authority', pp. 47–9. Both provide other examples of radical uses of Hooker during the Interregnum. See also Brydon, *Evolving Reputation of Hooker*, pp. 57–8, on Henry Parker, and J. Champion, *The Pillars of Priestcraft Shaken: The Church of England and its enemies, 1660–1730* (Cambridge, 1992), p. 204, on James Harrington.

98. C. McKelvie, 'Jeremy Taylor's recommendations for a library of Anglican theology (1660)', *Irish Booklore* 4, ii (1980), pp. 96–103 (I owe this reference to Jessica Martin).

99. Eccleshall, 'Hooker', p. 72 and n.31.

100. Trevor-Roper, *Catholics, Anglicans and Puritans*, p. 191.

101. J. Martin, *Walton's Lives: Conformist commemorations and the rise of biography* (Oxford, 2001), pp. 81–2, 231.

102. T. Fuller, *The Church-History of Britain . . . until the year MDCXLVIII* (London, 1655), Book ix, pp. 216–19, 235. Cf. discussion in Brydon, *Evolving Reputation of Hooker*, pp. 75–6. It is interesting that Fuller did not attempt a life of Hooker in his *Abel Redevivus* of 1651, even though he did include lives of Lancelot Andrewes and Hooker's tormentor Andrew Willet.

103. Fuller, *Worthies*, ed. Freeman, p. 133. Still in this post-Restoration work, despite a snarl against Presbyterians, Fuller could add 'But be it reported to the judicious whether, when all is done, a reserve must not be left for prudential supplies in church government.': p. 134. This is clearly a reference to 'judicious' Hooker.

104. Brydon, *Evolving Reputation of Hooker*, pp. 85–6; Eccleshall, 'Hooker', p. 70.

105. *Works of Hooker*, ed. Gauden, *Life*, pp. 7, 32–3.

106. *Works of Hooker*, ed. Gauden, *Life*, p. 22.

107. *Works of Hooker*, ed. Gauden, *Life*, pp. 4, 5.

108. *Works of Hooker*, ed. Gauden, *Life*, pp. 25, 40.

109. Equally masterly are the accounts of that shaping now provided by Martin, *Walton*, pp. 227–72, and by Brydon, *Evolving Reputation of Hooker*, pp. 105–22. An older account is D. Novarr, *The Making of Walton's Lives* (Ithaca, NY, 1958).

110. The epistle to the reader of 1670 and 1675 is more outspoken, and also openly says that Sheldon commissioned Walton to correct Gauden.

111. Eccleshall, 'Hooker', pp. 74–5.

112. For Coleridge and Hallam, see Sisson, *Judicious Marriage*, pp. 186–7. Sisson misdated the Coleridge remark, which is a marginalium to British Library, Ashley 5175, biographical preface to the 1682 edition of Hooker's *Works*, p. 28; this can be dated to Coleridge's radical years in 1790s Cambridge, not to the period of his later Toryism. I am indebted to Luke Wright for discussions on this point.

113. The 1906 Everyman edition of Hooker printed only the first five books. Cargill Thompson still felt constrained to argue against the fallacy in 1973: Cargill Thompson, 'Hooker's knowledge of Marsilius of Padua', p. 81 and n.2.

114. Cf. J. Edwards, *Veritas Redux* ... (London, 1707), p. 539; Edwards, *The Doctrine of Faith* ... (London, 1708), pp. 313–14. I am indebted to Stephen Hampton for pointing me to these references.

115. For a discussion of Hooker, Baxter and late seventeenth-century nonconformity, see Brydon, *Evolving Reputation of Hooker*, pp. 60–61, 125–33, 141–4; Condren, 'Hooker's public authority', pp. 50–51.

116. Brydon, *Evolving Reputation of Hooker*, pp. 146–8.

117. Eccleshall, 'Hooker', pp. 95–6; Brydon, *Evolving Reputation of Hooker*, pp. 136–7.

118. Eccleshall, 'Hooker', pp. 95–6; A. P. Monahan in *Hooker*, ed. McGrade, p. 215. Michael Brydon, *Evolving Reputation of Hooker*, pp. 139–40, speculates as to how extensive or profound Locke's reading of Hooker really was. However, Steven McGrade points out to me that Locke at various times did at least possess three different editions of Hooker's works: *The Library of John Locke*, ed. J. Harrison and P. Laslett (Oxford Bibliographical Society publications new series 13, 1965), p. 157, nos. 1490–92.

119. Eccleshall, 'Hooker', p. 98; Condren, 'Hooker's public authority', p. 53; Brydon, *Evolving Reputation of Hooker*, pp. 160–65; T. Claydon, *William III and the Godly Revolution* (Cambridge, 1996), pp. 4–6, 28–33, 83–7. Even the image of Charles I could be pressed into service to defend

the Revolution: see K. Sharpe, '"So hard a text"? Images of Charles I, 1612–1700', *Historical Journal* 43 (2000), pp. 383–407, at pp. 401–3.

120. *Charges to the Grand Jury 1689–1803*, ed. G. Lamoine (Camden 4th series 43, 1992), pp. 30–31, 41–2. For later Whig uses of Hooker in Grand Jury Charges, see Lamoine (ed.), pp. 255, 267, 434–5.

121. '... there is not any man of the Church of England, but the same man is also a member of the *Commonwealth,* nor any man a member of the *Commonwealth* which is not also of the *Church of England*': in *FLE,* vol. 3, p. 319.

122. J. Maltby, *Prayer Book and People in Elizabethan and early Stuart England* (Cambridge, 1998), p. 235.

123. Brydon, *Evolving Reputation of Hooker,* pp. 168–9; J. Gascoigne, 'The Unity of Church and State challenged: responses to Hooker from the Restoration to the Nineteenth-Century age of reform', *Journal of Religious History* 21 (1997), pp. 60–79, see p. 62.

124. For use by the Erastian Deist Matthew Tindal, see Gascoigne, 'Unity of Church and State', 61.

125. *The present Constitution and the Protestant Succession vindicated: in Answer to a late Book intituled "The Hereditary Right of the Crown of England asserted"* (London, 1714), p. 1, and see Brydon, *Evolving Reputation of Hooker,* pp. 193–4.

126. Brydon, *Evolving Reputation of Hooker,* pp. 176–97.

127. Condren, 'Hooker's public authority', p. 55; Eccleshall, 'Hooker', pp. 102–5.

128. W. Warburton, *The Alliance between Church and State: or the Necessity and Equity of an established religion and a Test-Law demonstrated* ... (editions from 1736). Principal enlargements of the *Alliance* as an independent text after 1736 are 1748 and 1766. Its original text had been designed as part of Warburton's much larger work, *The Divine Legation of Moses,* which first appeared in full in print in 1738, although it was begun at the end of the 1720s. Cf. useful discussion in Gascoigne, 'Unity of Church and State', pp. 63–6, and J. Van Den Berg, 'Thomas Morgan versus William Warburton: a conflict the other way round', *Journal of Ecclesiastical History* 42 (1991), pp. 82–5, at p. 84.

129. Warburton, *Alliance* (1748 edn), dedication to Philip, Earl of Chesterfield, unpaginated.

130. Warburton, *Alliance* (1741 edn), pp. 63, 88n.

131. Warburton, *Alliance* (1741 edn), pp. 113–114, to which the index entry refers. Obviously the relationship with the Church of Scotland was not the only issue shaping Warburton's distinctive alliance theory. Unnameable in his text, although undoubtedly in his mind, was the confessional

Lutheranism of the first Hanoverian monarchs. However, this was a diminishing reality (unlike the Church of Scotland) as the *Alliance* underwent its years of extended development.

132. Warburton, *Alliance* (1741 edn), p. 30; Eccleshall, 'Hooker', p. 76. On Neal and Warburton, see *The Ecclesiastical Polity and other works of Richard Hooker . . .*, ed. B. Hanbury (3 vols, London, 1830), vol. 1, pp. xxxvii–xxxix, and Warburton, *Works* (1788 edn), vol. 7, p. 898.

133. Condren, 'Hooker's public authority', p. 56.

134. The new excursus on Hooker occupies pp. 180–87 of Warburton, *Alliance* (vol. 4 of 1788 edn of Warburton, *Works,* reprinting the 1766 edn).

135. Warburton, 1788 edn of *Works*, vol. 4, pp. 180–81, 186–7, 243, 304. Gascoigne, 'Unity of Church and State', p. 65, suggests that Hooker may have primarily been a straw man for Warburton to make a veiled attack on Hoadly. This may well have been part of his intention, but 1766 seems a late date for such an impulse, and at *Works*, vol. 4, pp. 180–81, Warburton explicitly makes the connection to his clash with Bolingbroke, referring to material found in his Postscript from the 1766 edn, printed in ibid. vol. 4, pp. 300–304.

136. S. Taylor, 'William Warburton and the alliance of Church and State', *Journal of Ecclesiastical History* 43 (1992), pp. 271–86; P. Nockles, *The Oxford Movement in Context: Anglican High Churchmanship, 1760–1857* (Cambridge, 1994), p. 56.

137. Nockles, *Oxford Movement in Context*, p. 63; cf. Gascoigne, 'Unity of Church and State', pp. 67–8.

138. Nockles, *Oxford Movement in Context*, pp. 64–5. Gascoigne, 'Unity of Church and State', p. 67; Condren, 'Hooker's public authority', p. 56.

139. Gascoigne, 'Unity of Church and State', pp. 69–70.

140. Gascoigne, 'Unity of Church and State', p. 76.

141. *Works of Hooker*, ed. Keble, vol. 1, p. li.

142. *Works of Hooker*, ed. Keble, vol. 1, p. cv. *Works of Hooker*, ed. Hanbury, vol. 1, p. xiii.

143. *Works of Hooker*, ed. Keble, vol. 1, pp. ii, civ. Contrast Hanbury's trenchant criticism of Walton: *Works of Hooker*, ed. Hanbury, vol. 1, pp. cxviii–cxxii.

144. *Works of Hooker*, ed. Keble, vol. 1, pp. lii, lviii, lxxxiii, xcvi.

145. Cf. Keble's Preface in *Works of Hooker*, ed. Keble, *passim,* but esp. vol. 1, pp. lxi–lxii, lxvii, lxix, lxxii–lxxviii, lxxxi, xcii. For useful comment, see also Gascoigne, 'Unity of Church and State', pp. 73–4; Brydon, *Evolving Reputation of Hooker*, pp. 13–14; Nockles, *Oxford Movement in Context*, pp. 242, 250, 256, 264.

146. *Works of Hooker*, ed. Keble, vol. 1, p. lxxxix; cf. Nockles, *Oxford Movement in Context*, p. 207.

147. H. Froude, *Remains*, ed. J. H. Newman and J. B. Mozley (4 vols, Oxford, 1837–9), vol. 1, p. 415. For Froude's evolving attitude to Hooker and his influence on Keble, see Nockles, *Oxford Movement in Context*, p. 80, and W. J. Baker, 'Hurrell Froude and the Reformers', *Journal of Ecclesiastical History* xxi (1970), pp. 243–59, esp. pp. 251, 255.

148. J. H. Newman, *Lectures on Justification* (London, 1838), p. 442; this is in an Appendix to the actual lectures. I am grateful to Peter Nockles for leading me to this reference.

149. Nockles, *Oxford Movement in Context*, p. 242.

150. H. Fish, *Jesuitism traced in the movements of the Oxford Tractarians* (London, 1842), p. 61; cf. p. 26. Oxford, Pusey House, Pusey–Tyndale correspondence (uncatalogued). I am indebted to Peter Nockles for alerting me to these references, and for letting me see his so far unpublished article 'Anglicanism "Represented" or "Misrepresented"? The Oxford Movement, the Reformation and the 17th-century Divines'.

151. For useful discussion on this theme, together with a listing of Hooker statuary, see Brydon, *Evolving Reputation of Hooker*, pp. 15–16. To analyse the use of Hooker in Anglican contributions to ecumenical dialogue in the twentieth century would require another extended paper.

152. A. P. d'Entrèves, 'Richard Hooker: a study in the history of political philosophy', Oxford D.Phil. thesis, 1932: published and translated as *Ricardo Hooker* (Turin, 1932). Cf. W. J. T. Kirby, *Richard Hooker's Doctrine of the Royal Supremacy* (Leiden, 1990), p. 12.

21. Forging Reformation History: a cautionary tale

1. In the following references to Robert Ware's original works, it is necessary to make precise references to the bibliographically complicated publications associated with it, so I have given references to *Short-title Catalogue of Books printed in England, Scotland, Wales, and British America, and of English books printed in other countries, 1641–1700*, ed. D. G. Wing (2nd edn, ed. J. J. Morrison and C. W. Nelson with M. Seccombe, assistant editor, 4 vols, New York, 1972, 1982, 1988, 1998). These are made in the form 'Wing' plus reference. There is no account of Robert Ware in the *Oxford Dictionary of National Biography*, but there is a good entry in the *Dictionary of Irish Biography from the earliest times to the year 2002*, ed. J. McGuire and J. Quinn (9 vols, Cambridge, 2009), s.v. Ware,

Robert, 9/799–800. It gives his death as 1696, but he actually died in March 1696 Old Style, i.e. 1697.

2. The definitive account of Ussher is now A. Ford, *James Ussher: theology, history and politics in early-modern Ireland and England* (Oxford, 2007).

3. Margaret Statham has pointed out to me that this Reformed scholarly ethos extended as far as the community of Robert Ware's great-grandfather, the Suffolk haberdasher Ambrose Briden, one among the Puritan elite of the Suffolk town of Bury St Edmunds, who was one of a consortium of Bury worthies who in 1637 presented to the newly founded library of St James's Bury a set of M. de la Bigne (ed.), *Bibliothecae veterum patrum et auctorum ecclesiasticorum* (8 vols and supplementary vol., Paris, 1609–24).

4. An excellent treatment of this is A. Ford, 'The Irish historical renaissance and the shaping of Protestant history', in *The Origins of Sectarianism in Early Modern Ireland*, ed. A. Ford and J. McCafferty (Cambridge, 2005), pp. 127–57, with discussion of Sir James Ware at pp. 152–7.

5. Sir James Ware is listed as resident in Castle Street in St Werburgh's parish in the 1659 Dublin census: *Calendar of ancient records of Dublin*, ed. J. T. Gilbert and R. M. Gilbert (18 vols, Dublin, 1889–1903), vol. 4, p. 564.

6. Oxford, Bodleian Library MS Carte 30, fo. 634: Sir James Ware to the Duke of Ormond, 9 May 1660.

7. For a useful short discussion of Sir James Ware's meticulous antiquarianism in the tradition of William Camden, and also his friendly relations with and patronage to scholarly Gaelic historians, see M. Herity, 'Rathmulcah, Ware and Macfirbisigh', *Ulster Journal of Archaeology* 33 (1970), pp. 49–53.

8. W. O'Sullivan, 'A finding list of Sir James Ware's manuscripts', *Proceedings of the Royal Irish Academy* 97 section C (1997), pp. 69–99, at pp. 84–99. For a sample description of one of the unsullied manuscripts from Sir James's collections, see Kathleen Hughes, 'A manuscript of James Ware, British Museum, Additional 4788', *Proceedings of the Royal Irish Academy* 55 section C (1952–53), pp. 111–16.

9. *The whole works of Sir James Ware concerning Ireland Revised and improved, in three volumes*, ed. W. Harris (3 vols in 2, Dublin, 1739–46), vol. 3, pp. 155–6, augmented in J. Burke, *A genealogical and heraldic history of the commoners of Great Britain* (4 vols, London, 1833–8), vol. 4, p. 498. Robert's first appearance on the public stage seems to be an incident in April 1664, when he struck a Dublin waterman and was roundly

abused, subsequently with his father's aid securing the man's imprisonment and abject apology: Oxford, Bodleian Library MS Carte 159, fos 237r, 239r.

10. *Dictionary of Irish Biography*, ed. McGuire and Quinn, vol. 9, p. 799.

11. *The Irish statute staple books, 1596–1687*, ed. J. Ohlmeyer and E.Ó. Ciardha (Dublin, 1998), p. 155. The range is 13 December 1666 to 17 November 1669, with one £400 sum as creditor on 5 January 1684. Robert's father was a creditor in the enormous sum of £10,000 on 12 May 1665, which is likely to have been in connection with the settlement on Robert.

12. *Historical Manuscripts Commission: Calendar of the Manuscripts of the Marquess of Ormonde, K.P., preserved at Kilkenny Castle* (new series, 8 vols, 1902–20), vol. 4, p. 170: Earl of Arran to Duke of Ormond, London, 20 July 1678. The index to this volume identifies 'Mr Ware' as Robert's elder brother James, but on 18 October 1681, Ormond writing to Arran described Robert Ware as 'your landlord': *HMC Ormonde* new series, 6/200.

13. London, British Library, MS Additional 4813, fo. 3r.

14. Oxford, Bodleian Library MS Carte 45, fos 210 (Ormond to Archbishop of Canterbury, 11 February 1667), and see a less personal letter about the reversion from Ormond to the Duke of Albemarle (whose secretary Matthew Locke was seeking the post, MS Carte 45, fo. 204), same day and place, MS Carte 49, fo. 389. For the Archbishop of Canterbury's request on Locke's behalf, 31 December 1666, MS Carte 45, fo. 204, enclosing Locke's own petition, ibid., fo. 206. Earlier Ormond had described James as 'a person very uncapable of dischargeing it [the Auditor-Generalship] in his own person, but that defect is supplyed by a very able and a very honest officer, bred upp by the father': MS Carte 51, fos 263–4, Ormond to Arlington, Dublin, 17 December 1666.

15. O'Sullivan, 'A finding list of Sir James Ware's manuscripts', p. 73 and n, but see the careful but still too sympathetic analysis of a manifest forgery in Robert Ware's history of Dublin, R. Gillespie, 'Robert Ware's telling tale: a medieval Dublin story and its significance', in *Medieval Dublin V: Proceedings of the Friends of Medieval Dublin Symposium 2003*, ed. S. Duffy (Dublin, 2004), pp. 291–301. For Ware's pride in Dublin, see ibid., p. 300.

16. Armagh Public Library, 'Ware's history and antiquities', p. 6, quoted in Gillespie, 'Robert Ware's telling tale', p. 292.

17. Armagh Public Library, 'Ware's history and antiquities', p. 94, quoted in Gillespie, 'Robert Ware's telling tale', p. 301.

18. Oxford, Bodleian Library MS Tanner 114, no. 5, fo. 4; MS Tanner 90, no. 56, fo. 181. Tanner notes at the end of the latter, 'Out of Sir Ja. Ware's MSS Collections Vol 20. fo. 35 etc.' It was this same material which deceived Philip Wilson a century before, via a different source-collection: see P. Wilson, 'The writings of Sir James Ware and the forgeries of Robert Ware', *Transactions of the Bibliographical Society* 15 (1917–20), pp. 83–94; and compare his acknowledgement of having being deceived, ibid., p. 88, with the deception at P. Wilson, *The Beginnings of Modern Ireland* (Dublin, 1912), pp. 325–9.

19. These examples from London, British Library MS Additional 4797, fos 131r, 135r.

20. *Strange and remarkable prophesies and predictions of . . . James Ussher* (London, 1678; Wing U.225).

21. Cf. N. Bernard, *The life and death of the Most Reverend and learned father of our Church Dr James Usher . . .* (London, 1656; Wing B. 2012), pp. 38–40. Bernard's account is unclear as to whether he is describing two sermons, one in 1602 and a second in 1641–2, and unsurprisingly the redactor of *Strange and remarkable prophesies* has simplified his account.

22. Ford, *Ussher*, pp. 30–31, and cf. his comments on the prophecies and their afterlife at ibid., pp. 274–5. A. Ford in the *Oxford Dictionary of National Biography*, s.v. Ussher, James, 'Death and afterlife', seems to accept all the prophetic material more or less at face value, which is unwise.

23. The Oxford copies of various 1678 editions are Oxford, Bodleian Library Vet. A3 e.237 (19), Vet. A4 fo.1427, Wood 646 (14), Ashm. 1070 (21), Ashm. 1062 (3), Pamph. C 140 (6); G.Pamph. 1364 (1); New College BT3.199.5(6). There were subsequent editions in 1679 (Cork), 1681 (no place of publication), 1682 (London), 1687 (London; significantly paired with other Ware forgeries of material relating to Sir William Boswell and Bishop Bramhall), 1688 (London; same pairing), 1689 and 1691 (London). Later editions were 1697 (London); 1701 (Dublin), 1702? (Dublin), 1708 (Edinburgh), 1717 (Dublin), 1734 (London), 1745 (London), 1770 (Dublin), 1779 (Leeds), 1780? (Dublin), 1793 (London), 1797 (Bristol), 1800 (Edinburgh), c. 1825 (Dublin), 1843 (Dublin), 1860 (pr., Middle Hill).

24. [Anon. and Robert Ware], *Bishop Usshers second prophesie* (London, 1681; Wing U.222).

25. *The examinations of Faithful Commin Dominican fryer* (?Dublin, 1679; Wing W.847AC). Wing is not certain in attributing this to Dublin, but *The whole works of Sir James Ware*, ed. Harris (1739–46), vol. 3, p. 256 gives it a Dublin place of publication, while nevertheless mis-dating it to 1671.

26. On Jones, see *Oxford Dictionary of National Biography*, s.v. Jones, Henry; on his role in the plot, J. Gibney, *Ireland and the Popish Plot* (Basingstoke, 2009), *passim*.

27. T. C. Barnard, 'The uses of the 23rd of October 1641 and Irish Protestant celebrations', in Barnard, *Irish Protestant ascents and descents* (Dublin, 2004), pp. 111–42, at p. 115. It might be thought significant that the Irish publication of the prophecies came not in Dublin but in that rather amateurish edition in Cork, but Dr Barnard has reminded me that the edition advertises itself as a reprint, and this may indicate a previous edition in Dublin of which no copy has survived.

28. Gibney, *Ireland and the Popish Plot*, pp. 13–14, 20.

29. Oxford, Bodleian Library MS Carte 39, fos 146–70r is a file of papers from June and July 1680 intended for Bishop Jones but intercepted by agents of the Duke of Ormond and copied for his son the Earl of Ossory, concerning Mansell and Ware and their dealings with Shaftesbury. On Mansell and the contact and chief agitator in the 'Irish Plot' fabrication William Hetherington, whom Ware mentions in this correspondence, see Gibney, *Ireland and the Popish Plot*, pp. 80, 88.

30. Oxford, Bodleian Library MS Carte 39, fo. 152r (extracts of Ware's letters, 26 and 29 June 1680), 170r (memorandum about a letter of Bishop Jones, 24 July 1680). On the background, see Gibney, *Ireland and the Popish Plot*, pp. 88–9.

31. R. C. Richardson, 'Re-fighting the English Revolution: John Nalson (1637–1686) and the frustrations of late seventeenth-century English historiography', *European Review of History/Revue européenne d'histoire* 14 (2007), pp. 1–20, at p. 16.

32. For examples, see J. Scott, *England's troubles: 17th century English political instability in European context* (Cambridge, 2000), esp. p. 441. On Nalson and Danby, see M. Goldie, 'John Locke and Anglican Royalism', *Political Studies* 31 (1983), pp. 61–85, at p. 67.

33. On Shaftesbury's criticism of Ussher and royalist reprints of Ussher's works in the 1680s, see Goldie, 'John Locke and Anglican Royalism', pp. 66–7.

34. On Nalson's conceptualization of Whigs and liberty in terms of the 1640s, see T. Harris, '"Lives, Liberties and Estates": rhetorics of liberty in the Reign of Charles II', in *The Politics of Religion in Restoration England*, ed. T. Harris, P. Seaward and M. Goldie (Oxford, 1990), pp. 217–41, at pp. 231–4.

35. J. Nalson, *The common interest of King and People* . . . (London, 1677; Wing N.92), p. 257. For similar comments, cf. Scott, *England's troubles*, pp. 164–5, and J. Rose, 'Robert Brady's intellectual history and

Royalist antipopery in Restoration England', *English Historical Review* 122 (2007), pp. 1287–1317, esp. p. 1294.

36. J. Nalson with Robert Ware, *Foxes and firebrands* . . . (London, 1680; Wing N.102). The publisher, Benjamin Tooke, was much occupied with official printing for the government in England and also for Lord Lieutenant Ormond in Ireland.

37. Rose, 'Robert Brady's intellectual history', p. 1307.

38. Nalson with Ware, *Foxes and firebrands*, p. 7: the Ware and Heath materials together occupy pp. 6–22.

39. Richardson, 'Re-fighting the English Revolution', p. 14, points out that Nalson explicitly distanced himself from being identified as a 'Tory', even though Richardson constructs a portrait of an archetypal Tory historian of his period. A fine overview of the fluid politics of this era is the review article by T. Harris, 'From rage of party to age of oligarchy? Rethinking the later Stuart and early Hanoverian period', *Journal of Modern History* 64 (1992), pp. 700–720.

40. J. Nalson, ed., *A True copy of the journal of the High Court of Justice for the tryal of K. Charles I* . . . (London, 1684; Wing T.2645), Epistle Dedicatory, and Introduction, p. xiv.

41. J. Scott, 'England's Troubles: exhuming the Popish Plot', in *The Politics of Religion in Restoration England*, ed. Harris, Seaward and Goldie, pp. 107–31, at p. 126.

42. R. Ware, *The prophecy of Gnatus a Brittish prophet* (Dublin, 1681; Wing W.850A), sig. A2v. See MS versions of this at London, British Library MS Additional 4792, fo. 113 and MS Additional 4821, fos 209v–212v reversed.

43. R. Ware, *The Conversion of Philip Corwine* (Dublin, 1681; Wing G.278).

44. R. Ware, *The Reformation of the Church of Ireland, in the Life and Death of George Browne* (Dublin, 1681; Wing W.851), printed in London as *Historical Collections of the Church in Ireland* (London, 1681; Wing W.848). This was another long-lived success, achieving a reprint by Samuel Johnson in the *Harleian Miscellany* (1745), 5, no. lxxiii, and a translation into Latin in D. Gerdes, *Scrinium Antiquarium sive miscellanea Groningana nova ad historiam Reformationis* (Groningen and Bremen, 1749–65). On Sir James Ware's praise of Martin, see *The whole works of Sir James Ware*, ed. Harris (1739–46), vol. 1, p. 157.

45. The material of this complex affair is to be found in *HMC Ormonde* new series, vol. 6, pp. 153, 157, 180, 189, 194, 200, 203, ranging in date from 18 September to 19 October 1681 and looking back to an incident

of 7 July 1681. It is not clear what living or cure in Dublin Theophilus Harrison then held (from 1696 he would be Rector of St John's Dublin), but the affidavit of Fr Bartholomew St Lawrence, *HMC Ormonde* new series, vol. 6, p. 157, would suggest that he was associated with St Audoen's church. The events described in the affidavit seem to be set in St Audoen's parish; Harrison came to a house in Cook Street to perform a baptism, and most of Cook Street was situated in St Audoen's.

46. [Anon.], *The mischiefs and unreasonableness of endeavouring to deprive his majesty of the affections of his subjects . . . printed by Joseph Ray at Colledge-Green, for Samuel Helsham Bookseller in Castle-street* (Dublin, 1681; Wing M.2238). See Raymond Gillespie, *Devoted People: belief and religion in early modern Ireland* (Manchester, 1997), p. 43, and Gillespie, 'The religion of the first Duke of Ormond', in *The Dukes of Ormonde, 1610–1745*, ed. T. Barnard and J. Fenlon (Woodbridge, 2000), pp. 101–14, at p. 104.

47. *Mischiefs and unreasonableness*, p. 3.

48. *Mischiefs and unreasonableness*, pp. 3, 10–11.

49. I owe this point to Robin Usher.

50. R. Ware [and J. Nalson], *Foxes and Firebrands . . . In Two Parts* (Dublin, 1682; Wing N.104), sig. A3r. The second part has a separate pagination, title-page and dedication initialled by Robert Ware to the archbishops, bishops and 'the rest of the Reverend Divines of the Reformed Church of Ireland'.

51. Ware [and Nalson], *Foxes and Firebrands . . . In Two Parts*, Preface to Part 1, sig. A4rv.

52. Ware [and Nalson], *Foxes and Firebrands . . . In Two Parts*, p. 120.

53. R. Ware, *The hunting of the Romish fox* (Dublin, 1683; Wing W.849). William Turner's first effort in a sequence of similar titles was *The huntyng and fyndyng out of the Romyshe foxe which more then seuen yeares hath bene hyd among the bisshoppes of Englonde, after that the Kynges hyghnes had commanded hym to be dryuen owt of hys realme.* (Antwerp, 1544). T. Bell, *The hunting of the Romish foxe Presented to the popes holines, with the kisse of his disholy foote, as an odoriferous & redolent posie verie fit for his grauitie, so often as he walketh right stately, in his goodly pallace Bel-vidêre* (London, 1598).

54. On Jervis, see *Dictionary of Irish Biography*, ed. McGuire and Quinn, s.v. Jervis, Humphrey, and on Jervis and the Ormond Market scheme, *Calendar of ancient records of Dublin*, ed. Gilbert and Gilbert, vol. 6, pp. 582–605; vol. 5, pp. 302–4, 313–15, 603–8.

55. The quotation is *HMC Ormonde* new series, vol. 6, p. 543 (Arran to Ormond, Dublin, 13 March 1683). For further material on the Ormond

Market project between 1682 and 1683, see ibid., pp. 421–2, 524, 530. Robin Usher suggests to me that some of the Dublin pamphlet or MS attacks on Sir Humphrey Jervis may be by Robert Ware.

56. D. Armitage, *The Ideological Origins of the British Empire* (Cambridge, 2000), Ch. 2 and pp. 67, 170–71. L. Colley, *Britons: forging the nation 1707–1837* (New Haven, CT, and London, 1992), pp. 5–6, 11–18.

57. *The Hunting of the Romish Fox*, Preface to the Reader. The signatures are very confused in the Preface. At pp. 233–5 there is one of the very few stories in Ware's publications which is related from his personal experience and which sounds authentic, since there is nothing necessarily polemical about it in itself, relating to his employment of a Carmelite convert from Rome, Gerrard Moor, as a Latin and French teacher for his children, in the previous year.

58. *The Hunting of the Romish Fox* (pp. 250–51). *Historical collections* had already anticipated the publication of the history of Dublin as 'ready for the press' in 1681: *Historical collections*, p. 7.

59. Harris, ed., *The whole works of Sir James Ware* (1739–46), vol. 3, p. 256. See also the account in *A genealogical and heraldic history of the commoners of Great Britain*, ed. Burke, vol. 4, p. 498.

60. The complicated story is unravelled in O'Sullivan, 'A finding list of Sir James Ware's manuscripts', pp. 73–6.

61. O'Sullivan, 'A finding list of Sir James Ware's manuscripts', pp. 78–83.

62. O'Sullivan, 'A finding list of Sir James Ware's manuscripts', p. 77. The Irish publications are *The antiquities and history of Ireland, by . . . Sir James Ware* (1 vol. in 5, Dublin, 1705) and *The whole works of Sir James Ware concerning Ireland*, ed. and trans. W. Harris (2 vols in 3, Dublin, 1739); revd edn (1764). A useful compendium of MS sources for both James and Robert Ware and other members of the Ware family is provided in *Manuscript sources for the history of Irish civilisation*, ed. R. J. Hayes (11 vols, 1965 and 1979, available on microfiche), vol. 4, pp. 814–18, s.v. Ware (James) and Ware (Robert). These include Hayes's notice of a further apparently unpublished anti-Catholic MS by Robert, 'Rome's monarchical power blasted': Queen's University Library Belfast MS 1/149.

63. R. Ware [and J. Nalson], *Foxes and Firebrands . . . the Third and Last Part* (London, 1689; Wing W.847B). Churchill also brought out the first and second parts separately. In his Preface, Ware used the pseudonym 'Philirenes' which Nalson had used in the first part.

64. R. Ware [and J. Nalson], *Foxes and Firebrands . . . the Third and Last Part*, pp. 19–23.

65. R. Ware, *Pope Joan* (London, 1690, Wing W.850); it bears licence 31 January 1689 Old Style. *A history of Pope Joan and the Whores of Rome*, referred to in Ware's dedicatory Preface to *Pope Joan* as of 1687, appears only to survive in a second edition of 1687, without place of publication (Wing H.2132).

66. For background on the English use of the Pope Joan legend, see T. S. Freeman, 'Joan of contention: the myth of the female Pope in early modern England', in *Religious Politics in post-Reformation England: essays in honour of Nicholas Tyacke*, ed. K. Fincham and P. Lake (Woodbridge, 2006), pp. 60–79.

67. In two of history's pleasant coincidences, Jeremiah Milles, the purchaser of the Ware MSS which ended up in the British Library, was a passionate defender of the authenticity of Chatterton's spurious medieval poet, Thomas Rowley, as well as being successor to John Strype as Rector of West Tarring in Sussex: see *Oxford Dictionary of National Biography*, s.v. Milles, Jeremiah. Lovers of irrelevant conjunctions might also note that Chatterton was caught out in and had to explain an error about the gender of St Werburgh (a parish dedication as prominent in Bristol as in Dublin, thanks to the medieval links of the two cities): J. Rosenblum, *Practice to deceive: the amazing stories of literary forgery's most notorious practitioners* (New Castle, DE, 2000), p. 67.

68. A good assessment of Strype is W. D. J. Cargill Thompson, 'John Strype as a source for the study of sixteenth-century English Church History', in *The materials, sources and methods of ecclesiastical history*, ed. D. Baker (Studies in Church History xi, Oxford, 1975), pp. 237–47, reprinted in Thompson, *Studies in the Reformation: Luther to Hooker*, ed. C.W. Dugmore (London, 1980), pp. 192–201.

69. J. Strype, *Memorials of . . . Thomas Cranmer . . .* (London, 1694; Wing S.6024), pp. 144–5.

70. Strype, *Memorials of Cranmer*, p. ix. Strype's use of an anecdote about Archbishop Arundel from 'an Ancient MS Fragment, . . . formerly belonging to the Church of Worcester', in his Epistle Dedicatory to Archbishop Tenison, looks alarmingly like a borrowing from Ware. I am also suspicious of Strype's uncharacteristically colourful 'Sun of Truth . . . through the thick Mists of that Idolatry' metaphors characterizing the incomplete nature of Henry VIII's Reformation, Strype, *Memorials of . . . Thomas Cranmer . . .* Ch. 11, p. 45, but have not so far tracked this material down in Ware.

71. On Strype's dealings with in particular Sir William Hickes, see *Oxford Dictionary of National Biography*, s.v. Strype John, 'Biographical

Works', and Cargill Thompson, 'John Strype as a source for the study of sixteenth-century English Church History'.

72. [A. Collins], *An answer to Dr. Scot's cases against dissenters concerning forms of prayer. And the fallacy of the story of Commin, plainly discovered* (London, 1700; Wing C.5356), pp. 3–17. The *Oxford Dictionary of National Biography* account of Collins, s.v. Collins, Anthony, does not notice this pamphlet, anonymous as was always the case with Collins, and makes his earliest publication one of 1706. I am very grateful to Mark Williams for alerting me to the work's existence. On the Collins family property at Sandon, see P. Morant, *The history and antiquities of the county of Essex* . . . (2 vols, London, 1768), vol. 2, p. 27.

73. [J. Scott], *Certain cases of conscience resolved, concerning the lawfulness of joyning with forms of prayer in publick worship. Part II* . . . (London, 1684; Wing S.2042), pp. 59–60.

74. [Collins], *An answer to Dr. Scot's cases against dissenters*, p. 5. Collins's repeated use of the words 'Romance' and 'Romantick' is an interesting echo of Robert Ware's 'Romantick' in his Preface to *The hunting of the Romish fox*, but is probably coincidental.

75. E. Stillingfleet, *The unreasonableness of separation* (London, 1681; Wing S.5675), pp. xii–xiii, all of whose references rightly point back to the first source of the names, W. Camden, *Annales rerum Anglicarum, et Hibernicarum* . . . (Frankfurt-am-Main, 1616), p. 149. In 1694, John Scott preached at Stillingfleet's consecration as Bishop of Worcester (Gilbert Ironside and Simon Patrick were also being consecrated).

76. J. Strype, *The Life and Acts of Matthew Parker* . . .(London, 1711), p. iv.

77. Strype, *Life and Acts of Matthew Parker*, p. iii.

78. Strype's correspondence is Cambridge University Library, Additional MSS 1–10, and Harrison's letters to Strype between 1689 and 1719 are to be found in vols 1, 4, 6, 8 and 9. London, British Library MS Additional 5853 is William Cole's not altogether accurate transcripts of some of this correspondence. Harrison repeatedly describes himself as Strype's 'Brother', but the exact relationship is not clear, and probably refers merely to their common clerical status. Harrison makes frequent references in later years, e.g. to the 'few now at Low Layton that know me' (Cambridge University Library, MS Additional 6, fo. 808; London, British Library, MS Additional 5830, fo. 94v, Harrison to Strype, 29 August 1711), which probably relates to time spent in Strype's Essex benefice during his exile from Ireland in James II's reign. On Harrison's work on subscriptions for Strype's publications, see Cambridge University Library, MS Additional 6, fos 640, 700, 732, 741, 771 (transcribed in London, British Library, MS Additional 5853, fos 86, 88, 89, 90, 91,

94): Harrison to Strype, 10 April 1710, 29 August 1710, 14 November 1710, 29 December 1710, 3 April 1711, 4 August 1711); also Cambridge University Library, MS Additional 5 no. 247, Additional 8, nos. 203, 263, 269, 277, 290, 296, Additional 9, nos. 327, 333, 341, 342, 343, 351 (Harrison to Strype, 26 February 1709, 23 August 1715, 5 June 1717, 3 July 1717, 3 August 1717, 5 October 1717, 25 November 1717, 3 March 1718, 22 April 1718, 21 June 1718, 5 August 1718, 28 August 1718, 22 January 1719; the 1717 campaign extended Harrison's subscription efforts to the West of England).

79. Cambridge University Library, MS Additional 4, fo. 205v (not transcribed by Cole). The letter (unusually for Harrison) is undated, but the postmark and an endorsement by Strype reveal that he received it on 9 May 1709: he also endorsed the letter 'Fox's and Firebrands'.

80. [?J.C. Cox], 'Notes on the smaller Cathedral Churches of Ireland', *Reliquary*, new series 5 (1891), pp. 163–77, at p. 165. Of all Dean Harrison's many letters to Strype, only one is addressed from Clonmacnoise rather than Dublin or some place in England: Cambridge University Library, MS Additional 4, no. 311, 14 September 1709.

81. S. C. Hughes, *The Church of St John the Evangelist, Dublin* (Dublin, 1889), pp. 58, 97; by then, St John's parish had been amalgamated with St Werburgh's. Harrison graduated at Trinity College, Dublin around 1672; he held the Deanery of Clonmacnoise from 1682 until his death in 1720, with an interval and an intruder in the Deanery (Stephen Handcock) perhaps caused by his flight under James II (J. Healy, *History of the Diocese of Meath* (2 vols, Dublin, 1908), vol. 2, p. 278). Harrison married the daughter of Dean Jonathan Swift's uncle in 1702, in St John's Church, and the families were close.

82. Harrison's vivid narrative to Strype of the aftermath of James II's campaign in Ireland, Dublin 23 August 1690, is printed in *Original Letters illustrative of English History . . .*, ed. H. Ellis (second series, London, 1827), vol. 4, no. 389, pp. 209–13, from London, British Library MS 5853, fos 26v–7r, old pagination pp. 392–3 (a transcript of the original in Cambridge University Library, MS Additional 1, fo. 145).

83. On Bonnell, see the *Oxford Dictionary of National Biography*, s.v. Bonnell, James. His correspondence with Strype can be found in Cambridge University Library, MS Additional 1, fos 35–129, transcribed not accurately but supplying some lacunae in London, British Library MS Additional 5853, fos 5v–23v, and Cole's comment on Archdeacon Hamilton's biography of Bonnell can be found at ibid., fo. 5v.

84. Cambridge University Library, MS Additional 1, fo. 93r, Bonnell to Strype, Dublin, 24 April 1691: 'The opportunity of Dean Harisons

hand obliges me no longer to delay answering yours of 24 past'; ibid.,
fo. 89r, Bonnell to Strype, Dublin, 13 February 1691/2: 'I have not
heard of Dean Harison since I writ to you by him . . .'. Many similar
examples follow.

85. Cambridge University Library, MS Additional 1, fo. 110r, transcribed in
London, British Library MS Additional 5853, fo. 20r: Bonnell to Strype,
Dublin 26 June 1693. In his letter of 26 May 1697 (Cambridge University Library, MS Additional 1, fo. 124r, transcribed in London, British
Library MS Additional 5853, fo. 21v), Bonnell was judiciously warm
about Harrison's pastoral abilities: 'He acquits himself very well to the
satisfaction of his people, tho' in his Preaching least of all, having a
heaviness in speaking in the Pulpit, quite different from what he has in
conversation. He is a truly good Man, and zealous for promoting goodness among his people.'

86. Cambridge University Library, MS Additional 1, fos 94r, 96r, 100r,
transcribed in London, British Library MS Additional 5853, fos 17r,
18v, 19r.

87. Cambridge University Library, MS Additional 1, fo. 104r, transcribed
and shortened in London, British Library MS Additional 5853, fo. 19r.

88. A useful treatment of Dopping is J. I. Peacocke, 'Anthony Dopping,
Bishop of Meath', *Irish Church Quarterly* 2 (1906), pp. 120–33.

89. London, British Library MS Additional 4797, fo. 131r. The note appears
to be in a different hand either from the entry at the head of the document which says mendaciously 'Ex Bib. Cottonens. I got thes memories
on the 6th Oct., 1657' or from the more formal hand of the main body
of the text, both of which seem to be variants of Ware's hand.

90. G. Burnet, ed. O. Airy and H. C. Foxcroft, *History of my own Time* (3
vols, Oxford, 1897–1902), vol. 2, pp. 171, 174, 178–81.

91. G. Burnet, *A sermon preached before the House of Commons, on the
31st of January, 1688* . . . (London, 1689; Wing B.5885), p. 15. T. E.
Bridgett first made these connections: Bridgett, *Blunders and Forgeries:
historical essays* (London, 1890), pp. 213–14. W. Goode, *Rome's tactics: or, A lesson for England from the past . . . with a brief notice of
Rome's allies in the Church of England* (London, 1867), p. 6, noted
Burnet's reference to letters of the bishops.

92. Bridgett, *Blunders and Forgeries*, pp. 277–8. The original Latin text of
John Jewel's letter in Zürich is in G. Burnet, *History of the Reformation
of the Church of England. The Third Part* . . . (London, 1715), Records
no. 51 [second pagination], p. 275, which should be compared with the
text of Burnet's commentary at 6th book, ibid., [first pagination], p. 277.
Burnet's account of Edward VI's Coronation in the 1681 edition of his

History (Wing B.5798A), Pt II, Bk 1, p. 15, is notably brief, based on a single document from the Privy Council (*Collections* no. 4, pp. 93–6) and that may have inspired Ware to create the speech for Cranmer which he published as the very opening of his second part of *Foxes and Firebrands* in 1682 (Part II, pp. 1–9) – abruptly beginning that text, it stands as something of an anomaly in a volume mostly given over to seventeenth-century 'documentation'.

93. *Calendar of ancient records of Dublin*, ed. Gilbert and Gilbert, vol. 6, p. 349: resolution of 24 March 1706 (I am grateful to Toby Barnard for pointing me to this reference).

94. [J. Ware et al.], *The Antiquities and History of Ireland, by the Right Honourable Sir James Ware, Knt* . . . (Dublin, 1705), and [J. Ware et al.], *The antiquities and history of Ireland, by the Right Honourable Sir James Ware, Knt* . . . (London, 1705). For the Browne reference, ibid., second pagination, p. 147, introductory to the reprint of the two collections of spurious material on Archbishop Browne, pp. 147–55, 155–64. Dean Theophilus Harrison's name is notably not among the subscribers to the work listed in the Irish edition preliminaries.

95. [Ware et al.], *The Antiquities and History of Ireland*, Life of James Ware, after Preface, no pagination. Mary's brother Ambrose, mentioned in their father's will of 6 February 1640 (Suffolk Record Office, Bury Wills, Muriell 157), has become described (perhaps in Ware family lore) as Sir Ambrose Briden of Maidstone, Kent. There is no record of an Ambrose Briden being knighted in the period.

96. *The whole works of Sir James Ware*, ed. Harris (1739–46), and see in particular the Preface to vol. I. The spurious material on Archbishop George Browne, vol. 1, pp. 349–51, is shortened and more integrated in the main text than in the 1704–5 edition. The account of Archbishop Garvey, vol. 1, p. 96 merely describes Robert Ware's publication of the treatise attributed to him. The further edition in 2 vols, Dublin, 1764, has new preliminaries. On Harris, see *Oxford Dictionary of National Biography*, s.v. Harris, Walter, and useful background in T. C. Barnard, 'Improving Ireland's past', in *Improving Ireland? Projectors, prophets and profiteers, 1641–1786*, ed. T. C. Barnard (Dublin, 2008), pp. 89–119, esp. pp. 112–19.

97. *The whole works of Sir James Ware*, ed. Harris (1739–46), vol. 3, Preface.

98. Barnard, 'Improving Ireland's past', p. 113 and n.

99. The silence was noticed (p. 499n) amid a genealogical account of the Wares in *A genealogical and heraldic history of the commoners of Great Britain*, ed. Burke, vol. 4, pp. 498–500, and Burke also at p. 500, chronicles the lawsuits which the entail continued to cause right to the

end of the seventeenth century. Cf. *The whole works of Sir James Ware*, ed. Harris (1739–46), vol. 3, pp. 145–6 and 256–7.

100. Bridgett, *Blunders and Forgeries*, p. 215, first noticed the nexus of malice around the parliamentary castration bill and its connection to Ware. Ware's original forgery of Buckingham's proposal, embedded in a spurious Privy Council letter, is in London, British Library MS Additional 4791 fo. 38, and also in Ware, *Foxes and Firebrands . . . The Second Edition*, pp. 127–8. The proposal is associated with a pre-Ware forged letter attributed maliciously to the Jesuits, printed in ibid., pp. 118–24, and it may have given Ware particular pleasure to be able to cite this earlier forgery from the *Collections* of his collaborator John Nalson's *bête noire,* and an historian overly favourable to Dissent, John Rushworth (ibid., p. 129).

101. Bridgett, *Blunders and Forgeries*, pp. 218–21, usefully gathers together examples.

102. *Works of Archbishop Cranmer*, ed. Cox, vol. 2, p. 126n. The editor of Alexander Nowell's Catechism judiciously ignored the anecdote about Nowell and Queen Elizabeth in his biographical preface: *A catechism in Latin by Alexander Nowell . . . together with the same catechism translated into English by Thomas Norton . . .,* ed. G. E. Corrie (Parker Society, Cambridge, 1853), pp. i–ix.

103. J. Strype, *Memorials . . . of . . . Thomas Cranmer . . .,* ed. P. E. Barnes (2 vols, London, 1853), vol. 1, p. 205n.

104. Bridgett, *Blunders and Forgeries*, pp. 223–4. W. Goode, *Rome's tactics: or, A lesson for England from the past . . . with a brief notice of Rome's allies in the Church of England* (London, 1867); for his use of Ware both via Strype and directly from *Foxes and Firebrands*, see ibid., pp. 5–24, 45–51, 53.

105. R. Churton, *The Life of Alexander Nowell, Dean of St Pauls . . .* (Oxford, 1809), pp. 71–3.

106. *Oxford Dictionary of National Biography*, s.v. Bridgett, Thomas.

107. R. Marius, *Thomas More: a biography* (London, 1986), p. xix.

108. It is most easily sampled in its London reprint of 1890: Bridgett, *Blunders and Forgeries*, Ch. 7: 'Robert Ware; or, a rogue and his dupes', pp. 209–96.

109. Bridgett, *Blunders and Forgeries*, p. 245.

110. G. F. Warner, 'A forged account of the demolition of the shrine of St Thomas of Canterbury', *English Historical Review* 6 (1891), pp. 754–6. On Kegan Paul, see *Oxford Dictionary of National Biography*, s.v. Paul (Charles) Kegan.

111. On Warner, *Oxford Dictionary of National Biography*, s.v. Warner, Sir George Frederic.

112. Wilson, 'The writings of Sir James Ware and the forgeries of Robert Ware', in particular his note of being deceived, p. 88, as at Wilson, *The Beginnings of Modern Ireland*, pp. 325–9. B. Bradshaw, 'George Browne, first Reformation Archbishop of Dublin, 1536–1554', *Journal of Ecclesiastical History* 21 (1970), pp. 301–26, at pp. 301–2, drew historians' attention to Wilson's work and to Ware's forgeries in relation to George Browne, but wider lessons failed to be drawn. It is also cited briefly, though not wholly accurately, in J. Rosenblum, *Practice to deceive*, p. xvii.

113. R. Dudley Edwards, 'The Dictionary of National Biography', *Bulletin of the Institute of Historical Research* 15 (1933), pp. 54–6.

114. W. B. Stanford, *Ireland and the classical tradition* (Dublin, 1976), pp. 20–21, 41–2n, uses London, British Library MS 4813 fos 157v–8r, Robert Ware's supposed translation of Sir James Ware's Latin account of the teaching of a 'newe grammar' by Richard Owde at St Patrick's Grammar School in Dublin in 1587, and the ensuing controversy, arbitrated in favour of the older grammar of Lily (1540) by Archbishop Loftus since 'diversities of grammars would be destructive of learning'. Stanford notes Robert's dubious reputation but unwisely chooses to give credit to this tempting morsel of evidence. Equally, without corroboration, it is unsafe to take the testimony of Ware manuscripts to the first instance of morality or mystery plays in Ireland in 1528, cited by J.C. Walker, 'An historical essay on the Irish Stage', *Transactions of the Royal Irish Academy*, 2 (1788), 3d pagination ('Antiquities'), pp. 75–90, at pp. 78–80.

115. *Field Day Anthology of Irish Writing*, ed. S. Deane (5 vols, Derry and Cork, 1991–2002), vol. 5, pp. 264–5, quoting Robert Ware's 'translation' from the 1705 version of Ware's *De Hibernia*. R. Gillespie, *Devoted people: belief and religion in early modern Ireland* (Manchester, 1997), p. 118, is unduly indulgent in saying that 'the virulent Protestant Robert Ware invented at least one story to discredit Catholicism'.

116. In chronological order, P. Hughes, *The Reformation in England* (3 vols, London, 1950–54), vol. 2, p. 81; J. Ridley, *Thomas Cranmer* (Oxford, 1962), pp. 262–3; John M. King, *English Reformation Literature: the Tudor origins of the Protestant tradition* (Princeton, 1982), p. 67; M. Aston, *England's Iconoclasts I. Laws against images* (Oxford, 1988), pp. 249–50; MacCulloch, *Thomas Cranmer*, pp. 349, 364–5; C. Bradshaw, 'David or Josiah? Old Testament kings as exemplars in Edwardian religious polemic', in *Protestant history and identity in sixteenth-century Europe*, ed. B. Gordon (2 vols, Aldershot, 1996), vol. 2, pp. 77–90, at p. 84; G. Murdock, 'The importance of being Josiah: an image of Calvinist

identity', *Sixteenth Century Journal* 29 (1998), pp. 1043–59, at p. 1048; J. Loach, *Edward VI* (New Haven, CT, and London, 1999), pp. 37, 48–9 (with some characteristic but not absolute reservations); D. MacCulloch, *Tudor Church Militant: Edward VI and the Protestant Reformation* (London, 1999), pp. 62 and 231 n. 8 (by now my faith in the speech was wavering); S. Alford, *Kingship and politics in the reign of Edward VI* (Cambridge, 2002), p. 52; F. Heal, *Reformation in Britain and Ireland* (Oxford, 2003), pp. 157–8; C. Skidmore, *Edward VI: the lost king of England* (London, 2007), pp. 61–2; A. Hunt, *The drama of coronation: medieval ceremony in early modern England* (Cambridge, 2008), pp. 78–98; K. Sharpe, *Selling the Tudor monarchy: authority and image in sixteenth-century England* (New Haven, CT, and London, 2009), pp. 212, 236; E. Duffy, *Fires of Faith: Catholic England under Mary Tudor* (London and New Haven, CT, 2009), p. 88. We should all have heeded the scepticism of A. F. Pollard, *Thomas Cranmer and the English Reformation 1489–1556* (London, 1904), p. 186n.

117. C. Bradshaw, 'David or Josiah? Old Testament kings as exemplars in Edwardian religious polemic', is a good treatment of the Josiah theme in relation to Edward VI.

118. In chronological order of last appearance, J. Phillips, *The Reformation of Images: destruction of art in England, 1535–1660* (London, 1973), pp. 127–8; W. S. Hudson, *The Cambridge Connection and the Elizabethan Settlement of 1559* (Durham, NC, 1980), pp. 142–3 ('the story undoubtedly was embellished in the telling of it'); P. Collinson, *Godly people: essays on English Protestantism and Puritanism* (London, 1983), pp. 109–33, at p. 132, reprinted from Collinson, 'If Constantine, then also Theodosius: St Ambrose and the integrity of the Elizabethan *Ecclesia Anglicana*', *Journal of Ecclesiastical History* 30 (1979), pp. 205–29; D. MacCulloch, *The Later Reformation in England, 1547–1603* (Basingstoke, 1990), p. 25; *Oxford Dictionary of National Biography*, s.v. Nowell, Alexander.

119. Bridgett, *Blunders and Forgeries*, pp. 294–5. A more recent and rather acute amateur consideration of the work of Robert Ware is to be found on the internet, a blog by Owen Roberts on 7 August 2009; http://thisrecording.com/today/2009/8/7/in-which-a-forgery-just-breaks-our-heart.html, in which he not unjustly describes Robert Ware's *oeuvre* as 'crazy shit'.

Index

All dates are CE unless stated as BCE. Popes are cross-referenced from their entry under their birth-name to their papal name, under Rome, Popes; monarchs are gathered under their principal territory, and Archbishops of Canterbury gathered under Canterbury. Members of European nobility are indexed under their surnames. Those who have been declared saints by one or other Christian Church are indexed either under their first names or their surnames, not at 'Saint'.

à Lasco, Johannes *see* Łaski
Abbasid dynasty 19
Abelard, Peter 55
Abraham 23, 25
Adiaphora 285
Africa 6
Ainsworth, Henry 190, 192
Albigensian Crusade *see* Cathars
Aldobrandini, Ippolito *see* Rome: Popes: Clement VIII
Alexandria 20
allegory in Bible 33–4, 36
Alsace 46–7
Ambrose (Bishop of Milan) 59
Anabaptists 32, 51, 58–63, 107–8, 122, 130–34, 208, 232–3, 236, 323
see also radical Reformation
Andrewes, Lancelot (Bishop of Winchester) 54, 215–16, 225–6, 228, 238, 289, 298, 300–301, 318, 409, 415
Angelic Salutation *see* Hail Mary
angels and archangels 23–31
Anglicanism and Anglican Communion 145, 164, 209, 216–56, 266–79, 297, 303, 307, 359–62
   origins of word 219, 252, 359
   see also England, Church of; episcopacy; Evangelicalism; Ireland, Church of; High Churchmanship; United States of America: Episcopal Church
Anglo-Catholicism 96, 197–8, 212, 224, 254, 318, 361
   see also High Church Anglicanism; Oxford Movement
Anglo-Saxon Church 16
Anglo-Saxon language 16
Anna, prophetess 53
Annunciation *see* Mary, Blessed Virgin
'Anointed One' *see* Jesus Christ
anti-Catholicism 209, 321–58
   see also Popish Plot
anti-Semitism 37, 83

Anti-Trinitarians 232
   see also Arianism; Socinianism; Unitarianism; Valdés
Antichrist 28, 91, 121, 280–81, 287
anticlericalism 102, 114
Apocrypha and apocryphal writings 33, 48, 183
apostles (disciples) 120–21
Apostles' Creed 57
apostolic succession in ministry 120, 301
Appenzell 368
ARCIC (Anglican-Roman Catholic International Commission) 197, 246
Arianism 60
Aristotle 57, 286, 288, 303
   see also scholasticism
Armagh 341
   see also Boyle; Dowdall; Garvey; Plunket; Ussher
Arminianism 54, 215–16, 235–6, 241, 265, 307, 338
   see also 'Avant-garde conformists'; High Churchmanship; Canterbury, Archbishops: Laud; Methodism
Arnold, Jonathan 31
Arran *see* Butler
art 83, 162
Ascendancy *see* Ireland
Asia 6
Askew, Reginald 237
Aston, Margaret 253–4
Athanasian Creed 61
Atlantic Isles 223, 252, 254–5, 339
   see also Celtic Church; England; Great Britain; Ireland; Scotland; Wales
Augsburg: Confession (1530) 111
Augustine of Canterbury *see under* Canterbury, Archbishops
Augustine of Hippo 4, 44, 56, 63, 66, 118, 131
   see also Latin Doctors
authority *see* Bible; Church; tradition

437